100 Activities for Teaching Research Ethics and Integrity

Sara Miller McCune founded SAGE Publishing in 1965 to support the dissemination of usable knowledge and educate a global community. SAGE publishes more than 1000 journals and over 800 new books each year, spanning a wide range of subject areas. Our growing selection of library products includes archives, data, case studies and video. SAGE remains majority owned by our founder and after her lifetime will become owned by a charitable trust that secures the company's continued independence.

Los Angeles | London | New Delhi | Singapore | Washington DC | Melbourne

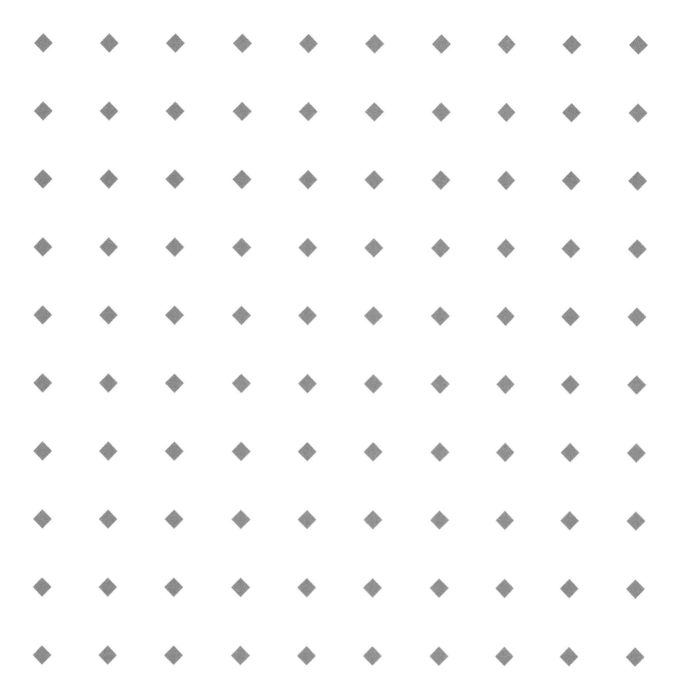

100

Activities for Teaching Research Ethics and Integrity

Catherine Dawson

Los Angeles | London | New Delhi
Singapore | Washington DC | Melbourne

Los Angeles | London | New Delhi
Singapore | Washington DC | Melbourne

SAGE Publications Ltd
1 Oliver's Yard
55 City Road
London EC1Y 1SP

SAGE Publications Inc.
2455 Teller Road
Thousand Oaks, California 91320

SAGE Publications India Pvt Ltd
B 1/I 1 Mohan Cooperative Industrial Area
Mathura Road
New Delhi 110 044

SAGE Publications Asia-Pacific Pte Ltd
3 Church Street
#10-04 Samsung Hub
Singapore 049483

Editor: Kirsty Smy
Assistant editor: Jessica Moran
Production editor: Sarah Cooke
Copyeditor: Elaine Leek
Proofreader: Salia Nessa
Indexer: Silvia Benvenuto
Cover design: Shaun Mercier
Typeset by: C&M Digitals (P) Ltd, Chennai, India
Printed in the UK

Library of Congress Control Number: 2022930172

British Library Cataloguing in Publication data

A catalogue record for this book is available from the British Library

ISBN 978-1-5297-7394-1
ISBN 978-1-5297-7395-8 (pbk)

At SAGE we take sustainability seriously. Most of our products are printed in the UK using responsibly sourced papers and boards. When we print overseas we ensure sustainable papers are used as measured by the PREPS grading system. We undertake an annual audit to monitor our sustainability.

Contents

Activity Level Index

This index helps educators to find activities that are aimed at the right level for the course they teach. It is not ideal: some may be uncomfortable with the terms (in particular, the term 'elementary', which was felt to be preferable to 'beginner'). Others may feel that it is impossible to categorize learners in this way or that the categories do not translate to a higher education context. However, this simple categorization is necessary to help educators find the right activities for their particular cohort. It is important to note, also, that these categories are only included in educator's notes and, therefore, will not be seen by, or discussed with, students. Many activities presented in this book are suitable for all three levels: this will be made clear in the relevant activity when it occurs.

DEFINITION OF CATEGORIES

- **Elementary:** students who are new to issues of ethics and integrity in research. This could be first-year undergraduate students or adults who have returned to education after some time away, for example.
- **Intermediate:** students who have a little more experience of research ethics and integrity, perhaps in their second or third year of undergraduate study. Many of these activities are aimed at students who are planning or undertaking their undergraduate dissertation/research project.
- **Advanced:** students studying at postgraduate level. Many of these activities are aimed at students who are planning or undertaking their master's or doctoral thesis/research project.

Elementary

Intermediate

Advanced

Activity Type Index

(in alphabetical order)

This index helps educators to choose the type of activity that most suits their students, course, subject area, and teaching and learning preferences. Some activities are listed in more than one category: this is because these activities can be run in more than one way. Digital activities (or digital alternatives when in-class activities are given) or self-guided options are provided so that activities are still available if in-class teaching is not possible.

Digital poster presentation (group activity, online asynchronous)

Digital storytelling (group activity, online asynchronous)

Discussion (group activity, in-class)

Discussion (group activity, online synchronous)

Discussion (informal, for invited students, in-class or online synchronous)

Discussion (whole-class activity, in-class)

Discussion (whole-class activity, online synchronous)

Game (group activity, in-class or online synchronous)

Game development and presentation/sharing (group activity in-class or online asynchronous)

Imagining the future: group presentation and class discussion (in-class or online synchronous)

Interviewing and videoing senior researchers (group activity, in-class or online asynchronous)

Online study and support group (asynchronous)

Personal journal or diary (self-guided activity during independent study)

Peer support group (in-class or online synchronous)

Podcast production and sharing (group activity, online asynchronous)

Poster presentations (group activity, in-class)

Presentations (group activity, in-class)

Presentations (individual activity, in-class)

Question-and-answer session (whole-class activity, in-class)

Question-and-answer session (whole-class activity, online synchronous or asynchronous)

Quiz (in-class or online synchronous or asynchronous)

Role-play and class discussion (in-class)

Scenario-based individual exercise

Scenario-based student-centred digital resource

Scenarios developed by students for discussion (in-class or online synchronous or asynchronous)

Scenarios for group discussion (in-class)

Scenarios for group discussion (online synchronous)

Scenarios for discussion (online asynchronous)

Self-guided individual exercise

Self-guided individual exercise with PDF production and sharing

Self-guided individual exercise with information sharing and discussion (in-class or online synchronous or asynchronous)

Tip exchange (student-centred, online asynchronous)

Vlog production and sharing (group activity, online asynchronous)

Video production and sharing (group activity, online asynchronous)

Wiki creation and editing

Wordsearch and discussion (in-class or online asynchronous)

Worksheet (individual activity during independent study)

Workshop (in-class)

Workshop (online synchronous)

Written assignment (individual self-guided activity during independent study)

Online Resources

Head online to **https://study.sagepub.com/dawsonresearchethics** to download and print all the student handout pages from the book and use them in your lessons!

Activity · · · · · · · · · · → 7

Promoting Social Good through Research Practice

STUDENT HANDOUT

This activity is called 'Promoting social good through research practice'. Craft a story with your group members that illustrates, explains or discusses how research practice can promote social good. The specific topic, style, structure, content and genre of your story are a group choice. It can be invented or based on real examples: if you choose to use a real example, make sure that the source is cited correctly. Try to be creative and imaginative: your story should be entertaining, informative and memorable.

Consider the following questions when you craft your story:

1. What is the key lesson that you wish to convey?
2. What do you want your peers to learn from your story?
3. How are you going to ensure that others learn from your story?
4. Will your story stimulate thought and reflection? Will it have an emotional and/or intellectual impact?
5. Will your story enable your peers to achieve the learning outcome given below?

Prepare your story for our next session: you can use props, visual aids or presentation software if you wish. Your group will be given up to 10 minutes to tell your story and a further five minutes for peers to ask questions and discuss your story. You will also be able to listen to the stories told by other groups and ask questions.

Learning outcome: By the end of this activity, you will be able to identify, explain and discuss how social good can be promoted through research practice.

About the Author

Dr Catherine Dawson studied at university in the UK for an undergraduate degree in Combined Humanities, a master's degree in Social Research and a PhD researching the learning choices of adults returning to education. She has worked as a research assistant, research associate and educator at various UK universities, and as a research and training officer in both the public and private sectors. Over the years, she has developed and taught research methods courses for undergraduate and postgraduate students, and has designed and delivered bespoke research methods courses to employees in the private sector. At this present time, Catherine is writing online courses in research methods, study skills and intellectual property in the research context, and continuing to write research methods books for students and educators.

Introduction

100 Activities for Teaching Research Ethics and Integrity is a sourcebook of original activities for educators teaching research ethics and integrity at undergraduate and postgraduate levels. It is not country-specific and, therefore, will be of use to educators across the globe. Each activity contains detailed educator notes, providing information about the purpose, level, type and alternative type of activity; the duration; a detailed description; key issues; related activities; preparatory reading; and useful resources. A learning outcome is given for each activity along with ready-made student handouts, where relevant. These provide worksheets, scenarios, descriptions of role-play and advice about how to complete the activity.

The book is divided into eight sections covering a wide range of research ethics and integrity topics:

Section 1: Moral and social imperatives

Section 2: Researcher and institution conduct

Section 3: Compliance with policy, standard or law

Section 4: Digital technology, software and tools

Section 5: Data collection

Section 6: Data analysis

Section 7: Data management

Section 8: Results and outputs

Educators can use a pick and mix approach to the book, dipping in and out of relevant sections when required. An 'activity type' index and an 'activity level' index make it easy for educators to choose the right type and level of activity for their student cohort. Each activity has been designed as a standalone activity that can, on occasions, be combined with another relevant activity for greater coverage of the topic: clear signposting is provided to enable effective use of related activities when they occur.

A wide variety of activity types is provided in the book, including blog production, brainstorms, collaborative dialogue, discussions, digital collage production, debates, digital storytelling, game development, peer support groups, digital presentations, quizzes, role-plays, scenarios, self-guided individual exercises, workshops, worksheets and video production. The 'activity type' index enables educators to choose the type of activity that most suits their students and subject area. It is also possible for educators to mix and match type of activity with topic (in cases where an activity is of interest, but the specific topic is not relevant, for example).

The coronavirus pandemic has necessitated a rapid move to online learning, which has been difficult for educators who are not used to online delivery. Therefore, every activity in this book has an online option (or a self-guided individual activity option) so that the activities can still be used if in-class teaching is not possible. Specific guidance is given about how to run the online activity, along with advice about relevant platforms, software products and tools (various options are given, enabling educators to use web-based tools or those integrated with learning management systems, for example). Advice and tips are provided, where relevant, for educators who are new to online delivery.

This book is not discipline-specific and will, therefore, be of use to educators who teach in the social sciences, sciences and humanities. It is aimed at anyone who teaches research ethics and integrity: for early-career educators it will provide original and ready-made materials that can be used when developing and designing modules, and for more experienced educators it can be used as a complementary resource to support existing programmes or to help adapt or develop new modules. Activities presented in this book have been tried, tested, modified, refined and updated over time. They are presented in a clear and concise way to ease the workload of busy educators, and provide useful activities and learning materials that can be used to inspire, engage and motivate students.

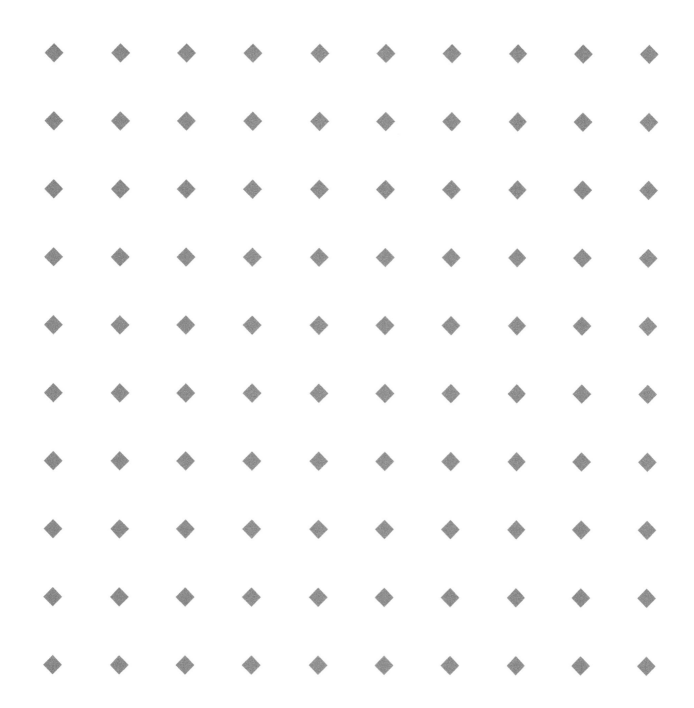

Section 1

Moral and Social
Imperatives

Activity • • • • • • • • • • → 1

Respecting Human Dignity, Privacy and Rights

The activity

Begin this activity by explaining to your students that an important ethical issue they need to address when undertaking their research with human subjects is respect for human dignity, privacy and rights, which must be considered and addressed early in their research planning. Ask them first to think about these issues in relation to their proposed project on an individual basis: they should identify issues relevant to human dignity, privacy and rights, and illustrate how they intend to address these issues in their research.

Your students should produce a summary of no more than 600 words (for undergraduates) or 1,000 words (for postgraduates). Explain that their work will be read and discussed by their peers: it should be interesting and informative, enabling students to learn from each other.

Once complete, work should be uploaded using an appropriate asynchronous tool. This could be a discussion board facility that enables students to attach files to threads (Blackboard Discussion Board or Discussions in Canvas, for example: you will need to ensure that the settings are changed in Canvas to enable files to be attached to threads). Or you could use group functions that enable file exchange, or a peer assessment tool integrated with your learning management system (LMS) that enables peers to view work created by their peers (Groups and File Exchange in Blackboard or Peer Assessment on Canvas, for example). Alternatively, you could ask students to upload their work to a virtual bulletin or post board such as Padlet for sharing and discussion (ensure that you choose 'Secret' in privacy settings so that only users with a link can view the information and remind students not to post personal details). Give a date by which time this must be done.

Once all summaries have been uploaded, ask students to read the summaries presented. Open a discussion or thread to discuss pertinent ideas. Encourage students to read and digest the information posted by their peers, and ask them to make comments, ask questions, discuss ideas and provide constructive advice, based on what they have learnt during the individual exercise. If you have not already done so, ensure that students understand how to offer respectful feedback to their peers (the CORBS model from the University of Alberta provides useful guidance: https://sites.ualberta.ca/~hsercweb/viper/CORBS_Feedback.pdf). Monitor posts to ensure that information is useful, constructive, respectful and correct.

If you choose the student presentation option, ask students to prepare a 10-minute presentation instead of the written summary. They can use any presentation materials they wish, and these should be made available for their use, if required. When you meet in-class, allocate 10 minutes for each student, with five minutes for discussion after each presentation. Summarize the session with a discussion of the pertinent points raised, or by addressing some of the questions listed below.

Key issues

Students approach this activity in a variety of ways, depending on their research topic, research question, methodology, subject of study and level of study. Some concentrate on practical methods issues, such as seeking informed consent and ensuring anonymity, whereas others consider deeper theoretical and philosophical issues, such as competing definitions and contrasting theories. Some concentrate on identifying and meeting legal obligations.

Below is a selection of questions that can be explored further during the online discussion: pick those that are most appropriate for your cohort. These can also be produced as a handout, if you think your students need more guidance for this activity.

1. What is meant by the term 'human dignity'? How might this fit with social dignity and personal dignity? Is dignity bestowed on a person or attained? In what ways might research threaten human dignity (and social and personal dignity)? How can you avoid this in your research?

2. To what does the term 'privacy' refer in relation to your research (spatial privacy, relating to a person's body or mind, or information privacy, relating to a person's personal, sensitive or intimate data, for example)? Do different types of privacy require different types or levels of respect and protection? How will you ensure that relevant types of privacy are met in your research (data protection, anonymity and respect of values, for example)?

3. What is meant by human rights? What are the nature and scope of these rights? How do you intend to respect these rights in your research? For example, might you have to consider how the rights of one participant might be balanced against the rights of another? Or is there a possibility that you could be duty-bound to act in a certain way, irrespective of the rights of your research participants?

4. What local, national and international rules, regulations and legislation are relevant to your research in terms of human dignity, privacy and rights? What action do you need to take to ensure that you adhere to all relevant rules, regulations and legislation?

5. What frameworks or norms already exist to protect dignity, privacy and rights? How might these inform and guide your research methodology and methods?

→ **Related activities**

Activity 9: Discussing privacy and confidentiality in the research context

Activity 31: Identifying and complying with local, regional and national law

Activity 32: Understanding and adhering to relevant human rights legislation

Activity 50: Evaluating privacy policies of software companies and third-party providers

Activity 57: Seeking informed consent

Activity 1

→ **Preparatory reading**

Educators: All the resources listed below provide useful preparatory reading for this activity.

Students: Should be encouraged to find their own resources. Once the activity has concluded, undergraduate students with little experience of this topic might find it useful to refer to this book:

Anderson, E. and Corneli, A. (2018) *100 Questions (and Answers) About Research Ethics*. Thousand Oaks, CA: Sage.

....

→ **Useful resources**

Constantin, A. (2018) 'Human subject research: International and regional human rights standards', *Health and Human Rights Journal*, 4 December 2018, www.hhrjournal.org/2018/12/human-subject-research-international-and-regional-human-rights-standards.

De Koninck, T. (2009) 'Protecting human dignity in research involving humans', *Journal of Academic Ethics*, 7 (1–2): 17, published 4 August 2009, doi: 10.1007/s10805-009-9086-z.

Floridi, L. (2016) 'On human dignity as a foundation for the right to privacy', *Philosophy and Technology*, 29: 307–12, published 26 April 2016, doi: 10.1007/s13347-016-0220-8.

Kirchhoffer, D. (2019) 'Dignity, being and becoming in research ethics'. In D. Kirchhoffer and B. Richards (eds), *Beyond Autonomy: Limits and Alternatives to Informed Consent in Research Ethics and Law* (Cambridge Bioethics and Law, pp. 117–32). Cambridge: Cambridge University Press, doi: 10.1017/9781108649247.008.

Pieper, I.J. and Thomson, C.J.H. (2014) 'The value of respect in human research ethics: A conceptual analysis and a practical guide', *Monash Bioethics Review*, 32: 232–53, published 13 January 2015, doi: 10.1007/s40592-014-0016-5.

Activity 1

Activity • • • • • • • • • • • → 2

Discussing the Ethics of Consent and Purpose

ACTIVITY 2: EDUCATOR NOTES

Purpose: This activity enables students to explore the ethics of consent and purpose, encouraging them to think about these issues in relation to research in general and to their research project in particular. This is a theoretical (and part practical) discussion about the ethics of consent and purpose: the practical application of informed consent is covered in Activity 57: Seeking informed consent, which can be run together with this activity, if required.

Type: Discussion (online synchronous).

Alternative type(s): In-class discussion; student worksheet.

Level: Intermediate and advanced (this activity is of particular use for students who are beginning to think about their dissertation or thesis).

Duration: Fifty minutes to one hour for both the online and in-class discussions. If the worksheet option is chosen students can work at their own pace.

Equipment/materials: A suitable online synchronous video/web conferencing tool to host the discussion in real-time.

Learning outcome: By the end of this activity, students will be able to explain what is meant by the ethics of consent and purpose, discuss the importance of consent and purpose in research and explain how they intend to address issues of consent and purpose in their own research.

The activity

Choose a suitable tool to host your online synchronous discussion (Zoom Meetings, Blackboard Collaborate, Conferences in Canvas or a tool integrated with Moodle, such as BigBlueButton, Adobe Connect or BigMarker, for example). This activity will use breakout rooms (smaller groups of students) for the first part of the discussion. These can be set automatically or manually: ensure that breakout rooms are enabled and pre-assign students to rooms prior to your session (or if you prefer, you can enable software to split students evenly into groups).

Provide a brief introduction to the session and set guidelines for constructive and supportive online discussion. Open the breakout rooms and broadcast questions to your students (see below, for examples). Questions can be sent altogether or one at a time, after a five-minute interval. Ask groups to discuss each question, taking notes as they hold their discussion: they will need to report back to their peers later. You can develop and use an online spreadsheet or document note catcher to organize note-taking for each group, if required. This can be used to monitor their discussions and see how they are progressing. It can also help you to decide which breakout rooms to visit during the session. Alternatively, you can visit rooms one-by-one, or ask that groups request help, if required.

When all questions have been asked and discussed, end the breakout session. Ask a member from each group to report some of their main findings and hold a short discussion on the issues that have been raised. Summarize these points to conclude the session.

If you choose the in-class option, divide your students into pairs or small groups (depending on the number of students), ask them to discuss each question, taking notes as they go. Walk among groups answering questions and offering advice, where required. Bring the groups back together after 30 minutes, or when you think the discussion has run its course. Ask a member of each group to report their main findings, then open up the discussion to the whole class. Conclude the session with a summary of the main points.

Key issues

The type, content and depth of discussion for this activity tends to depend on students' discipline, research subject and level of study. Several questions have been presented below as a guide, covering consent to undertake research, consent to take part in research and the purpose of research. Possible discussion points are listed after each question: these can be used as prompts if the discussion stalls. Pick those that are most suitable for your cohort and add questions that are specific to your discipline, if required. Ensure that you include one or two questions that relate specifically to students' research projects. Four to eight questions are usually enough for this activity. However, if you feel that all the questions below are relevant for your cohort, you could produce a worksheet for students to work through on an independent basis, in addition to, or instead of, the discussions.

1. What do we mean by consent to undertake research?

Permissions, approval and consent that must be sought and given before research can go ahead: ethical approval from universities and national bodies and necessary permissions or approvals (from individuals, organizations, government agencies and associations) that own data, data collection instruments and research sites, for example.

2. Why does consent to undertake research matter?

Ethical standards and requirements are met; adherence to rules, regulations and legislation; protect individuals, vulnerable people, researchers, organizations and society; avoid harm; respect for others as autonomous, rational and self-governing individuals.

3. Do all types of research require consent before they can begin?

Ethical approval required for all research involving human subjects (from universities and relevant national bodies); research that might not need consent (theoretical research, computer modelling and simulation, 3D modelling, research that uses anonymized data that cannot be traced back to the individual); research in which it is impractical or meaningless to obtain consent (crowd behaviour research, for example); in cases where consent might compromise the research; where consent might cause harm to participants.

4. Do you need to obtain consent to undertake *your* research and, if so, what type of consent?

Ethical approval from the University Ethics Committee, Institutional Review Boards or equivalent, and any relevant national body such as the Health Research Authority in England (or national equivalents); permissions from any relevant organization (data access and use permission or permission to conduct research on site, for example); revised approval/reconsent if the research changes as it gets under way.

5. What do we mean by consent to participate in research?

Agreement based on understanding of what is involved (informed consent); the difference between consent and assent (who is able to give informed consent, and researching with children and vulnerable people, for example); the ethics of research without consent.

6. Are there different types of consent required from those who participate in research?

Informed consent, process consent, dynamic consent, verbal consent, written consent, assent (affirmative agreement), post-hoc consent, consent of those who lose capacity to consent during a project.

Activity 2

7. Why do participants consent to take part in research?

Interest; altruism; boredom; perks and benefits (or perceived perks and benefits); to learn more; to help others; to help researchers increase knowledge and understanding; coercion or perception of little choice.

8. What will *your* research participants need to consent to?

Taking part in the research (the specific methods chosen); sharing their data; your privacy policy; anything else relevant to the topic/subject of research.

9. What is the purpose of research?

Identify problems; find solutions/answers; add to knowledge; benefits people, communities, industry, the economy and/or the environment; enables researchers to contribute to humanity.

10. In what ways are consent and purpose connected?

Participants must understand (and potentially agree with) the purpose to be able/willing to give consent; they must be able to understand and weigh-up benefits versus burden.

11. What is the purpose of *your* research?

Undergraduate/postgraduate course requirements; interest; related to future employment; fill a gap in the literature; innovative, creative and intellectually stimulating undertaking; collaboration on a national and international basis; other purposes related specifically to the subject/topic of research.

12. How will you enable participants to understand the purpose of *your* research, and know that they do understand the purpose?

Work out what they need to know and produce this information in an appropriate way (producing an information sheet, using appropriate language and providing alternative languages/formats, if required); undertaking a participant comprehension assessment (checking their ability to understand, retain, weigh-up and communicate purpose and their consent, for example). See Activity 57: Seeking informed consent.

→ **Related activities**

Activity 7: Promoting social good through research practice

Activity 13: Creating social change through research practice

Activity 42: Obtaining informed consent in the digital world

Activity 57: Seeking informed consent

Activity 65: Assessing the ethical implications of incentives and rewards

→ **Preparatory reading**

Educators: All the resources listed below provide useful preparatory reading.

Students: None required.

→ **Useful resources**

Luger, E. and Rodden, T. (2020) 'Ethics and consent in the (sociotechnical) wild'. In A. Chamberlain and A. Crabtree (eds), *Into the Wild: Beyond the Design Research Lab* (Studies in Applied Philosophy, Epistemology and Rational Ethics, 48). Cham: Springer.

Activity 2

Miller, F. and Wertheimer, A. (eds) (2010) *The Ethics of Consent: Theory and Practice*. New York, NY: Oxford University Press.

Nairn, K., Showden, C., Sligo, J., Matthews, K. and Kidman, J. (2020) 'Consent requires a relationship: Rethinking group consent and its timing in ethnographic research', *International Journal of Social Research Methodology*, 23 (6): 719–31, published online 7 May 2020, doi: 10.1080/13645579.2020.1760562.

Teare, H.J.A., Prictor, M. and Kaye, J. (2020) 'Reflections on dynamic consent in biomedical research: The story so far', *European Journal of Human Genetics*, Open Access, published 28 November 2020, doi: 10.1038/s41431-020-00771-z.

West-McGruer, K. (2020) 'There's "consent" and then there's consent: Mobilising Māori and Indigenous research ethics to problematise the western biomedical model', *Journal of Sociology*, 56 (2): 184–96, first published 13 January 2020, doi: 10.1177/1440783319893523.

Activity 2

Activity • • • • • • • • • • • • • ➔ 3

Assessing the Complexities and Tensions of Research Ethics

The activity

Ask your students to prepare for this activity by reading your university's and/or department's research ethics policy, procedures and guidelines (or similar). When you meet, divide your students into groups and ask them to work through the Student Handout (the number of groups depends on the number of students in your class, but four to five groups are usually good numbers for this activity). Allow 40 minutes for this part of the activity. Walk among the groups to check on their discussion, ask questions and address queries.

Once the groups have finished discussing the six complexities and tensions outlined in the Student Handout, bring the groups back together and lead a discussion on the issues raised. During this discussion, ask your students whether they can think of any other complexities and tensions that are relevant to their research.

This activity can be run as an online activity if you prefer. Choose a suitable synchronous tool to host the group discussion (Zoom Meetings, Blackboard Collaborate, Conferences in Canvas or Google Meet, for example). Use breakout rooms for students to work through the complexities and tensions listed in the Handout. These can be set automatically or manually: ensure that breakout rooms are enabled prior to your session. Provide a brief introduction to the session and set guidelines for constructive and supportive online discussion. Open the breakout rooms and broadcast the complexities and tensions in the Handout to your students. Ask groups to discuss each one, taking notes as they hold their discussion: they will need to discuss these issues with the whole class later. You can develop and use an online spreadsheet or document note-catcher to organize note-taking for each group, if required. This can be used to monitor their discussions and see how they are progressing. They can also help you to decide which breakout rooms to visit during the session.

This activity can also be run as a student worksheet, if contact time is not available. Use the complexities and tensions provided in the Handout to develop an appropriate worksheet to give to your students. Add other complexities and tensions that are relevant to your discipline, if required.

Key issues

This activity is of particular use for students who are in the process of thinking about, or developing, their application for ethical approval. It enables them to become familiar with your university's and/or department's research ethics policy, procedures and guidelines, while thinking more deeply about the complexities and tensions within research ethics. The activity starts with a short discussion on what they think about their university's policy, before moving to other complexities and tensions that they may not have considered. Reading the university's policy first gives context to the activity and enables them to relate the ensuing discussion to their own research.

Six broad areas have been covered in the Student Handout, but these can be modified if there are complexities and tensions that are specific to your discipline (those related to medicine and healthcare, for example). Delete the extra information provided in Question 1 on the Handout, if you think that students should be able to work this out for themselves.

→ **Related activities**

Activity 6: Aligning with the UN's Sustainable Development Goals

Activity 12: Comparing codes of ethics

Activity 33: Knowing about the General Data Protection Regulation (GDPR)

Activity 36: Working within the European Code of Conduct for Research Integrity

Activity 37: Aligning with the Concordat to Support Research Integrity

....

→ **Preparatory reading**

Educators: Ensure you are familiar with your university's and/or department's research ethics policy, procedures and guidelines (or similar).

Students: Should read their university's and/or department's research ethics policy, procedures and guidelines (or similar) in preparation for this activity.

....

→ **Useful resources**

Hammersley, M. and Traianou, A. (2012) *Ethics in Qualitative Research: Controversies and Contexts*. London: Sage.
Kara, H. (2018) *Research Ethics in the Real World: Euro-Western and Indigenous Perspectives*. Bristol: Policy Press.
Oyinloye, B. (2021) 'Towards an Ọmọlúàbí code of research ethics: Applying a situated, participant-centred virtue ethics framework to fieldwork with disadvantaged populations in diverse cultural settings', *Research Ethics*, first published 16 April 2021, doi: 10.1177/17470161211010863.
Taylor, A., Taylor-Neu, R. and Butterwick, S. (2020) '"Trying to square the circle": Research ethics and Canadian higher education', *European Educational Research Journal*, 19 (1): 56-71, first published 4 July 2018, doi: 10.1177/1474904118785542.
The Ethics Codes Collection, produced by the Center for the Study of Ethics in the Professions, Illinois Institute of Technology can be found at http://ethicscodescollection.org [accessed 2 November 2021].
Detailed ethical guidelines are provided by the Social Research Association in the UK: https://the-sra.org.uk/SRA/Ethics/Research-ethics-guidance/SRA/Ethics/Research-Ethics-Guidance [accessed 2 November 2021].

Activity 3

Activity • • • • • • • • • • • → 3

Assessing the Complexities and Tensions of Research Ethics

STUDENT HANDOUT

This activity is called 'Assessing the complexities and tensions of research ethics'. Some of these complexities and tensions are listed below. Discuss each one with your group members: identify difficulties that could arise and suggest possible ways to overcome these difficulties.

1. Understanding and following your university's and/or department's research ethics policy, procedures and guidelines.

    a. Are they simple to understand and follow?

    b. Are they cut and dried? Are there any grey areas?

    c. Do they address all research approaches and methodologies?

    d. Are they suitable for all disciplines?

2. Matching ethical standards of professional practice with ethical standards required to pass university ethical review.

3. Bringing together ethical practice or standards from different disciplines when undertaking interdisciplinary, multidisciplinary or transdisciplinary research.

4. Reconciling research approaches and methodologies that might focus on different aspects of ethical practice.

5. Balancing different cultural, social and political perceptions and beliefs about research ethics.

6. Integrating personal virtues, judgements and beliefs with those of collaborators, peers and the wider research community.

Learning outcome: By the end of this activity, you will be able to identify and assess the complexities and tensions of research ethics.

Activity • • • • • • • • • • • • → 4

Meeting the Ethical Needs of Stakeholders

The activity

Give a copy of the Student Handout to your students and ask them to work through the questions during independent study. Give a date by which time the work should be submitted, and provide assessment criteria if you choose to make this an assessed piece of work. Once the worksheets have been returned, go through them to check that students are clear about the ethical needs of stakeholders: if not, meet individually with students or hold an in-class or online discussion to clarify points.

This activity can also be run as a whole-class online synchronous discussion, using video conferencing/webinar tools such as Zoom Meetings, Google Meet, Blackboard Collaborate or the appropriate tool integrated with Moodle. Set guidelines for constructive and supportive online discussion. Introduce the session and work through the questions provided in the Student Handout. This works best if there are no more than eight students: if you have more than this number, divide your students into groups of up to eight and use breakout rooms for students to work through the questions, before bringing them back together to discuss the issues raised.

Key issues

Students should be encouraged early in their research to think about stakeholders: who they are, their interests and their ethical needs. This activity does not take up too much time, but raises important issues that are sometimes not considered fully by students.

A stakeholder is a person, a group of people, a community or an organization that has an interest in (or is implicated by) the topic, methods, results and/or outcomes of students' research. Students might decide to engage stakeholders because co-productive and/or participatory approaches help to increase impact and enable research to be aligned to the needs of users (Activities 29, 30 and 94). Stakeholder-driven research shares knowledge, power and decision-making, and encourages ethical research (Corbie-Smith et al., 2018). Sharing data with stakeholders increases transparency; enables others to replicate the work; reduces participant burden; helps to build science, capacity, fairness and respect; reduces the costs of further research; saves time and resources; and increases collaboration (Activity 89).

However, engaging stakeholders may not be straightforward: participants might hinder the research process or misunderstand the process, and research settings might not be suitable for stakeholders (for example, den Houting et al., 2021). This activity enables students to consider all these points in relation to their own research.

→ Related activities

Activity 2: Discussing the ethics of consent and purpose

Activity 5: Assessing research accountability

Activity 7: Promoting social good through research practice

Activity 82: Aligning with the FAIR principles

Activity 89: Assessing the ethical implications of data sharing

Activity 94: Ensuring against exploitation of results and outputs

→ Preparatory reading

Educators: Useful preparatory reading is provided by Robert Borst and Annette Boaz, who reflect on their research on stakeholder engagement in their blog: https://blogs.lse.ac.uk/impactofsocialsciences/2019/11/01/who-are-stakeholders-in-research-a-science-and-technology-studies-approach-to-navigating-research-impact/, 1 November 2019 [accessed 22 March 2021].

Students: Can find their own resources for this activity, or you can add some of the resources listed below to the Student Handout.

→ Useful resources

Boaz, A., Hanney, S., Borst, R., O'Shea, A. and Kok, M. (2018) 'How to engage stakeholders in research: Design principles to support improvement', *Health Research Policy and Systems*, 16 (60), published 11 July 2018, doi: 10.1186/s12961-018-0337-6.

Corbie-Smith, G., Wynn, M., Richmond, A., Rennie, S., Green, M., Hoover, S.M., Watson-Hopper, S. and Nisbeth, K.S. (2018) 'Stakeholder-driven, consensus development methods to design an ethical framework and guidelines for engaged research', *PLoS ONE*, 13 (6): e0199451, published online 21 June 2018, doi: 10.1371/journal.pone.0199451.

Hoover, S.M., Tiwari, S., Kim, J., Green, M., Richmond, A., Wynn, M., Nisbeth, K.S., Rennie, S. and Corbie-Smith, G. (2019) 'Convergence despite divergence: Views of academic and community stakeholders about the ethics of community-engaged research', *Ethnicity and Disease*, 29 (2): 309–16, published online 18 April 2019, doi: 10.18865/ed.29.2.309.

den Houting, J., Higgins, J., Isaacs, K., Mahony, J. and Pellicano, E. (2021) ''I'm not just a guinea pig': Academic and community perceptions of participatory autism research', *Autism*, 25 (1): 148–63, first published 27 August 2020, doi: 10.1177/1362361320951696.

Kelly, E.L., Davis, L., Holguin, M., Gaona, L., Pahwa, R., Lee, S., Pancake, L., Murch, L., Giambone, L. and Brekke, J. (2020) 'Practice-based research networks in stakeholder-driven social work research', *Research on Social Work Practice*, 30 (8): 819–31, first published 24 July 2020, doi: 10.1177/1049731520942591.

Neale, B. (2013) 'Adding time into the mix: Stakeholder ethics in qualitative longitudinal research', *Methodological Innovations Online*, 8 (2): 6–20, first published 1 August 2013, doi: 10.4256/mio.2013.010.

Penuel, W.R., Riedy, R., Barber, M.S., Peurach, D.J., LeBouef, W.A. and Clark, T. (2020) 'Principles of collaborative education research with stakeholders: Toward requirements for a new research and development infrastructure', *Review of Educational Research*, 90 (5): 627–74, first published 3 July 2020, doi: 10.3102/0034654320938126.

Ward, C.L., Shaw, D., Anane-Sarpong, E., Sankoh, O., Tanner, M. and Elger, B. (2018) 'The ethics of health care delivery in a pediatric malaria vaccine trial: The perspectives of stakeholders from Ghana and Tanzania', *Journal of Empirical Research on Human Research Ethics*, 13 (1): 26–41, first published 28 November 2017, doi: 10.1177/1556264617742236.

Activity 4

Meeting the Ethical Needs of Stakeholders

STUDENT HANDOUT

This activity is called 'Meeting the ethical needs of stakeholders'. Work through the following questions during independent study and return them to me by the given date.

1. When thinking about your research, what is a 'stakeholder'?
2. Who are the stakeholders of your research?
3. What interests do these stakeholders have in your research (or how are stakeholders implicated in your research)?
4. Can you identify any tensions between the interests of different stakeholders?
5. Can you identify any tensions between the interests of stakeholders and your research (or the way you intend to conduct and report your research)?

6. Should these stakeholders be engaged in your research?
   a. If yes, in what way?
   b. If no, why not?
7. Can you identify any problems that might be encountered when engaging stakeholders?
8. What are the ethical needs of the stakeholders you have identified?
9. Why is it important to think about the ethical needs of these stakeholders?
10. What action do you intend to take to meet the ethical needs of stakeholders?

Learning outcome: By the end of this activity, you will be able to define what is meant by a stakeholder; identify stakeholders, their interests and possible tensions in relation to your research; assess stakeholder engagement; and explain how to meet the ethical needs of stakeholders.

Activity • • • • • • • • • • • → 5

Assessing Research Accountability

The activity

Choose whether to run this activity as an online asynchronous activity or as an in-class activity. If you choose the online activity, use a suitable tool for students to upload their work, share and discuss with their peers (Discussions in Canvas, Forum in Moodle or Discussions in Brightspace, for example). Check that settings enable files to be added to discussions. Give your students a copy of the Student Handout and ask them to work through the questions on their own during independent study. Give a deadline by which time work should be completed, uploaded and discussions held. If you choose to make this an assessed piece of work, provide specific activity requirements and assessment criteria. If you choose the in-class activity, adapt the Handout slightly and lead a class discussion on the issues raised from the self-guided exercise.

Key issues

This activity asks students to spend a little time thinking about research accountability on their own, before coming together to discuss thoughts with their peers. This enables them to develop their thoughts, pool ideas, learn from each other and consolidate learning. Issues that arise in this activity include:

- Researchers must be accountable for their actions. They must be responsible, act with integrity (Activities 19 and 20) and ensure that their research is open and transparent (Activity 17). All actions and decisions must be justifiable, based on acceptable standards.
- Accountability is important because it helps to avoid research misconduct (Activity 22) and address conflicts of interest (Activity 25). It addresses problems with unethical practice in data collection (Activity 67) and data analysis (Activity 71). Accountability builds trust in inferences and conclusions (Activity 91) and helps to ensure against exploitation of results and outputs (Activity 94).
- Researchers are accountable to themselves, their institution, their discipline/profession, their participants, the wider public and all stakeholders (Activity 4).
- Individuals, groups and communities expect and deserve accountability, in particular, in cases where their lives are affected by research outcomes. Researchers must take responsibility for possible social, economic and political consequences of their research.
- Accountability can be developed through a better understanding of the research process (Wagner, 2020). Students and researchers should ensure that they receive appropriate research methods training and view integrity as an individual and collective responsibility (Activity 19).
- Students and researchers can ensure accountability by adhering to all institutional/professional policies and guidelines. They should take note of disciplinary standards of acceptable academic conduct (Activity 18), and foster research integrity through practice (Activity 20). The processes of editing and reviewing can help to build accountability.

→ Related activities

Activity 4: Meeting the ethical needs of stakeholders

Activity 17: Cultivating transparency and openness

Activity 18: Appraising disciplinary standards of acceptable academic conduct

Activity 19: Viewing integrity as an individual and collective responsibility

Activity 20: Fostering research integrity through practice

Activity 21: Developing a resilient integrity culture

→ Preparatory reading

Educators: Read your university policy and guidelines on research accountability, if you have not already done so. All the resources listed below provide useful preparatory reading.

Students: None required. Students will find their own resources for this activity. They should be made aware of your university policy and guidelines on research accountability.

→ Useful resources

Jarzabkowski, P., Langley, A. and Nigam, A. (2021) 'Navigating the tensions of quality in qualitative research', *Strategic Organization*, 19 (1): 70–80, first published 4 February 2021, doi: 10.1177/1476127020985094.

Komporozos-Athanasiou, A., Thompson, M. and Fotaki, M. (2018) 'Performing accountability in health research: A socio-spatial framework', *Human Relations*, 71 (9): 1264–87, first published 4 December 2017, doi: 10.1177/0018726717740410.

Mayernik, M.S. (2017) 'Open data: Accountability and transparency', *Big Data & Society*, first published 4 July 2017, doi: 10.1177/2053951717718853.

Pardee, J.W., Fothergill, A., Weber, L. and Peek, L. (2018) 'The collective method: Collaborative social science research and scholarly accountability', *Qualitative Research*, 18 (6): 671–88, first published 19 December 2017, doi: 10.1177/1468794117743461.

Romm, N. (2001) *Accountability in Social Research: Issues and Debates*. New York, NY: Springer.

Romm, N. (2010) *New Racism: Revisiting Researcher Accountabilities*. Dordrecht: Springer.

Wagner, B. (2020) 'Accountability by design in technology research', *Computer Law & Security Review*, 37, July 2020, 105398, doi: 10.1016/j.clsr.2020.105398.

Activity 5

Activity • • • • • • • • • • • → 5

Assessing Research Accountability

STUDENT HANDOUT

This activity is called 'Assessing research accountability'. Work through the following questions on an individual basis. Once you have done this, upload your answers using the tool that has been set up for this purpose. Read the responses uploaded by your peers and enter into online discussion, where appropriate. Ensure that posts are constructive and informative, and enable your peers to work towards meeting the learning outcome given below. Remember to be courteous and respectful in all the posts you make.

1. What is meant by research accountability?
2. Why is research accountability important?
3. To whom are researchers accountable?

4. How can researchers ensure accountability?
5. What specific action will you take to ensure accountability when researching?

Learning outcome: By the end of this activity, you will be able to define what is meant by research accountability, describe why it is important and explain how to be accountable when researching.

Activity • • • • • • • • • • • • • → 6

Aligning with the UN's Sustainable Development Goals

ACTIVITY 6: EDUCATOR NOTES

Purpose: This activity encourages students to find out about the United Nations (UN) Sustainable Development Goals (SDGs) and think about how research can be aligned with these goals through producing a podcast aimed at members of the public. Podcasts are shared and discussed with peers for deeper coverage and greater understanding.

Type: Podcast production and sharing.

Alternative type(s): Poster presentation.

Level: Elementary, intermediate and advanced.

Duration: Students will spend a few hours during independent study working with group members to research, produce, share and discuss podcasts. Educators will spend one or two hours listening to podcasts and monitoring online discussions. If the poster presentation option is chosen, students will spend a few hours during independent study working with their group members to research and produce their poster presentation. Fifty minutes to two hours of contact time will be required to present, view and discuss posters (depending on the number of student groups).

Equipment/materials: Students can use smartphones, tablets or laptops for this activity; however, recording equipment should be made available if students do not possess this technology. You will need a suitable tool to upload and discuss podcasts.

Learning outcome: By the end of this activity, students will be able to describe the UN's SDGs and illustrate, with examples, how research can be aligned with these goals.

The activity

Divide your students into small groups (three to five students in each group is a good number for this activity, but if you have only a few students in your cohort, this activity can be carried out in pairs). Give each group a copy of the Student Handout. This asks them to produce a podcast that explains to members of the public how research can be aligned with the UN's SDGs. Students can choose the structure, style and content of their podcasts: a few examples are given in the handout, along with information about how to produce their podcasts (check that the editing tools mentioned in the Handout are still available when you run the activity).

Set up a suitable tool for students to upload, listen to and discuss podcasts (Discussions in Canvas or Forum in Moodle that enable messages to be posted with media file attachments, for example). Students should upload their podcasts by your given deadline, then spend some time listening to, and discussing, the podcasts of their peers. Listen to all podcasts and monitor online discussions to ensure that information is correct, supportive and respectful. If appropriate, ask students to vote on the most informative or creative podcast at the end of the activity (if you choose to do this, add a sentence to the Student Handout).

This activity can also be run as a poster presentation. Ask students, in their groups, to produce a poster that illustrates or explains how research can be aligned to the UN's SDGs. Groups should produce their poster during independent study. Give a date and time when the posters are to be presented so that each group can work to the deadline (if you choose a time that is outside your usual teaching hours, ensure that all students are able to attend the session). Provide venue details so that groups know what space and equipment is available for their poster presentation. If students are unfamiliar with the poster presentation technique, give them a copy of the Student Handout in Activity 26, which gives advice and information about producing a poster presentation. More information for educators about running a poster presentation session is also provided in Activity 26.

Key issues

There are 17 SDGs that students can consider for this activity: some students choose to concentrate on one of the goals and look at research projects that align with that goal. Others choose to look at all 17 goals and illustrate why it is important that research aligns with these goals. Some students choose a disciplinary approach (biology or economics for example), discussing research projects within these disciplines and illustrating how they align with relevant goals. Some choose, instead, to focus on why it is important to align with SDGs and how this can be achieved in research and in research methods training.

Producing a podcast aimed at the wider public encourages students to think about the impact of research and how it can affect people's lives. It also encourages them to think about how research projects and methods are discussed in a way that is interesting and can be understood by those who do not have any research methods training. It enables them to be creative and imaginative, producing podcasts that are both entertaining and informative. Students are asked to work in groups for this activity as it helps to pool ideas and build understanding, while enabling students to help and support each other with the technical aspects of podcast production.

→ Related activities

Activity 4: Meeting the ethical needs of stakeholders

Activity 7: Promoting social good through research practice

Activity 13: Creating social change through research practice

→ Preparatory reading

Educators: Visit the UN's website for a list of the 17 SDGs, along with videos, campaign information and resources (details below). Section 2.2 of SDSN Australia/Pacific (2017) provides useful material on action that can be taken to align research to SDGs (and align SDGs to research), including interdisciplinary and transdisciplinary approaches, and co-design and co-production approaches.

Students: None required. Students will find their own resources for this activity.

→ Useful resources

The UN's Sustainable Development Goals can be found on the UN website at www.un.org/sustainabledevelopment [accessed 5 November 2021]. Informative videos can also be found on this site.

Section 2.2 of this report from Sustainable Development Solutions Network – Australia/Pacific covers research, illustrating how research is relevant to SDGs, how it can support their implementation and what action can be taken by researchers.

SDSN Australia/Pacific (2017) *Getting Started with the SDGs in Universities: A Guide for Universities, Higher Education Institutions, and the Academic Sector*, Australia, New Zealand and Pacific Edition. https://resources.unsdsn.org/getting-started-with-the-sdgs-in-universities [accessed 8 March 2022].

Activity 6

Annan-Diab, F. and Molinari, C. (2017) 'Interdisciplinarity: Practical approach to advancing education for sustainability and for the Sustainable Development Goals', *The International Journal of Management Education*, 15 (2): 73–83, doi: 10.1016/j.ijme.2017.03.006.

Hewitt, M., Molthan-Hill, P., Lomax, R. and Baddley, J. (2019) 'Supporting the UN's Sustainable Development Goals: Reconceptualising a "sustainable development assessment tool" for the health and care system in England', *Perspectives in Public Health*, 139 (2): 88–96, first published 11 July 2018, doi: 10.1177/1757913918786523.

Useh, U. (2021) 'Sustainable Development Goals as a framework for postgraduate future research following COVID-19 pandemic: A new norm for developing countries', *Higher Education for the Future*, 8 (1): 123–32, first published 8 December 2020, doi: 10.1177/2347631120972064.

Activity 6

Activity · · · · · · · · · · · · · → 6

Aligning with the UN's Sustainable Development Goals

STUDENT HANDOUT

This activity is called 'Aligning with the UN's Sustainable Development Goals' (SDGs). Work with your group members to produce a podcast aimed at members of the public, which lets them know how research can be aligned with the SDGs. The structure, content and style of podcast is a group choice: all you need to do is ensure that your podcast enables your peers to meet the learning outcome given below. You might decide, for example, to focus on a specific research project, illustrating how it aligns with the SDGs. Or you might decide to explain more about the SDGs, what they are, why they are important, why research should be aligned to them and how this can be achieved. Or perhaps you might focus in on one particular SDG and think about how research can be aligned to that goal. Provide practical examples that members of the public can understand and to which they can relate.

Podcasts can be recorded using smartphones, tablets or laptops, but if you do not have any of this equipment, or feel it to be inadequate, come to me for help. This activity does not require professionally produced podcasts: instead, just make sure that the audio recording is clear enough to be heard easily by your peers. This requires a quiet space for the recording, a stable mount for your device, suitable microphone placement and a little practice to get it right.

Once you have produced your podcast, edit as required (using free online audio editing tools such as Audacity, Auphonic or Beautiful Audio Editor) and upload it using the tool provided for this purpose by the deadline given. Listen to the podcasts produced by your peers and enter into online discussion, where appropriate. You will be listening to a number of podcasts, therefore, try to make yours stand out: ensure that it is entertaining and enables your peers to learn something new. If all podcasts are dull, this will be a rather boring activity!

Learning outcome: By the end of this activity, you will be able to describe the UN's Sustainable Development Goals and illustrate, with examples, how research can be aligned with these goals.

Activity · · · · · · · · · · · → 7

Promoting Social Good through Research Practice

The activity

Divide your students into small groups and give each group a copy of the Student Handout. This asks them to craft a story that illustrates, explains or discusses how research practice can promote social good. They should make their story entertaining, informative and memorable. When you next meet, ask them to tell their stories, allocating up to 10 minutes for each story. Allocate five minutes after each story for discussion, with a few minutes at the end of the session to summarize the issues raised. Ensure that presentation equipment is available for their use, if required.

Questions that can be asked after each story include:

1. What did you learn from the story?
2. What is the key lesson conveyed by the story?
3. Do you think the story is memorable? Why?

You can ask students to produce a digital story instead, if this is a more suitable option (the Student Handout will need to be adapted accordingly). Explain that students can use any technology or features that they wish to bring their digital story to life (graphics, video, audio and photography, for example). Give a deadline for stories to be uploaded and ask students to spend time reading, commenting on and discussing each group's story. This can be done using open-source software and publishing tools such as Pageflow or WeVideo, or by using learning management system (LMS) discussion tools that enable the attachment of media files (Discussions in Canvas, for example). Read each story and monitor comments to ensure that information is correct, supportive and encouraging and to check that students are able to learn from the stories presented.

Key issues

Students enjoy this activity. It enables them to think about the different ways in which social good can be promoted through research practice, while working out the most creative way to tell a story. Stories can be told in a number of different ways, including anecdotes, case studies, life histories, reflective accounts, fiction, myth, scenarios and personal examples from experience. Some students choose to use real examples, whereas others decide to use their imagination to create memorable stories. See Gersie and Schiefflin (2014) for examples of how storytelling can be used, in their case, to promote a greener world.

If the digital storytelling option is chosen, students have the opportunity to produce interactive and meaningful stories, using a wide variety of features such as narration, title screens, photography, music, text, graphics and sound effects. However, students should not get too caught up in the technical production aspects of their story development. The goal is to craft a story that is memorable and enables their peers to learn something new. Technology can help to meet this goal, but should not detract from it.

Both the in-class and digital activities require students to work in groups because some people are better at telling stories than others. Working in groups helps to pool strengths and provides a variety of roles so that if a student does not feel comfortable telling the story, they can adopt another role within the group. Producing a story in a group can help students to understand others, help group cohesion, aid collaborative learning and enhance learning among group members.

→ Related activities

Activity 13: Creating social change through research practice

Activity 46: Reclaiming datasets for social justice

Activity 80: Avoiding unethical or inappropriate action resulting from analyses

Activity 94: Ensuring against exploitation of results and outputs

Activity 96: Discussing Open Research, Open Science and Open Access

→ Preparatory reading

Educators: If you are new to using storytelling in the classroom you might find Alterio and McDrury (2003) useful preparatory reading for storytelling activities as it outlines the different models of storytelling and explains how techniques can be used. A useful activity for educators who are interested in using storytelling with their students is Activity 46: Learning through storytelling, in Dawson (2019).

Students: None required. Students will find their own resources for this activity.

→ Useful resources

Alterio, M. and McDrury, J. (2003) *Learning Through Storytelling in Higher Education: Using Reflection and Experience to Improve Learning*. London: Routledge.

Dawson, C. (2019) *100 Activities for Teaching Study Skills*. London: Sage, pp. 131–3.

Gersie, A. and Schiefflin, E. (2014) *Storytelling for a Greener World: Environment, Community and Story-Based Learning*. Stroud: Hawthorn Press.

Activity 7

Huffman, T. and Tracy, S.J. (2018) 'Making claims that matter: Heuristics for theoretical and social impact in qualitative research', *Qualitative Inquiry*, 24 (8): 558-70, first published 11 December 2017, doi: 10.1177/1077800417742411.

Lee, J.S. and Wolf-Branigin, M. (2020) 'Innovations in modeling social good: A demonstration with juvenile justice intervention', *Research on Social Work Practice*, 30 (2): 174-85, first published 30 May 2019, doi: 10.1177/1049731519852151.

Mor Barak, M.E. (2020) 'The practice and science of social good: Emerging paths to positive social impact', *Research on Social Work Practice*, 30 (2): 139-50, first published 3 January 2018, doi: 10.1177/1049731517745600.

Examples of digital stories can be found at www.storycenter.org/stories [accessed 29 September 2021].

Activity 7

Activity · · · · · · · · · · · → 7

Promoting Social Good through Research Practice

STUDENT HANDOUT

This activity is called 'Promoting social good through research practice'. Craft a story with your group members that illustrates, explains or discusses how research practice can promote social good. The specific topic, style, structure, content and genre of your story are a group choice. It can be invented or based on real examples: if you choose to use a real example, make sure that the source is cited correctly. Try to be creative and imaginative: your story should be entertaining, informative and memorable.

Consider the following questions when you craft your story:

1. What is the key lesson that you wish to convey?
2. What do you want your peers to learn from your story?
3. How are you going to ensure that others learn from your story?

4. Will your story stimulate thought and reflection? Will it have an emotional and/or intellectual impact?
5. Will your story enable your peers to achieve the learning outcome given below?

Prepare your story for our next session: you can use props, visual aids or presentation software if you wish. Your group will be given up to 10 minutes to tell your story and a further five minutes for peers to ask questions and discuss your story. You will also be able to listen to the stories told by other groups and ask questions.

Learning outcome: By the end of this activity, you will be able to identify, explain and discuss how social good can be promoted through research practice.

Activity ‧ ‧ ‧ ‧ ‧ ‧ ‧ ‧ ‧ ‧ → 8

Conducting Discrimination-Aware and Fairness-Aware Research

ACTIVITY 8: EDUCATOR NOTES

Purpose: This activity is aimed at students who are about to start the research for their dissertation or thesis. It is a workshop that requires them to develop an action plan that will help to ensure that they undertake discrimination-aware and fairness-aware research.

Type: Workshop (in-class).

Alternative type(s): Workshop (online synchronous); self-guided individual exercise.

Level: Intermediate and advanced.

Duration: Fifty minutes to one hour for the workshop. If the self-guided individual exercise is chosen students will spend up to two hours during independent study working on their action plan.

Equipment/materials: A suitable video/web conferencing tool, if the online option is chosen.

Learning outcome: By the end of this activity, students will be able to describe what is meant by discrimination-aware and fairness-aware research and will have produced an action plan that will help them to conduct their research fairly and without discrimination.

The activity

Hold a workshop with students who are about to begin their research. Introduce the session with a brief description of what is meant by discrimination-aware and fairness-aware research. Divide your students into pairs or small groups and ask them to spend 10 minutes listing examples of ways in which discrimination and unfairness can affect research, or be incorporated into any part of the research process. Bring the small groups back together to discuss the issues raised for a further 10 minutes.

Once this has been completed, ask your students to return to their pairs or small groups to discuss how they can ensure that their research is discrimination-aware and fairness-aware. After 10 minutes, bring them back together to discuss the issues raised for a further five minutes. Then ask your students to work independently to develop an action plan for their research that will help them to carry out discrimination-aware and fairness-aware research. Spend a little time at the end of the session to check that students are happy with their action plan and are clear about how to proceed once they have finished in the workshop.

This workshop can be held online, if you prefer, using a video/web conferencing tool such as Zoom Meetings, Blackboard Collaborate or Meetings in Microsoft Teams for Education. Set guidelines for constructive and supportive online discussion, use breakout rooms and follow the same structure as that given for the in-class workshop, above.

This activity can also be run as a self-guided individual exercise. Ask your students to think about, and research, what is meant by discrimination-aware and fairness-aware research before going on to build an action plan that will help them to conduct discrimination-aware and fairness-aware research.

Key issues

A variety of issues can be raised in this activity depending on your students' understanding, knowledge, discipline and subject of study. Some students choose to concentrate on how researcher bias can lead to discrimination, highlighting the importance of a careful and full evaluation of biases. This can be done with reference to equality, diversity and inclusion (Activity 28) or through recognizing bias when collecting data (Activity 63) and when analysing data (Activities 73 and 74), for example. Students highlight the importance of ensuring that researchers are well trained and well versed in equality, diversity and human rights. Other groups raise the issue of dealing with discriminatory comments or action by research participants or when using co-researchers in a collaborative project, for example.

A topic that is discussed by students interested in digital research methods involves big data, artificial intelligence and machine learning: how historical biases, racism and sexism can influence machine training and outputs (see O'Neil, 2017 for examples). The topics of discrimination-aware data mining and fairness, accountability and transparency in machine learning can be introduced into the discussion, if they are not raised by students and if you feel they are relevant to your cohort. More information about these topics can be obtained from Chapter 29 in Dawson (2020: 194–9) and from the Fairness, Accountability, and Transparency in Machine Learning website (www.fatml.org).

→ Related activities

Activity 28: Evaluating biases with reference to equality, diversity and inclusion

Activity 45: Designing inclusive data systems

Activity 52: Assessing bias in search tools

Activity 54: Understanding problems associated with unequal access to data

Activity 55: Assessing the ethical implications of ownership and use of digital technology

Activity 63: Recognizing and addressing bias when collecting data

Activity 73: Recognizing and addressing bias when analysing qualitative data

Activity 74: Avoiding bias in quantitative analyses

→ Preparatory reading

Educators: Most of the books and papers listed below discuss discrimination and fairness in big data, artificial intelligence and machine learning and provide useful preparatory reading. Further references relating to bias can be found in the relevant activities listed above.

Students: None required at the start of the workshop. Some of the resources listed below can be recommended once the workshop has concluded.

→ Useful resources

Banaji, M. and Greenwald, A. (2016) *Blindspot: Hidden Biases of Good People*, reprint edition. New York, NY: Bantam Books.
Broussard, M. (2019) *Artificial Unintelligence: How Computers Misunderstand the World*. Cambridge, MA: MIT Press.
Criado Perez, C. (2020) Invisible Women: Exposing Data Bias in a World Designed for Men. London: Vintage.
Dawson, C. (2020) *A–Z of Digital Research Methods*. Abingdon: Routledge.
Kearns, M. and Roth, A. (2020) *The Ethical Algorithm: The Science of Socially Aware Algorithm Design*. New York, NY: Oxford University Press.
Mann, M. and Matzner, T. (2019) 'Challenging algorithmic profiling: The limits of data protection and anti-discrimination in responding to emergent discrimination', *Big Data & Society*, first published 16 December 2019, doi: 10.1177/2053 951719895805.
O'Neil, C. (2017) *Weapons of Math Destruction: How Big Data Increases Inequality and Threatens Democracy*. London: Penguin.
Veale, M. and Binns, R. (2017) 'Fairer machine learning in the real world: Mitigating discrimination without collecting sensitive data', *Big Data & Society*, first published 20 November 2017, doi: 10.1177/2053951717743530.
Zuiderveen Borgesius, F.J. (2020) 'Strengthening legal protection against discrimination by algorithms and artificial intelligence', *International Journal of Human Rights*, 24 (10): 1572–93, published online 25 March 2020, doi: 10.1080/ 13642987.2020.1743976.

Activity 8

Activity • • • • • • • • • • → 9

Discussing Privacy and Confidentiality in the Research Context

The activity

Give your students a copy of the Student Handout. This asks them to think about, and research, what is meant by privacy and confidentiality in the research context. They are to produce three questions on this topic that they would like to discuss with their peers when you next meet (in-class or online). The Handout encourages them to develop questions that will lead to an informative, interesting and thought-provoking discussion. This activity works best if there are 8-10 students in the discussion group. If you have more than this number in your cohort, divide your students into groups (use a room big enough for separate groups if you choose the in-class option, and use breakout rooms if you choose the online option).

Your role is to act as facilitator. Set guidelines for constructive, respectful and courteous discussion. Ask a student to pose their first question, then encourage students to answer the questions and/or discuss issues raised by the question. Move on to the next student when you feel it to be appropriate (depending on the content of discussion and whether you feel it has run its course). Students might not have time to pose all three questions, but they are asked to produce three in case one of their questions is posed by another student. Continue with the discussion until the session is almost over: conclude with a summary of the main points raised.

Key issues

This activity has been designed as a student-led activity because it enables students to raise and discuss aspects of privacy and confidentiality that are important to their research and studies. Questions that are asked and topics that are discussed tend to depend on discipline, methodology, research approach and level of study. They cover issues of privacy and confidentiality when:

- recruiting participants (Activity 62);
- considering cultural and social norms (some groups/individuals are more private than others, for example);
- considering age and different attitudes towards privacy and confidentiality;
- considering legal and policy requirements (Section 3);
- obtaining informed consent (how to talk about issues of privacy and confidentiality, and convince participants that the researcher will be able to protect privacy and confidentiality, for example: Activity 57);
- using digital technology (various aspects of privacy and confidentiality when undertaking online research, social media research and mobile app research, and when data mining or undertaking data analytics: Section 4);
- undertaking interviews (physical privacy in terms of where to hold interviews and confidentiality in terms of what is shared and how interviews are recorded, transcribed, analysed and stored, for example: Section 5);
- removing and destroying identifiers (what type of data can be used to identify participants and how these can be de-identified, including names, addresses, dates, records, codes, numbers and images: Activity 84);
- considering the risk of disclosure (in community-based research or social networks, for example);
- considering the risk of harm if information is made public (Activity 11);
- researching dangerous, illegal or illicit behaviour (Activity 34) and what should be done if students feel behaviours should be reported because someone is being harmed or is in danger, for example;
- undertaking third-party research or secondary analysis (Activity 79);
- managing and protecting data, and keeping them secure (Section 7);
- sharing research (Activity 89);
- working with the media (or when media report the results of research);
- publishing research (Activity 95);
- considering whether privacy and confidentiality are achievable and desirable in some types of research (see Kamanzi and Romania, 2019 for a discussion on this point).

Cautionary note

Some topics raised in this activity can be emotive: monitor discussions to ensure that students are acting in a courteous, responsible and respectful manner (and adhering to the guidelines you have set). If you notice that the discussion is getting heated or arguments are developing, refer students back to the guidelines and move the discussion on to the next question.

→ **Related activities**

Activity 1: Respecting human dignity, privacy and rights

Activity 11: Avoiding harm to others

Activity 50: Evaluating privacy policies of software companies and third-party providers

Activity 62: Addressing issues of anonymity and confidentiality

Activity 79: Discussing the ethics, integrity and practice of anonymization in analysis, secondary analysis, re-analysis and third-party analysis

Activity 84: Anonymizing qualitative and quantitative data

→ **Preparatory reading**

Educators: All the resources listed below provide useful preparatory material.

Students: None required. Students will find their own resources for this activity.

Activity 9

→ **Useful resources**

Brear, M. (2018) 'Swazi co-researcher participants' dynamic preferences and motivations for, representation with real names and (English-language) pseudonyms – an ethnography', *Qualitative Research*, 18 (6): 722–40, first published 30 November 2017, doi: 10.1177/1468794117743467.

Jacobs, B. and Popma, J. (2019) 'Medical research, Big Data and the need for privacy by design', *Big Data & Society*, first published 18 January 2019, doi: 10.1177/2053951718824352.

Kamanzi, A. and Romania, M. (2019) 'Rethinking confidentiality in qualitative research in the era of Big Data', *American Behavioral Scientist*, 63 (6): 743–58, first published 8 February 2019, doi: 10.1177/0002764219826222.

Lowrance, W. (2012) *Privacy, Confidentiality, and Health Research*. Cambridge: Cambridge University Press.

Oberski, D.L. and Kreuter, F. (2020) 'Differential privacy and social science: an urgent puzzle', *Harvard Data Science Review*, 2 (1), published 31 January 2020, doi: 10.1162/99608f92.63a22079.

Surmiak, A. (2020) 'Should we maintain or break confidentiality? The choices made by social researchers in the context of law violation and harm', *Journal of Academic Ethics*, 18: 229–47, published 16 July 2019, doi: 10.1007/s10805-019-09336-2.

Tovino, S.A. (2020) 'Privacy and security issues with mobile health research applications', *Journal of Law, Medicine & Ethics*, 48 (1_suppl): 154–8, first published 28 April 2020, doi: 10.1177/1073110520917041.

Useful information and links can be obtained from the guest blog post of the Digital Curation Centre: IDCC13 on the issues of confidentiality and open research data by Limor Peer, Associate Director for Research, Institution for Social and Policy Studies, Yale University: www.dcc.ac.uk/blog/idcc13-panel-confidentiality-and-open-access-research-data [accessed 4 April 2021].

Activity 9

Activity • • • • • • • • • • → 9

Discussing Privacy and Confidentiality in the Research Context

STUDENT HANDOUT

This activity is called 'Discussing privacy and confidentiality in the research context'. It is a student-led activity in which you and your peers will decide on, and lead, the discussion. Take a little time before we next meet to think about, and research, what is meant by privacy and confidentiality in the research context. Once you have done this, develop three questions related to this topic that you would like to explore with your peers.

When we next meet, each student, in turn, will have the chance to pose one of their questions, which will then be discussed by the group. It is important that we have an interesting, informative and thought-provoking discussion, so think about this when developing your questions. Try to choose something that will not have been chosen by your peers, while ensuring that your questions are related, in some way, to privacy and confidentiality in the research context.

You have been asked to produce three questions, but may have the chance to ask only one or two of them. It is important, however, that you produce three, so that you can choose which to ask and have alternatives available if one of your questions has already been posed by one of your peers.

Learning outcome: By the end of this activity, you will be able to explain what is meant by privacy and confidentiality in the research context and discuss and appraise a number of privacy and confidentiality issues that have been introduced by your peers.

Activity · · · · · · · · · · → 10

Working within the Principle of Beneficence

> **ACTIVITY 10: EDUCATOR NOTES**
>
> **Purpose:** This activity has been designed for postgraduate students who are in the process of planning their research. It is an informal discussion (in-class or online) for invited students who have an interest in this topic. This activity is closely aligned with Activity 11: Avoiding harm to others. The activities can be combined for greater coverage, if required.
>
> **Type:** Informal discussion (in-class or online).
>
> **Alternative type(s):** Self-guided individual exercise.
>
> **Level:** Advanced.
>
> **Duration:** Fifty minutes to one hour for the discussion. If you choose the self-guided individual exercise you will need to spend a little time producing guidelines for students, based on the questions given below. Students will spend one or two hours working on the questions during independent study.
>
> **Equipment/materials:** A suitable venue, if the in-class option is chosen, or a suitable video/web conferencing tool if the online option is chosen.
>
> **Learning outcome:** By the end of this activity, students will be able to explain and assess the principle of beneficence, and illustrate how they intend to address this principle in their research.

The activity

Invite together a group of postgraduate students who want to know more about working within the principle of beneficence (if you feel that this topic is relevant to all your students, or that voluntary attendance might not work for your students, make this session compulsory instead). Explain that this session is an informal discussion that will enable them to understand what is meant by beneficence, discuss the relevance to their research and think about the action they need to take to ensure that they work within the principle of beneficence. This activity can be run as an in-class session or as a synchronous online discussion (using a video/web conferencing tool such as Zoom Meetings, Blackboard Collaborate, Meetings in Microsoft Teams for Education, or Google Meet). Set guidelines for constructive, supportive and respectful interaction and use the questions given below as a basis for your discussion.

This activity can also be run as a self-guided individual exercise, if you prefer. Use the questions given below to produce a handout to give to your students so that they can work on the activity during independent study.

Key issues

This activity has been designed as an informal discussion for invited students because some research projects may not be relevant to the topic (the research does not involve human subjects) or students may already be familiar with what is required (those from medicine, healthcare or social work professions, for example). It is informal because there is no set structure: students should be encouraged to raise issues pertinent to their research.

Questions that can be used to guide the discussion, if required, include:

1. What is meant by beneficence?
2. Why is beneficence important in research?
3. Should all researchers work within the principle of beneficence? Why (not)?
4. Do beneficence and avoiding harm differ? If so, in what way?
5. Is it possible to work within the principle of beneficence yet still cause harm? Can you provide examples of when this might occur?
6. To whom does beneficence apply? How might it apply to research participants, stakeholders and future individuals and groups (those who might benefit or be harmed by the research later on, for example)?
7. Is it possible that the researcher's view of beneficence might differ from the views of research participants, stakeholders and future beneficiaries? If so, in what way? How can researchers address different views?
8. Is the principle of beneficence relevant to your research? If so, in what way?
9. How can you ensure that you work within the principle of beneficence in your research? What action do you need to take?

→ Related activities

Activity 7: Promoting social good through research practice

Activity 8: Conducting discrimination-aware and fairness-aware research

Activity 11: Avoiding harm to others

Activity 13: Creating social change through research practice

→ Preparatory reading

Educators: All the references listed below provide useful preparatory reading.

Students: None required prior to this activity. Relevant resources listed below can be recommended after the activity, if required.

→ Useful resources

Avant, L.C. and Swetz, K.M. (2020) 'Revisiting beneficence: What is a "benefit", and by what criteria?', *American Journal of Bioethics*, 20 (3): 75-7, published online 27 February 2020, doi: 10.1080/15265161.2020.1714808.

Bester, J.C. (2020) 'Beneficence, interests, and wellbeing in medicine: What it means to provide benefit to patients', *American Journal of Bioethics*, 20 (3): 53-62, published online 27 February 2020, doi: 10.1080/15265161.2020.1714793.

Brothers, K.B., Rivera, S.M., Cadigan, R.J., Sharp, R.R. and Goldenberg, A.J. (2019) 'A Belmont reboot: Building a normative foundation for human research in the 21st century', *Journal of Law, Medicine & Ethics*, 47 (1): 165-72, first published 17 April 2019, doi: 10.1177/1073110519840497.

Kirchhoffer, D., Favor, C. and Cordner, C. (2019) 'Beneficence in research ethics'. In D. Kirchhoffer and B. Richards (eds), *Beyond Autonomy: Limits and Alternatives to Informed Consent in Research Ethics and Law* (Cambridge Bioethics and Law, pp. 96-116). Cambridge: Cambridge University Press, doi: 10.1017/9781108649247.007.

Pieper, I. and Thomson, C.J.H. (2016) 'Beneficence as a principle in human research', *Monash Bioethics Review*, 34: 117-35, published 16 July 2016, doi: 10.1007/s40592-016-0061-3.

Ruch, G. (2014) 'Beneficence in psycho-social research and the role of containment', *Qualitative Social Work*, 13 (4): 522-38, first published 13 August 2013, doi: 10.1177/1473325013497390.

Activity 10

Activity • • • • • • • • • • → 11

Avoiding Harm to Others

ACTIVITY 11: EDUCATOR NOTES

Purpose: This activity is a brainstorm that encourages students to think about the different types of harm to others that can be caused by research, and discuss ways to mitigate harm in research.

Type: Brainstorm (in-class or online synchronous).

Alternative type(s): None.

Level: Elementary, intermediate and advanced.

Duration: Fifty minutes to one hour.

Equipment/materials: Interactive whiteboard, flipchart or chalkboard. A synchronous online brainstorming tool and a suitable video/web conferencing tool, if the online option is chosen.

Learning outcome: By the end of this activity, students will be able to list the different types of harm to others that can be caused by research and explain how to mitigate harm in research.

The activity

Introduce the topic and explain to your students that you are going to run a brainstorm for the first part of the session. Let them know that you require one-word answers for this brainstorm: students can provide them as soon as they think of something. Explain that they will not be criticised or judged by others for what they say, and they should not criticise or judge the answers given by other students (even if they do not agree with what has been said). All contributions will be written down without comment, until you have a full list that can be discussed when the brainstorm has concluded.

Pose the question: 'What harm to others can research cause?'. Ask students to give any one-word answer they can think of in relation to the question (you can give a couple of examples from the list below, if you think this will help to get the brainstorm started). Write down each one-word answer they give: the goal is to pool ideas and come up with a comprehensive list of types of harm that can be caused by research. This usually takes 10–15 minutes. Once you have created a suitable list (or students cannot think of other examples) work through each word, unpacking what is meant by the type of harm listed and asking students to suggest ways to mitigate this type of harm. Conclude the session with a summary of the main points raised.

This activity can be run as an online brainstorm, if you prefer. Find a suitable online brainstorming tool (Stormboard, MindMeister, SpiderScribe, Popplet or Miro are examples, but there are plenty more available). Practise with the tool if you have not used it before. Choose a suitable video/web conferencing tool for your discussion (Zoom Meetings, Blackboard Collaborate or Meetings in Microsoft Teams for Education, for example) and check that your chosen brainstorming tool is compatible. Again, practise with the tools, if required. Send your students the time, date and joining instructions. Introduce the session by explaining that the session is about avoiding harm to others in research, then run the brainstorm in the same way as the in-class session, described above.

Key issues

A wide variety of types of harm to others can be mentioned in the brainstorm. When working through your brainstorm list it is important to point out that harm avoidance must be considered at all stages of the research process: early in the planning stages, when applying for ethical approval (Activity 41), when collecting and analysing data, and when sharing and publishing research. Examples of harm and possible action include:

- Stress: this can be avoided through putting participants at ease, building trust, using appropriate methods and cultivating sensitivity in method (Activities 58 and 60). Participants must be given the right to withdraw at any time if their participation is too stressful (Activity 57).
- Discomfort: researchers should pay attention to location and venue, ensuring participants are comfortable; to methods of data collection and recording, ensuring participants are aware of, and comfortable with, all methods, and that they understand the process; to body language, taking note when a participant becomes uncomfortable.
- Anxiety: researchers should be open, transparent and sensitive. Building rapport can help to put people at ease. Appropriate researcher training is required. Participants must be given the right to withdraw at any time if they become too anxious.
- Helplessness: researchers must ensure that participants are not bullied or cajoled into taking part in research. They should not feel pressurized or exploited, or feel that they have no choice but to take part (researchers should choose gatekeepers or co-researchers with care).
- Embarrassment: researchers must consider the research context and situation, and how this might lead to embarrassment (when participants communicate with a researcher or when peers or colleagues might find out about the research, for example). Issues that can cause embarrassment should be avoided or approached only if absolutely necessary and when trust has been built.
- Injury: participants should not be put in physical danger. Researchers must carry out a risk assessment (Activity 27). This includes injury to animals in animal research.
- Illness: all potential risks must be identified, evaluated and managed, with ongoing assessment throughout the research. A comprehensive risk assessment must be carried out to identify risks (Activity 27).
- Trauma: participants might re-live trauma or might be traumatized by the research process. Researchers must carry out a detailed risk assessment and ensure that participants are fully informed about the research process and understand their right to withdraw.
- Prosecution: researchers must understand what can happen when they research illegal, unlawful, illicit or dangerous behaviour (Activity 34) and they must make consequences clear to participants before informed consent is requested and obtained.
- Demotion: researchers must be aware of the wider consequences of their research and assess how the results of their research can impact on employees (or others who have not been involved in the research). Researchers must pay attention to anonymity and confidentiality (Activity 62) and report research carefully (Activity 94).
- Redundancy: researchers must be aware of the consequences of their research, both for employees who have taken part in the research and for those who might be affected by the results of the research (in cases where decisions might be based on data analytics, for example: Activity 72). Again, researchers must pay attention to anonymity and confidentiality (Activity 62) and report research carefully (Activity 94). A comprehensive risk assessment will enable them to mitigate potential problems (Activity 27).
- Identification: researchers must pay close attention to the risk of identification throughout the research project, from design, through data collection, analysis and reporting, and when storing and sharing data (Activities 9, 62, 79 and 84). Care must be taken when using digital technologies, software companies and third-party providers (Activity 50) and when undertaking data analytics (Activity 72), data mining (Activity 49) or social media research, for example.
- Discrimination: researchers must ensure that they avoid all types of discrimination and act fairly (Activity 8). Evaluating bias with reference to equality, diversity and inclusion (Activity 28), and recognizing and addressing bias when collecting data (Activity 63) and analysing data (Activity 73) will help researchers to avoid this.

→ **Related activities**

Activity 8: Conducting discrimination-aware and fairness-aware research

Activity 10: Working within the principle of beneficence

Activity 14: Working with vulnerable people

Activity 15: Conducting research with children

Activity 27: Carrying out a risk assessment

Activity 30: Researching cross-culturally

Activity 11

→ Preparatory reading

Educators: Dixon and Quirke (2018) provide an interesting preparatory paper.

Students: None required. Some of the resources listed below can be recommended to students once the activity has concluded.

....

→ Useful resources

Bonell, C., Jamal, F. and Melendez-Torres, G.J. (2015) '"Dark logic": Theorising the harmful consequences of public health interventions', *Journal of Epidemiology and Community Health*, 69 (1): 95–8, Epub, 17 November 2014, doi: 10.1136/jech-2014-204671.

Dixon, S. and Quirke, L. (2018) 'What's the harm? The coverage of ethics and harm avoidance in research methods textbooks', *Teaching Sociology*, 46 (1): 12–24, first published 2 June 2017, doi: 10.1177/0092055X17711230.

Kennan, D. and Dolan, P. (2017) 'Justifying children and young people's involvement in social research: Assessing harm and benefit', *Irish Journal of Sociology*, 25 (3): 297–314, first published 29 May 2017, doi: 10.1177/0791603517711860.

Kostovicova, D. and Knott, E. (2020) 'Harm, change and unpredictability: The ethics of interviews in conflict research', *Qualitative Research*, first published 8 December 2020, doi: 10.1177/1468794120975657.

Ogden, J. (2019) 'Do no harm: Balancing the costs and benefits of patient outcomes in health psychology research and practice', *Journal of Health Psychology*, 24 (1): 25–37, first published 31 May 2016, doi: 10.1177/1359105316648760.

Pound, P. and Nicol, C.J. (2018) 'Retrospective harm benefit analysis of pre-clinical animal research for six treatment interventions', *PLoS ONE*, published 28 March 2018, doi: 10.1371/journal.pone.0193758.

Wood, E.J. (2006) 'The ethical challenges of field research in conflict zones', *Qualitative Sociology*, 29: 373–86, published 20 June 2006, doi: 10.1007/s11133-006-9027-8.

Activity 11

Activity · · · · · · · · · · · · → 12

Comparing Codes of Ethics

The activity

Divide your students into small groups. The number of groups depends on the size of your cohort: make sure that you have enough time for each group to make a 10-minute presentation with five minutes for discussion after each presentation.

Give each group a copy of the Student Handout. This asks them to visit the Ethics Codes Collection, produced by the Center for the Study of Ethics in the Professions, Illinois Institute of Technology: http://ethicscodescollection.org. They should work together with their group members to choose two codes of ethics that they would like to assess, compare and contrast. They must then present their findings to their peers when you next meet. Instructions are provided in the Handout to help them do this.

When you meet, ask each group to present their findings. Allocate 10 minutes for their presentation and five minutes for questions from their peers. Lead a discussion on the issues raised (questions for discussion are provided below, if required) and conclude the session with a summary of the main points.

If you choose the video production and sharing activity, explain the activity to groups, ask that they work in their groups (either online or face-to-face) to choose, assess, compare and contrast two codes. As they do this, they should think about what constitutes a viable, workable and comprehensive code of ethics, and think about how this relates to their research practice (the Student Handout can be modified slightly to provide this instruction). They should then produce a video of their findings (of no more than 10 minutes) that should be uploaded by the given date, using a dedicated video viewing and sharing tool such as WeVideo, or using a suitable tool integrated with your university learning management system (LMS). Students tend to use smartphones, laptops or tablets to produce videos, but equipment should be made available for those who do not have this technology.

The structure, style and content of the video is a group choice. Ask students to view the uploaded videos of other groups and open a discussion thread or chat room to talk about the issues raised. The goal is to deepen understanding through discussion and collaboration. Therefore, students should be encouraged to enhance the discussion rather than merely repeat or affirm comments. If you have not already done so, ensure that students understand how to offer respectful feedback to their peers (the CORBS model from the University of Alberta provides useful guidance: https://sites.ualberta.ca/~hsercweb/viper/CORBS_Feedback.pdf).

Key issues

The Ethics Codes Collection contains over 2,500 codes from around the world since 1887. Students undertake this activity in a variety of ways:

- They choose codes to assess, compare and contrast on a historical basis, illustrating how issues have changed over the years and demonstrating which of these are pertinent to their own research practice in the 21st century.
- They choose what they perceive to be one 'good' and one 'bad' code, comparing the good with the bad and illustrating how these comparisons can provide useful guidance for their research practice.
- They choose codes based on subject, with a comparison of factors that are given prominence in one subject, but are less prominent in another subject, and relate these findings to factors that are important in their own subject or discipline.

- They choose organizations that are of interest, relevant to their field of study or are the professional body for their area of practice. They highlight areas that can be considered to be examples of good or best practice. Some of these students illustrate how these codes are of importance not only to their research practice, but also to the profession they intend to enter on completion of their studies.
- Codes are chosen because they enable students to show that, in relation to research, codes can be problematic (this type of presentation and discussion tends to be raised by those studying at advanced level).

Examples of questions that can be raised and discussed during this activity (or in a follow-up session if you have only one hour of contact time) are listed below. If you feel that your students need more guidance, add relevant questions to the Student Handout. These questions can also be posted in your online discussion, if this option is chosen.

1. What is a code of ethics?
2. What is the purpose of a code of ethics? What should it do?
3. How are ethical issues articulated, parcelled and communicated in codes?
4. Is it actually possible or desirable to include all ethical issues in a code of ethics?
5. Who decides what issues should be included and what should be left out?
6. Will all employees/students/researchers/participants understand and adhere to codes?
7. Are codes adaptable? Can they be refined, modified and changed? Is this desirable? Why (not)?
8. Can historical codes teach us about modern codes?
9. How much impact do codes have on ethical decision-making?
10. In what way do codes reflect differences and challenges of disciplines, professional groups and organizations?

→ **Related activities**

Activity 36: Working within the European Code of Conduct for Research Integrity

Activity 37: Aligning with the Concordat to Support Research Integrity

Activity 79: Producing a code of ethics, in Dawson, C. (2016) *100 Activities for Teaching Research Methods*. London: Sage, pp. 214-15.

Activity 12

→ **Preparatory reading**

Educators: If you are new to the Ethics Codes Collection there is an article in the 'Learn' section of the website that is useful preparatory reading for this activity (it is an old article, but is still of relevance): Andrew Olson (1998) 'Authoring a code of ethics: Observations on process and organization', http://ethicscodescollection.org/authoringcode [accessed 3 September 2021]. The resources listed below also provide useful preparatory reading.

Students: None required.

→ **Useful resources**

Detailed ethical guidelines are provided by the Social Research Association in the UK: https://the-sra.org.uk/SRA/Ethics/Research-ethics-guidance/SRA/Ethics/Research-Ethics-Guidance [accessed 3 September 2021].

In the UK, guidance on ethical issues can be obtained from the UK government's Data Ethics Framework: www.gov.uk/government/publications/data-ethics-framework/data-ethics-framework#the-data-ethics-framework-principles [accessed 3 September 2021].

In Australia, the National Statement on Ethical Conduct in Human Research (2007 – Updated 2018) provides comprehensive information: www.nhmrc.gov.au/about-us/publications/national-statement-ethical-conduct-human-research-2007-updated-2018 [accessed 3 September 2021].

In the USA, the Belmont Report sets out guidelines that address ethical issues arising from the conduct of research with human subjects: www.hhs.gov/ohrp/regulations-and-policy/belmont-report/read-the-belmont-report/index.html [accessed 3 September 2021].

The British Psychological Society has produced a comprehensive Code of Ethics and Conduct: www.bps.org.uk [accessed 3 September 2021].

Professional codes of ethics are discussed in Chapter 2 of Ransome, P. (2013) *Ethics and Values in Social Research*. Basingstoke: Palgrave Macmillan.

Activity 12

Activity • • • • • • • • • • → 12

Comparing Codes of Ethics

STUDENT HANDOUT

This activity is called 'Comparing Codes of Ethics'. Visit the Ethics Codes Collection website: http://ethicscodescollection. org, which has been produced by the Center for the Study of Ethics in the Professions, Illinois Institute of Technology. Work with your group members to find two codes to assess, compare and contrast. The choice of codes is a group decision: there are over 2,500 available on the website. You can browse codes or search by institution, topic, fields and sub-fields.

   Once you have chosen two codes, work through each, assessing, comparing and contrasting information, styles and content. As you do so, think about what constitutes a viable, workable and comprehensive code of ethics, and think about how this relates to your research practice.

   When we next meet, your group will make a short presentation on your findings to your peers. The presentation should be up to 10 minutes in length with five minutes allocated at the end for questions. You can use any presentation materials you wish. Ensure that your presentation is interesting, creative and informative, providing useful information that will enable your peers to learn something new, increase their understanding of the topic presented and meet the learning outcome given below.

Learning outcome: By the end of this activity, you will be able to assess, compare and contrast codes of ethics; identify what constitutes a viable, workable and ethically comprehensive code; and relate these findings to your research practice.

Activity · · · · · · · · · · · · · · · · · · → 13

Creating Social Change Through Research Practice

The activity

Divide your students into small groups. Three to five students in each group is a good number for this activity: however, the number of groups depends on the size of your cohort and the amount of contact time you have available. Ideally, each group will need up to 10 minutes for their presentation, with a further five minutes for discussion after each presentation.

Give each group a copy of the Student Handout. This describes how this activity is old school, or retro, asking students to produce a paper collage that illustrates how social change is (or can be) created through research practice. When you meet, ask each group in turn to present their collage, explaining why items have been included, what they represent and how they help to illustrate how social change is (or can be) created through research practice. Allocate up to 10 minutes for each presentation with a further five minutes for discussion and questions. Conclude the session with a summary of the issues raised.

This session works best when students are asked to produce a paper collage. However, if this is not possible and you have to run this activity online, ask students to use a suitable collage maker tool to produce a digital collage that can be presented and discussed online (Canva or PicCollage, for example). Set up a suitable asynchronous tool to host collages and discussions and ensure that all students have access details (a discussion tool integrated with your university

_____ACTIVITY 13: CREATING SOCIAL CHANGE THROUGH RESEARCH PRACTICE ○ 45

learning management system (LMS) that enables media file attachments, for example). Adapt the Student Handout and provide a deadline by which time all collages should be presented and discussed.

Key issues

This activity provides an entertaining and creative way for students to think about how social change is (or can be) created through research practice. Paper collages are memorable, both in the production stage and when they are presented to peers. Students enjoy this activity even though they are sometimes surprised and consider it to be old-fashioned (this is why this point is emphasized in the Student Handout).

Some groups take time to think about what is meant by social change, discussing whether, how and why it is desirable, before assessing how research practice might bring this about. Some choose to find examples of research projects that have brought about social change, finding items for their collage that represent outcomes such as societal benefits and economic progress. Others choose to focus on the research process itself, illustrating how taking part in research, or reading about research, can change public perceptions, behaviour and actions. Some groups choose instead to consider specific cultures, organizations or groups, illustrating how their lives have been transformed through research. Others concentrate on certain methodologies that help to initiate social change (action research or participatory methods, for example).

→ **Related activities**

Activity 6: Aligning with the UN's Sustainable Development Goals

Activity 7: Promoting social good through research practice

Activity 46: Reclaiming datasets for social justice

→ **Preparatory reading**

Educators: If you are new to using collages for teaching and research you might find the article by Lahman et al. (2020) interesting.

Students: None required. Students will find their own resources for this activity.

→ **Useful resources**

Bartels, K. (2020) 'Transforming the relational dynamics of urban governance: How social innovation research can create a trajectory for learning and change', *Urban Studies*, 57 (14): 2868-84, first published 9 January 2020, doi: 10.1177/0042098019889290.

Chan, C.L.W. (2021) 'My personal journey of generating evidence in social work practice for social change', *Research on Social Work Practice*, 31 (1): 6-13, first published 30 September 2020, doi: 10.1177/1049731520961166.

Darder, A. (ed.) (2019) *Decolonizing Interpretive Research: A Subaltern Methodology for Social Change.* Abingdon: Routledge.

Lahman, M.K.E., Taylor, C.M., Beddes, L.A., Blount, I.D., Bontempo, K.A., Coon, J.D., Fernandez, C. and Motter, B. (2020) 'Research falling out of colorful pages onto paper: Collage inquiry', *Qualitative Inquiry*, 26 (3-4): 262-70, first published 2 April 2019, doi: 10.1177/1077800418810721.

Mcnamee, S. (2012) *Research and Social Change: A Relational Constructionist Approach.* New York, NY: Routledge.

Mitchell, C., De Lange, N. and Moletsane, R. (2017) *Participatory Visual Methodologies: Social Change, Community and Policy.* London: Sage.

Sharp, C., Dewar, B., Barrie, K. and Meyer, J. (2018) 'How being appreciative creates change – theory in practice from health and social care in Scotland', *Action Research*, 16 (2): 223-43, first published 1 May 2017, doi: 10.1177/1476750316684002.

Activity 13

Activity • • • • • • • • • • • → 13

Creating Social Change Through Research Practice

STUDENT HANDOUT

This activity is called 'Creating social change through research practice'. For this activity we're going old school, or perhaps you prefer the term retro. You're going to channel your inner child to create an old-fashioned, paper collage (yes, a collage: a collection or combination of various things such as photos, fabric and news items) that illustrates how social change is (or can be) created through research practice. No digital collage makers allowed, just old-fashioned paper and glue: I can provide these for you, if you need them.

   Work with your group members to create your collage. When we next meet you will be asked to present your collage to your peers, explaining why items have been included, what they represent and how they help to illustrate how social change is (or can be) created through research practice. You will be given up to 10 minutes to present your collage, with a further five minutes for your peers to ask questions. Be creative and have fun!

Learning outcome: By the end of this activity, you will be able to discuss, and provide examples of, how social change is (or can be) created through research practice.

Activity • • • • • • • • • • • → 14

Working with Vulnerable People

ACTIVITY 14: EDUCATOR NOTES

Purpose: This activity is an online study and support group that is available for invited students who intend to conduct research with vulnerable people. The study part of the group is educator-led, and enables students to learn more about what is meant by 'vulnerable' and the challenges of conducting this type of research. The support part of the group is student-led and is available throughout students' research to offer peer support and encouragement.

Type: Online study and support group.

Alternative type(s): None.

Level: Intermediate and advanced.

Duration: This activity will be available throughout the duration of students' research. Students will choose the amount of time they wish to spend. Educators will spend one or two hours a week hosting the educator-led part of the activity and monitoring posts on the student-led part of the activity.

Equipment/materials: A suitable online discussion tool.

Learning outcome: By the end of this activity, students will be able to explain what is meant by vulnerability, identify the challenges of researching vulnerable people and describe how challenges have been addressed in their research.

The activity

Invite together a group of students who intend to conduct research with vulnerable people: it does not matter how many students decide to take part in this activity, as long as there is more than one. Students can be from one course and one level or from a range of courses and levels. Explain that you intend to set up an online study and support group. The study part of the group will be educator-led. Students will be required to read papers and enter into online asynchronous discussion on specific topics. Decide whether to make participation compulsory or voluntary in this part of the activity, and whether to make this an assessed piece of work. If so, provide students with assessment criteria, participation requirements and deadlines that will need to be met for specific components of the activity.

The support part of the group will be student-led and provides the opportunity for students to offer information, advice, guidance, support and encouragement to their peers as their research progresses. Students will be able to share worries and concerns, and discuss issues that they might find difficult or upsetting, as they collect and analyse data.

Set up an appropriate tool for the activity (Blackboard discussion boards or Moodle discussion forums, for example) and divide into two separate discussions. Ensure that all students know where to find the discussions and know how to access them. Set guidelines for respectful and supportive discussion, or negotiate and agree on a suitable code of conduct as the first part of the activity.

Begin the educator-led study group by providing a paper for students to read and discuss: some examples of suitable papers are given in the useful resources below. Continue to provide papers, references, discussion points and useful exercises as the activity progresses. Relevant questions, discussion points, definitions and more useful resources can be found in Activity 88: Conducting research with vulnerable people, in Dawson (2016: 235-7).

Encourage students to enter into discussion for the student-led part of the activity. This should be voluntary: students can seek advice, support and encouragement from their peers at any time during their research. Some students might use this resource more than others, and some might not enter into discussion at all. The level of involvement should be an individual choice and students should not be forced to take part if they do not wish to do so. Monitor posts from time-to-time to ensure that students are being constructive, encouraging and helpful, and to ascertain whether a student might need individual, face-to-face support.

Key issues

There are a wide variety of issues that can be raised in this activity, depending on students' research topics and methodologies. Examples include:

- defining vulnerability (Racine and Bracken-Roche, 2019; Gordon, 2020);
- ensuring the physical, social and psychological well-being of vulnerable people (Activity 10);
- avoiding harming participants and others who might be affected by the research (Activity 11);
- concern that the research process might cause unnecessary stress, anxiety, negative emotions or secondary traumatization;
- concerns about level of personal competence to deal with traumatic or upsetting issues that might be raised;
- worries about becoming emotional during interviews;
- ensuring support arrangements are in place for participants, and finding support for researchers;
- avoiding labelling and stereotyping vulnerable people (Humpage et al., 2019);
- asking for, and obtaining, informed consent: explaining what is required in a way that can be understood and ensuring that vulnerable people do not feel pressurized to take part (Activity 57);
- ensuring anonymity and confidentiality, and providing this information in a way that can be understood (Activity 62);
- finding a suitable venue in which participants feel comfortable and not under pressure;
- knowing about, and adhering to, all legal obligations (Activity 31).

Cautionary note

Some types of research with vulnerable people can be very upsetting for students. It is important that the support group part of the activity is monitored carefully. If you feel a student is struggling, meet with them face-to-face. Provide a list of people/organizations that can help if students find it difficult to cope on their own.

→ **Related activities**

Activity 1: Respecting human dignity, privacy and rights

Activity 10: Working within the principle of beneficence

Activity 11: Avoiding harm to others

Activity 15: Conducting research with children

Activity 57: Seeking informed consent

Activity 58: Cultivating sensitivity in method

Activity 62: Addressing issues of anonymity and confidentiality

→ **Preparatory reading**

Educators: Become familiar with your university guidelines on researching vulnerable people, if you have not already done so (a link to these should be provided in the educator-led part of the activity). The following paper is useful preparatory reading for educators who have an interest in teaching about vulnerability in research:

Activity 14

Loue, S. and Loff, B. (2019) 'Teaching vulnerability in research: A study of approaches utilized by a sample of research ethics training programs', *Journal of Empirical Research on Human Research Ethics*, 14 (4): 395-407, first published 17 August 2019, doi: 10.1177/1556264619869130.

Students: Should read papers and relevant book chapters as the activity progresses. Provide useful resources relevant to the discussion as it unfolds.

→ **Useful resources**

Bashir, N. (2020) 'The qualitative researcher: The flip side of the research encounter with vulnerable people', *Qualitative Research*, 20 (5): 667-83, first published 9 December 2019, doi: 10.1177/1468794119884805.

Cascio, M.A., Weiss, J.A. and Racine, E. (2020) 'Person-oriented ethics for autism research: Creating best practices through engagement with autism and autistic communities', *Autism*, 24 (7), 1676-90, first published 18 June 2020, doi: 10.1177/1362361320918763.

Dawson, C. (2016) *100 Activities for Teaching Research Methods*. London: Sage.

Gordon, B. (2020) 'Vulnerability in research: Basic ethical concepts and general approach to review', *Ochsner Journal*, 20 (1): 34-8, doi: 10.31486/toj.19.0079.

Humpage, L., Fozdar, F., Marlowe, J. and Hartley, L. (2019) 'Photovoice and refugee research: The case for a "layers" versus "labels" approach to vulnerability', *Research Ethics*, 15 (3-4): 1-16, first published 19 September 2019, doi: 10.1177/1747016119864353.

Liamputtong, P. (2007) *Researching the Vulnerable: A Guide to Sensitive Research Methods*. London: Sage.

Racine, E. and Bracken-Roche, D. (2019) 'Enriching the concept of vulnerability in research ethics: An integrative and functional account', *Bioethics*, 33 (1): 19-34, first published 23 August 2018, doi: 10.1111/bioe.12471.

Roffee, J.A. and Waling, A. (2017) 'Resolving ethical challenges when researching with minority and vulnerable populations: LGBTIQ victims of violence, harassment and bullying', *Research Ethics*, 13 (1): 4-22, first published 18 August 2016, doi: 10.1177/1747016116658693.

Shaw, R.M., Howe, J., Beazer, J. and Carr, T. (2020) 'Ethics and positionality in qualitative research with vulnerable and marginal groups', *Qualitative Research*, 20 (3): 277-93, first published 16 April 2019, doi: 10.1177/1468794119841839.

Webber-Ritchey, K.J., Simonovich, S.D. and Spurlark, R.S. (2021) 'COVID-19: Qualitative research with vulnerable populations', *Nursing Science Quarterly*, 34 (1): 13-19, first published 21 December 2020, doi: 10.1177/0894318420965225.

Activity 14

Activity • • • • • • • • • • • → 15

Conducting Research with Children

ACTIVITY 15: EDUCATOR NOTES

Purpose: This activity is an informal discussion (in-class or online) for invited students that enables them to talk about ethical issues involved in research with children. They prepare for the session by reading relevant papers, which are then used as the basis for discussion. Students are able to raise concerns, bounce ideas and seek advice from their peers about their own research involving children.

Type: Informal discussion for invited students (in-class or online).

Alternative type(s): None.

Level: Intermediate and advanced (students from different levels and subjects of study can get together for this activity).

Duration: Students will spend an hour or two reading and digesting their allocated paper during independent study. Educators will spend a few hours choosing and reading suitable papers. Fifty minutes to one hour of contact time will be required to hold the discussion (in-class or online).

Equipment/materials: Access to relevant journal papers.

Learning outcome: By the end of this activity, students will be able to identify ethical issues relevant to research with children and describe how they intend to tackle these issues in their research.

The activity

Invite together students who are intending to undertake research with children. These can be students from different levels, subject areas and methodologies. The group should not be too large: up to eight students is ideal (you will probably find that the number is quite small as only a few students may decide to undertake research with children, and some of these might choose not to attend the session if you make it voluntary).

Find an equivalent number of research papers that cover ethics and research with children (use papers listed in the resources section below, or choose others that are more suited to your students). Allocate one paper to each student prior to the session: ask them to read their allocated paper and be prepared to discuss aspects of the paper when you meet. Try to ensure that there are a variety of topics and methodologies covered in the papers as these will be used as the basis for your discussion. Read each paper yourself, taking note of the ethical issues raised and listing relevant points for discussion.

Begin the in-class or online synchronous discussion by asking students about the ethical issues that have been raised in the paper they were allocated. Discuss each issue, asking whether it is something they need to consider for their own research and, if so, what they need to think about, or do, to address the issue. Use the list you developed from reading the papers to keep the discussion going, if it stalls. Once this part of the discussion has concluded, ask students whether they have any specific worries or concerns about undertaking research with children. Encourage them to bounce ideas off each other, while offering support and advice to their peers.

Key issues

The key issues raised in this activity depend on the papers you have chosen and the research topics and methodologies of your students. Examples include:

- finding 'safe and easily accessible locations' to undertake research with children (Maglio and Pherali, 2020: 10);
- finding the right physical and social environments for children (Water et al., 2020: 40-2);
- assessing safety, vulnerability and well-being (Maglio and Pherali, 2020: 7);
- assessing the challenges of recruitment (Water et al., 2020: 37-40);
- engaging 'critically about possibilities beyond the notion of voluntary participation' (Maglio and Pherali, 2020: 7);
- reflecting on consent/assent-related boundaries and dilemmas (Gaches, 2020: 9-11);
- assessing the challenges of consent and assent when using digital data collection methods with children (Facca et al., 2020: 5-8);
- safeguarding data and minors' data rights (Facca et al., 2020: 8-10);
- maintaining user privacy and limiting potential harm when using social media for research with children (Facca et al., 2020: 11-12);

- using children as co-researchers and assessing pressures, burdens and stress placed on them (Spriggs and Gillam, 2019: 10);
- providing support and training for child co-researchers (Spriggs and Gillam, 2019: 10-11);
- balancing time restrictions with the need for rapport-building (Water et al., 2020: 42);
- ensuring representation: how to present the views and voices of younger children (Gaches, 2020: 7-9);
- reflecting on the politics of interpretation and representation (De Wilde et al., 2020: 301-4);
- assessing multidirectional relationships and shared authority of researcher and participants (De Wilde et al., 2020: 298-301);
- reflecting on issues of power and hierarchy (Webber, 2020: 348-9);
- assessing the emotive impact of child research on parents (Webber, 2020: 349-50).

Cautionary note

This activity provides the opportunity to explore worries and concerns about undertaking research with children. It also provides the opportunity for you to find out which students may need further monitoring and support as their research progresses. Let your students know that you will be available if they need help, and encourage students to offer support to each other as their research progresses.

→ Related activities

Activity 14: Working with vulnerable people

Activity 89: Conducting research with children, in Dawson (2016: 238-41)

....

→ Preparatory reading

Educators: Read all the papers that you recommend for this activity. You might also find it useful to read Activity 89: Conducting research with children, in Dawson (2016: 238-41). This activity provides five examples of research projects that involve children for students to discuss.

Students: Each student will need to read the paper allocated to them as preparatory reading.

....

→ Useful resources

Dawson, C. (2016) *100 Activities for Teaching Research Methods*. London: Sage.
De Wilde, L., Roets, G. and Vanobbergen, B. (2020) 'Discovering dimensions of research ethics in doing oral history: Going public in the case of the Ghent orphanages', *Qualitative Research*, 20 (3): 294-306, first published 27 May 2019, doi: 10.1177/1468794119851330.

Activity 15

Facca, D., Smith, M.J., Shelley, J., Lizotte, D. and Donelle, L. (2020) 'Exploring the ethical issues in research using digital data collection strategies with minors: A scoping review', *PLoS ONE*, 15 (8): e0237875, published 27 August 2020, doi: 10.1371/journal.pone.0237875.

Gaches, S. (2020) 'Using critically reflexive ethics in practice to address issues of representation in children's rights-based research', *Global Studies of Childhood*, first published 1 October 2020, doi: 10.1177/2043610620959679.

Greig, A., Taylor, J. and Mackay, T. (2013) *Doing Research with Children: A Practical Guide*, 3rd edition. London: Sage.

Groundwater-Smith, S., Dockett, S. and Bottrell, D. (2015) *Participatory Research with Children and Young People*. London: Sage.

Maglio, F. and Pherali, T. (2020) 'Ethical reflections on children's participation in educational research during humanitarian crises', *Research Ethics*, 16 (1-2): 1-19, first published 22 January 2020, doi: 10.1177/1747016119898409.

Sargeant, J. and Harcourt, D. (2012) *Doing Ethical Research with Children*. Maidenhead: Open University Press.

Spriggs, M. and Gillam, L. (2019) 'Ethical complexities in child co-research', *Research Ethics*, 15 (1): 1-16, first published 20 December 2017, doi: 10.1177/1747016117750207.

Water, T., Payam, S., Tokolahi, E., Reay, S. and Wrapson, J. (2020) 'Ethical and practical challenges of conducting art-based research with children/young people in the public space of a children's outpatient department', *Journal of Child Health Care*, 24 (1): 33-45, doi: 10.1177/1367493518807318.

Webber, L. (2020) 'Researching with children using Skype interviews and drawings: Methodological and ethical issues explored', *Journal of Early Childhood Research*, 18 (4): 339-53, first published 27 July 2020, doi: 10.1177/1476718X20938084.

Activity 15

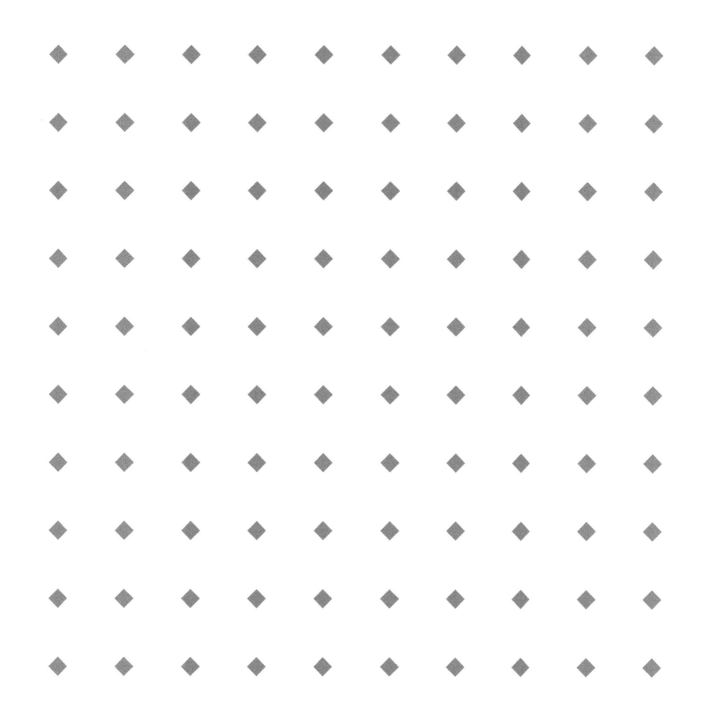

Section 2

Researcher and
Institution Conduct

Activity ● ● ● ● ● ● ● ● ● ● ● → 16

Discussing Epistemic Norms

ACTIVITY 16: EDUCATOR NOTES

Purpose: This activity encourages students to explore epistemic norms by asking them, in pairs, to undertake collaborative dialogue (using the Socratic Method as a tool) about epistemic norms that provide standards, licences or allowances for their beliefs, actions and/or assertions in relation to their research. This will help them to focus their thoughts, clarify ideas and develop further insight.

Type: Collaborative dialogue (in-class).

Alternative type(s): Collaborative dialogue (online); student worksheet.

Level: Advanced.

Duration: Several hours during independent study and up to one hour in class or online.

Equipment/materials: Students will need access to epistemic literature and information about the Socratic Method.

Learning outcome: By the end of this activity, students will be able to identify, evaluate and judge epistemic norms that provide standards, licences or allowances for their beliefs, actions and/or assertions in relation to their research.

The activity

Give a copy of the Student Handout to your students a week before you intend to meet. Ask them to prepare for the session following the guidelines given. These ask students to find out what is meant by epistemic norms and think about how these relate to their research. They are also to find out more about the Socratic Method, which will be used for this activity. A wide variety of questions are included in the Handout for complete coverage: however, if you think there are too many or that some are too complex, delete as appropriate.

When you meet, divide your students into pairs. Ask one student to describe the epistemic norms that provide standards, licences or allowances for their beliefs, actions and/or assertions in relation to their research. The other student should listen to this description, asking questions when appropriate to help the first student focus in on their assumptions, clarify thoughts and develop further insights. The pairs of students are to do this for up to 20 minutes. Once they have completed this task, ask them to reverse roles and continue with the dialogue for another 20 minutes.

Encourage your students to be thought-provoking, challenging and stimulating, in a constructive and supportive manner. Derogative, cantankerous or quarrelsome dialogue must be avoided. Follow their collaborative dialogue with a discussion on the issues raised.

If you choose to run this activity online, choose a suitable tool to host the collaborative discussion (Zoom Meetings, Blackboard Collaborate or Google Meet, for example). Use breakout rooms for pairs to undertake their collaborative dialogue. These can be set automatically or manually: ensure that breakout rooms are enabled prior to your session. Provide a brief introduction to the session and set guidelines for constructive and supportive online discussion. Open the breakout rooms and monitor discussions. Ask students to reverse roles after 20 minutes. Let them continue for another 20 minutes, before ending the breakout session. Summarize the main points to conclude the session.

This activity can be run as a student worksheet, if you prefer. Use the questions provided in the Student Handout to develop an appropriate worksheet to give to your students and ask that they work on it during independent study. Provide assessment criteria if you intend to make this an assessed piece of work.

Key issues

This activity provides the opportunity for students to think about issues that they might not previously have thought about, or that are taken for granted in their subject area. It encourages them to think more deeply about why they believe something to be true, or why they might judge that it is true, and to think about the evidence that has been provided to enable them to reason that what they have been told is true. It also provides them with the opportunity to cover related issues such as epistemic trust, mis-trust and self-trust, and other types of norms that relate to, or influence, their research practice (moral norms, legal norms, social norms and norms of etiquette, for example).

The nature and type of questions asked by students depends on their subject area, research topic, background reading, and epistemic norms and epistemic questions asked about, and within, their research or subject area. The Socratic Method enables students to ask different types of question for different purposes, and follow a line of reasoning or thought that is of interest to them, or relevant to their research. These questions can:

- help to clarify concepts;
- probe existing assumptions and reasoning;
- probe rationale;
- query evidence;
- test viewpoint and perspective;

- probe relevance;
- ask about alternatives;
- query implications and consequences;
- query the questions that are being asked.

Cautionary note

Some students find this task intellectually stimulating and extremely worthwhile. Others find it daunting and irrelevant. If you feel that any of your students might be in the latter category, ask them to come to you with any questions, doubts or difficulties they might have prior to your session. It might be prudent to think about how your students should be paired, if cases such as this arise.

→ Related activities

Activity 18: Appraising disciplinary standards of acceptable academic conduct

Activity 91: Asking epistemological questions, in Dawson (2016: 247-8)

⋯⋯⋯⋯⋯⋯⋯⋯⋯⋯⋯⋯⋯⋯⋯⋯⋯⋯⋯⋯⋯⋯⋯⋯⋯⋯⋯⋯⋯⋯⋯⋯⋯⋯⋯⋯⋯⋯⋯

→ Preparatory reading

Educators: All the resources listed below provide useful preparatory reading for this activity. Chapter 34 in Hannon and de Ridder (2021) provides an interesting discussion on epistemic norms of political deliberation and Part 5 of the same book covers useful information on epistemic virtues and vices in politics.

Students: None required. Students will find their own resources for this activity.

⋯⋯⋯⋯⋯⋯⋯⋯⋯⋯⋯⋯⋯⋯⋯⋯⋯⋯⋯⋯⋯⋯⋯⋯⋯⋯⋯⋯⋯⋯⋯⋯⋯⋯⋯⋯⋯⋯⋯

→ Useful resources

Cohen, S. (2016) 'Theorizing about the epistemic', *Inquiry*, 59 (7-8): 839-57, published online 11 August 2016, doi: 10.1080/0020174X.2016.1208903.

Activity 16

Dawson, C. (2016) *100 Activities for Teaching Research Methods*. London: Sage.

Gerken, M. (2015) 'The epistemic norms of intra-scientific testimony', *Philosophy of the Social Sciences*, 45 (6): 568-95, first published 24 August 2015, doi: 10.1177/0048393115600527.

Hannon, M. and de Ridder, J. (eds) (2021) *The Routledge Handbook of Political Epistemology*. Abingdon: Routledge.

Kauppinen, A. (2018) 'Epistemic norms and epistemic accountability', *Philosopher's Imprint*, 18 (8): 1-16, open access, www.philosophersimprint.org/018008/.

Littlejohn, C. and Turri, J. (eds) (2014) *Epistemic Norms: New Essays on Action, Belief, and Assertion*. Oxford: Oxford University Press.

Activity 16

Activity • • • • • • • • • • • → 16

Discussing Epistemic Norms

STUDENT HANDOUT

Our next session is about epistemic norms and how these provide standards (or licences) for our research beliefs, actions and/or assertions. Take the next week to think more deeply about what is meant by 'epistemic norms' and how these relate to what you think, or believe, about your research topic, approach and methods. The following questions provide guidance for your thinking:

- What are epistemic norms?
- Why is an epistemic norm 'epistemic'?
- How do 'epistemic' and 'epistemological' differ?
- What epistemic norms relate specifically to your research beliefs, actions and/or assertions? Are they possible to identify? Should they be identified? Why (not)?
- In what way are epistemic norms connected to the nature of the scientific process?
- How are they connected to different stages of your research?

  o How have you justified the importance of your topic?
  o How have you chosen your methodology and methods? How do you know that these are the correct procedures to use?
  o How will you analyse your data? How do you know that you have chosen the right or correct methods?

  o How will you interpret your results and form conclusions? How will you convince others of the value of your research?

- How might epistemic norms ensure that you conform to the rules? What are the rules? Where have they come from? Is it necessary to conform to the rules? Why (not)?
- What other types of norm relate to (or influence) your research actions and/or assertions (moral norms, legal norms, social norms, norms of etiquette, etc.)?
- How do epistemic norms relate to epistemic trust? How do we build epistemic trust?
- How do epistemic norms relate to epistemic self-trust? If we find our beliefs have been influenced by bias, do we need to lower our epistemic self-trust and/or undertake an epistemic self-evaluation?
- What is the difference between epistemic norms and epistemic values?

Take time to research these issues, or any others related to this topic that you find interesting and relevant. Think about them ready for our next session. When we meet you will be divided into pairs to undertake collaborative dialogue, following the Socratic Method. This is a tool that is used to draw individual answers and encourage fundamental insight into the topic. Using this tool, a problem (or issue) is broken down into a series of questions that are asked to help you determine your underlying beliefs or the extent of your knowledge. This enables your ideas, thoughts, beliefs or hypotheses to be narrowed and refined.

Take a little time to read up about the Socratic Method. When we meet you will be paired together with a peer. You will be given 20 minutes for one of you to describe the epistemic norms that provide standards, licences or allowances for your beliefs, actions and/or assertions in relation to your research. Your peer will listen to this description, asking questions when appropriate to help you focus in on your assumptions, clarify thoughts and develop further insights. After 20 minutes the roles will be reversed.

Take some time to think about your description and to develop questions that you can ask your peer. These should be questions that will enable your peer to process, interpret and analyse information and build a deeper understanding of epistemic norms in relation to their research. Keep the discussion focused and intellectually responsible, enabling and encouraging a deeper search for intellectual knowledge and insight.

Learning outcome: By the end of this activity, you will be able to identify, evaluate and judge epistemic norms that provide standards, licences or allowances for your beliefs, actions and/or assertions in relation to your research.

Activity · · · · · · · · · · · · → 17

Cultivating Transparency and Openness

ACTIVITY 17: EDUCATOR NOTES

Purpose: This is a practical activity for students studying at advanced level who are in the design stage of their research. It is a workshop that enables them to discuss what is meant by transparency and openness in research, before going on to develop and discuss a plan of action that will help them to cultivate transparency and openness in their research.

Type: Workshop (in-class).

Alternative type(s): Workshop (online); self-guided individual exercise with information sharing and discussion (in-class or online).

Level: Advanced.

Duration: Fifty minutes to one hour for the workshops (in-class or online). If the self-guided exercise is chosen, students will spend one or two hours working on their action plan, followed by 50 minutes to one hour of contact time for information sharing and discussion (in-class or online).

Equipment/materials: A suitable synchronous video/web conferencing tool, if the online option is chosen.

Learning outcome: By the end of this activity, students will be able to list a variety of ways to cultivate transparency and openness in research and summarize the action they intend to take to ensure that their research is transparent and open.

The activity

Invite students to a workshop about transparency and openness in research. This can be either in-class or online (using a suitable video/web conferencing tool such as Zoom Meetings, Blackboard Collaborate or Meetings in Microsoft Teams for Education). Begin by holding a short discussion about what is meant by transparency and openness and why it is important that these are cultivated in research. This discussion should last for 10–15 minutes. After this time, ask students to spend 10 minutes on an individual basis thinking about what they can do in their own research to cultivate transparency and openness. Bring them back together to discuss their ideas, asking each student, in turn, to present their ideas to their peers. Make sure that all students have enough time to present their ideas: this will depend on the number of students in your group and on the amount of discussion generated by each student. Take note of the Transparency and Openness Promotion (TOP) Guidelines (see the useful resources below) and, if these issues are not raised by students, ensure that they are covered when you summarize the session.

This activity can be run as a self-guided individual exercise if you prefer. Ask students to work on a plan of action, which will enable them to cultivate transparency and openness in their research, during independent study. Once they have done this, their plans should be shared and discussed with their peers. This can be done in-class or online (using a synchronous video tool or an asynchronous text-based tool). Ensure that the TOP Guidelines, or similar issues, are discussed at some point during the session.

Key issues

This activity encourages students to think about what is meant by transparency and openness, and why these are important in research. The initial discussion can include issues such as building trust in inferences and conclusions (Activity 91), avoiding research misconduct (Activity 22), recognizing and declaring conflict of interest (Activity 25) and ensuring that research can be reproduced or replicated (Activities 92 and 93). It might also include a discussion on whether (and how) ideas and intellectual property might be negatively impacted by transparency and openness (Activity 38), and whether transparency and openness is always desirable (see John, 2018 for a discussion on climate science and how he thinks that openness and transparency can be epistemologically and politically dangerous).

A variety of topics can be mentioned in action plans and these include the following (if these are not mentioned by students, they can be introduced by you and given as further reading: see the useful resources below):

- using language that can be understood by the lay person;
- producing a lay summary targeted at a wider audience (see Activity 67: Presenting to a lay audience, in Dawson, 2016: 181-2);
- paying attention to correct referencing and citation, including digital tools and software (Activities 23 and 56);
- understanding anonymization techniques (Activities 62, 79 and 84);
- consulting and using the Centre for Open Science (www.cos.io/);
- preregistering research designs, research questions, hypotheses, data collection methods and data analysis plans (see TOP Guidelines, below);

- ensuring all data, codes and analyses are made available (Activity 89 and TOP Guidelines);
- providing all the information required to ensure that research can be reproduced and replicated (Activities 92 and 93);
- sharing pre-print journal articles;
- depositing work in public access depositories and publishing in Open Access journals (Activity 96);
- explaining why data or results cannot be shared (confidentiality or consent has not been given for sharing data, for example).

→ **Related activities**

Activity 82: Aligning with the FAIR principles

Activity 83: Producing a data access (or availability) statement

Activity 89: Assessing the ethical implications of data sharing

Activity 91: Building trust in inferences and conclusions

Activity 92: Repeating, reproducing and replicating research

Activity 93: Debating the replication crisis

Activity 96: Discussing Open Research, Open Science and Open Access

→ **Preparatory reading**

Educators: The TOP Guidelines provide useful preparatory reading.

Students: None required for the workshop. Relevant resources listed below can be recommended once the workshop has taken place.

→ **Useful resources**

Dawson, C. (2016) *100 Activities for Teaching Research Methods*. London: Sage.
Grahe, J. (2022) *A Journey into Open Science and Research Transparency in Psychology*. Abingdon: Routledge.
John, S. (2018) 'Epistemic trust and the ethics of science communication: Against transparency, openness, sincerity and honesty', *Social Epistemology*, 32 (2): 75-87, published online 8 December 2017, doi: 10.1080/02691728.2017.1410864.
Lewandowsky, S. and Bishop, D. (2016) 'Research integrity: Don't let transparency damage science', *Nature* 529, 459-61, published online 28 January 2016, doi: 10.1038/529459a.

Activity 17

McVay, M.A. and Conroy, D.E. (2021) 'Transparency and openness in behavioral medicine research', *Translational Behavioral Medicine*, 11 (1): 287-90, published online 1 November 2019, doi: 10.1093/tbm/ibz154.

Tackett, J.L. and Miller, J.D. (2019) 'Introduction to the special section on increasing replicability, transparency, and openness in clinical psychology', *Journal of Abnormal Psychology*, 128 (6): 487-92, doi: 10.1037/abn0000455.

The Transparency and Openness Promotion (TOP) Guidelines have been created by journal editors, funders and researchers. They include eight modular standards for journal articles: citation, data transparency, analytics methods (code) transparency, research materials transparency, design and analysis transparency, preregistration of studies, preregistration of analysis plans and replication: www.cos.io/initiatives/top-guidelines [accessed 22 March 2022]. Information about Open Science Badges, providing incentives for researchers to preregister, share data and share materials, is also available on this site: www.cos.io/initiatives/badges [accessed 22 March 2022].

ClinicalTrials.gov contains information about medical studies in human volunteers in the USA. It enables researchers to meet ethical obligations and ensures that research is open and transparent: www.clinicaltrials.gov [accessed 22 March 2022].

Activity 17

Activity · · · · · · · · · · · · · → 18

Appraising Disciplinary Standards of Acceptable Academic Conduct

The activity

Divide your students into pairs or small groups (this depends on the size of your student cohort: ideally you need at least six different groups/pairs to add variety to this activity). Give them a copy of the Student Handout. This asks them to find a senior researcher at your university who is willing to be interviewed about what they consider to be standards of acceptable academic conduct within their discipline. Students should prepare a few questions ready for the interview and choose who will undertake the interview and who will record it.

Once groups have completed their interviews, they should upload their videos using the tool you have set up for this purpose to share with their peers (internal VLE or external such as a Facebook group or Vimeo, for example). Advice about producing the video is given in the Handout. Give a deadline by which time this task should be completed. Ask students to view the videos produced by their peers and open a discussion board or thread so that they can discuss the issues raised.

This activity can be run in-class, if you prefer. Ask students to produce and upload videos as above, then play them in class. Allocate at least 20 minutes to hold a discussion on the issues raised.

Key issues

This activity is an entertaining way to introduce students to disciplinary standards of acceptable academic conduct. Some groups are quite inventive about whom they decide to interview: this provides interest and variety, and illustrates how researchers from different disciplines answer questions in different ways. Students are also creative about the questions they ask, obtaining useful and interesting information to share with their peers.

Interviews can cover a wide variety of topics, some of which may not seem to be so relevant, until they are unpacked and discussed. Examples include:

- Expected standards, behaviour and conduct in all disciplines:

    o   avoiding research misconduct (Activity 22);
    o   avoiding plagiarism (Activity 23);
    o   avoiding contract cheating (Activity 24);
    o   avoiding conflict of interest (Activity 25);
    o   cultivating transparency and openness (Activity 17);
    o   avoiding sampling bias (Activity 64);
    o   recognizing and addressing bias when collecting and analysing data (Activities 63, 73 and 74);
    o   avoiding wrong conclusions (Activity 75);
    o   avoiding falsification, fabrication or misleading analysis (Activity 76);
    o   building trust in inferences and conclusions (Activity 91).

- Undertaking responsible research, complying with and following all necessary regulatory, legal, professional and disciplinary obligations (all activities in Section 3 and the European Code of Conduct for Research Integrity: see useful resources).
- How researchers are trained in the responsible conduct of research: effects and attitudes (Kalichman and Plemmons, 2015).
- Methods and methodologies favoured by different disciplines (see, for example, Piekkari et al., 2009, who discuss the use of case studies in business), and using them correctly.
- The importance of cross-disciplinary, transdisciplinary and interdisciplinary research, and how these enable researchers to work together to build better standards of acceptable academic conduct.
- The importance of avoiding methodological fundamentalism (strict adherence to one methodology that is seen to be the only true and correct methodology). Being open to other methodologies that are favoured in certain disciplines and accepting that different types of research (and standards) are just as valid (Anders and Lester, 2015 provide an interesting paper that illustrates these points well).
- Disciplines that prize scientific rigour and emphasize the importance of the scientific method. How to work within these standards and produce statistically significant results when researching in challenging circumstances (Peterson, 2016).
- Scientific instruction and the disciplinary literacy skills required to engage in scientific research (Hayden and Eades-Baird, 2020). Aligning disciplinary literacy and core standards (Paugh and Wendell, 2021).

→ **Related activities**

Activity 16: Discussing epistemic norms

Activity 19: Viewing integrity as an individual and collective responsibility

Activity 20: Fostering research integrity through practice

Activity 21: Developing a resilient integrity culture

....

→ **Preparatory reading**

Educators: Become familiar with your university/departmental guidelines concerning acceptable academic conduct. Links to these can be provided for students as part of this activity.

Students: None required. Students will find their own resources for this activity, if required.

....

→ **Useful resources**

Anders, A.D. and Lester, J.N. (2015) 'Lessons from interdisciplinary qualitative research: Learning to work against a single story', *Qualitative Research*, 15 (6): 738-54, first published 18 December 2014, doi: 10.1177/1468794114557994.

Hayden, H.E. and Eades-Baird, M. (2020) 'Disciplinary literacy and the 4Es: Rigorous and substantive responses to interdisciplinary standards', *Literacy Research: Theory, Method, and Practice*, 69 (1): 339-57, first published 2 July 2020, doi: 10.1177/2381336920937258.

Activity 18

Kalichman, M.W. and Plemmons, D.K. (2015) 'Research agenda: The effects of responsible-conduct-of-research training on attitudes', *Journal of Empirical Research on Human Research Ethics*, 10 (5): 457–9, first published 9 March 2015, doi: 10.1177/1556264615575514.

Paugh, P. and Wendell, K. (2021) 'Disciplinary literacy in STEM: A functional approach', *Journal of Literacy Research*, 53 (1): 122–44, first published 21 January 2021, doi: 10.1177/1086296X20986905.

Peterson, D. (2016) 'The baby factory: Difficult research objects, disciplinary standards, and the production of statistical significance', *Socius*, first published 22 January 2016, doi: 10.1177/2378023115625071.

Piekkari, R., Welch, C. and Paavilainen, E. (2009) 'The case study as disciplinary convention: Evidence from international business journals', *Organizational Research Methods*, 12 (3): 567–89, first published 9 June 2008, doi: 10.1177/1094428108319905.

The European Code of Conduct for Research Integrity provides a framework for self-regulation, describing ethical, legal and professional responsibilities for researchers: www.allea.org/wp-content/uploads/2017/05/ALLEA-European-Code-of-Conduct-for-Research-Integrity-2017.pdf [accessed 22 March 2022].

Activity 18

Activity • • • • • • • • • • • → 18

Appraising Disciplinary Standards of Acceptable Academic Conduct

STUDENT HANDOUT

This activity is called 'Appraising disciplinary standards of acceptable academic conduct'. Work together to find a senior researcher who is willing to be interviewed about what they consider to be disciplinary standards of acceptable academic conduct. This researcher can be from your department and discipline, or from another department and discipline (if you are intending to undertake interdisciplinary research, for example). As there are several groups undertaking this activity you will need to hunt around for someone who has not already said yes (or no) to being interviewed. The activity works best if there is variety, so think about interviewing someone whom your peers might not have considered.

Develop a number of suitable questions that you can ask during the interview. Use the learning outcome given below to guide you and help you to keep your questions relevant. The interview does not have to be very long: two to four minutes is a good length, so make sure that you have enough questions for the interview and work out how to probe for more information, if required. Decide who is going to ask the questions.

The interview will need to be videoed so that it can be shared with your peers. Smartphones or webcams are fine for this activity: if you don't have this equipment, I can provide it for you. Decide who is going to record the interview. Ensure that you pay attention to audio, lighting and camera stabilization, and use basic editing software, if required.

Once you have produced your video, share it with your peers by uploading it using the tool provided. Make sure that this is done by the deadline. View the videos that are uploaded by your peers and, if you want to make any comments, you can do so on the discussion board. Ensure that you have viewed the videos and participated in the discussion by the given deadline.

Learning outcome: By the end of this activity, you will be able to identify, discuss and appraise disciplinary standards of acceptable academic conduct.

Activity • • • • • • • • • • • → 19

Viewing Integrity as an Individual and Collective Responsibility

ACTIVITY 19: EDUCATOR NOTES

Purpose: This activity is a group discussion that encourages students to view integrity as an individual and collective responsibility. It requires students, in small groups, to approach integrity from a number of different roles and positions, before pooling ideas to assess similarities and connections between roles and positions. This activity covers similar ground to that covered in Activities 20 and 21. Therefore, choose the activity that is best suited to your course, or combine activities for greater coverage of this topic.

Type: Group discussion (in-class).

Alternative type(s): Group discussion (online).

Level: Elementary, intermediate and advanced.

Duration: Fifty minutes to one hour.

Equipment/materials: A whiteboard or flip chart for the in-class session and a suitable video/web conferencing tool and note-catcher for the online session.

Learning outcome: By the end of this activity, students will be able to explain why integrity is important for people from a number of different positions and roles, and discuss how people within these different positions and roles can work individually and collectively to maintain and/or increase integrity.

The activity

This activity is a group discussion that can be run in-class or online. If you choose the online option, use a suitable synchronous video/web conferencing tool such as Zoom Meetings, Blackboard Collaborate or Meetings in Microsoft Teams for Education. Begin the session by explaining its purpose: to enable students to view integrity as an individual and collective responsibility. Divide your students into five groups (or pairs or individuals, if you only have a small number of students) and use breakout rooms if you are running this activity online. Explain that you are going to pose two questions that must then be considered by each group. However, each group will be given a different position, or role, from which to consider the questions. The positions are:

1. research students;
2. university administrators or directors;
3. members of the public;
4. funding organizations;
5. research participants.

Allocate a position to each group, then pose the question 'From your position/role, why is integrity important?'. Ask students to discuss this question and write down a list of reasons why integrity is important from their position/role (note-catchers can be used to develop these lists, if you choose to run this activity online). This discussion should last 10-15 minutes: if students struggle to get the discussion started, introduce some of the topics provided in key issues, below.

Then ask 'From your position/role, how can you work individually and collectively to maintain and/or improve integrity?'. Ask groups to develop another list of points that answer this question. This should take another 10-15 minutes. After this time, bring groups back together and ask each group, one at a time, to present their first list. Lead a class discussion on the issues raised, then repeat with the second question and lists. Conclude the session by illustrating that items listed are relevant to all groups and emphasizing the importance of viewing integrity as an individual and collective responsibility.

Key issues

This activity illustrates that even though students approach the questions from different positions or roles, they find that issues surrounding integrity are very similar. Integrity is seen to be important because it:

- builds or enhances reputations (of universities, researchers and funding bodies);
- is good for public relations and building positive perceptions (of universities, funding bodies and individual researchers);
- builds trust (among researchers, funding bodies, research participants and members of the public);
- increases the chance of funding (for universities and researchers);
- increases career prospects (of researchers);
- benefits society, nature and the environment;
- encourages others to take part in research.

People can work individually and collectively to maintain and/or improve integrity through:

- understanding, discussing and reaching agreement on what is meant by integrity;
- developing and adhering to guidelines, codes of conduct and/or policy (that cover issues such as honour, trust, rigour, transparency, respect and accountability: Activities 12, 36 and 37);
- ensuring that researchers receive the best training and support;
- ensuring that students are introduced early to issues of integrity, and know how to avoid plagiarism (Activity 23), research misconduct (Activity 22), cheating (Activity 24) and conflict of interest (Activity 25);
- monitoring and taking immediate action when problems occur;
- working together to build a resilient integrity culture (Activity 21).

→ **Related activities**

Activity 18: Appraising disciplinary standards of acceptable academic conduct

Activity 20: Fostering research integrity through practice

Activity 21: Developing a resilient integrity culture

Activity 36: Working within the European Code of Conduct for Research Integrity

Activity 37: Aligning with the Concordat to Support Research Integrity

→ **Preparatory reading**

Educators: Read your university's research integrity statement. You might also find it useful to read the *Concordat to Support Research Integrity, European Code of Conduct for Research Integrity and/or Australian Code for the Responsible Conduct of Research* (details in useful resources below). Links to your university's statement and to relevant national frameworks can be provided for students once the activity has concluded.

Students: None required.

→ **Useful resources**

Bowden, J.A. and Green, P.J. (2019) *Playing the PhD Game with Integrity: Connecting Research, Professional Practice and Educational Context*. Singapore: Springer Nature.

Activity 19

Bretag, T. (ed.) (2020) *A Research Agenda for Academic Integrity*. Cheltenham: Edward Elgar.

The *Australian Code for the Responsible Conduct of Research*, 2018 (the 2018 Code) provides a framework for responsible research conduct and covers issues of integrity: www.nhmrc.gov.au/about-us/publications/australian-code-responsible-conduct-research-2018 [accessed 27 April 2021].

The *Concordat to Support Research Integrity*, 2019 (revised edition) has been developed by Universities UK, funding bodies and UK Government departments. It provides a national framework for the conduct of research and its governance: www.universitiesuk.ac.uk/topics/research-and-innovation/concordat-research-integrity [accessed 8 March 2022].

The *European Code of Conduct for Research Integrity*, 2017 (revised edition), published by the All European Academies, provides a framework for self-regulation for the research community: https://ec.europa.eu/info/funding-tenders/opportunities/docs/2021-2027/horizon/guidance/european-code-of-conduct-for-research-integrity_horizon_en.pdf   [accessed 27 April 2021].

The UK Research Office provides a wide range of information, resources and links about research integrity: https://ukrio.org [accessed 27 April 2021].

Activity 19

Activity • • • • • • • • • • • • → 20

Fostering Research Integrity Through Practice

The activity

Set up a suitable asynchronous, text-based tool for running the tip exchange (a VLE-hosted discussion board, chat room or Facebook group, for example). Provide instructions on what is required: this is a tip exchange about how to foster research integrity through practice. Students read tips and post a tip. Each tip should be different from those that have gone before, or they can build on previous tips. Students must post five tips over the period of the activity (give a deadline by which time tips must be posted: this depends on your course or students' research – it is useful to have the final list of tips available for when students begin their research or relevant assignments).

Give students joining instructions and set guidelines for constructive, supportive and respectful online collaboration. Place one or two tips as examples and to get the exchange started (see below). Monitor posts from time to time, to check that information is correct, useful and supportive. Remove any inappropriate posts and explain why this has been done. Check that all students have posted their five tips a few days before the deadline, and send reminders if they have not done so. This tip exchange can remain available throughout students' course or research, if required.

This activity can also be run as a class brainwave. Divide your students into small groups and ask them to develop a list of tips about how to foster research integrity through practice. Walk among the groups, answering questions or offering advice, if required. Once the groups have developed a suitable list (after about 15 minutes), bring the groups back together and start the brainwave. Ask the first group to provide a tip, then ask another group to provide a second tip, ensuring that they give a different tip to those that have come before. This continues until all groups have offered several tips and it is no longer possible to give tips without repetition. Conclude the session with a summary of the issues raised.

Key issues

This activity enables students to exchange useful tips that they can assess and put into practice, if they feel the tip is useful and relevant to their studies, research or professions. The tips offered tend to depend on subject of study, research approach, discipline and level of study. The following list provides an edited snapshot of the type of tips that can be included (some of these can be used to get the tip exchange started, if required):

- Enrol on relevant research methods training courses (students provide links to relevant courses) so that you know what you are doing and can work to the highest standards.
- Read as much as you can (students provide references and resources that they have found useful: some of the resources listed below can be posted, if you feel this would be of use to your students).
- Find and adhere to best practice guidelines (students give links to those provided at their university or in their department).
- Find out about cases of bad practice or questionable practice and learn from them: make sure you don't make the same mistakes (students provide links to some cases of malpractice).
- Ensure that you are honest, open and accountable.
- Do the best you can.
- Be proud of your work.
- Think about software, codes and algorithms developed by others and try to work out whether there are any problems written into them. You might act with integrity, but others might not.
- Remember that just because information is freely available on the internet, you're not freely available to do what you want with it. Know what you can and can't do with what you find on the net.

- Read licences: know what they mean and don't just agree to everything.
- Make sure your analyses are correct. Ask your supervisor or team members to check all your workings and take time to correct any errors.
- Avoid p-hacking.
- Don't change your hypothesis to fit your findings.
- Don't cook data.
- Don't cut corners.
- Don't be tempted to falsify or fabricate results.
- Give yourself plenty of time to do your research: you won't be rushed and feel the need to compromise on methods and procedures.
- Work with your friends.
- Ask for advice.
- Don't be afraid to say you don't know how to do something.
- Watch out for vested interests.
- Be wary of senior researchers/professors/supervisors wanting to be the first author on *your* paper.
- Join forces with other students and researchers to push for changes in the system that encourage bad practice or force researchers to cut corners, such as the pressure to publish or the pressure to conform to a certain methodology.

→ **Related activities**

Activity 18: Appraising disciplinary standards of acceptable academic conduct

Activity 19: Viewing integrity as an individual and collective responsibility

Activity 21: Developing a resilient integrity culture

Activity 36: Working within the European Code of Conduct for Research Integrity

Activity 37: Aligning with the Concordat to Support Research Integrity

→ **Preparatory reading**

Educators: All the resources listed below provide useful preparatory reading.

Students: None required. Students will find their own resources for this activity, and some might mention these in their tips (see key issues, above).

Activity 20

→ **Useful resources**

Aubert Bonn, N. and Pinxten, W. (2019) 'A decade of empirical research on research integrity: What have we (not) looked at?', *Journal of Empirical Research on Human Research Ethics*, 14 (4): 338–52, first published 30 July 2019, doi: 10.1177/1556264619858534.

Bouter, L. (2020) 'What research institutions can do to foster research integrity', *Science and Engineering Ethics*, 26: 2363–9, published 21 January 2020, doi: 10.1007/s11948-020-00178-5.

Bukusi, E.A., Manabe, Y.C. and Zunt, J.R. (2019) 'Mentorship and ethics in global health: Fostering scientific integrity and responsible conduct of research', *American Journal of Tropical Medicine and Hygiene*, 100 (1): 42–7, doi: 10.4269/ajtmh.18-0562.

National Academies of Sciences, Engineering, and Medicine (2017) *Fostering Integrity in Research*. Washington, DC: The National Academies Press, doi: 10.17226/21896.

Roberts, L.L., Sibum, H.O. and Mody, C.C.M. (2020) 'Integrating the history of science into broader discussions of research integrity and fraud', *History of Science*, 58 (4): 354–68, first published 10 December 2020, doi: 10.1177/0073275320952268.

The Royal Society and the UK Research Integrity Office have produced an Integrity in Practice Toolkit, which can be accessed at https://royalsociety.org/topics-policy/projects/research-culture/changing-expectations/integrity-in-practice [accessed 28 April 2021].

The UK Research Office provides a wide range of information, resources and links about research integrity: https://ukrio.org [accessed 28 April 2021].

Information about the Concordat to Support Research Integrity, European Code of Conduct for Research Integrity and Australian Code for the Responsible Conduct of Research can be found in Activity 19, along with other relevant resources.

Activity 20

Activity • • • • • • • • • • • → 21

Developing a Resilient Integrity Culture

The activity

Ask your students to produce a blog of no more than 600 words (for undergraduates) or 800 words (for postgraduates) about developing a resilient integrity culture. If you have a large number of students in your cohort, ask students to complete this activity in small groups (later, they are asked to read the blogs produced by their peers: if there are too many, they might not complete the activity). Encourage students to produce an informal, imaginative, creative and memorable blog from which their peers can learn. 'Developing a resilient integrity culture' has been given as the title as it enables students to approach this from different standpoints (professional, student or researcher, for example). However, if you would like this activity to be a little more specific, you can change it to 'developing a resilient integrity culture in research'.

Once students have produced their blogs, they should be uploaded using a suitable tool (the blog tool in Moodle or Blackboard Learn, for example). Some universities now have their own blogging service that can be used for teaching and learning, and these contain useful templates, guidance notes and advice on setting up the service for assessed and non-assessed work. If you decide to make this an assessed piece of work, explain the process to your students and give guidance on standards required. Students can use the dashboard to customize their blogs: for example, add features such as images, links and multimedia; edit their work; and receive comments from their peers.

Give a deadline by which time all blogs should be uploaded. Ask students to read the blogs of their peers, and post constructive and informative comments, where relevant (check that the right visibility option is chosen so that students can read each other's blogs: default settings might enable blogs to be shared only between student and educator). Read all blogs when they have been posted to ensure that information is correct and does not breach copyright rules. Monitor comments to make sure that they are supportive and constructive, and delete comments that do not meet these criteria, explaining why this has been done.

This activity can be run as a simple written assignment (assessed or non-assessed). Ask your students to produce a written piece of work about developing a resilient integrity culture. Give guidance on length (appropriate to your cohort), include assessment criteria if this is to be an assessed piece of work, and give a date by which time assignments should be submitted.

Key issues

Producing and sharing blogs encourages students to think about how to communicate relevant issues effectively, creatively and imaginatively, in a way that can be understood by those who are new to these issues. This activity provides the opportunity for them to undertake self-guided individual work, before sharing their ideas with their peers. This enables them to complete the work independently, share their knowledge, learn from each other, respond to each other and reinforce their learning. A variety of issues can be discussed in student blogs, including:

- definitions and examples, enabling students to understand what is meant by integrity and why it is important in their studies and research;
- the importance of aligning integrity with students' goals;
- promoting a culture of integrity in studies, research, professions and life in general;
- integrity by example, highlighting excellent practice within the university (observation and improvement);
- high-quality education, training and mentorship, and support in writing papers;
- effective leadership and governance, making good practice the norm;
- clear departmental guidelines;
- effective support structures/support for students who are struggling;
- encouragement and reassurance, inspiring students to work with integrity;

- recognition of, and reward for, good work/excellence (incentives and motivation);
- institution-wide adherence to best practice;
- helpful and constructive one-to-one guidance and timely feedback;
- cultivating trust, openness, honesty and transparency;
- stress/anxiety management, training and support;
- good levels of pay and/or enough student financial support (students can work better and are not tempted to cut corners if they are not in financial difficulty);
- constructive criticism when mistakes are made;
- support for whistle-blowers;
- effective disciplinary procedures;
- research and monitoring of policy, procedures and activity so that changes and improvements can be made.

Cautionary note

Check blog visibility in your chosen tool. It is a good idea to ensure that blogs can be viewed only by students on your course and by yourself, at least until you have checked for potential problems such as breach of copyright, slander, libel or plagiarism. Educators have control over this activity: you have the opportunity to create or edit content; monitor comments; remove posts or blogs that are misleading, unsupportive or wrong; or prohibit users if they break the rules.

→ **Related activities**

Activity 18: Appraising disciplinary standards of acceptable academic conduct

Activity 19: Viewing integrity as an individual and collective responsibility

Activity 20: Fostering research integrity through practice

Activity 36: Working within the European Code of Conduct for Research Integrity

Activity 37: Aligning with the Concordat to Support Research Integrity

→ **Preparatory reading**

Educators: All the resources listed below provide useful preparatory reading (Hooper et al., 2018 will be of particular relevance to those interested in innovative and creative teaching methods).

Students: None required. Students will find their own resources for this activity.

Activity 21

➜ Useful resources

Braun, R., Ravn, T. and Frankus, E. (2020) 'What constitutes expertise in research ethics and integrity?', *Research Ethics*, 16 (1-2): 1-16, first published 13 January 2020, doi: 10.1177/1747016119898402.

Eury, J.L. and Treviño, L.K. (2019) 'Building a culture of honor and integrity in a business school', *Journal of Management Education*, 43 (5): 484-508, first published 20 May 2019, doi: 10.1177/1052562919850223.

Hooper, M., Barbour, V., Walsh, A., Bradbury, S. and Jacobs, J. (2018) 'Designing integrated research integrity training: Authorship, publication, and peer review', *Research Integrity and Peer Review*, 3 (2), published 26 February 2018, doi: 10.1186/s41073-018-0046-2.

Kraemer Diaz, A.E., Spears Johnson, C.R. and Arcury, T.A. (2015) 'Perceptions that influence the maintenance of scientific integrity in community-based participatory research', *Health Education & Behavior*, 42 (3): 393-401, first published 14 January 2015, doi: 10.1177/1090198114560016.

Langlais, P.J. and Bent, B.J. (2014) 'Individual and organizational predictors of the ethicality of graduate students' responses to research integrity issues', *Science and Engineering Ethics*, 20: 897-921, published 19 September 2013, doi: 10.1007/s11948-013-9471-2.

Plemmons, D.K. and Kalichman, M.W. (2018) 'Mentoring for responsible research: The creation of a curriculum for faculty to teach RCR in the research environment', *Science and Engineering Ethics*, 24: 207-26, published 9 March 2017, doi: 10.1007/s11948-017-9897-z.

The UK Research Integrity Office provides a comprehensive list and links to useful resources about various topics under the heading of research culture, including questionable research practices, open access and doctoral theses, and predatory journals and publishers: https://ukrio.org/research-integrity-resources/ [accessed 22 March 2022].

Information about the Concordat to Support Research Integrity, European Code of Conduct for Research Integrity and Australian Code for the Responsible Conduct of Research can be found in Activity 19, along with other relevant resources.

Activity 21

Activity · · · · · · · · · · · → 22

Avoiding Research Misconduct

The activity

Ask your students to complete the wordsearch given in the Student Handout. They are to find 20 words that relate to research misconduct. Once they have completed this task, ask them to choose two of the words. They should then produce a description/definition of the words, give a specific example of these types of misconduct (invented or real) and describe how these types of misconduct can be addressed and avoided. Ask students to share their ideas with their peers on the discussion board or forum that you have set up for this activity (add a sentence to the Handout, informing students of the tool to be used, along with access details). Set a deadline by which time the task should be completed and ask students to read the posts of their peers, again by a specific deadline. Encourage constructive discussion on the issues raised. Monitor posts to ensure that information is correct and constructive.

This activity can be run in-class, if you prefer. Divide students into small groups or pairs (depending on the size of your student cohort). Give them a copy of the Student Handout and ask them to work through the activity in their group/pairs. Again, ask them to choose two words, produce a description/definition of the words, give a specific example of these types of misconduct (invented or real) and describe how these types of misconduct can be addressed and avoided. There is no need to assign words to each individual/group for both the online and in-class versions of this activity. There tends to be a good coverage of words chosen, but if some words are not chosen by any group/individual they can be discussed towards the end of the discussion board/in-class activity if you feel it is important.

The wordsearch provides an entertaining and enjoyable way to introduce different types of research misconduct. However, if you feel that the wordsearch is not appropriate for your students (you have students with dyslexia, for example), allocate each individual/group/pair with two of the following:

Bias	Cheating
Concoction	Corruption
Deception	Dishonesty
Distortion	Evasion
Fabrication	Fakery
Falsehood	Falsification
Forgery	Fraud
Inaccuracy	Negligence
Piracy	Plagiarism
Slander	Untruth

Key issues

The solution to the wordsearch is:

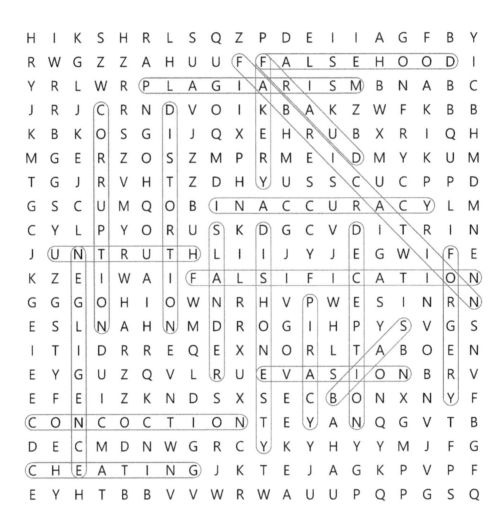

This activity enables students to explore and discuss different types of research misconduct in-depth, with their peers. Issues covered tend to depend on level of study and discipline. Examples include:

- students buying essays from essay mills;
- scientists fabricating results of experiments;
- researchers who are paid by corrupt organizations;
- students using software in their research without correct citation or acknowledgement;
- students copying the work of others and passing it off as their own;
- mistakes made due to lack of training and misunderstanding;
- researchers making-up results to receive funding;
- making defamatory statements about colleagues/peers;
- displaying prejudice and bias that influence research.

Activity 22

➜ Related activities

Activity 17: Cultivating transparency and openness

Activity 18: Appraising disciplinary standards of acceptable academic conduct

Activity 20: Fostering research integrity through practice

Activity 23: Avoiding plagiarism

Activity 24: Critiquing contract cheating

Activity 76: Recognizing false, fabricated or misleading analyses

➜ Preparatory reading

Educators: A comprehensive discussion about research misconduct in the sciences, including some interesting case studies, can be found in: D'Angelo, J. (2019) *Ethics in Science: Ethical Misconduct in Scientific Research*, 2nd edition. Boca Raton, FL: CRC Press.

Students: None required. Students can find their own resources during the individual exercise, if required.

➜ Useful resources

Aubert Bonn, N., Godecharle, S. and Dierickx, K. (2017) 'European universities' guidance on research integrity and miscon-duct: Accessibility, approaches, and content', *Journal of Empirical Research on Human Research Ethics*, 12 (1): 33-44, doi: 10.1177/1556264616688980.

Faria, R. (2018) *Research Misconduct as White-Collar Crime: A Criminological Approach*. Cham: Palgrave Macmillan.

Holtfreter, K., Reisig, M., Pratt, T. and Mays, R. (2020) 'The perceived causes of research misconduct among faculty members in the natural, social, and applied sciences', *Studies in Higher Education*, 45 (11): 2162-74, doi: 10.1080/03075079.2019.1593352.

Tourish, D. and Craig, R. (2020) 'Research misconduct in business and management studies: Causes, consequences, and possible remedies', *Journal of Management Inquiry*, 29 (2): 174-87, doi: 10.1177/1056492618792621.

Velliaris, D. (ed.) (2017) *Handbook of Research on Academic Misconduct in Higher Education*. Hershey, PA: IGI Global.

Activity 22

Activity → 22
Avoiding Research Misconduct

STUDENT HANDOUT

This activity is called 'Avoiding research misconduct'. Find 20 words that relate to research misconduct in the following wordsearch.

```
H  I  K  S  H  R  L  S  Q  Z  P  D  E  I  I  A  G  F  B  Y
R  W  G  Z  Z  A  H  U  U  F  F  A  L  S  E  H  O  O  D  I
Y  R  L  W  R  P  L  A  G  I  A  R  I  S  M  B  N  A  B  C
J  R  J  C  R  N  D  V  O  I  K  B  A  K  Z  W  F  K  B  B
K  B  K  O  S  G  I  J  Q  X  E  H  R  U  B  X  R  I  Q  H
M  G  E  R  Z  O  S  Z  M  P  R  M  E  I  D  M  Y  K  U  M
T  G  J  R  V  H  T  Z  D  H  Y  U  S  S  C  U  C  P  P  D
G  S  C  U  M  Q  O  B  I  N  A  C  C  U  R  A  C  Y  L  M
C  Y  L  P  Y  O  R  U  S  K  D  G  C  V  D  I  T  R  I  N
J  U  N  T  R  U  T  H  L  I  I  J  Y  J  E  G  W  I  F  E
K  Z  E  I  W  A  I  F  A  L  S  I  F  I  C  A  T  I  O  N
G  G  G  O  H  I  O  W  N  R  H  V  P  W  E  S  I  N  R  N
E  S  L  N  A  H  N  M  D  R  O  G  I  H  P  Y  S  V  G  S
I  T  I  D  R  R  E  Q  E  X  N  O  R  L  T  A  B  O  E  N
E  Y  G  U  Z  Q  V  L  R  U  E  V  A  S  I  O  N  B  R  V
E  F  E  I  Z  K  N  D  S  X  S  E  C  B  O  N  X  N  Y  F
C  O  N  C  O  C  T  I  O  N  T  E  Y  A  N  Q  G  V  T  B
D  E  C  M  D  N  W  G  R  C  Y  K  Y  H  Y  Y  M  J  F  G
C  H  E  A  T  I  N  G  J  K  T  E  J  A  G  K  P  V  P  F
E  Y  H  T  B  B  V  V  W  R  W  A  U  U  P  Q  P  G  S  Q
```

When you have found the words, pick two to explore further and undertake the following:

1. Produce a description/definition of the words.
2. Find (or invent) examples of both types of research misconduct.
3. Discuss how these types of misconduct can be addressed and avoided.
4. Upload your work using the tool provided.
5. Read contributions from your peers and enter into online discussion to explore the issues further, remembering to be respectful and courteous.
6. Complete the work by the given date.

Learning outcome: By the end of this activity, you will be able to list, and provide examples of, different types of research misconduct, and explain how to address and avoid the types of research misconduct identified.

Activity ・・・・・・・・・・・ → 23

Avoiding Plagiarism

The activity

A week before your next contact session, divide your students into groups (three to five students in each group is a good number for this activity). Ask each group to prepare a 10-minute session that will teach their peers how to avoid plagiarism. Presentation equipment and materials should be made available for their use, if required. When you next meet, ask each group to deliver their teaching session, in turn. Allocate five minutes at the end of each session for students to ask questions and receive answers. Conclude the session with a summary of the main points raised.

You can ask students to produce and upload a digital presentation (video or text-based) if contact time is unavailable. Provide information about where, how and when to upload presentations. Give a deadline by which time sessions should be uploaded, viewed and commented on. Monitor teaching sessions, posts and comments, to ensure that information is correct, supportive and respectful.

An alternative way to run this session is to ask students to develop a student-centred resource where they provide advice, guidance, information and tips about how their peers can avoid plagiarism. The resource can be edited, modified and built over students' courses, and provides a useful resource to reference if students are struggling with any issues relating to plagiarism during their studies and research. Activity 78: Avoiding plagiarism, in Dawson (2016: 211-13) provides specific details about how to run this activity.

Key issues

This activity requires students to develop an understanding of, and become familiar with, what is meant by plagiarism before they can teach this topic to their peers. This student-centred approach highlights issues of deliberate and/or unintentional plagiarism, while providing advice and guidance about how to recognize these problems and avoid them in students' work. The focus, structure, content and method of delivery are a group choice: students tend to produce informative, creative and imaginative teaching sessions that engage their peers, increase motivation and consolidate learning. Issues that are covered in sessions include definitions, examples, case studies, citing, referencing, deterrents and adopting good practice.

➜ Related activities

Activity 22: Avoiding research misconduct

Activity 24: Critiquing contract cheating

Activity 35: Seeking permission with regard to data ownership

Activity 39: Avoiding copyright infringement

Activity 56: Citing digital tools and software correctly

➜ Preparatory reading

Educators: Read your university's rules and guidance about plagiarism if you have not already done so. A link to these can be given to your students at the end of the session, along with some of the useful resources listed below.

Students: The following books can be recommended to students either before or after the activity:

Harris, R. (2017) *Using Sources Effectively: Strengthening Your Writing and Avoiding Plagiarism*, 5th edition. New York, NY: Routledge.
Neville, C. (2016) *The Complete Guide to Referencing and Avoiding Plagiarism*, 3rd edition. London: Open University Press.
Pears, R. and Shields, G. (2019) *Cite Them Right: The Essential Referencing Guide*, 11th edition. London: Palgrave.
Williams, K. and Davis, M. (2017) *Referencing and Understanding Plagiarism*, 2nd edition. London: Palgrave.

➜ Useful resources

Cleary, M.N. (2017) 'Top 10 reasons students plagiarize & what teachers can do about it (with apologies to David Letterman)', *Phi Delta Kappan*, 99 (4): 66-71, first published 27 November 2017, doi: 10.1177/0031721717745548.
Dawson, C. (2016) *100 Activities for Teaching Research Methods*. London: Sage.
Fazilatfar, A.M., Elhambakhsh, S.E. and Allami, H. (2018) 'An investigation of the effects of citation instruction to avoid plagiarism in EFL academic writing assignments', *SAGE Open*, first published 11 April 2018, doi: 10.1177/2158244018769958.
Moskovitz, C. and Hall, S. (2021) 'Text recycling in STEM research: An exploratory investigation of expert and novice beliefs and attitudes', *Journal of Technical Writing and Communication*, 51 (3): 252-72, first published 30 March 2020, doi: 10.1177/0047281620915434.
Obeid, R. and Hill, D.B. (2017) 'An intervention designed to reduce plagiarism in a research methods classroom', *Teaching of Psychology*, 44 (2): 155-9, first published 20 February 2017, doi: 10.1177/0098628317692620.
Strangfeld, J.A. (2019) 'I just don't want to be judged: Cultural capital's impact on student plagiarism', *SAGE Open*, first published 14 January 2019, doi: 10.1177/2158244018822382.
Suter, W.N. and Suter, P.M. (2018) 'Understanding plagiarism', *Home Health Care Management & Practice*, 30 (4): 151-4, first published 4 June 2018, doi: 10.1177/1084822318779582.

Activity 23

Activity • • • • • • • • • • → 24

Critiquing Contract Cheating

The activity

Divide your students into small groups (three to four groups is a good number for this activity). Give them a copy of the Student Handout. This asks them to produce a video that critiques contract cheating and addresses the learning outcome given above. They need to upload their video using an appropriate tool so that it can be shared with their peers (internal VLE or external such as a Facebook group or Vimeo, for example). Advice about producing the video is given in the handout. Give a deadline by which time this task should be completed. Ask students to view the videos produced by their peers and open a discussion board or thread, to spend a little time discussing the issues raised.

This activity can be run as a poster presentation session, if you prefer. Ask students to produce a poster presentation called 'Critiquing Contract Cheating'. The style and content of the poster is a group choice. If your students are new to poster presentations, give them a copy of the Student Handout in Activity 26, which offers tips and advice. Groups should produce their poster during independent study. Give a date, time and venue when the posters are to be presented so that each group can work to the given deadline (if you choose a time that is outside your usual teaching hours, ensure that all students are able to attend). Provide details of the venue so that groups understand what equipment and space is available for their presentation. Decide how you wish to run the session: keep it free-flowing and informal, enabling students to wander between posters to discuss them with presenters, or ask each group to present their poster in turn, allowing enough time for discussion, questions and feedback, after each presentation.

Key issues

This activity enables students to use their imagination and creativity to produce an entertaining video (or poster) from which their peers can learn. The style and content of the video is a group choice: some choose to role-play a student deciding to contract cheat, and the consequences of this decision. Others choose to approach this task by discussing the ethics of contract cheating and the moral choices students should make. Some consider the increasing availability of contract cheating websites and the influence these might have on studies, whereas others consider the reasons why people decide to cheat and what can be done to address these issues.

→ Related activities

Activity 19: Viewing integrity as an individual and collective responsibility

Activity 22: Avoiding research misconduct

Activity 23: Avoiding plagiarism

→ Preparatory reading

Educators: A useful guide to contract cheating has been produced by the Quality Assurance Agency for Higher Education in the UK: *Contracting to Cheat in Higher Education: How to Address Essay Mills and Contract Cheating*, 2nd edition, 2020, www.qaa.ac.uk/docs/qaa/guidance/contracting-to-cheat-in-higher-education-2nd-edition.pdf [accessed 12 November 2021].

Students: None required. Groups find their own resources.

→ Useful resources

Bretag, T., Harper, R., Burton, M., Ellis, C., Newton, P., Rozenberg, P. Saddiqui, S. and van Haeringen, K. (2019) 'Contract cheating: A survey of Australian university students', *Studies in Higher Education*, 44 (11): 1837-56, published online 17 April 2018, doi: 10.1080/03075079.2018.1462788.

Draper, M. and Newton, P. (2017) 'A legal approach to tackling contract cheating?', *International Journal of Educational Integrity*, 13 (11), published 29 November 2017, doi: 10.1007/s40979-017-0022-5.

Newton, P. (2018) 'How common is commercial contract cheating in higher education and is it increasing? A systematic review', *Frontier in Education*, 3 (67), published 30 August 2018, doi: 10.3389/feduc.2018.00067.

Steel, A. (2017) 'Contract cheating: Will students pay for serious criminal consequences?', *Alternative Law Journal*, 42 (2): 123-9, first published 18 September 2017, doi: 10.1177/1037969X17710627.

Activity 24

Activity • • • • • • • • • • • • → 24

Critiquing Contract Cheating

STUDENT HANDOUT

This activity is called 'Critiquing contract cheating'. Work with your group members to produce a video that critiques contract cheating and addresses the learning outcome given below. Your video can be any length, up to 10 minutes. The approach, style and content of your video is a group choice: use your creativity and imagination to produce a video that is entertaining, informative and memorable. If you need to borrow video equipment, please contact me, otherwise smartphones or webcams are fine for this activity. Ensure that you pay attention to audio, lighting and camera stabilization, and use basic editing software, if required.

Once you have produced your video, share it with your peers by uploading it using the given tool. Make sure that this is done by the deadline. View the videos that are uploaded by your peers and, if you want to make any comments, you can do so on the discussion board. Ensure that you have viewed the videos and participated in the discussion by the given deadline.

Learning outcome: By the end of this activity, you will be able to describe what is meant by contract cheating, identify different types of contract cheating and discuss why contract cheating should be avoided.

Activity • • • • • • • • • → 25

Recognizing Conflict of Interest

ACTIVITY 25: EDUCATOR NOTES

Purpose: This activity helps students to recognize conflict of interest by asking them to work independently to produce a definition, provide specific examples, identify effects and list ways in which conflict can be avoided in others' research and their own. Their work is shared and discussed with their peers (in-class or online). This activity can be expanded by combining it with Activity 82: Avoiding conflict of interest, in Dawson (2016: 221-2), which asks students to find, analyse and critique some research (current or historical) in which conflict of interest has occurred.

Type: Self-guided individual exercise with information sharing and discussion (in-class or online).

Alternative type(s): None.

Level: Intermediate and advanced.

Duration: Students will spend a few hours producing, uploading, sharing and discussing their work. Educators will spend one to two hours monitoring posts and leading the online discussion. If the in-class option is chosen you will need 50 minutes to one hour of contact time.

Equipment/materials: A suitable online asynchronous tool, if the online option is chosen.

Learning outcome: By the end of this activity, students will be able to define what is meant by conflict of interest in research; provide examples; list ways in which conflict can influence the research process; explain how conflict can be avoided or managed; and describe how to avoid or manage conflict of interest in their own research.

The activity

Choose whether to run this activity online or in-class. If you choose the online option, set up a suitable tool for students to upload their work, share and discuss with their peers (Discussions in Canvas, Blackboard Discussion Board or Forum in Moodle, for example). Give your students a copy of the Student Handout and ask them to work through the questions and tasks on their own during independent study. Provide a deadline by which time work should be completed, uploaded and discussions held. If you choose to make this an assessed piece of work, provide specific activity requirements and assessment criteria. If you choose the in-class activity, adapt the Student Handout slightly and lead a class discussion on the issues raised from the self-guided exercise.

Activity 82: Avoiding conflict of interest, in Dawson (2016: 221-2) asks students to find, analyse and critique some research (current or historical) in which conflict of interest has occurred, relate this to their own research and share this information with their peers. Therefore, it can be combined with this activity to provide greater coverage and deeper insight on this topic, if required.

Key issues

This activity enables students to think about conflict of interest on an individual basis, before pooling and discussing ideas with their peers. It is interesting for students to see that their peers often come up with quite different ideas and examples. Issues that can be raised and discussed online or in-class include:

- 'Conflict of interest' occurs when a researcher, team member, funding body, journal editor, reviewer or organization has conflicting interests that influence the integrity or publication of research. These people or organizations are in a position to derive some kind of personal (or organizational) benefit from research outcomes or publication.
- Conflicts can be personal, political, financial or to do with loyalty or commitment, for example.
- Conflicts can occur at all stages of a research project, from choosing a topic through to disseminating (or withholding) and publishing results.
- Conflicts can be actual or perceived (by the wider public): public trust can be damaged and negative perceptions can be harmful even if they are incorrect.
- People have different perceptions of conflict of interest, depending on their own politics and bias. Neill et al. (2020) provides an interesting discussion on how clinical expertise is seen as a conflict of interest for clinician-researchers undertaking abortions, but not for surgeons involved in other areas of medicine.

- Researchers and institutions should act with integrity to avoid conflict of interest (Activities 20 and 21).
- Current ethical standards require full written disclosure of conflicts in all scientific reports and reputable journals insist that conflicts of interest are declared. However, standards and procedures are not infallible as Bruton and Sacco (2018) illustrate.
- Some types of conflict are acceptable: researchers must be open and transparent, and manage the conflict with care so that the integrity of research is not compromised.
- Students should pay attention to who has funded the research, why the research has been commissioned and the credentials of the person or people undertaking the research.
- Students should obtain all relevant information on conflict of interest before beginning their research (funding body guidelines, university policy/code of practice and journal policies, for example).
- Students should understand how to cultivate transparency and openness (Activity 17) and foster research integrity through practice (Activity 20).

→ Related activities

Activity 22: Avoiding research misconduct

Activity 82: Avoiding conflict of interest, in Dawson (2016: 221-2)

Activity 97: Recognizing reporting bias

Activity 98: Understanding the influence of publication bias

→ Preparatory reading

Educators: Read your university's policy/code of conduct on conflicts of interest, if you have not already done so (and provide a link for your students). All the resources listed below provide useful preparatory reading.

Students: None required. Students will find their own resources for this activity.

→ Useful resources

Abbas, M., Pires, D., Peters, A. et al. (2018) 'Conflicts of interest in infection prevention and control research: No smoke without fire. A narrative review', *Intensive Care Medicine*, 44: 1679-90, published 11 September 2018, doi: 10.1007/s00134-018-5361-z.

Bruton, S.V. and Sacco, D.F. (2018) 'What's it to me? Self-interest and evaluations of financial conflicts of interest', *Research Ethics*, 14 (4): 1-17, first published 10 November 2017, doi: 10.1177/1747016117739940.

Dawson, C. (2016) *100 Activities for Teaching Research Methods*. London: Sage.

John, L.K., Loewenstein, G., Marder, A., and Callaham, M.L. (2019) 'Effect of revealing authors' conflicts of interests in peer review: randomized controlled trial', *BMJ 2019*, 367: l5896, published 6 November 2019, doi: 10.1136/bmj.l5896.

Neill, S., Martin, L. and Harris, L. (2020) 'Is clinical expertise a conflict of interest in research?', *Women's Health*, first published 3 November 2020, doi: 10.1177/1745506520969616.

Rodwin, M.A. (2019) 'Conflicts of interest in human subject research: The insufficiency of U.S. and international standards', *American Journal of Law & Medicine*, 45 (4): 303-30, first published 23 January 2020, doi: 10.1177/0098858819892743.

Activity 25

Activity • • • • • • • • • • → 25

Recognizing Conflict of Interest

STUDENT HANDOUT

This activity is called 'Recognizing conflict of interest'. Work through the following questions and tasks on an individual basis. Once you have done this, post your answers using the tool that has been set up for this purpose. Read the responses posted by your peers and enter into online discussion, where appropriate.

1. When thinking about research, what is meant by 'conflict of interest'?
2. Provide examples of two research projects in which conflict of interest has occurred (these can be real or invented).
3. List three ways in which conflict of interest can influence the research process.
4. List three ways in which conflict of interest can be avoided or managed.
5. Describe how you will avoid (or manage) conflict of interest in your own research.

Learning outcome: By the end of this activity, you will be able to define what is meant by conflict of interest in research; provide examples; list ways in which conflict can influence the research process; explain how conflict can be avoided or managed; and describe how to avoid or manage conflict of interest in your own research.

Activity · · · · · · · · · · · → 26

Ensuring Researcher Safety

The activity

Divide your students into small groups and ask them to research, prepare and produce a poster presentation that will enable them to recognize and address issues of researcher safety. This could include physical, emotional, social, economic and psychological aspects, for example. The focus of the poster is a group choice. They could consider one specific project and highlight potential safety issues; view the task from a disciplinary perspective; think about the safety implications of a number of different research methods; or identify a number of risks and threats and assess how these might impact researchers, for example.

Groups should produce their poster during independent study. Provide a date and time when the posters are to be presented so that each group can work to the given deadline (if you choose a time that is outside your usual teaching hours, check that all students are happy and able to attend the session). Give details of the venue so that students know what materials, equipment and space are available for their presentation. Decide how to run the poster presentation session: free-flowing and informal, enabling students to wander between posters to discuss them with the presenters, or by asking each group to present their poster in turn to their peers, allowing enough time for discussion and questions after each presentation. Once students have had time to view all posters, sum up the findings by relating what has been covered in the posters to students' research projects.

Some students may be unfamiliar with the poster presentation technique. If this is the case, give them a copy of the Student Handout, which gives advice and information about producing a poster presentation. This handout can be used for all poster presentation activities in this book.

This activity can be run as an online question-and-answer session, if you prefer. Ask students to think about useful questions they want answered about researcher safety. These can relate to dilemmas associated with personal safety in their research project, or to researcher safety issues in general. Ask students to post answers, encouraging discussion and reflection on pertinent topics. If necessary, begin the session with a few of your own questions. Decide whether to run the session in real-time using a video/web conferencing tool, or over a period of time using a discussion board. Also, decide whether to make the activity compulsory (a set number of questions and answers must be given) or voluntary. Monitor the posts or video discussion to make sure that information is correct, supportive, constructive and useful.

Key issues

This activity engages and motivates students, enabling them to produce imaginative and creative posters from which their peers can learn (graphic comic strip styles, spider diagrams, flow charts and posters that tell a story have been produced previously for this activity). Examples of issues that have been identified and addressed in poster presentations include:

- dangerous situations when meeting participants for face-to-face interviews (meeting alone, unsafe venues and dangerous pets, for example);
- physical violence when in the field (actual or perceived);
- emotional distress when researching harrowing accounts or distressing situations (and having the professional competence to work with, and support, participants);
- entering war zones, areas of armed conflict or dangerous neighbourhoods;
- arrest, detention, expulsion or deportation of researchers by authoritarian or semi-authoritarian regimes;
- threats from activists who disagree with the research project or results;
- threats and abuse from online trolls;
- risk of being put in a compromising position or being accused of something that has not happened;
- risk of infectious disease or illness;
- tabloid newspapers twisting and manipulating facts and damaging researcher reputations;
- prolonged and bitter disputes with other researchers;
- loss of self-esteem through research going badly;
- suffering sexual or other types of harassment.

→ Related activities

Activity 11: Avoiding harm to others

Activity 27: Carrying out a risk assessment

Activity 34: Researching illegal, unlawful, illicit or dangerous behaviour

Activity 94: Ensuring against exploitation of results and outputs

→ Preparatory reading

Educators: The resources listed below all provide useful preparatory reading.

Students: Groups find their own resources if they need to read up on the subject before producing their poster presentation. If you decide to run an online question-and-answer session, students can choose resources that will help them to answer the specific questions posed.

→ Useful resources

Arias, E. (2015) 'Managing researcher safety'. In R. Dingwall and M.B. McDonnell (eds), *The SAGE Handbook of Research Management* (pp. 173–84). London: Sage.
Bashir, N. (2018) 'Doing research in people's homes: Fieldwork, ethics and safety – on the practical challenges of researching and representing life on the margins', *Qualitative Research*, 18 (6): 638–53, first published 21 September 2017, doi: 10.1177/1468794117731808.

Activity 26

Bloor, M., Fincham, B. and Sampson, H. (2010) 'Unprepared for the worst: Risks of harm for qualitative researchers', *Methodological Innovations Online*, 5 (1): 45–55, first published 1 April 2010, doi: 10.4256/mio.2010.0009.

Roguski, M. and Tauri, J. (2013) 'Key issues effecting field researcher safety: A reflexive commentary', *New Zealand Sociology*, 28: 18–35, published January 2013, https://search.informit.org/doi/10.3316/informit.494950171546442.

Stahlke, S. (2018) 'Expanding on notions of ethical risks to qualitative researchers', *International Journal of Qualitative Methods*, first published 10 July 2018, doi: 10.1177/1609406918787309.

Tolich, M., Tumilty, E., Choe, L., Hohmann-Marriott, B. and Fahey, N. (2020) 'Researcher emotional safety as ethics in practice'. In R. Iphofen (ed.), *Handbook of Research Ethics and Scientific Integrity* (pp. 589–602). Cham: Springer.

Williamson, A.E. and Burns, N. (2014) 'The safety of researchers and participants in primary care qualitative research', *British Journal of General Practice*, 64 (621): 198–200, doi: 10.3399/bjgp14X679480.

The Social Research Association has produced a *Code of Practice for the Safety of Social Researchers*, which can be found in the resources section of their website: https://the-sra.org.uk [accessed 12 November 2021].

Activity 26

Activity • • • • • • • • • • • • → 26

Ensuring Researcher Safety

STUDENT HANDOUT

This handout has been produced for those of you who are new to making poster presentations.

- Poster presentations are used to share information with peers and colleagues in seminars, at conferences and at exhibitions. They present complex or in-depth material in a user-friendly, accessible and legible form, with the purpose of imparting information and/or starting a conversation. Therefore, close attention must be paid to both content and visual appearance.
- There are different styles of poster presentation (different templates are available, depending on the tools and software used). Examples include:

  o one-piece posters that are produced in A3 or A4 size and enlarged at the print-out stage;
  o column styles that present information in columns arranged in a logical sequence;
  o panel styles that incorporate a number of separately produced panels or pages that are printed and mounted on a background;
  o digital posters that are projected rather than printed (static or dynamic).

- When planning a poster, think about the following:

  o know your audience and pitch content accordingly;
  o be clear about the purpose of your poster;
  o work out the specific point(s) you wish to get across;
  o keep focused on the topic and ensure that you concentrate on the specific point(s);
  o work out an explicit 'take-home' message, clear conclusion or summary of implications;

  o ensure that images reinforce your message and do not detract from it;
  o create an obvious path for the viewer to follow.

- When designing a poster, think about the following:

  o keep words to a minimum and keep language simple and clear;
  o ensure the font is suitable and large enough to be read at a distance;
  o don't mix too many fonts and font sizes;
  o ensure there is plenty of open space (or white space);
  o structure it well, with appropriate titles, headings and sub-headings, and a logical flow (keep connected items together);
  o make it stimulating visually;
  o use charts, graphs, diagrams, illustrations or photographs, if possible (simplify them, remove non-essential information, crop and edit, adjust colour and contrast, where appropriate);
  o make it colourful but don't mix too many colours: use bright colours sparingly;
  o high contrast helps text to stand out (notice that screen and paper may look a little different);
  o ensure all work is acknowledged and include references, when required.

- An important part of producing a poster presentation is the opportunity for creativity. Therefore, try to produce a poster presentation that is exciting, creative, interesting, informative and memorable.

Activity • • • • • • • • • • → 27

Carrying out a Risk Assessment

┌───┐

ACTIVITY 27: EDUCATOR NOTES

Purpose: This activity is aimed at students who are planning their research (at undergraduate or postgraduate level). It is a practical workshop that encourages them to think about what is meant by risk; introduces them to your university's policy and requirements concerning risk; enables them to consider (with the help and support of their peers) what aspects of risk might be associated with their research; and assess which forms will need to be completed.

Type: Workshop (in-class or online).

Alternative type(s): Self-guided individual exercise with information sharing and discussion.

Level: Intermediate and advanced.

Duration: Fifty minutes to one hour for the workshop followed by one or two hours of independent study to complete the necessary forms. If the self-guided individual exercise is chosen, students will spend one or two hours producing their list of potential risks and up to an hour sharing and discussing their list with their peers.

Equipment/materials: All relevant university guidelines, templates and risk assessment forms.

Learning outcome: By the end of this activity, students will be able to define what is meant by risk, identify risks associated with their research and list university forms that will need to be completed for their risk assessment.

└───┘

The activity

Gather together all the relevant risk assessment information from your university. The information available depends on your university, but might include flowcharts that illustrate the risk assessment process; risk estimation toolkits; examples and cases studies of risk; examples of completed risk assessment forms; risk assessment templates and forms (travel abroad risk, event risk, computer-based risk and microscope-based risk, for example); and university's risk policy and procedures.

Hold a workshop with students who are at the planning stages of their research (before they have applied for ethical approval as they will need to consider aspects of risk, and produce a risk assessment, before they make their application). This workshop can be held in-class or online (if the online option is chosen use a synchronous video/web conferencing tool such as Zoom Meetings, Meetings in Microsoft Teams for Education, Google Meet or Blackboard Collaborate). Begin the session by holding a short brainstorm on what is meant by risk. Once this has been completed (after about 5–10 minutes), ask students to provide specific examples of types of risk that could be faced by participants and/or researchers (these can be real examples or invented by students). This will take around 10 minutes.

Then introduce your university's risk assessment policy and guidelines, explaining the process that students must work through and the information they must provide. Show them some of the forms they will need to complete. Ask students to digest this information and start to think about risk associated with their own research. Suggest that they consider all stages of their research project, including dissemination of results and beyond. Give them up to 15 minutes to think about, and list, areas of risk they might need to consider (working independently or in pairs). Once they have done this, bring students back together to discuss items on their lists. This will take up to 20 minutes. Conclude the session by asking whether students have any questions, concerns or worries about the risk assessment process. Provide details of further risk assessment training courses that might be available at your university (this is useful for students who have higher levels of risk in their research as there is not enough time in this activity to cover this type of research and risk).

This activity can be run as a self-guided individual exercise with information sharing and discussion, if you prefer. Ask students to obtain all the necessary guidance and forms from your university, digest the information and produce a list of potential risks they could encounter in their research (risks to participants and/or researcher). Once they have done this, they should upload their list using a suitable asynchronous tool that you have set up for this purpose (Discussions in Brightspace, Forum in Moodle or Discussions in Canvas, for example). Ask students to read and comment on the lists of their peers by a given deadline. This will enable them to find out whether there are areas of risk they have not considered, bounce ideas off one another and consolidate their learning. Provide links to relevant resources and university forms and policy for students who need this information.

Key issues

Your university's guidance will cover all the key areas of risk that students should consider. These include social, economic, legal, physical, psychological, reputational and safeguarding risks, for example. Guidance will also include information about different levels of risk (insignificant, minor, moderate and major, for example). Risk assessment forms and templates provide further guidance, along with questions that students must answer, or details they must provide. A bullet point list of specific types of risk and harm that could be faced by researchers and participants is provided in Activity 26.

→ Related activities

Activity 14: Working with vulnerable people

Activity 15: Conducting research with children

Activity 26: Ensuring researcher safety

Activity 34: Researching illegal, unlawful, illicit or dangerous behaviour

→ Preparatory reading

Educators: Become familiar with your university's risk assessment guidelines, policy, procedures and forms, if you have not already done so.

Students: None required. Relevant resources listed below can be recommended after the activity, if required.

→ Useful resources

The Office for Human Research Protections (OHRP) provides information and guidance, maintains regulatory oversight and develops educational materials in biomedical and behavioural research conducted or supported by the US Department of Health and Human Services (HHS). Useful information about risk in research can be obtained from their website: www.hhs.gov/ohrp [accessed 12 November 2021].

Atkins, M.S. and LeGrow, C. (2018) 'Risk perceptions for trauma-related research: An exploratory study of undergraduate student researchers in psychology', *Journal of Empirical Research on Human Research Ethics*, 13 (5): 537-45, first published 25 October 2018, doi: 10.1177/1556264618805282.

Butler, A.E., Copnell, B. and Hall, H. (2019) 'Researching people who are bereaved: Managing risks to participants and researchers', *Nursing Ethics*, 26 (1): 224-34, first published 3 April 2017, doi: 10.1177/0969733017695656.

DeGroot, J.M. and Carmack, H.J. (2020) 'Unexpected negative participant responses and researcher safety: "Fuck your survey and your safe space, trigger warning bullshit"', *Journal of Communication Inquiry*, 44 (4): 354-75, first published 1 May 2020, doi: 10.1177/0196859920921752.

Activity 27

Novek, S. and Wilkinson, H. (2019) 'Safe and inclusive research practices for qualitative research involving people with dementia: A review of key issues and strategies', *Dementia*, 18 (3): 1042-59, first published 28 March 2017, doi: 10.1177/1471301217701274.

Orr, E., Durepos, P., Jones, V. and Jack, S.M. (2021) 'Risk of secondary distress for graduate students conducting qualitative research on sensitive subjects: A scoping review of Canadian dissertations and theses', *Global Qualitative Nursing Research*, first published 12 February 2021, doi: 10.1177/2333393621993803.

Sampson, H. (2019) '"Fluid fields" and the dynamics of risk in social research', *Qualitative Research*, 19 (2): 131-47, first published 21 December 2017, doi: 10.1177/1468794117746085.

Activity 27

Activity • • • • • • • • • • • → 28

Evaluating Biases with Reference to Equality, Diversity and Inclusion

The activity

Ask your students, at the start of their course (or at the start of their research), to keep a learning journal or diary that will enable them to recognize and critique their own bias, and the bias of others, with reference to equality, diversity and inclusion (EDI). Explain that the journal or diary is a personal endeavour that will not be seen by others or assessed by you. It should be kept throughout their course (or their research) and should be completed on a regular basis to get the maximum benefit. If you feel your students need a little more structure and guidance for this activity, give them a copy of the Student Handout.

Key issues

Personal journals encourage students to reflect on their learning, reading, behaviour and actions with reference to equality, diversity and inclusion through the process of writing down their thoughts and reflections. The journal should not be a descriptive account of their course or research project, but should indicate an active process of thought, reflection, recognition, analysis and understanding (this is made clear in the Student Handout, if you choose to use it). The journal helps students to:

- think about what is meant by bias, equality, diversity and inclusion;
- evaluate their biases and the biases of others with reference to equality, diversity and inclusion;
- consider bias in relation to their research, studies and life in general;
- address or make plans for problems that have been identified;

- develop their skills of reflection, critical thinking and reflective writing;
- become actively involved in learning;
- increase personal development and self-empowerment;
- analyse, evaluate and weigh evidence;
- question and solve problems;
- take control of their own learning.

Cautionary note

This activity can uncover biases of which students were previously unaware. It should be made clear that this is a good thing: the first step to addressing bias is recognition. This issue is covered in the Student Handout, if you intend to give it to students. It might be helpful to let students know that you are available to discuss any issues that might arise from this activity, if required.

→ Related activities

Activity 8: Conducting discrimination-aware and fairness-aware research

Activity 30: Researching cross-culturally

Activity 51: Assessing the neutrality of online platforms, tools and data

Activity 52: Assessing bias in search tools

Activity 63: Recognizing and addressing bias when collecting data

Activity 73: Recognizing and addressing bias when analysing qualitative data

Activity 74: Avoiding bias in quantitative analyses

→ Preparatory reading

Educators: None required for this activity. However, if you are new to learning journals and reflective writing, Bassot (2020a) and Moon (2006) provide useful reading.

Students: None required. Students will find their own resources as this activity progresses, if required (although Bantam, 2016 might be useful to stimulate thought and reflection and Bassot, 2020b could be recommended for students who need guidance on using journals in research).

→ Useful resources

Bassot, B. (2020a) *The Reflective Journal*, 3rd edition. London: Red Globe Press.

Bassot, B. (2020b) *The Research Journal: A Reflective Tool for Your First Independent Research Project*. Bristol: Policy Press.

Banaji, M. and Greenwald, A. (2016) *Blindspot: Hidden Biases of Good People*, reprint edition. New York, NY: Bantam Books.

Booysen, L., Bendl, R. and Pringle, J. (eds) (2018) *Handbook of Research Methods in Diversity Management, Equality and Inclusion at Work*. Cheltenham: Edward Elgar.

Köllen, T., Kakkuri-Knuuttila, M.-L. and Bendl, R. (2018) 'An indisputable "holy trinity"? On the moral value of equality, diversity, and inclusion', *Equality, Diversity and Inclusion*, 37 (5): 438-49, published 18 June 2018, doi: 10.1108/EDI-04-2018-0072.

Moon, J. (2006) *Learning Journals: A Handbook for Reflective Practice*, 2nd edition. Abingdon: Routledge.

Equality, Diversity and Inclusion (www.emerald.com/insight/publication/issn/2040-7149) is a peer-reviewed journal published by Emerald that provides a 'platform for critical and rigorous exploration of equal opportunities concerns including gender, ethnicity, class, disability, age, sexual orientation, religion, as well as other nascent forms of inequalities in the context of society'.

Activity 28

Activity •••••••••• → 28

Evaluating Biases with Reference to Equality, Diversity and Inclusion

STUDENT HANDOUT

This activity is called 'Evaluating biases with reference to equality, diversity and inclusion'. Please keep a learning journal or diary that will enable you to recognize and critique your own bias, and the bias of others, with reference to equality, diversity and inclusion (EDI). Your journal or diary is a personal endeavour that will not be seen by your peers, or assessed or seen by me (unless, of course, you wish to discuss any issues raised within your journal). Keep your journal throughout your course (or research project): it should be completed on a regular basis to get the maximum benefit.

   The content, structure and style of your journal is up to you. The journal should not be a descriptive account of your course or research project, but should indicate an active process of thought, reflection, recognition, analysis and understanding. Below are some ideas that might help you to get started and encourage you to make entries as your course progresses.

1. When you begin your learning journal, define what is meant by bias, equality, diversity and inclusion. Return to these definitions as your course progresses: add to, modify or change them as your knowledge and understanding grows.

2. Try to make an entry at least once a week. This enables you to keep these issues in mind: for example, you might notice how issues of inclusion have been addressed when you read a book or a research paper, which stimulates reflection on possible biases relating to inclusion in your work. Or you might notice someone, or an organization, that has treated someone unequally due to their own bias or institutional bias. Write down your thoughts and reflections while they are fresh in your mind. Perhaps, at this stage, definitions of issues such as 'institutional bias', might be useful to include in your journal.

3. We all have biases of which we are unaware. Through careful reflection and increased understanding some of these biases might become visible. This is a good thing: don't be hard on yourself. Remember that recognition is the first step to addressing bias. Reflect on these biases and write down your thoughts. Think about how you can address this bias in your research, studies and life in general.

4. Keep in mind the learning outcome given below. You will be able to achieve this outcome through deep reflection and regular entry into your journal.

Learning outcome: By the end of this activity, you will be able to recognize and critique your own bias, and the bias of others, with reference to equality, diversity and inclusion; and plan how to address your own bias in your research, studies and life in general.

Activity • • • • • • • • • • • → 29

Collaborating Ethically in Research

The activity

Divide your students into small groups. Set or agree guidelines for constructive and respectful discussion. Give each group a copy of the Student Handout and ask them to work through the scenarios in their groups for 20 minutes. After this time, bring the groups back together to hold a whole-class discussion on the issues raised. This activity can be run in-class or online (using a video/web conferencing tool such as Zoom Meetings, Blackboard Collaborate or Meetings in Microsoft Teams for Education, with breakout rooms used for the small group discussion).

Two activities in Dawson (2016) also cover working collaboratively. If you require fuller coverage of this topic, combine one or more of these activities. Alternatively, you might find that one of the activities in Dawson (2016) is better suited to your students:

- *Activity 32: Working collaboratively with others* (pp. 81-3) is a ball game that highlights the importance of making new members feel welcome and part of the team, and illustrates the significance of providing an adequate induction when working collaboratively with an existing research team or student group.

- *Activity 86: Collaborating and cooperating ethically* (pp. 230-1) is a role-play that helps students to think about the issues involved in collaborating and cooperating ethically. They are asked to develop a 'Code of Ethical Cooperation', which is presented to, and discussed with, their potential collaborators.

This activity can also be run as a scenario-based individual exercise. Give a copy of the Student Handout to your students and ask them to work on the scenarios on an individual basis. If you want to make this an assessed piece of work, provide assessment criteria and a deadline by which time the work should be submitted.

Key issues

The key issues raised in this activity are provided as options in the first three scenarios presented in the Student Handout. However, if you feel that these issues should be discovered and explored by students rather than provided as options, remove them from the Handout. Key issues that could be discussed in Scenario 4 are:

- acting with courtesy and respect;
- building trust;
- being open and transparent (Activity 17);
- reaching agreement on roles and ensuring that everyone understands their role;
- setting up suitable communication channels;
- agreeing on budgets and equipment ownership;
- agreeing author and publication protocols;
- discussing and agreeing on Open Access, Open Science and Open Research (Activity 96);
- discussing and reaching agreement on intellectual property ownership and rights (Activity 38);
- developing and adhering to a Code of Ethical Conduct;
- developing and reaching agreement on a Data Management Plan (Activity 81) and a data access (or availability) statement (Activity 83);
- reaching agreement on FAIR principles (findable, accessible, interoperable and reusable: Activity 82);
- respecting different cultures (Activity 30).

Cautionary note

Walk among groups or visit breakout rooms during the group part of this activity to monitor discussions. On occasions, students might disagree about the solutions to the challenges and dilemmas. If students are unable to agree, let them know that there are no specific right or wrong answers. Ask them to move on to the next scenario, then lead a class discussion on the issues raised, bringing in other groups who may have found it easier to reach a consensus.

→ Related activities

Activity 1: Respecting human dignity, privacy and rights

Activity 17: Cultivating transparency and openness

Activity 30: Researching cross-culturally

....

→ Preparatory reading

Educators: The resources listed below provide useful preparatory reading for this activity and further resources can be found in Activities 32 and 86 in Dawson (2016).

Students: None required, although the useful resources listed below can be recommended on conclusion of the activity.

....

→ Useful resources

Clerke, T. and Hopwood, N. (2014) *Doing Ethnography in Teams: A Case Study of Asymmetries in Collaborative Research*. Cham: Springer.

Dawson, C. (2016) *100 Activities for Teaching Research Methods*. London: Sage.

Flammia, M., Cleary, Y. and Slattery, D. (2016) *Virtual Teams in Higher Education: A Handbook for Students and Teachers*. Charlotte, NC: Information Age Publishing, Inc.

Olechnicka, A., Ploszaj, A. and Celi ska-Janowicz, D. (2019) *The Geography of Scientific Collaboration*. Abingdon: Routledge.

Reeves, J., Starbuck, S. and Yeung, A. (2020) *Inspiring Collaboration and Engagement*. London: Sage.

Methods and tools for collaboration projects and the co-production of knowledge can be found on the Swiss Academy of Arts and Sciences website: https://naturalsciences.ch/co-producing-knowledge-explained [accessed 12 November 2021].

Activity 29

Activity • • • • • • • • • → 29
Collaborating Ethically in Research

STUDENT HANDOUT

This activity is called 'Collaborating ethically in research'. Work through the following scenarios with your group members, discussing each of them and finding possible solutions. After 20 minutes of discussion, we will come back together as a class to discuss the issues raised. Remember to be courteous and respectful in your discussion: listen to what others have to say and let everyone make a contribution. There are no right or wrong answers, although you will find that some answers are more appropriate than others.

Scenario 1

Mafalda is a postgraduate student in a Portuguese research team working together with a US research team. Kya is a student in the US team. She has made contact with Mafalda, suggesting that they build an informal relationship, outside the formal structure of the collaboration. Mafalda thinks this is a good idea as networking and informal collaboration will be good for the research project. However, during their informal exchanges, Kya makes discriminatory and defamatory remarks about a member of the US research team. What should Mafalda do?

1. Break informal ties and adhere to the formal collaboration agreement. This should include a Code of Ethical Conduct (or equivalent), which will cover issues such as respect, courtesy, fairness and non-discriminatory behaviour.
2. Seek advice from her supervisor or team leader.
3. Explain to Kya that she is not comfortable with discrimination and ask that she ceases if they are to continue with their informal relationship.

4. Refer Kya to the collaboration agreement and to university policy covering issues such as mutual respect, integrity and transparency, shared goals, a legacy of goodwill and lasting partnerships.
5. Report Kya's behaviour to her university in the USA.
6. Report Kya's behaviour to Mafalda's university in Portugal.
7. A combination of the above.
8. Something else.

Scenario 2

Noah is a student member of a research team collaborating with industry. He is extremely enthusiastic about his work and wants to share what he is doing with others, perhaps through a podcast, vlog or blog. He has a chat with his mates who say that a YouTube video would be a great way to share his research with a wider audience. He works with a friend to produce, edit and upload a video. Has Noah done the right thing?

1. Yes, Noah has done the right thing: it's great to share research with a wider audience.
2. No, he has not done the right thing. He should have spoken to his supervisors first, asking them to view and comment on the video before it was uploaded.
3. No, he has not done the right thing. He should have checked whether there was a confidentiality agreement,

or non-disclosure agreement, in place before sharing any of his research. University and industry often agree on this type of agreement to protect sensitive or commercial data in collaboration projects.
4. Yes, it's good to share information and it doesn't matter if he's broken an agreement: what can the university do? He would rather make sure that people know about his vital research than face sanctions.

5. No, he has not done the right thing. It would have been better to speak to all members of the research team to find out about publishing protocols and intellectual property.

6. A combination of the above.

7. Something else.

Scenario 3

Andy is collaborating on a research paper with several other researchers. One of the senior researchers insists that his name comes first on the paper, even though he has not written any of the paper. Another insists that a previous paper of hers is referenced, even though it is not relevant. What should Andy do?

1. Walk away. Find someone else to collaborate with as these people seem to be ethically unsound.
2. Agree to all the demands, after all, Andy is only a student and these researchers are much more experienced. It will be good to have the senior researcher's name on a paper, even if there are a few problems with it.
3. Arrange a meeting with all the contributors. Set guidelines for courteous and respectful discussion, and try to reach consensus about the issues under debate.

4. Ask his supervisor for advice and guidance.
5. Write his own paper on the topic and submit it to a journal before his colleagues.
6. Write a blog and publish it quickly.
7. A combination of the above.
8. Something else.

Scenario 4

Hathai has been told by her supervisor that it would be beneficial to her research and potential academic career to collaborate with other researchers. What ethical issues should she consider, if she decides to collaborate with others?

Learning outcome: By the end of this activity, you will be able explain how to collaborate ethically in research; identify challenges and dilemmas associated with collaborating ethically in research; and list possible solutions to these challenges and dilemmas.

Activity 29

Activity • • • • • • • • • • → 30

Researching Cross-Culturally

The activity

Give a copy of the Student Handout to your students and ask that they work on the tasks by your given deadline. A quotation is provided in the Handout that introduces a number of issues related to cross-cultural research: an alternative quotation can be used if you prefer. If you think that there is too much work involved for your students, choose the last item on the Handout, which asks students to find and critique an example of cross-cultural research.

Once your students have completed the work, compile their answers and examples into a PDF and send it to all your students to read and digest. If you have the contact time available, and if it better suits your students, meet to share and discuss students' work (either in-class or online), instead of producing a PDF. Set guidelines for constructive and respectful interaction and lead a whole-class discussion on the answers and examples produced by students. If you decide to make this an assessed piece of work, provide assessment guidelines with the handout.

Key issues

This activity provides the opportunity for students to work on the task on an individual basis, before pooling work and consolidating their learning. A wide variety of topics and tasks can be covered, including:

- developing cultural sensitivity in method (Activity 58);
- communicating cross-culturally (using appropriate language for interviews and questionnaires, for example);
- paying attention to the presentation and representation of the researcher (Activity 70);
- respecting local knowledge and understanding;
- respecting beliefs, values and customs;
- building cultural knowledge (learning a language, living in the community, participatory methods and the benefits of insider status, for example);
- building trust among different cultures (in the researcher, the research process, data sharing and publication);
- addressing and overcoming researcher misunderstandings, preconceptions and/or bias;
- adhering to local rules, regulations and laws (Activity 31);
- identifying and critiquing research projects that have been carried out in a culturally sensitive way;
- identifying and critiquing research projects that have displayed poor cultural integrity (displaying a lack of cultural understanding or the use of inappropriate research methods, for example).

→ Related activities

Activity 1: Respecting human dignity, privacy and rights

Activity 7: Promoting social good through research practice

Activity 13: Creating social change through research practice

Activity 94: Ensuring against exploitation of results and outputs

→ Preparatory reading

Educators: Liamputtong (2010) provides a comprehensive guide for educators who are new to teaching this topic. You might also find it useful to read the paper that provides the quotation for the student activity (Pelzang and Hutchinson, 2018).

Students: None required. Students will find their own resources for this activity and most will read the full paper from which the quotation originates (Pelzang and Hutchinson, 2018).

→ Useful resources

Griffin, G. (ed.) (2018) *Cross-Cultural Interviewing: Feminist Experiences and Reflections*. Abingdon: Routledge.

Kowal, S.P., Bubela, T. and Jardine, C. (2017) 'Experiences in broker-facilitated participatory cross-cultural research: overcoming practical and ethical challenges', *International Journal of Qualitative Methods*, first published 4 May 2017, doi: 10.1177/1609406917706883.

Liamputtong, P. (2010) *Performing Qualitative Cross-Cultural Research*. Cambridge: Cambridge University Press.

Milfont, T.L. and Klein, R.A. (2018) 'Replication and reproducibility in cross-cultural psychology', *Journal of Cross-Cultural Psychology*, 49 (5): 735–50, first published 21 May 2018, doi: 10.1177/0022022117744892.

Nakray, K., Alston, M. and Whittenbury, K. (eds) (2020) *Social Science Research Ethics for a Globalizing World: Interdisciplinary and Cross-Cultural Perspectives*. New York, NY: Routledge.

Pelzang, R. and Hutchinson, A.M. (2018) 'Establishing cultural integrity in qualitative research: Reflections from a cross-cultural study', *International Journal of Qualitative Methods*, first published 2 January 2018, doi: 10.1177/1609406917749702.

Reid, C., Calia, C., Guerra, C., Grant, L., Anderson, M., Chibwana, K., Kawale, P. and Amos, A. (2021) 'Ethics in global research: Creating a toolkit to support integrity and ethical action throughout the research journey', *Research Ethics*, first published 27 February 2021, doi: 10.1177/1747016121997522.

Schrauf, R.W. (2018) 'Mixed methods designs for making cross-cultural comparisons', *Journal of Mixed Methods Research*, 12 (4): 477–94, first published 20 November 2017, doi: 10.1177/1558689817743109.

Activity 30

Activity • • • • • • • • • • → 30

Researching Cross-Culturally

STUDENT HANDOUT

This activity is called 'Researching cross-culturally'. Read the following quotation, then work through the questions and tasks given below:

'Cultural integrity cannot be achieved without adapting and applying research in a culturally meaningful way and without an in-depth knowledge and understanding of the sociocultural and political dynamics of a particular research setting' (Pelzang and Hutchinson, 2018: 1):

1. What do the authors mean by 'cultural integrity'?
2. Why is cultural integrity important?
3. Give three examples of how research can be adapted and applied 'in a culturally meaningful way'.
4. Give three examples of how a researcher can develop an 'in-depth knowledge and understanding of the sociocultural and political dynamics of a particular research setting'.
5. Find an example of a cross-cultural research project. Produce a critique of the research, paying particular attention to the points raised in the quotation above. Your critique should be no longer than 800 words.

Once you have completed these tasks, hand your work into me by the given deadline. I will compile your work into a PDF that will be sent to you all. Once I have done this, read the entries from your peers as this will enable you to develop a deeper understanding of what is involved when researching cross-culturally.

Learning outcome: By the end of this activity, you will be able to describe what is meant by cultural integrity and explain why it is important; illustrate how research methods can be adapted and applied in a culturally meaningful way; list ways that researchers can improve their knowledge and understanding in different cultural settings; and identify and critique specific examples of cross-cultural research.

Reference

Pelzang, R. and Hutchinson, A.M. (2018) 'Establishing cultural integrity in qualitative research: Reflections from a cross-cultural study', *International Journal of Qualitative Methods*, first published 2 January 2018, doi: 10.1177/1609 406917749702.

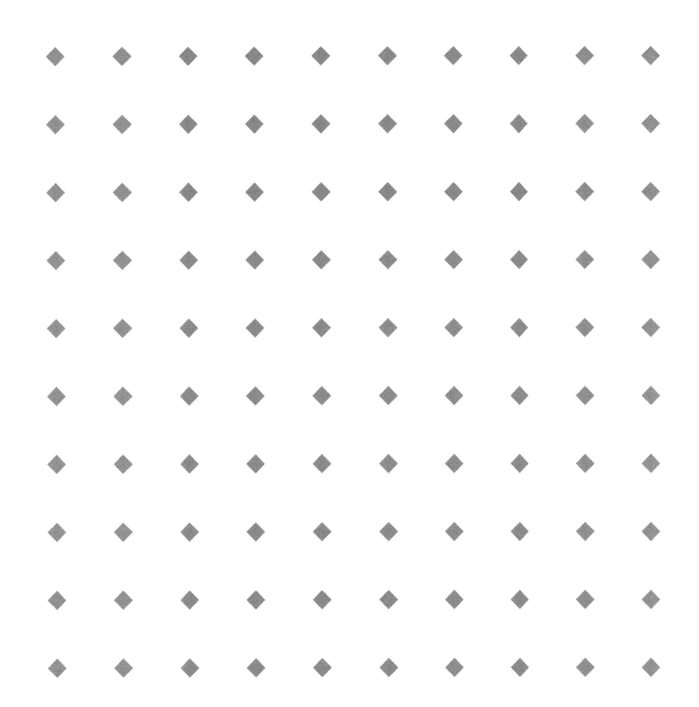

Section 3

Compliance with
Policy, Standard
or Law

Activity • • • • • • • • • • • → 31

Identifying and Complying with Local, Regional and National Law

ACTIVITY 31: EDUCATOR NOTES

Purpose: This activity helps students to identify local, regional and national law that is relevant to their research, and understand how to comply with relevant law. They build a student-centred digital resource that can be accessed throughout the planning stages of their research and beyond.

Type: Student-centred digital resource.

Alternative type(s): None.

Level: Intermediate and advanced (this activity works best when students are in the planning stages of their research).

Duration: Students will spend two or three hours during independent study researching relevant laws, uploading information and reading and discussing their peers' posts. Educators will spend up to an hour setting up the digital resource and monitoring posts.

Equipment/materials: A suitable digital tool for building the resource.

Learning outcome: By the end of this activity, students will be able to identify local, regional and national law that is relevant to their research, and explain how they will comply with relevant law.

The activity

When students are in the planning stages of their research ask them to work independently to identify local, regional and national law that is relevant to their research. Once they have identified relevant law, they should explain how they intend to comply with this law. Ask them to produce a summary of each law and intended compliance (this can be a bullet point list, if they wish) that they should upload using the tool you have set up for this purpose. Give a deadline by which time all summaries should be posted. Ask students to read, digest and comment on the summaries posted by their peers. Monitor posts to ensure that information is correct: add to, or modify, posts if required, and explain why this has been done. The digital resource can remain available to students throughout the planning stages of their research and beyond, if required.

Key issues

This activity encourages students to think about specific law that might be relevant to their research, and explain how they intend to comply with this law. Students are able to share their ideas and learn from each other. Often, students find that their peers have identified law that is relevant to their research that they have missed. They are able to discover and discuss relevant law, and work out together how to ensure that they comply with the law when undertaking their research.

Law that is identified tends to depend on discipline, research topic and methodology, but can include the following:

- human rights (Activity 32);
- data protection (Activity 33);
- indigenous law (tribal codes and constitutions);
- duty of confidentiality common law;
- law relating to consent (the Mental Capacity Act 2005 in England and Wales, for example);
- safeguarding requirements (Disclosure and Barring Service checks in the UK, for example);
- freedom of information;
- telecommunications law covering recording, privacy and protection such as the Telecommunications (Data Protection and Privacy) Regulations 1999 in the UK;
- health and safety;
- equality and diversity (the Equality Act 2010 in the UK, for example);
- intellectual property rights (Activity 38);
- law relating to security-sensitive research materials (commissioned by the military or concerning extreme groups, for example);
- law relating to health, medicine and social care;
- law relating to science and research.

→ Related activities

Activity 32: Understanding and adhering to relevant human rights legislation

Activity 33: Knowing about the General Data Protection Regulation (GDPR)

Activity 40: Understanding digital licences, laws and conventions

→ Preparatory reading

Educators: All the resources listed below provide useful preparatory reading.

Students: None required. Students will find their own resources for this activity.

→ Useful resources

Harrell, H.L. and Rothstein, M.A. (2016) 'Biobanking research and privacy laws in the United States', *Journal of Law, Medicine & Ethics*, 44 (1): 106-27, first published 1 March 2016, doi: 10.1177/1073110516644203.

Hawkins, S. (ed.) (2021) *Access and Control in Digital Humanities.* Abingdon: Routledge. Part V: Access, control, and the law, is of particular relevance to this activity.

Tovino, S.A. (2020) 'Mobile research applications and state research laws', *Journal of Law, Medicine & Ethics*, 48 (1_suppl): 82-6, first published 28 April 2020, doi: 10.1177/1073110520917032.

The NHS Health Research Authority in the UK provides information about policies, standards and legislation for researchers working in health and medicine: www.hra.nhs.uk/planning-and-improving-research/policies-standards-legislation [accessed 27 May 2021].

All UK legislation can be accessed on the Government legislation website. Searches can be made by title, year, number and type: www.legislation.gov.uk [accessed 27 May 2021].

Information about legislation in force, and legislation under preparation, in the European Union can be obtained from the official website of the EU: https://europa.eu/european-union/law/find-legislation_en [accessed 27 May 2021].

The Federal Register of Legislation is a government website for Commonwealth legislation and related documents in Australia: www.legislation.gov.au [accessed 27 May 2021].

Information about legislation in the USA can be obtained from Congress.gov, which is the official website for US federal legislative information: www.congress.gov [accessed 27 May 2021].

Activity 31

Activity • • • • • • • • • • → 32

Understanding and Adhering to Relevant Human Rights Legislation

The activity

Divide your students into small groups (three to five students in each group is a good number for this activity, but if you have only a few students in your cohort this activity can be carried out in pairs). Give each group a copy of the Student Handout. This asks them to produce a podcast that identifies human rights legislation that is relevant to their research and explains, or illustrates, how they can and should adhere to this legislation when undertaking their research. Students can choose the structure, style and content of their podcasts: all they need to ensure is that their podcast enables other students to meet the learning outcome given above. Free online audio editing tools such as Audacity, Auphonic or Beautiful Audio Editor can be used, if required.

Students should upload their podcasts by your given deadline, then spend some time listening to, and discussing, the podcasts of their peers (use tools such as Discussions in Canvas or Forum in Moodle that enable messages to be posted with media file attachments). Listen to all podcasts and monitor online discussion to ensure that information is correct, supportive and respectful. If appropriate, ask students to vote on the most informative or creative podcast at the end of the activity (if you choose to do this, add a sentence to the Student Handout).

Key issues

Students are asked to work in groups for this activity as it helps to pool ideas and build understanding, while enabling students to help each other with the technical aspects of podcast production. This activity encourages students to find, read and digest complex legislation, think about the relevance to their research and then present their ideas in a creative, entertaining and informative way.

When this activity has been undertaken in the UK, students discuss the Human Rights Act 1998. Articles that are of particular relevance to students are:

- Article 8: Right to respect for private and family life
- Article 9: Freedom of thought, conscience and religion
- Article 10: Freedom of expression
- Article 14: Prohibition of discrimination (this refers to the rights and freedoms set out in the Act, but students might choose to include additional legislation that covers discrimination in other areas of life, such as the Equality Act 2010)
- Article 17: Prohibition of the abuse of rights

Students might also refer to the United Nations Universal Declaration of Human Rights, the International Covenant on Economic, Social and Cultural Rights and the International Covenant on Civil and Political Rights, collectively known as the International Bill of Rights. They might also refer to the European Convention on Human Rights. Some students choose also to consider current human rights legislation in relation to digital research.

→ Related activities

Activity 1: Respecting human dignity, privacy and rights

Activity 31: Identifying and complying with local, regional and national law

Activity 33: Knowing about the General Data Protection Regulation (GDPR)

Activity 40: Understanding digital licences, laws and conventions

→ Preparatory reading

Educators: You might find it useful to read relevant human rights legislation, if you have not already done so.

Students: None required. Students will find their own resources for this activity.

→ Useful resources

Relevant human rights legislation can be found at:

UK: www.legislation.gov.uk/ukpga/1998/42/contents [accessed 28 May 2021];

Australia: https://humanrights.gov.au/our-work/rights-and-freedoms/how-are-human-rights-protected-australian-law [accessed 28 May 2021];

Canada: https://laws-lois.justice.gc.ca/eng/acts/h-6/ [accessed 28 May 2021];

New Zealand: www.legislation.govt.nz/act/public/1993/0082/latest/DLM304212.html [accessed 28 May 2021].

The Equality and Human Rights Commission in Great Britain provides a wide range of information on equality and human rights law, including a useful breakdown of the Human Rights Act 1998: www.equalityhumanrights.com/en/human-rights/human-rights-act [accessed 28 May 2021].

The Office of the High Commissioner for Human Rights (UN Human Rights) has a mission to promote and protect all human rights. Useful information and publications can be found on the website, including information about the International Bill of Rights: www.ohchr.org/EN/pages/home.aspx [accessed 28 May 2021].

A useful factsheet on the International Bill of Rights can be obtained from the Australian Human Rights Commission: https://humanrights.gov.au/our-work/education/human-rights-explained-fact-sheet-5the-international-bill-rights [accessed 28 May 2021].

Activity 32

The European Convention on Human Rights can be accessed at www.echr.coe.int/documents/convention_eng.pdf [accessed 28 May 2021].

Constantin, A. (2018) 'Human subject research: International and regional human rights standards', *Health and Human Rights Journal*, December 4, 2018, www.hhrjournal.org/2018/12/human-subject-research-international-and-regional-human-rights-standards [accessed 28 May 2021].

Susi, M. (ed.) *Human Rights, Digital Society and the Law: A Research Companion*. Abingdon: Routledge.

Wagner, B., Kettemann, M.C. and Vieth, K. (eds) (2019) *Research Handbook on Human Rights and Digital Technology: Global Politics, Law and International Relations*. Cheltenham: Edward Elgar.

Activity 32

Activity • • • • • • • • • • • • → 32

Understanding and Adhering to Relevant Human Rights Legislation

STUDENT HANDOUT

This activity is called 'Understanding and adhering to relevant human rights legislation'. Work with your group members to produce a podcast, aimed at other research students. It should identify human rights legislation that is relevant to your research and explain, or illustrate, how you can and should adhere to relevant human rights legislation when undertaking your research. The structure, specific content and style of podcast is a group choice: all you need to do is ensure that your podcast enables your peers to meet the learning outcome given below.

Podcasts can be recorded using smartphones, tablets or laptops: if you do not have any of this equipment, or feel it to be inadequate, come to me for help. This activity does not require professionally produced podcasts: instead, just make sure that the audio recording is clear enough to be heard easily by your peers. This requires a quiet space for the recording, a stable mount for your device, suitable microphone placement and a little practice to get it right.

Once you have produced your podcast, edit as required (using free online audio editing tools such as Audacity, Auphonic or Beautiful Audio Editor, if needed) and upload it by the deadline given. Listen to the podcasts produced by your peers and enter into online discussion, where appropriate. You will be listening to a number of podcasts, therefore, try to make yours stand out: ensure that it is entertaining, enables your peers to learn something new and meet the learning outcome given below.

Learning outcome: By the end of this activity, you will be able to identify human rights legislation that is relevant to your research and explain how you intend to adhere to this legislation when conducting your research.

Activity • • • • • • • • • • → 33

Knowing about the General Data Protection Regulation (GDPR)

ACTIVITY 33: EDUCATOR NOTES

Purpose: This activity enables students to find out more about the General Data Protection Regulation (GDPR) by working individually to produce a blog that is shared and discussed with peers.

Type: Blog production and sharing.

Alternative type(s): Vlog production and sharing.

Level: Intermediate and advanced (this activity has been designed for students who are planning their thesis or dissertation).

Duration: Up to three hours for students to produce, upload, share and discuss blogs (or vlogs, if this option is chosen).

Equipment/materials: A suitable tool to upload blogs (or vlogs).

Learning outcome: By the end of this activity, students will be able to explain the purpose of the GDPR, identify how it relates to their research and describe how they must adhere to it when conducting research.

The activity

Ask your students to produce a blog of no more than 600 words (for undergraduates) or 800 words (for postgraduates). The blog should do three things:

- explain the purpose of the GDPR;
- illustrate how the GDPR is relevant to their research;
- describe how they must adhere to the GDPR when conducting their research.

Blogs should be informal yet informative. Students should be encouraged to be imaginative and creative, producing a memorable blog from which their peers can learn. Once students have produced their blog it should be uploaded using the tool you have set up for this purpose (the blog tool in Moodle or Blackboard Learn, for example). Some universities now have their own blogging service that can be used for teaching and learning, and these contain useful templates, guidance notes and advice on setting up the service for assessed and non-assessed work. If you decide to make this an assessed piece of work, explain the process to your students and give guidance on the standards required. Students can use the dashboard to customize their blogs, edit their work and receive comments from their peers.

Give a deadline by which time all blogs should be posted. Ask students to read their peers' blogs, and post constructive and informative comments, where relevant (check that the right visibility option is chosen so that students can read each other's blogs: default settings might enable blogs to be shared only between student and educator). Read all blogs when they have been posted to ensure that information is correct and does not breach copyright rules. Monitor comments to make sure that they are supportive and constructive. Delete comments that do not meet these criteria, and explain why this has been done.

This activity can be run as a vlog production and sharing exercise, if this is better suited to your students or the facilities you have available. If you choose this option, run it as a small group exercise rather than on an individual basis: this allows for group help and support for students who do not have the necessary technology, or for those who are unfamiliar with the technology.

Key issues

This activity provides the opportunity for students to learn about what can, for some, be a rather bland and uninteresting topic in a creative way. Students must first get to grips with the purpose of the GDPR and then understand how it relates to their research, before thinking about how they can best communicate this to their peers, in an interesting, creative and memorable way. Blogs have been chosen as a way to do this because they encourage students to think about how complex and detailed issues can be communicated concisely in a way that can be understood by those who are new to these issues, but who need to know about them.

The activity title refers to the GDPR. However, since the UK left the European Union, and the transition period ended, there is now a UK-GDPR together with an amended version of the Data Protection Act 2018. While principles, research/organization obligations and participant rights remain the same, students should be aware of the implications for data transfer between the UK and member countries of the European Economic Area (EEA) (depending on when data were gathered). If this is relevant to your students, it can be pointed out prior to them writing their blogs, or you could wait to see if it is raised in blogs. If not, this issue could be discussed further once blogs have been shared.

➜ Related activities

Activity 9: Discussing privacy and confidentiality in the research context

Activity 31: Identifying and complying with local, regional and national law

Activity 50: Evaluating privacy policies of software companies and third-party providers

Activity 81: Producing a Data Management Plan

Activity 83: Producing a data access (or availability) statement

Activity 85: Keeping research data protected and secure

Activity 87: Assessing short-term storage and long-term data preservation strategies

....

➜ Preparatory reading

Educators: Contact your university Data Protection Office (or equivalent) for advice. The guide that has been produced by the Information Commissioner's Office (ICO) provides useful preparatory reading for those new to the UK-GDPR (see below).

Students: The resources given below can be provided for your students, if required.

....

➜ Useful resources

The official PDF of Regulation (EU) 2016/679 (General Data Protection Regulation) can be found at https://gdpr-info.eu/ [accessed 16 November 2021].

A useful guide to the UK-GDPR has been produced by the ICO and can be found at https://ico.org.uk/for-organisations/guide-to-data-protection/guide-to-the-general-data-protection-regulation-gdpr [accessed 16 November 2021].

The UK Data Service gives detailed information about applying the GDPR in research: www.ukdataservice.ac.uk/manage-data/legal-ethical/gdpr-in-research.aspx [accessed 16 November 2021].

Activity 33

Activity · · · · · · · · · · · → 34

Researching Illegal, Unlawful, Illicit or Dangerous Behaviour

ACTIVITY 34: EDUCATOR NOTES

Purpose: This activity is for students who intend to undertake research into illegal, unlawful, illicit or dangerous behaviour. It is a structured peer support group that enables students to assess the potential challenges and risks involved, develop a plan that will help them to address these issues, undertake their data collection with access to support when required, and reconvene when the data collection phase has ended. It is both a 'structured' group because students are required to meet on two occasions and develop an action plan, and a peer support group because students can offer support throughout the duration of their research, if required.

Type: Structured peer support group (in-class and/or online) for invited students.

Alternative type(s): None.

Level: Intermediate and advanced (students can be from different levels of study and disciplines).

Duration: Fifty minutes to one hour for an initial meeting and for a concluding meeting. Additional sessions throughout the research period, if and when required.

Equipment/materials: A suitable synchronous or asynchronous tool, if any part of this activity is to be run online.

Learning outcome: By the end of this activity, students will be able to identify potential challenges and risks associated with undertaking research into illegal, unlawful, illicit or dangerous behaviour, and explain how to address challenges and risks that have been identified.

The activity

Invite a group of students together who intend to undertake research into behaviour that may be illegal, unlawful, illicit or dangerous (this activity should begin before students apply for ethical approval as it enables them to anticipate challenges and outline possible solutions, which can be included in their application). Students can be from one course and one level or from a range of courses, levels and proposed methodologies. The group should not be too large: seven to 14 participants is a good number. Explain the purpose and format of the structured peer support group:

- first, you will meet in a 50-minute to one-hour session (in-class or online) to assess potential challenges and risks of researching illegal, unlawful, illicit or dangerous behaviour;
- second, students will work on an action plan that will help them to overcome problems that have been identified (during independent study): these can be shared online to benefit other students;

- third, students will undertake their data collection (the timescale here depends on the type and level of research);
- fourth, the group will reconvene for another 50-minute to one-hour session (in-class or online) to discuss their data collection and any problems they may have encountered.

Students can also meet on an informal basis (face-to-face or online) at any time as the activity progresses and after the activity, if they feel that support and encouragement from group members would be of use.

Decide how you would like to run the sessions. They can be informal, enabling students to raise issues that are of concern in any order they wish, or you can develop a list of topics or questions to cover (see key issues, below). Encourage students to meet with their peers if they need support as their data collection progresses and be flexible about calling another meeting part-way through their research, if students feel this would be of help (if some students are researching in the field, this can be undertaken online if they have equipment available).

A similar structured support group is used in Activity 69: Assessing the challenges of potential negative effects of fieldwork. Some research projects may cover both this activity and Activity 69, and similar issues can be raised in each. Therefore, take a little time to look at students' proposed research and choose the activity that is the most appropriate to run with your students.

Key issues

This activity enables students to discuss their concerns and worries about undertaking research into illegal, unlawful, illicit or dangerous behaviour. They are able to pool experiences, knowledge and understanding so that they can develop and implement a constructive and effective plan of action. Group members are available for support and encouragement throughout the activity (and often throughout their research). This provides the opportunity for peers to offer support if unforeseen problems occur during and after their research.

Issues that are raised and discussed in this activity depend on research topic and methodologies, but can include:

- personal risk and personal safety (Activity 26);
- undertaking a risk assessment (Activity 27);
- the protection of participants and collaborators (in cases where the researcher has information that could cause harm, prove dangerous or compromise those taking part in the research, for example);
- legal responsibilities (national and international law relating to child protection, abuse of vulnerable people, money laundering and terrorism, for example: Activity 31);
- moral obligations (disciplinary traditions that warn participants that certain criminal behaviour will be reported if disclosed or promises to gatekeepers that dangerous behaviour will be reported, for example);
- issues of confidentiality and how this might be affected by legal responsibilities or moral obligations (Activity 9);
- how issues of confidentiality might have a negative effect on obtaining informed consent (Activity 57);
- relationships with participants (Pérez-Y-Pérez and Stanley, 2011);
- what happens if a researcher is expected to undertake illegal or dangerous actions;
- ensuring that researchers do not encourage illegal, unlawful, illicit or dangerous behaviour for the purposes of their research;
- whether researchers are covered by legal privilege;
- whether researchers can be prosecuted;
- whether researchers' findings can be used in a court of law;
- how to ensure anonymity (Activity 62);
- how to avoid, or what to do with, problematic information;
- what methods to use for collecting data, and how methods might influence results (Bowman-Bowen and Menard, 2016);
- how to record, store and publish information safely (for researcher and participants);
- how to write up research sensitively (illustrating why the research is important, but taking care not to be seen to condone illegal, unlawful, illicit or dangerous behaviour);
- if undertaking fieldwork, how to withdraw safely while ensuring that participants are not put at risk (Activity 69);
- the ethical review process and how to be successful (Activity 41).

Cautionary note

It is important that you are present for discussions in this activity and monitor what students have to say. Ensure that all proposed methods adhere to university policy, and that information and advice shared between students are correct and supportive. Ask students to provide support to each other and make yourself available (or ensure that personal tutors/supervisors are available) if problems arise.

→ **Related activities**

Activity 26: Ensuring researcher safety

Activity 27: Carrying out a risk assessment

Activity 31: Identifying and complying with local, regional and national law

Activity 69: Assessing the challenges and potential negative effects of fieldwork

Activity 34

→ Preparatory reading

Educators: Take time to become familiar with your university ethics policy concerning illegal, unlawful, illicit or dangerous behaviour in preparation for this activity, if you have not already done so. All the resources listed below provide useful preparatory reading.

Students: None required for the first stage of the activity. Some of the references listed below can be recommended if they are relevant to the challenges and concerns that have been raised in the first stage of this activity.

→ Useful resources

Boratto, R. and Gibbs, C. (2019) 'Advancing interdisciplinary research on illegal wildlife trade using a conservation criminology framework', *European Journal of Criminology*, first published 22 November 2019, doi: 10.1177/147737081988751.

Bowman-Bowen, L.C. and Menard, S. (2016) 'Survey design elements as influences on estimates of self-reported illicit substance use and other illegal activities', *Journal of Drug Issues*, 46 (3): 178-97, first published 16 February 2016, doi: 10.1177/0022042616629513.

Downes, J., Kelly, L. and Westmarland, N. (2014) 'Ethics in violence and abuse research – a positive empowerment approach', *Sociological Research Online*, 19 (1): 29-41, first published 5 March 2014, doi: 10.5153/sro.3140.

Ford, M. and Lyons, L. (2020) 'The illegal as mundane', *Indonesia and the Malay World*, 48 (140): 24-39, published online 28 October 2019, doi: 10.1080/13639811.2019.1648006.

Pérez-Y-Pérez, M. and Stanley, T. (2011) 'Ethnographic intimacy: Thinking through the ethics of social research in sex worlds', *Sociological Research Online*, 16 (2): 39-48, first published 6 June 2011, doi: 10.5153/sro.2310.

Ward, J. (2008) 'Researching drug sellers: An "experiential" account from "the field"', *Sociological Research Online*, 13 (1): 31-42, first published 11 December 2017, doi: 10.5153/sro.1673.

Ethical codes that cover the main issues raised in this activity include:

The British Society of Criminology: www.britsoccrim.org/ethics/ [accessed 16 November 2021].

The Australian and New Zealand Society of Criminology: https://anzsoc.org/about/ethics/ [accessed 16 November 2021].

The American Society of Criminology: https://asc41.com/wp-content/uploads/Core_Documents/ASC_Code_of_Ethics.pdf [accessed 16 November 2021].

Activity 34

Activity · · · · · · · · · · · · → 35

Seeking Permission with Regard to Data Ownership

The activity

Give your students a copy of the Student Handout and ask them to work through the activity during independent study (you may need to adjust the Handout slightly, depending on your university thesis publishing policy). Students are told why they must think about whether and how to obtain permission to use data in their thesis. Then they are asked to produce a plan of action, or a strategy, which outlines how they will obtain permission. They should also provide a contingency plan if they are unable to obtain permission. This activity works best if students are nearing completion of their research as it encourages them to think about data they are using and whether they need to seek permission to publish them in their thesis.

   Set up a suitable tool for students to upload their work. Give a deadline by which time this should be done. Ask them to read the work of their peers and make constructive and supportive comments. Monitor posts to ensure that information is correct and supportive. If you find information that is incorrect, edit or delete the comments, giving an explanation as to why this has been done. If you prefer, you can ask students to hand their work into you, which you then edit and collate into a PDF to send to all students. Hold an informal discussion on the contents of the PDF if you think it will benefit your students.

This activity can be run as a self-guided individual exercise followed by an in-class discussion, if you prefer. Ask students to work on the activity for a few hours before the session, then ask each, in turn, to present their plan of action or strategy. Allocate a few minutes after each presentation for questions and comments. Conclude the session with a summary of the main points raised.

Key issues

This activity encourages students to think about different types of data ownership and types of permission that they must seek with regard to this ownership. It can include copyright permission, database rights permission and licensing, depending on the type of data students intend to use. The activity asks them to go through their own work, identifying data that may require permission, think about how they can obtain permission, and think about what they will do if they are unable to get permission. Sharing and discussing plans with their peers enables them to bounce ideas off each other, learn from each other and consolidate their learning.

Cautionary note

Monitor students' work and discussions carefully to ensure that information is correct. Some permissions and rights issues can be quite complex: it is important that students share the correct information with their peers, and that they are able to understand exactly what permissions they need to obtain before they publish their thesis.

➜ Related activities

Activity 23: Avoiding plagiarism

Activity 39: Avoiding copyright infringement

Activity 40: Understanding digital licences, laws and conventions

Activity 56: Citing digital tools and software correctly

....

➜ Preparatory reading

Educators: Read your university thesis publication policy and your university intellectual property (IP) policy and permissions guidance, if you have not already done so.

Students: None required. Students will find their own resources for this activity.

....

➜ Useful resources

Information about copyright and copyright permissions can be obtained from the relevant national and international organizations:

Australia: www.copyright.com.au/about-copyright/permission/ [accessed 12 May 2021]

Canada: www.ic.gc.ca/eic/site/cipointernet-internetopic.nsf/eng/h_wr00003.html [accessed 12 May 2021]

Global: www.wipo.int/copyright/en/ [accessed 12 May 2021]

India: https://copyright.gov.in [accessed 12 May 2021]

UK: www.gov.uk/copyright [accessed 12 May 2021]

US: www.copyright.gov [accessed 12 May 2021]

Activity 35

Information about copyright and copyright licensing in the UK can be obtained from the Copyright Licensing Agency: www.cla.co.uk/what-is-copyright [accessed 12 May 2021].

Information about Creative Commons licensing can be obtained from https://creativecommons.org/licenses/ [accessed 12 May 2021].

Bogre, M. and Wolff, N. (eds) (2021) *The Routledge Companion to Copyright and Creativity in the 21st Century.* Abingdon: Routledge.

Goldstein, P. and Hugenholtz, P.B. (2019) *International Copyright: Principles, Law, and Practice,* 4th edition. New York, NY: Oxford University Press.

Karapapa, S. (2020) *Defences to Copyright Infringement: Creativity, Innovation and Freedom on the Internet.* Oxford: Oxford University Press.

Netanel, N.W. (2018) *Copyright: What Everyone Needs to Know.* New York, NY: Oxford University Press.

Stokes, S. (2021) *Art and Copyright,* 3rd edition. Oxford: Hart.

Other useful references and resources relating to copyright can be found in Activity 39.

Activity 35

Activity • • • • • • • • • • • • → 35

Seeking Permission with Regard to Data Ownership

STUDENT HANDOUT

This activity is called 'Seeking permission with regard to data ownership'. Most universities make it a condition of enrolment that you agree to deposit a digital copy of your thesis in the university repository, many of which are open access. Your digital thesis will be freely available online to anyone who wishes to access it, and a printed copy of your thesis will be available for inter-library loan. Therefore, you must ensure that you obtain all the necessary permissions for data you intend to publish in your thesis. If you are unable to obtain permission, data will need to be removed (and you could instead insert a link to the original copy of data). Alternatively, you might need to consider an embargo on the publication of your thesis until you are able to obtain the necessary permissions.

This activity asks you to provide details of how you intend to seek permission with regard to data ownership. There are a number of questions you may need to consider:

1. What are 'data' and what do we mean by 'data ownership'?
2. What are 'copyright' and 'copyright permission'?
3. What type of data can and cannot be copyrighted?
4. What is the difference between copyright, database rights and a licence?
5. Who owns the data you intend to use? Are these data copyrighted, covered by database rights or available for use under some kind of licence (if so, do you understand the terms of the licence)?
6. What is meant by 'fair use' or 'fair dealing' and do these have an influence on the permissions you need to obtain?
7. If you do need to seek permission, how will you go about doing so? Whom do you need to contact? How will you contact them?

Produce a plan of action, or outline a strategy, which illustrates how you will obtain all the necessary permissions. This should include a contingency plan that outlines the action you will take if you are unable to secure permission. Your plan of action or strategy should be no more than 500 words and can be a bullet point list, if you wish.

Once you have produced the work, upload it using the tool set up for this purpose by the given date. Read the work produced by your peers as this will introduce you to other strategies or plans that you may not have previously considered and highlight permissions you may not have thought about. Add constructive and supportive comments or advice, if appropriate.

Learning outcome: By the end of this activity, you will be able to discuss whether or not you need to seek permission to publish data in your thesis, summarize strategies you will use to obtain the necessary permissions and outline a contingency plan if you are unable to obtain the necessary permissions.

Activity • • • • • • • • • • • • → 36

Working within the European Code of Conduct for Research Integrity

The activity

Ask your students to read through the European Code of Conduct on Research Integrity (provide a link so that they work with the correct version: see below). Once they have done this, they should produce a short, written piece of no more than 800 words (for postgraduates) or 600 words (for undergraduates) that illustrates how they intend to work within this code when conducting their research: they should provide specific details that relate to their topic and methods. Bullet point lists are acceptable for this piece of work.

Set up a suitable tool for students to upload their work, share and discuss with their peers. Give a deadline by which time work should be completed and uploaded. Once this has been done, encourage students to make comments and discuss the ideas presented by their peers. If you choose to make this an assessed piece of work, provide specific activity requirements and assessment criteria.

It is possible to hold an in-class discussion on the topics raised by the self-guided individual exercise, if you prefer. Ask students to post their work a few days before you meet so that they have time to digest each other's ideas prior to the class. Ask them to think of any questions or issues they wish to discuss when you meet. When you get together, lead an informal discussion on the issues raised by the self-guided individual exercise, and discuss and answer students' questions.

Key issues

Most students tend to find this Code straightforward, relevant and easy to understand. However, they also point out that it is extremely comprehensive: they sometimes struggle to include everything they wish to include in under 800 or 600 words. This limit has been given for two reasons: 1) students are required to read the work of their peers and might struggle to complete the task if there is a higher word count; 2) it forces students to focus their thoughts and provide a summary of the most pertinent issues relevant to their research. However, the word count can be increased if you have only a small number of students studying at postgraduate level, and you feel it will be of benefit to students.

This activity is similar to that provided in Activity 37: Aligning with the Concordat to Support Research Integrity, so choose the activity that is best suited to your geographical location and/or to your students. Alternatively, choose your national Code if you are not based in the UK or the European Union (EU).

➜ **Related activities**

Activity 19: Viewing integrity as an individual and collective responsibility

Activity 20: Fostering research integrity through practice

Activity 21: Developing a resilient integrity culture

Activity 37: Aligning with the Concordat to Support Research Integrity

➜ **Preparatory reading**

Educators: Read through the European Code of Conduct for Research Integrity, if you have not already done so (details below).

Students: Will need to read the European Code of Conduct for Research Integrity (see below).

➜ **Useful resources**

The revised edition of the European Code of Conduct for Research Integrity can be found at www.allea.org/wp-content/uploads/2017/05/ALLEA-European-Code-of-Conduct-for-Research-Integrity-2017.pdf [accessed 15 June 2021]. This link was correct at the time of writing: ensure that this is the correct link when you run this activity.

Aubert Bonn, N., Godecharle, S. and Dierickx, K. (2017) 'European Universities' Guidance on Research Integrity and Misconduct: Accessibility, approaches, and content', *Journal of Empirical Research on Human Research Ethics*, 12 (1): 33–44, first published 1 February 2017, doi: 10.1177/1556264616688980.

Bretag, T. (ed.) (2020) *A Research Agenda for Academic Integrity*. Cheltenham: Edward Elgar.

National Academies of Sciences, Engineering, and Medicine (2017) *Fostering Integrity in Research*. Washington, DC: The National Academies Press, doi: 10.17226/21896.

Tijdink, J.K., Horbach, S.P.J.M., Nuijten, M.B. and O'Neill, G. (2021) 'Towards a research agenda for promoting responsible research practices', *Journal of Empirical Research on Human Research Ethics*, first published 26 May 2021, doi: 10.1177/15562646211018916.

Zeljic, K. (2020) 'Research integrity awareness among biology students – experience from the University of Belgrade', *Accountability in Research*, published online 23 November 2020, doi: 10.1080/08989621.2020.1843445.

Activity 36

Activity • • • • • • • • • • • ➔ 37

Aligning with the Concordat to Support Research Integrity

The activity

Give your students a copy of the Student Handout. This asks them to work independently to find and read a copy of the Concordat to Support Research Integrity. They should then produce a piece of written work of no more than 1,000 words that provides a description of the Concordat; explains how universities, funding bodies and researchers align with the Concordat; and identifies how they, as researchers, can align with the Concordat when undertaking their research. Give a deadline for submission and, if you choose to make this an assessed piece of work, provide assessment criteria.

Key issues

This is a simple activity that introduces students to important issues of research integrity. It encourages them to consider university and funding body statements and commitments, and think about how they can ensure that they act with integrity when undertaking their research. It is a similar activity to Activity 36: Working within the European Code of Conduct for Research Integrity, so choose the activity that is best suited to your geographical location and/or to your students. Alternatively, choose your national Code or Concordat if you are not based in the UK or the EU.

→ Related activities

Activity 19: Viewing integrity as an individual and collective responsibility

Activity 20: Fostering research integrity through practice

Activity 21: Developing a resilient integrity culture

Activity 36: Working within the European Code of Conduct for Research Integrity

→ Preparatory reading

Educators: Read the Concordat and become familiar with your university statements and commitments, if you have not already done so.

Students: None required. Students are instructed to find and read a copy of the Concordat and work independently to find other useful information, such as university and funding body statements or commitments.

→ Useful resources

The Concordat to Support Research Integrity, 2019 (revised edition) has been developed by Universities UK, funding bodies and UK Government departments. It provides a national framework for the conduct of research and its governance: www.universitiesuk.ac.uk/topics/research-and-innovation/concordat-research-integrity [accessed 8 March 2022].

Activity 37

Activity · · · · · · · · · · → 37

Aligning with the Concordat to Support Research Integrity

STUDENT HANDOUT

This activity is called 'Aligning with the Concordat to Support Research Integrity'. The Concordat to Support Research Integrity, 2019 (revised edition) has been developed by Universities UK, funding bodies and UK Government departments. It provides a national framework for the conduct of research and its governance.

Find and read a copy of the Concordat, then produce a piece of written work of no more than 1,000 words that provides a description of the Concordat and explains how universities, funding bodies and researchers align with the Concordat (you might find it useful to consider our university statement or commitments, and look at funding body statements or commitments, for example). Once you have done this, go on to identify how you, as a researcher, can align with the Concordat when conducting your research.

The structure and style of the written piece is up to you: just ensure that your work enables you to meet the learning outcome given below, and that you submit your work by the given deadline.

Learning outcome: By the end of this activity, you will be able to provide a description of the Concordat to Support Research Integrity; explain how universities, funding bodies and researchers align with the Concordat; and identify how you can align with the Concordat when conducting your research.

Activity · · · · · · · · · · · → 38

Protecting Intellectual Property

ACTIVITY 38: EDUCATOR NOTES

Purpose: This activity introduces students to protecting intellectual property (IP) by asking them to imagine that they work as an IP Officer for an organization of their choice. In this role they must produce a document that explains what is meant by protecting IP, aimed at employees who know little about the subject. All documents are uploaded to build a useful student-centred digital resource. This is an entertaining way to introduce issues about protecting IP to students who are unfamiliar with this topic.

Type: Text-based role-play (self-guided individual exercise with digital document sharing).

Alternative type(s): Written assignment (assessed).

Level: Intermediate and advanced.

Duration: Students will spend a few hours during independent study researching, producing and uploading their documents. They will also spend some time reading, reviewing and voting on the documents produced by their peers. Educators will spend one or two hours setting up the digital resource and monitoring uploaded documents.

Equipment/materials: A suitable digital tool and access for all students. Polling/voting tool if this option is chosen.

Learning outcome: By the end of this activity, students will be able to discuss what is meant by protecting IP.

The activity

Give a copy of the Student Handout to your students. This asks them to imagine that they have obtained a job as an IP Officer at an organization of their choice. For their first task they must produce a document that explains what is meant by protecting IP, aimed at employees who are unfamiliar with the issues. The documents are to be shared by uploading them using a suitable asynchronous tool. Give a deadline by which time all documents should be uploaded. Students should read and review the documents produced by their peers and vote on the best, if appropriate. This will be the document that explains protecting IP in a clear, succinct and user-friendly way. It should be imaginative, creative and hold the interest of their peers.

This activity can be run as an assessed written assignment, if you prefer. Adapt the Student Handout to make it more specific, include the assessment criteria and give a date by which time assignments should be submitted.

Key issues

This activity enables students to learn by researching and producing their own documents before reinforcing their learning by reading and assessing the documents produced by their peers. Topics that can be covered in this activity include:

- a definition of IP;
- why employees need to know about IP;
- why IP is relevant to their work;
- how IP relates to research and publications;
- specific examples related to their chosen organization;
- rights of ownerships (by the company/organization/university);
- assignment of rights;
- publication rights;
- copyright;
- trademarks;
- patents;
- confidentiality;
- costs;
- how to deal with disputes;
- useful contacts (national IP offices, for example).

Cautionary note

This activity initially asked students to imagine that they had obtained a job as a university IP Officer and they were to produce a document aimed at students and researchers. However, this did not work very well: universities produce their own documents for students and staff and it was too easy for students to use existing documents. Also, there was not much variety: students covered very similar issues, which made the activity rather monotonous. Once the activity had been modified to include any company or organization of their choice, much more variety appeared: students were able to invent an organization, or use an existing organization, which produced a more informative and entertaining activity.

However, it is important that you become familiar with some university and organization documents on protecting IP (in particular, those that are highly ranked in search engines) so that you can check that students have not merely copied an existing document. You might also find it useful to provide a link to (or a copy of) your university document on protecting IP at the end of the activity so that students can see how this activity relates to them and their university work.

→ Related activities

Activity 29: Collaborating ethically in research

Activity 36: Working within the European Code of Conduct for Research Integrity

Activity 37: Aligning with the Concordat to Support Research Integrity

Activity 39: Avoiding copyright infringement

....

→ Preparatory reading

Educators: Op den Kamp and Hunter (2019), Vaidhyanathan (2017) and Bainbridge (2018) provide useful preparatory reading, and can be recommended after the activity for students who are interested in this topic.

Students: None required. Students will find their own resources for this activity.

....

→ Useful resources

Bainbridge, D. (2018) *Intellectual Property*, 10th edition. Harlow: Pearson Education.
Op den Kamp, C. and Hunter, D. (eds) (2019) *A History of Intellectual Property in 50 Objects*. Cambridge: Cambridge University Press.
Silvernagel, C.A., Olson, M.R. and Stupnisky, R.H. (2019) 'Mine, yours, or ours? Perceptions of student-created intellectual property ownership', *Entrepreneurship Education and Pedagogy*, first published 16 August 2019, doi: 10.1177/2515127419866426.
Vaidhyanathan, S. (2017) *Intellectual Property: A Very Short Introduction*. New York, NY: Oxford University Press.

Information about IP in specific countries, regions and worldwide can be obtained from:

Africa: www.aripo.org/ [accessed 16 November 2021]

Australia: www.ipaustralia.gov.au [accessed 16 November 2021]

Canada: www.ic.gc.ca/eic/site/cipointernet-internetopic.nsf/eng/Home [accessed 16 November 2021]

EU: https://euipo.europa.eu/ohimportal/en [accessed 16 November 2021]

Activity 38

New Zealand: www.iponz.govt.nz [accessed 16 November 2021]

UK: www.gov.uk/intellectual-property-an-overview/protect-your-intellectual-property [accessed 16 November 2021]

USA: www.uspto.gov [accessed 16 November 2021]

World Intellectual Property Organization: www.wipo.int [accessed 16 November 2021]

A guide called *How do I know if my research data is protected?* provides information about IP and can be obtained from OpenAIRE, the European project supporting Open Science: www.openaire.eu/how-do-i-know-if-my-research-data-is-protected [accessed 16 November 2021].

Activity 38

Activity • • • • • • • • • • → 38

Protecting Intellectual Property

STUDENT HANDOUT

This activity is called 'Protecting intellectual property'. Imagine that you have been successful in obtaining a job as an Intellectual Property Officer within an organization of your choice. Your first task within your new role is to produce a document that explains what is meant by protecting intellectual property (IP). It is aimed at employees within your organization who are unfamiliar with this issue. You can choose any type of organization: it could be an existing private company, a public sector organization, or a group, charity or an organization invented by yourself, for example.

The content, style, structure and length of the document is up to you. Think about the type of organization for which you work and think about what employees of that organization would want and need from this type of document. Ensure that it is informative, useful, interesting and creative.

Upload your document using the tool provided. Once this has been done, read/view the documents produced by your peers and vote on the best one. This will be the document that defines, describes and explains what is meant by protecting IP in a clear, succinct and user-friendly way. It should also be imaginative, creative and hold the interest of readers.

Learning outcome: By the end of this activity, you will be able to discuss what is meant by protecting IP.

Activity · · · · · · · · · · · → 39

Avoiding Copyright Infringement

The activity

This activity is a group discussion that can be run in-class or online. If you choose the online option, use a suitable synchronous video/web conferencing tool such as Zoom Meetings, Blackboard Collaborate or Meetings in Microsoft Teams for Education. Begin the session by explaining its purpose: to enable students to understand what is meant by copyright infringement and know how to avoid it. Divide your students into five groups (or pairs or individuals, if you have only a small number of students) and use breakout rooms if you are running this activity online.

Ask students to discuss and write down a list of different types and forms of copyright infringement (note-catchers can be used to develop these lists, if you choose to run this session online). This discussion should last 10-15 minutes: if students struggle to get the discussion started, introduce some of the topics provided in key issues, below. Walk among the groups, or visit breakout rooms, to check on discussions and to answer queries (this can be a complex issue and some students might need help in determining what is and what is not copyright infringement).

Then ask 'What can you do to avoid infringing copyright?'. Ask groups to develop another list of points that answer this question. This should take another 10-15 minutes. After this time, bring the groups back together and ask each group, one at a time, to present their first list. Lead a class discussion on the issues raised, then repeat with the second question and lists. Take time to spot, and rectify, any mistakes or misunderstandings. Conclude the session with a summary of the main points raised and provide useful links and resources for students to follow-up issues discussed (see below).

Key issues

Items that can be listed as examples of copyright infringement include:

- downloading videos at home, using pirate sites and BitTorrents;
- recording a film in the cinema using a smartphone or digital video recorder;
- downloading music without paying for it;
- downloading software without permission;
- playing someone else's music in a public performance without permission;
- performing someone else's play, without permission;
- pirating video games;
- using an image taken from Twitter or Facebook without permission;
- finding an image, editing it and using it on your own website;
- posting someone else's photo from a social media page, even if you are in it;
- copying a work of art without seeking permission;
- copying someone else's written work without a licence;
- quoting a poem without permission;
- photocopying too much of a book;
- cutting and pasting large amounts of text from copyrighted work, even if acknowledgement is given.

Items that can be listed as a way to avoid infringing copyright include:

- understand what is meant by copyright (and understand the difference between copyright and plagiarism – this might be a useful issue to raise if it is not raised by students: see Activity 23: Avoiding plagiarism);
- become familiar with copyright laws in your own country and globally;
- find out about the Copyright Licensing Agency and the Educational Recording Agency in the UK (or national equivalents);
- read your university policy on copyright;
- visit your university library website for information on copyright;
- make sure you obtain permission if you want to use copyrighted work in your dissertation or thesis (Activity 35);
- ask peers to check over your work to see if there are any problems;
- understand what is meant by 'fair use' or 'fair dealing' (the fair use of work without the need to seek permission);
- look for copyright symbols and statements;
- understand that copyrighted work does not need a copyright symbol or statement (this might need to be pointed out, if students presume a copyright symbol is required);
- try hard not to use other people's work;
- check licences, especially on open access works;
- assume all work is copyrighted, and treat it accordingly;
- speak to a librarian about the various types of licence that enable copying of works (Activity 40).

➜ Related activities

Activity 23: Avoiding plagiarism

Activity 35: Seeking permission with regard to data ownership

Activity 40: Understanding digital licences, laws and conventions

Activity 56: Citing digital tools and software correctly

➜ Preparatory reading

Educators: Read your university IP policy, if you have not already done so.

Students: None required at the start of this activity. Recommend useful links and resources at the end of the discussion, including a link to your university IP policy, if appropriate.

➜ Useful resources

The British Library in the UK provides useful information on fair use and fair dealing, including fair use for private study and exploration: www.bl.uk/business-and-ip-centre/articles/how-to-avoid-copyright-infringement# [accessed 10 March 2022].

The Berne Convention 'deals with the protection of works and the rights of their authors'. It was adopted in 1886. More information can be obtained from the WIPO website: www.wipo.int/treaties/en/ip/berne/ [accessed 20 September 2021].

Aufderheide, P. and Jaszi, P. (2018) *Reclaiming Fair Use: How to Put Balance Back in Copyright*, 2nd edition. Chicago, IL: University of Chicago Press.

Activity 39

Buskirk, M. (2022) *Is It Ours? Art, Copyright, and Public Interest*. Oakland, CA: University of California Press.

Egger, J.O. and Springer, D.G. (2019) 'Music educators' understanding and opinions of U.S. Copyright Law', *Update: Applications of Research in Music Education*, 37 (3): 20-7, first published 9 September 2018, doi: 10.1177/8755123318801064.

Geçer, A.K. and Topal, A.D. (2021) 'Academic and postgraduate student awareness of digital product copyright issues', *Information Development*, 37 (1): 90-104, first published 26 December 2019, doi: 10.1177/0266666919895550.

Gu, J. (2018) 'From divergence to convergence: Institutionalization of copyright and the decline of online video piracy in China', *International Communication Gazette*, 80 (1): 60-86, first published 1 January 2018, doi: 10.1177/1748048517742785.

Meese, J. and Hagedorn, J. (2019) 'Mundane content on social media: Creation, circulation, and the copyright problem', *Social Media + Society*, first published 4 April 2019, doi: 10.1177/2056305119839190.

Information about national and international copyright organizations, along with other relevant references and useful resources, can be found in Activity 35.

Activity 39

Activity • • • • • • • • • • • → 40

Understanding Digital Licences, Laws and Conventions

The activity

This activity is a simple quiz that provides a number of statements about digital licences, laws and conventions that students must work through, deciding whether the statements are correct or incorrect. The quiz can be educator-administered during an in-class session, with each answer discussed, or it can be self-administered online, with students reading the correct answer once they have made their choice (or at the end of the quiz). If you choose the online option, use tools such as Quiz in Moodle; Tests, Surveys or Pools in Blackboard; or open-source tools such as Quiz, Survey, Test (https://qstonline.ca). The statements and answers are provided in key issues, below.

Key issues

Statements (along with answers) that can be used in the quiz are given below. Students are to answer correct or incorrect for each statement. Add to, or delete, statements so that they suit your student cohort, level of study and country of study.

Statement 1: The 'database right', in the European Union, protects sets of data if they come within the definition of a database and if there has been substantial investment in the database.

Answer 1: This is *correct*. A database is a collection of data, information or independent works that have been brought together and organized in a structured or systematic way. Database rights, in the EU, protect these collections where there has been substantial investment in their creation (this can be financial, resources used or the amount of time involved, for example).

Statement 2: Software used in the creation of a database, in most cases, is not protected by database rights.

Answer 2: This is *correct*. Software is protected, in most cases, by copyright law as it is seen to be a literary work. There might be some cases where software is covered by database rights, such as software developed in modular or tabular form.

Statement 3: Individual components of a database are protected by database rights.

Answer 3: This is *incorrect*. Database rights only extend to the collection of data. Individual components (such as names and addresses) are not protected by database rights.

Statement 4: Creative Commons licences mean that a student can give away their copyright so that others can do what they want with their work.

Answer 4: This is *incorrect*. Creative Commons licences enable you to retain copyright while allowing others to use, distribute or copy your work.

Statement 5: Students will not have copyright protection on any written work they place online unless they include a copyright symbol '©'.

Answer 5: This is *incorrect*. Copyright comes into existence as soon as the original work is created. Students don't need to register or include the copyright symbol on any written work they place online. However, placing a symbol in a position that can be seen illustrates to others that the work is protected and it might help to stop readers presuming that they can do what they want with the work.

Statement 6: Digital copyrighted works can be used for illustrative purposes by educators as long as their use is fair, non-commercial and the copyright holder is acknowledged.

Answer 6: This is *correct*. This enables educators to use works without having to seek permission or pay rights holders.

Statement 7: A licence from the Copyright Licensing Agency in the UK allows the copying of digital content from e-books for educational purposes.

Answer 7: This is *correct*. The licence provides blanket coverage to use digital content from e-books. However, there are restrictions on the amount of original work that can be copied (10% of the total, or one chapter, whichever is the greater). At the time of writing, the licence enables the copying of publications from the UK and 38 international territories. Copyright holders are paid a royalty for their work.

Statement 8: The Educational Recording Agency (ERA) in the UK provides a policing service to ensure that online or on-demand services are not commercialized.

Answer 8: This is *incorrect*. The ERA provides a licence that allows access to online or on-demand services (and television and radio) for educational purposes. The licence is a legal requirement for any educational establishment that uses members' broadcasts for educational use.

Statement 9: Students can use any information they find on the internet in any way they wish under the 'fair dealing' policy.

Answer 9: This is *incorrect*. Although 'fair dealing' is a legal term that is used to establish whether or not copyright has been infringed, there is no statutory definition. However, under 'fair dealing' students are expected to act openly and honestly, only using what is reasonable and appropriate. An infringement is deemed to have occurred if using the work affects the market value of the original work.

Statement 10: Students can use third-party, copyrighted materials that have not been published in their thesis or dissertation under 'fair dealing'.

Answer 10: This is *incorrect*. If material has not been published, students must seek permission from the copyright holder as copyright includes the right to publish. However, students can use already published material under 'fair dealing for criticism or review' without permission, as long as the work is properly cited and the use is appropriate.

Statement 11: Open-Source software licences allow software to be freely used, modified, enhanced and/or shared under defined terms and conditions.

Answer 11: That is *correct*. Different licences are available that enable end users to use, modify and share the source code: some apply certain restrictions such as a stipulation that those who might have modified or enhanced the code must also share it without charging a licence fee.

Statement 12: A Public Domain Mark identifies works that are no longer covered by copyright.

Answer 12: That is *correct*. Creative Commons has produced a Public Domain Mark that can be tagged to items that are free of known copyright around the world. More information about this mark can be obtained from the Creative Commons website (details below).

Activity 40

→ Related activities

Activity 31: Identifying and complying with local, regional and national law

Activity 33: Knowing about the General Data Protection Regulation (GDPR)

Activity 35: Seeking permission with regard to data ownership

Activity 38: Protecting intellectual property

Activity 39: Avoiding copyright infringement

→ Preparatory reading

Educators: All the resources listed below are useful as preparatory reading (Hutchison, 2016 relates to Canada).

Students: None required. Some of the resources listed below can be recommended after the activity, if appropriate.

→ Useful resources

Hamilton, G. and Saunderson, F. (2017) *Open Licensing for Cultural Heritage.* London: Facet Publishing.
Hutchison, C. (2016) *Digital Copyright Law.* Toronto: Irwin Law.
Schwemer, S.F. (2019) *Licensing and Access to Content in the European Union: Regulation between Copyright and Competition Law.* Cambridge: Cambridge University Press.

The Copyright Licensing Agency in the UK provides rights and licences to enable institutions to share and use content without having to seek permission from copyright holders: www.cla.co.uk [accessed 11 May 2021].

The Educational Recording Agency in the UK provides a licence for the education sector to use audio-visual broadcast material for educational purposes: https://era.org.uk [accessed 11 May 2021].

Information about exceptions to copyright and fair dealing in the UK can be obtained from the Government website: www.gov.uk/guidance/exceptions-to-copyright#fair-dealing [accessed 11 May 2021].

Information about open-source licences and definitions can be obtained from the Open Source Initiative: https://open-source.org [accessed 11 May 2021].

Activity 40

Activity • • • • • • • • • → 41

Obtaining Ethical Approval

....

ACTIVITY 41: EDUCATOR NOTES

Purpose: This activity has been designed to encourage students to read and digest their university ethical approval policy and procedures, before developing a number of questions that they have about the process. Students are able to ask and answer questions, and discuss any concerns they might have. This will enable them to understand the action they need to take to obtain ethical approval for their research.

Type: Question-and-answer session (whole-class activity, in-class).

Alternative type(s): Question-and-answer session (whole-class activity, online, synchronous or asynchronous).

Level: Intermediate and advanced (this activity is aimed at students who are in the planning stages of their research, who need to apply for ethical approval).

Duration: Students will spend an hour or two during independent study reading and digesting university ethical approval policy and procedures, and developing their questions. Fifty minutes to one hour of contact will be required for questions and answers in class or synchronous online. If the asynchronous online option is chosen, educators will spend an hour or two setting up a suitable tool, monitoring posts and answering questions. Students will spend up to an hour posting and answering questions, and entering into online discussion.

Equipment/materials: A suitable video tool or discussion board if the online option is chosen.

Learning outcome: By the end of this activity, students will be able to describe their university ethical approval policy and procedures and discuss the action they need to take to obtain ethical approval.

....

The activity

Ask students to read your university policy and procedures for obtaining ethical approval. Once they have done this, they should think about useful questions they want answered about the approval process: these can be general questions about ethical approval or questions related specifically to their research. When you next meet, ask each student, in turn, to pose a question. Invite answers from other students before providing your own. If you feel that it would help, invite a member of your university ethics committee (or equivalent) to attend the session.

This activity can be run as an online question-and-answer session, if you prefer. Decide whether to run the session in real-time using a video/web conferencing tool, or over a period of time using a discussion board. Also, decide whether to make the activity compulsory (a set number of questions and answers must be given) or voluntary. Ask students to pose their questions and provide answers to the questions posed by their peers, encouraging discussion, reflection and support. If necessary, begin the question-and-answer session with a few of your own questions to get the session running. Monitor the posts or video discussion to make sure that information is correct, supportive, constructive and useful.

An alternative way to run this session is to invite a person from your research ethics committee (or similar body) to give a specialist talk to your students (see Activity 85: Knowing about the ethical approval process, in Dawson, 2016: 227–9).

Key issues

This activity encourages students to work independently to find out about their university policy and procedures concerning ethical approval. It enables them to ask questions about any issues that are unclear, clarify policy and procedures and find out about issues related specifically to their research topic or methods. Questions and topics raised in this session depend on type of research, subject, methodology and level of study. Examples include:

- understanding whether ethical approval is required (when undertaking research using data that are available online to the public, for example);
- overcoming problems with particular methodologies, approaches or topics that do not fit with required ethical processes and procedures (innovative approaches, ethnographic research, social enterprise, collaborations, engaged learning or entrepreneurship, for example);
- clarifying how much and what type of detail is required;
- knowing when approval is required from outside bodies and, if so, understanding what action needs to be taken to obtain approval;

- seeking approval for transnational research or international collaboration projects;
- approaching the issue of informed consent for different types of research (Activities 42 and 57);
- addressing issues of anonymity and confidentiality (Activity 62);
- using images ethically (Activity 68);
- knowing how to manage data ethically (and understanding the connection between Data Management Plans and ethical approval: Activity 81);
- obtaining approval for covert methods (Activity 59);
- overcoming worries and concerns about approval not being granted, and knowing what to do if approval is not given.

➜ **Related activities**

Activity 2: Discussing the ethics of consent and purpose

Activity 42: Obtaining informed consent in the digital world

Activity 57: Seeking informed consent

Activity 62: Addressing issues of anonymity and confidentiality

Activity 85: Knowing about the ethical approval process, in Dawson (2016: 227-9)

....

➜ **Preparatory reading**

Educators: Become familiar with your university's ethical approval policy and procedures, if you have not already done so. More information about the type of research that needs ethical approval can be found in Activity 85: Knowing about the ethical approval process, in Dawson (2016: 227-9).

Students: None required. Students should be encouraged to find their own way to your university's policy and procedures, or if you prefer, provide relevant links.

....

➜ **Useful resources**

Dawson, C. (2016) 100 *Activities for Teaching Research Methods*. London: Sage.

Griffin, G. and Leibetseder, D. (2019) '"Only applies to research conducted in Sweden ...": Dilemmas in gaining ethics approval in transnational qualitative research', *International Journal of Qualitative Methods*, first published 27 August 2019, doi: 10.1177/1609406919869444.

Harte, J.D., Homer, C.S., Sheehan, A., Leap, N. and Foureur, M. (2017) 'Using video in childbirth research: Ethical approval challenges', *Nursing Ethics*, 24 (2): 177-89, first published 24 July 2015, doi: 10.1177/0969733015591073.

Ingham-Broomfield, R. (2017) 'A nurse's guide to ethical considerations and the process for ethical approval of nursing research', *Australian Journal of Advanced Nursing, Australian Nursing and Midwifery Federation*, 35 (1): 40-7, first published 1 September 2017, doi: 10.3316/ielapa.509772218688556.

Mapedzahama, V. and Dune, T. (2017) 'A clash of paradigms? Ethnography and ethics approval', *SAGE Open*, first published 1 March 2017, doi: 10.1177/2158244017697167.

Padley, A. (2021) 'The agile ethics process: An oxymoron or a new paradigm in education?', *Industry and Higher Education*, first published 11 May 2021, doi: 10.1177/09504222211015606.

Activity 41

Ralefala, D., Ali, J., Kass, N. and Hyder, A. (2018) 'A case study of researchers' knowledge and opinions about the ethical review process for research in Botswana', *Research Ethics*, 14 (1): 1-14, first published 3 November 2016, doi: 10.1177/1747016116677250.

Raykov, M. (2020) 'Education researchers' perceptions of and experiences with the research ethics application process in Europe and beyond', *European Educational Research Journal*, 19 (1): 10-29, first published 8 December 2019, doi: 10.1177/1474904119893461.

Stommel, W. and Rijk, L. de (2021) 'Ethical approval: None sought. How discourse analysts report ethical issues around publicly available online data', *Research Ethics*, first published 19 January 2021, doi: 10.1177/1747016120988767.

Activity 41

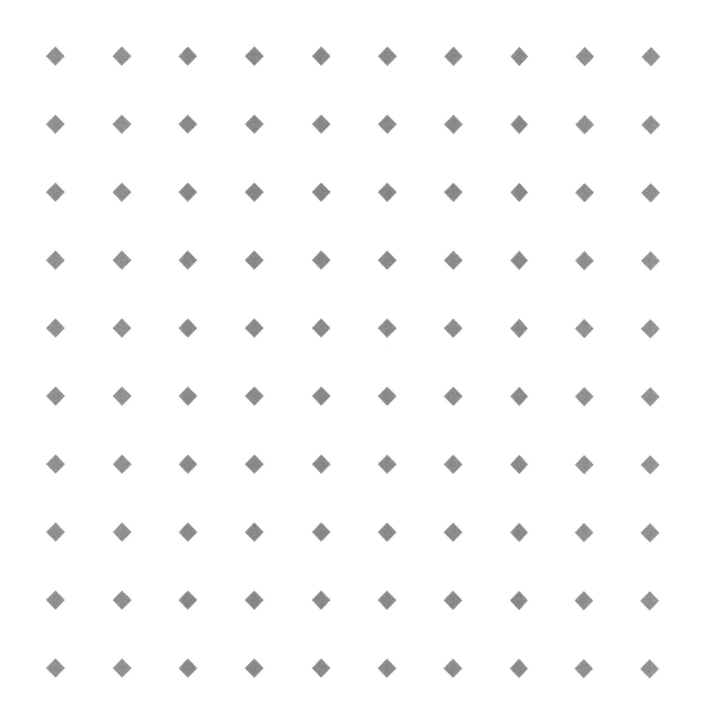

Section 4

Digital Technology, Software and Tools

Activity · · · · · · · · · · · → 42

Obtaining Informed Consent in the Digital World

The activity

This activity asks students to develop two scenarios that introduce a difficulty, problem or dilemma relating to obtaining informed consent in the digital world (they are asked to develop two scenarios to provide a back-up if their topic has already been introduced by another student, and in case you get through the first scenarios quicker than expected). Students work on the scenarios during independent study and present them to their peers when you next meet. This can be done in-class or online synchronous (using video/web conferencing software) or online asynchronous (using your VLE-hosted discussion board, for example). If the asynchronous option is chosen, give a deadline by which time all scenarios should be uploaded and discussed. Monitor discussions to ensure that information is correct and that discussions are supportive and constructive. Remove any incorrect posts and explain why this has been done.

Six to eight scenarios to discuss are good numbers for this activity if you are running it over 50 minutes to one hour. Therefore, ask your students to work in small groups, in pairs or on an individual basis, depending on the number of students in your cohort. Give them a copy of the Student Handout, which provides specific details about what is required (this will need to be adapted slightly, depending on whether you intend to run this activity in-class or online). You might also decide to adapt the Handout slightly, depending on the level at which your students are studying.

This activity can be run together with Activity 57: Seeking informed consent, for greater coverage of this topic, if required.

Key issues

This activity encourages students to think about what is meant by informed consent and how this translates to research in the digital world. Examples of issues that can be raised by the student-developed scenarios include:

- Dealing with issues of consent when undertaking data analytics. Have people given their consent for research purposes? They might have given consent for their data to be collected by a particular company or organization, but not for use in research, for example.
- Obtaining consent when undertaking covert research (as a participant in an online community, for example), and in research where participants are unaware that they are taking part (location tracking, researching browsing history or collecting sensor data, for example).
- Knowing what to do in digital storytelling when one person tells a story of another who has not given their consent to take part.
- Gaining consent from people who have been captured in digital images and the difficulties associated with this.
- Providing information to people in a way that they can understand and in a way that they can access digitally. This needs to be appropriate and easy: digital signatures, for example, can cause problems if people do not understand how to use the technology.
- Avoiding the use of data where consent has not been given or consent has been declined (when harvesting from social networks, for example).

- Knowing whether to ask for informed consent for the use of paradata or metadata and, if so, how to do this (how to explain what they are and how they will be used in a way that can be understood).
- Using opt-out clauses and how this can influence analyses.
- Considering legal issues and fair use policies when it is not possible to obtain informed consent (where thousands of posts are being analysed, for example).
- Ensuring that participants are given enough information that covers the whole research process, including data collection, data analysis, data sharing, data protection and disseminating results.
- Understanding the norms and practices of your target population, and adapting informed consent information, methods and procedures accordingly.
- Working with other organizations and third parties to ensure that they have obtained informed consent (placement of cookies, for example).
- Dealing with situations where a person may provide informed consent for issues of which they are aware, but the research finds something of which they are unaware (illness detected by wearable sensors, for example).

→ Related activities

Activity 11: Avoiding harm to others

Activity 14: Working with vulnerable people

Activity 15: Conducting research with children

Activity 57: Seeking informed consent

....

→ Preparatory reading

Educators: The i-CONSENT project provides some useful preparatory reading for educators (see useful resources). Become familiar with your university informed consent guidelines and templates, if you have not already done so.

Students: None required. Students will find their own resources for this activity. However, they can be directed to your university informed consent guidelines and templates on conclusion of the activity (check that these contain relevant information about informed consent in the digital world, as some do not).

....

→ Useful resources

Barrera, A.Z., Dunn, L.B., Nichols, A., Reardon, S. and Muñoz, R.F. (2016) 'Getting It "right": Ensuring informed consent for an online clinical trial', *Journal of Empirical Research on Human Research Ethics*, 11 (4): 291–8, first published 14 September 2016, doi: 10.1177/1556264616668974.

Activity 42

Geier, C., Adams, R.B., Mitchell, K.M. and Holtz, B.E. (2021) 'Informed consent for online research – is anybody reading?: Assessing comprehension and individual differences in readings of digital consent forms', *Journal of Empirical Research on Human Research Ethics*, first published 24 May 2021, doi: 10.1177/15562646211020160.

Kunz, T., Landesvatter, C. and Gummer, T. (2020) 'Informed consent for paradata use in web surveys', *International Journal of Market Research*, 62 (4): 396–408, first published 17 June 2020, doi: 10.1177/1470785320931669.

Mayne, F. and Howitt, C. (2022) *The Narrative Approach to Informed Consent: Empowering Young Children's Rights and Meaningful Participation*. Abingdon: Routledge.

McInroy, L.B. (2017) 'Innovative ethics: Using animated videos when soliciting informed consent of young people for online surveys', *Social Work Research*, 41 (2): 121–8, published 4 April 2017, doi: 10.1093/swr/svx004.

Norval, C. and Henderson, T. (2020) 'Automating dynamic consent decisions for the processing of social media data in health research', *Journal of Empirical Research on Human Research Ethics*, 15 (3): 187–201, first published 6 November 2019, doi: 10.1177/1556264619883715.

Wilbanks, J. (2018) 'Design issues in e-consent', *Journal of Law, Medicine & Ethics*, 46 (1): 110–18, first published 27 March 2018, doi: 10.1177/1073110518766025.

Wilbanks, J.T. (2020) 'Electronic informed consent in mobile applications research', *Journal of Law, Medicine & Ethics*, 48 (1 Suppl): 147–53, first published 28 April 2020, doi: 10.1177/1073110520917040.

i-CONSENT is a project funded by the European Union H2020 programme that 'aims to improve the information that patients receive from clinical studies'. The website contains useful information about informed consent, including workshop videos and publications: https://i-consentproject.eu [accessed 21 June 2021].

Activity 42

Activity • • • • • • • • • • • → 42

Obtaining Informed Consent in The Digital World

STUDENT HANDOUT

This activity is called 'Obtaining informed consent in the digital world'. First, ensure that you have a good idea about what is meant by informed consent in the research context. Questions to consider include:

1. What is meant by 'informed consent'?
2. How can researchers ensure that participants take part voluntarily and freely, and that they have all the information they require to make this decision?
3. What do participants need to know to give their informed consent?
4. How can researchers provide the necessary information (taking into account people who cannot read or speak English, for example)?
5. How should the issue of informed consent be approached with children and vulnerable populations?

Now think about informed consent for research in the digital world. This includes research that takes place using digital tools such as the Internet, smartphones, apps, email, social media, SMS, computer games and video tools. It can include research that gathers data through the use of online questionnaires, focus groups or interviews; digital ethnography that uses methods such as participant observation to observe virtual worlds, gaming or social networks; and research that uses techniques such as data mining or data analytics to examine datasets, find patterns, make inferences and draw conclusions.

There are a number of difficulties, problems or dilemmas associated with obtaining informed consent for research in the digital world, and these depend, in part, on the topic, research approach and research methods. For this activity you need to develop two scenarios that introduce a difficulty, problem or dilemma associated with obtaining informed consent in the digital world. You will then read one of your scenarios to your peers when we next meet so that we can discuss a solution to the difficulty, problem or dilemma you have identified. Be imaginative and creative, but make sure that your scenario is realistic and is a situation that could, potentially, be faced by student researchers. You are asked to produce two scenarios for two reasons: we will probably only have time to discuss one scenario from each group, but if time is available, we can move on to the second. Also, if your particular scenario has already been introduced by another group, you have an alternative available.

Learning outcome: By the end of this activity, you will be able to summarize what is meant by informed consent in the digital world and be able to identify, and explain how to overcome, a number of difficulties, problems and dilemmas when obtaining informed consent in the digital world.

Activity • • • • • • • • • ➔ 43

Critiquing the Presentation of Self in Online Worlds

ACTIVITY 43: EDUCATOR NOTES

Purpose: This activity encourages students, through group discussion, to critique the presentation of self in online worlds and think about the implications of self-presentation for online research. Definitions of 'online worlds' and 'online research' are given for students in the Student Handout.

Type: Group discussion followed by whole-class discussion (in-class).

Alternative type(s): Group discussion followed by whole-class discussion (online synchronous); self-guided individual exercise.

Level: Intermediate and advanced.

Duration: 50 minutes to one hour for the group discussion and up to two hours of work for students during independent study if the self-guided individual exercise option is chosen.

Equipment/materials: A suitable tool to host the online group discussion and a suitable note-catcher, if this option is chosen.

Learning outcome: By the end of this activity, students will be able to critique presentation of self in online worlds and summarize the implications of self-presentation for online research.

The activity

Divide your students into groups and ask them to work through the Student Handout (the number of groups depends on the number of students in your class, but four or five groups are usually a good number for this activity). Allow 20 minutes for this part of the activity. Walk among the groups to check on their discussion, ask questions and address queries. Once the groups have finished discussing the two topics given in the Student Handout, bring the groups back together to focus in on, and unpack, some of the pertinent issues raised by group discussions. Examples of questions and topics that can be asked are given below.

This activity can be run as an online activity if you prefer. Choose a suitable tool to host the group discussion (Zoom Meetings, Conferences in Canvas or Blackboard Collaborate, for example). Use breakout rooms for groups to work through the Student Handout. These can be set automatically or manually: ensure that breakout rooms are enabled prior to your session. Provide a brief introduction to the session and set guidelines for constructive and supportive online discussion. Open the breakout rooms and broadcast the questions in the Handout, one at a time, to your students. Ask groups to discuss each one, taking notes as they hold their discussion: they will need to discuss these issues with the whole class later. Develop and use an online spreadsheet or document note-catcher to organize note-taking for each group, if required. This can be used to monitor their discussions and see how they are progressing. It can also help you to decide which breakout rooms to visit during the session.

This activity can also be run as a self-guided individual exercise, if contact time is not available. Use the Student Handout and some of the questions provided below to develop an appropriate guide to give to your students and give a deadline by which time the work should be submitted. Provide assessment criteria if you choose to make this an assessed piece of work.

Key issues

Questions and topics that can be discussed in this activity include the following (several topics have been presented: choose those that are most suitable for the level at which your students are studying):

1. In what way do individuals present themselves online? What methods do they use? This can be text, images, sound, movement, for example. How can these methods be manipulated to present desired representations? How can researchers work with presentations that are manipulated or manufactured? Does it matter if they are manipulated (does this provide valuable research data, for example)?

2. Are self-presentations influenced by viewing platforms or media? Are they influenced by how many people view, at what time and on what device? How do actual or perceived number of views, likes or comments influence how, why and when individuals present themselves?

3. How does framing of self-presentation (the literal presentation and the interpretative markers) influence our interpretation of what we see?

4. Can presentations of self be a representation of reality? Can they be accurate and true? Do they provide a record of phenomena or social behaviour in an objective way? Can researchers trust what they are seeing or reading? Does it matter if a photograph has been altered digitally? What are the implications for transparency?

5. What information about self is presented and what is left out? How can researchers work with this?

6. How is self-presentation influenced by culture, society, history and politics (of the individual, viewer and researcher)? What are the implications for research?

7. Who is the audience or viewer? How and why are they looking at, or reading, self-presentations? What role does the gaze of the viewer or reader have in constructing meaning about self-presentation? What influence does the perceived audience or the viewer have on presentation of self? If the viewer is a researcher, how might this influence presentation of self? Might research have a performative effect on research participants, for example?

8. What motive do individuals have for their online presentation of self? This can include creating a desired image for others to see; meeting a specific goal, such as getting a job or a new partner; meeting new people; gaining help from others; and conveying an image of happiness or importance, for example. How might researchers deal with different types of motivation?

9. How and why do researchers present themselves online? If a researcher intends to undertake covert research, how will they present themselves online (Activity 59)? In overt research, how might researcher online visibility affect participant attitudes and participation levels?

10. What are the motivations for researchers presenting themselves online? How can this be done with transparency and integrity (Activities 17 and 19)?

→ **Related activities**

Activity 44: Managing the researcher's online presence

Activity 59: Critiquing overt and covert methods

Activity 70: Critiquing representation of the researcher in qualitative research

→ **Preparatory reading**

Educators: All the resources listed below provide useful preparatory reading.

Students: None required at the start of this activity. Useful resources relating to your discipline listed below can be recommended to students on completion of the activity, if required.

Activity 43

➜ Useful resources

Banwart, M.C. and Winfrey, K.L. (2013) 'Running on the web: Online self-presentation strategies in mixed-gender races', *Social Science Computer Review*, 31 (5): 614-24, first published 16 June 2013, doi: 10.1177/0894439313490390.

Bullingham, L. and Vasconcelos, A.C. (2013) '"The presentation of self in the online world": Goffman and the study of online identities', *Journal of Information Science*, 39 (1): 101-12, first published 4 January 2013, doi: 10.1177/0165551512470051.

Cheek, J. and Øby, E. (2019) '"Getting attention" creating and presenting the visible, online, researcher self', *Qualitative Inquiry*, 25 (6): 571-82, first published 31 October 2018, doi: 10.1177/1077800418806593.

D'Angelo, A. and Ryan, L. (2019) 'The presentation of the networked self: Ethics and epistemology in social network analysis', *Social Networks*, available online 24 July 2019, doi: 10.1016/j.socnet.2019.06.002.

van Dijck, J. (2013) '"You have one identity": Performing the self on Facebook and LinkedIn', *Media, Culture & Society*, 35 (2): 199-215, first published 14 March 2013, doi: 10.1177/0163443712468605.

Lin, C., Fang, W. and Jin, J. (2017) 'You are what you post in "circle of friends" of WeChat: Self-presentation and identity production from a personality perspective', *Global Media and China*, 2 (2): 138-52, first published 4 September 2017, doi: 10.1177/2059436417728855.

Michikyan, M., Dennis, J. and Subrahmanyam, K. (2015) 'Can you guess who I am? Real, ideal, and false self-presentation on Facebook among emerging adults', *Emerging Adulthood*, 3 (1): 55-64, first published 24 April 2014, doi: 10.1177/2167696814532442.

Schwarz, K.C. (2021) '"Gazing" and "performing": Travel photography and online self-presentation', *Tourist Studies*, 21 (2): 260-77, first published 18 January 2021, doi: 10.1177/1468797620985789.

Sibilla, F. and Mancini, T. (2018) 'I am (not) my avatar: A review of the user-avatar relationships in Massively Multiplayer Online Worlds', *Cyberpsychology: Journal of Psychosocial Research on Cyberspace*, 12 (3): Article 4, doi: 10.5817/CP2018-3-4.

Wright, E.J., White, K.M. and Obst, P.L. (2018) 'Facebook false self-presentation behaviors and negative mental health', *Cyberpsychology, Behavior, and Social Networking*, 21 (1): 40-9, first published 20 October 2017, doi: 10.1089/cyber.2016.0647.

Activity 43

Activity • • • • • • • • • • • → 43

Critiquing the Presentation of Self in Online Worlds

STUDENT HANDOUT

This activity is about critiquing the presentation of self in online worlds and the implications that self-presentation has for online research. For the purposes of this activity, 'online worlds' refers to any activity undertaken online and can include social media, social networks, online gaming, virtual worlds, discussion groups, forums and chat rooms. 'Online research' refers to any research that is undertaken online and can include, for example, online questionnaires, interviews and focus groups; social media research; data, web or mobile analytics; data mining; link analysis; and live audience response.

There are two topics that I would like you to discuss with your group members:

1. In what ways do individuals present themselves online? What are the implications for online research?

2. In what ways do researchers present themselves online? What are the implications for online research?

Take 20 minutes to discuss these questions in your groups. We will then come back together to hold a whole class discussion so that we can explore some of the pertinent issues in more depth. I will be walking among the groups during your discussions: if you have any questions, please ask.

Learning outcome: By the end of this activity, you will be able to critique the presentation of self in online worlds and summarize the implications of self-presentation for online research.

Activity • • • • • • • • • • • → 44

Managing the Researcher's Online Presence

The activity

Set up a suitable asynchronous, text-based tool to run the tip exchange (a VLE-hosted discussion board, chat room or Facebook group, for example). Provide instructions on what is required: this is a tip exchange about managing the researcher's online presence. Students can post tips about *why* it is important for researchers (including research students) to manage online presence and tips about *how to* manage their researcher online presence. Students read tips and post a tip. Each tip can be different from those that have gone before, or it can build on previous tips. Students must post five tips over the period of the activity (give a deadline by which time tips must be posted: this depends on your course or students' research – it is useful to have the final list of tips available for when students begin their research or relevant assignments).

Give students joining instructions and set guidelines for constructive, supportive and respectful online collaboration. Place one or two tips to get the exchange started (see below). Monitor posts from time-to-time, to check that information is correct, useful and supportive. Remove any inappropriate posts and explain why this has been done. Check that all students have posted their five tips a few days before the deadline, and send reminders if they have not done so. This tip exchange can remain available throughout students' course or research, if required.

This activity can also be run as a blog or vlog production and sharing activity (a vlog is an informal, 'chatty' style of video that is posted online: if you would like your students to produce something a little more formal, ask them to produce a 'video' instead). If you choose the blog or vlog option, divide your students into small groups or pairs so that they can help and support each other with technology and content. Ask students to produce a blog of no more than 600 words, or a vlog of no more than five minutes, which is informal and informative. They should explain why it is important to manage the researcher's online presence, and illustrate how this can be done. Ask students to upload their blog or vlog using a suitable tool (the blog tool in Moodle or Blackboard Learn, or Vimeo for vlogs, for example). Ensure that settings enable sharing and comments, and encourage students to read/view the work of their peers and enter into supportive and constructive online discussion.

Key issues

There are a wide variety of tips that can be included in the tip exchange and some examples are given below (these provide a mix relevant to students studying at different levels). They illustrate how students are able to build on the tips posted by their peers. They also illustrate that some tips veer slightly off topic: use your judgement on what to leave in the resource and what to remove. Use some of the following tips to get the tip exchange started, if required.

- An active presence is important to build networks and gain an 'audience' for your research.
- You can reach other students and researchers around the world to share your ideas and research results.
- You can contact global experts and, if you have a good online presence, they will take you more seriously. Publishers will also take you more seriously if you have a good online presence.
- If people know who you are and you have a good online image or reputation, you can be invited for conferences or to write book chapters, for example.
- Building and managing your online presence doesn't cost anything extra.
- Managing your online presence can stop false or misleading impressions, or stop others attributing something to you that does not belong to you (negative comments or poor research, for example).
- Keep public and private information separate. Keep your researcher information and your private life separate. Manage public and private information very carefully. Keep private information private.
- Engage with others, including academics, students and members of the public. Ask questions, answer questions, chat, send constructive comments and build networks.
- Think before you post: don't post when you are angry or upset; never be abusive or offensive; think about other people's feelings.
- Only appear online when you have something useful and constructive to say. Don't bombard others with pointless posts or chat.

- If you have doubts about posting something, delay acting: seek advice from others, especially your supervisor, and don't post if you still have doubts.
- Don't do anything online that would have a detrimental impact on your professional reputation (enter into personal arguments, rise to academic trolling or disrespect others, for example).
- Be very clear about rules and regulations. Make sure you don't accidentally share another person's work and infringe copyright, for example (Activity 39). Become knowledgeable about types of intellectual property and how they can be infringed (accidentally or on purpose). These can include copyright, trademarks and design rights, which can all be relevant to information posted online. Make sure you obtain all permissions before you post anything from other people online (Activity 38).
- Make sure you don't release data that your funding body or university doesn't want you to release: you should check everything with your supervisor first.
- Think about whether you might want to try publishing in an academic journal. If you do want to, don't publish your work online first as publishers might then not accept it.
- Check your online presence regularly. If you find problems, try to rectify them straight away.
- Find out about registering for an ORCID iD. The website provides information and your supervisor will give more advice: https://info.orcid.org.
- Make your work open access, where possible (Activity 96).

→ **Related activities**

Activity 17: Cultivating transparency and openness

Activity 38: Protecting intellectual property

Activity 39: Avoiding copyright infringement

Activity 40: Understanding digital licences, laws and conventions

Activity 44

→ Preparatory reading

Educators: Some universities provide guidelines about managing the researcher's online presence. If so, become familiar with your university guidelines and provide a link in the tip exchange for your students to follow. If any of the resources listed below are useful for your students, they can be posted on the tip exchange.

Students: None required.

→ Useful resources

Cheek, J. and Øby, E. (2019) '"Getting attention" creating and presenting the visible, online, researcher self', *Qualitative Inquiry*, 25 (6): 571-82, first published 31 October 2018, doi: 10.1177/1077800418806593.

Craft, A.R. (2020) 'Electronic Resources Forum - managing researcher identity: Tools for researchers and librarians', *Serials Review*, 46 (1): 44-9, published online 4 February 2020, doi: 10.1080/00987913.2020.1720897.

Pasquini, L.A. and Eaton, P.W. (2021) 'Being/becoming professional online: Wayfinding through networked practices and digital experiences', *New Media & Society*, 23 (5): 939-59, first published 14 February 2020, doi: 10.1177/1461444820902449.

Robards, B. (2013) 'Friending participants: Managing the researcher-participant relationship on social network sites', *YOUNG*, 21 (3): 217-35, first published 12 August 2013, doi: 10.1177/1103308813488815.

Ryan, F.V.C., Cruickshank, P., Hall, H. and Lawson, A. (2020) 'Blurred reputations: Managing professional and private information online', *Journal of Librarianship and Information Science*, 52 (1): 16-26, first published 13 May 2018, doi: 10.1177/0961000618769977.

Sheldon, J. and Sheppard, V. (2022) *Online Communities for Doctoral Researchers and Their Supervisors: Building Engagement with Social Media*. Abingdon: Routledge.

Activity 44

Activity · · · · · · · · · · → 45

Designing Inclusive Data Systems

The activity

Give a copy of the Student Handout to your students and ask that they work on the questions and tasks during independent study (the five IDC principles are given in the Handout: the questions and tasks relate to the principles and to students' research). Give a deadline for the work to be submitted and, if appropriate, share student answers online (if you choose to do this, make sure students know that their work will be shared).

   This activity can be run as a synchronous online discussion using a video/web conferencing tool such as Zoom Meetings, Google Meet or Blackboard Collaborate, if you prefer. Set guidelines for constructive and supportive online discussion. Introduce the session and then broadcast the questions in the Handout, one at a time. Invite students to discuss each (they can write answers using the chat facility or you can ask them to answer by video). When asking Question 6 (if any of the principles relate to students' research), use online polling tools such as Kwiqpoll, Mentimeter or Answer Garden so that students can see which of the principles are considered relevant to their peers. Conclude the session with a summary of the main points raised.

Key issues

This activity is a simple worksheet that raises important issues for students. At first, some might think that their research is not relevant to the five principles contained within the IDC. However, once they are encouraged to unpack each principle and think more about what they entail, relevance can become more visible.

There are a number of key issues that can be raised in this activity:

- the importance of global data for sustainable development (Activity 6);
- the importance of transparency and openness in data collection and analysis (Activity 17);
- collecting, analysing and disaggregating data with reference to equality, diversity and inclusion (Activity 28);
- undertaking discrimination-aware and fairness-aware research (Activity 8);
- political motivation, political culture and government commitment;
- public understanding and public pressure;
- the costs involved and who pays them, in particular, in poorer nations;
- how badly designed, restrictive or incomplete data systems can lead to disadvantage, perpetuate inequalities or cause harm to individuals and communities;
- the importance of comprehensive researcher training;
- the importance of research(er) integrity (Activities 19, 20 and 21);
- how the principles relate to qualitative and quantitative research (and whether all five principles relate to all types of student research).

→ Related activities

Activity 6: Aligning with the UN's Sustainable Development Goals

Activity 46: Reclaiming datasets for social justice

Activity 53: Overcoming problems with weak, restricted, non-existent or invisible data systems

Activity 54: Understanding problems associated with unequal access to data

Activity 72: Assessing ethical issues in data analytics

→ Preparatory reading

Educators: If you are new to teaching this topic, you might find it useful to read about the IDC (details below).

Students: None required. Students will find their own resources for this activity, although you can provide links to the IDC after the activity has taken place.

→ Useful resources

The IDC was developed by the GPSDD 'to mobilize political commitments and meaningful actions to advance inclusive and disaggregated data'. More information about the charter can be obtained from www.data4sdgs.org/inclusivedatacharter [accessed 21 September 2021].

Information about the Inclusive Data Charter Action Plan in the UK can be obtained from www.gov.uk/government/publications/leaving-no-one-behind-our-promise/inclusive-data-charter-action-plan [accessed 21 September 2021].

The Office for National Statistics (ONS) in the UK has partnered with the GPSDD 'to improve the quality, quantity and availability of inclusive data'. Information about their IDC action plan for the global Sustainable Development Goals can be obtained from www.ons.gov.uk/economy/environmentalaccounts/methodologies/inclusivedatacharteractionplan-fortheglobalsustainabledevelopmentgoals [accessed 21 September 2021].

Criado Perez, C. (2020) *Invisible Women: Exposing Data Bias in a World Designed for Men*. London: Vintage.

Mitra, S., Yap, J., Herve, J. and Chen, W. (2021) 'Inclusive statistics: Human development and disability indicators in low- and middle-income countries', *SSRN*, first published 6 May 2021, available at *SSRN*: https://ssrn.com/abstract=3840952 or doi: 10.2139/ssrn.3840952.

O'Neil, C. (2017) *Weapons of Math Destruction: How Big Data Increases Inequality and Threatens Democracy*. London: Penguin.

Activity 45

Activity · · · · · · · · · · · → 45

Designing Inclusive Data Systems

STUDENT HANDOUT

This activity is about designing inclusive data systems. The Inclusive Data Charter (IDC) was developed by the Global Partnership for Sustainable Development Data (GPSDD) 'to mobilize political commitments and meaningful actions to advance inclusive and disaggregated data'. The Charter sets out five principles:

Principle 1: All populations must be included in the data.

Principle 2: All data should, wherever possible, be disaggregated in order to accurately describe all populations.

Principle 3: Data should be drawn from all available sources.

Principle 4: Those responsible for the collection of data and production of statistics must be accountable.

Principle 5: Human and technical capacity to collect, analyse and use disaggregated data needs to be improved, including through adequate and sustainable financing.

Consider each of these principles and then answer the following questions.

Question 1

In Principle 1, why should all populations be included in the data? Give an example of a problem that might occur if all populations are not included in the data.

Question 2

In Principle 2, what does 'disaggregated' mean? Why is this important?

Question 3

In Principle 3, why should data be drawn from all available sources? Give an example of a problem that might occur if data are not drawn from all available sources.

Question 4

In Principle 4, why is accountability important for those responsible for the collection of data and production of statistics?

Question 5

In Principle 5, other than sustainable financing, in what way can human and technical capacity to collect, analyse and use disaggregated data be improved?

Question 6

Do any or all of these principles relate to your research? If so, in what way?

Question 7

How will you try to meet relevant principles when you conduct your research?

Learning outcome: By the end of this activity, you will be able to appraise the five principles presented in the IDC and demonstrate how these principles relate to your research.

Activity 45

Activity • • • • • • • • • • • → 46

Reclaiming Datasets for Social Justice

The activity

Divide your students into groups or pairs: it is useful to have at least six different groups or pairs for this activity to provide a variety of ideas and views (if you have only a small number of students in your cohort, ask them to work on an individual basis). Give each group a copy of the Student Handout and ask that they work on the tasks with their group members during independent study. The Handout asks them to provide a definition of 'dataset' and 'social justice' (you might choose to omit this part of the activity for students studying at advanced level); provide three imagined or real-world examples of ways in which the creation and/or use of datasets can lead to social injustice; and provide five ways in which datasets can be reclaimed for social justice.

Once they have completed the tasks, they should upload their work to the VLE-hosted discussion board or forum that you have set up for this purpose (Blackboard Discussion Board or Forum in Moodle, for example). Encourage them to enter into online discussion, reading, commenting and building on each group's ideas, so that a useful student-centred resource is built that can be accessed when required. Monitor posts to ensure that information is correct and that all discussion remains courteous, respectful, supportive and constructive. Remove any posts that do not meet these criteria and explain why this has been done. Set a deadline for work to be posted and, if you choose to make this an assessed piece of work, provide detailed assessment criteria.

This activity can also be run as a simple student worksheet. Use the tasks given in the Student Handout to develop a worksheet that students can work through individually during independent study. Alternatively, combine the tasks in this activity with those on the worksheet in Activity 45: Designing inclusive data systems, to give more complete coverage of the topics. If you have contact time available, meet to discuss and share ideas.

Key issues

In this activity it is useful to ask students to define what is meant by 'dataset' and 'social justice' as there can be slightly different opinions, which lead students to approach the next two tasks in slightly different ways. This is not a problem: it provides variety and enables students to enter into useful and constructive online discussion. It tends to provide a variety of examples of social injustice, and leads to different methods to reclaim datasets for social justice, including:

- better training in the creation, use and critique of datasets (teaching data literacy from an early age, for example);
- methods to help people recognize assumptions, flaws and prejudices in datasets (thinking about why and how data are produced, for example);
- giving individuals more and better control over their data (empowering individuals to control their digital lives, for example);
- ways to overcome oppression, inequality and exclusion that result from flawed analyses of flawed data (recognizing and challenging data-driven discrimination, for example);
- challenging datafication by the rich and powerful;
- recognizing and redressing political influence on data collection and analysis;
- addressing apathy of individuals about what happens to their data;
- empowering others to fight for data justice;
- critiquing and challenging the commercialization of data.

→ **Related activities**

Activity 6: Aligning with the UN's Sustainable Development Goals

Activity 45: Designing inclusive data systems

Activity 53: Overcoming problems with weak, restricted, non-existent or invisible data systems

Activity 54: Understanding problems associated with unequal access to data

Activity 72: Assessing ethical issues in data analytics

→ **Preparatory reading**

Educators: O'Neil (2017) provides an interesting and useful introduction.

Students: None required. Students will find their own resources for this activity, although useful resources listed below can be posted on the digital resource, if required.

→ **Useful resources**

Beraldo, D. and Milan, S. (2019) 'From data politics to the contentious politics of data', *Big Data & Society*, first published 7 November 2019, doi: 10.1177/2053951719885967.

Criado Perez, C. (2020) *Invisible Women: Exposing Data Bias in a World Designed for Men*. London: Vintage.

Gray, J., Gerlitz, C. and Bounegru, L. (2018) 'Data infrastructure literacy', *Big Data & Society*, first published 10 July 2018, doi: 10.1177/2053951718786316.

Lehtiniemi, T. and Ruckenstein, M. (2019) 'The social imaginaries of data activism', *Big Data & Society*, first published 7 January 2019, doi: 10.1177/2053951718821146.

Kazansky, B. and Milan, S. (2021) '"Bodies not templates": Contesting dominant algorithmic imaginaries', *New Media & Society*, 23 (2): 363-81, first published 25 February 2021, doi: 10.1177/1461444820929316.

Kearns, M. and Roth, A. (2020) *The Ethical Algorithm: The Science of Socially Aware Algorithm Design*. New York, NY: Oxford University Press.

Activity 46

Milan, S. and Treré, E. (2020) 'The rise of the data poor: The COVID-19 pandemic seen from the margins', *Social Media + Society*, first published 11 August 2020, doi: 10.1177/2056305120948233.

O'Neil, C. (2017) *Weapons of Math Destruction: How Big Data Increases Inequality and Threatens Democracy*. London: Penguin.

Stoner, M. (2017) 'Making sense of social justice: Reclaiming the subject', *The National Teaching & Learning Forum*, 27 (1): 1-4, first published 19 December 2017, doi: 10.1002/ntlf.30134.

Taylor, L. (2017) 'What is data justice? The case for connecting digital rights and freedoms globally', *Big Data & Society*, first published 1 November 2017, doi: 10.1177/2053951717736335.

Activity 46

Activity • • • • • • • • • • • • → 46

Reclaiming Datasets for Social Justice

STUDENT HANDOUT

This activity is about reclaiming datasets for social justice. Work through the following tasks with your group members, then upload your work using the tool provided. Read the work posted by your peers so that you can compare, contrast and discuss ideas and opinions. Remember to keep all online discussion courteous, respectful, supportive and constructive. This activity will build a useful student-centred resource that can be accessed when required.

1. Provide a definition of 'dataset'.
2. Provide a definition of 'social justice'.
3. Give three examples of ways in which the creation and/or use of datasets can lead to social injustice (these can be real-world examples or imagined).

4. List five ways in which datasets can be reclaimed for social justice.

Learning outcome: By the end of this activity, you will be able to give a definition of 'dataset' and 'social justice'; provide examples of ways in which the creation and/or use of datasets can lead to social injustice; and list ways in which datasets can be reclaimed for social justice.

Activity • • • • • • • • • • • • → 47

Evaluating Compliance of Software Companies and Third-Party Providers

The activity

Give your students a copy of the Student Handout and ask that they work on the task during independent study. If you intend to make this an assessed piece of work, provide assessment criteria and a submission deadline. The Handout provides information about what is meant by compliance, why it is important, gives examples of stages that can be worked through to evaluate compliance, and asks students to build a checklist of action they need to take to identify and evaluate compliance. If you think there is too much information provided in the Handout, or that students should find this information for themselves, delete accordingly.

Key issues

This activity has different levels of importance for students, depending on their research approach, topic and methods. Most will use some software, tools, equipment or secondary data and will, therefore, need to produce a checklist that will help them to identify and evaluate compliance. Others might not use any software companies or third-party providers and, therefore, will not need to produce a checklist, although this tends to be quite rare.

   Comprehensive information has been produced in the Handout because students, sometimes, do not see the relevance of what they are being asked to do. They believe they are working with reputable companies that comply with all rules, regulations and frameworks. Even if this is the case, they still need to check that their beliefs are correct and ascertain whether companies and providers work to the same standards as those required of researchers. Other students do not think about software, tools and data that are being used (and the implications of this use) until they take part in this activity.

→ Related activities

Activity 50: Evaluating privacy policies of software companies and third-party providers

Activity 56: Citing digital tools and software correctly

Activity 77: Critiquing the origin and provenance of data

→ Preparatory reading

Educators: Monciardini et al. (2021) provides interesting preparatory reading for this activity.

Students: None required.

→ Useful resources

The Open Compliance and Ethics Group (OCEG) 'is a non-profit think tank that is dedicated to achieving a world where every organization and every person strives to achieve objectives, address uncertainty and act with integrity'. Useful information and advice about ethics and compliance can be obtained from their website: www.oceg.org [accessed 29 June 2021].

Informal information about legal and regulatory compliance issues and/or business ethics can be obtained from the Compliance and Ethics blog, which is produced by the Society of Corporate Compliance and Ethics (SCCE) and the Health Care Compliance Association (HCCA): https://complianceandethics.org [accessed 29 June 2021].

Bicaku, A., Tauber, M. and Delsing, J. (2020) 'Security standard compliance and continuous verification for Industrial Internet of Things', *International Journal of Distributed Sensor Networks*, first published 20 June 2020, doi: 10.1177/1550147720922731.

Kamarinou, D., Millard, C. and Oldani, I. (2018) 'Compliance as a service', *Queen Mary School of Law Legal Studies Research Paper*, 287/2018, November 14, 2018, available at SSRN: https://ssrn.com/abstract=3284497.

Monciardini, D., Bernaz, N. and Andhov, A. (2021) 'The organizational dynamics of compliance with the UK Modern Slavery Act in the food and tobacco sector', *Business & Society*, 60 (2): 288–340, first published 30 December 2019, doi: 10.1177/0007650319898195.

Riehle, D. and Harutyunyan, N. (2019) 'Open-Source License compliance in software supply chains'. In B. Fitzgerald, A. Mockus and M. Zhou (eds), *Towards Engineering Free/Libre Open Source Software (FLOSS) Ecosystems for Impact and Sustainability*. Singapore: Springer, doi: 10.1007/978-981-13-7099-1_5.

Vitunskaite, M., He, Y., Brandstetter, T. and Janicke, H. (2019) 'Smart cities and cyber security: Are we there yet? A comparative study on the role of standards, third party risk management and security ownership', *Computers & Security*, 83: 313–31, doi: 10.1016/j.cose.2019.02.009.

Activity 47

Activity • • • • • • • • • • • → 47

Evaluating Compliance of Software Companies and Third-Party Providers

STUDENT HANDOUT

This activity is about evaluating the compliance of software companies and third-party providers that you intend to use in your research. Compliance refers to regulatory compliance (to local, regional, national and international law), ethical compliance (to ethical codes and standards, or within ethical frameworks) and integrity compliance (to codes of professional, organization and/or research integrity). This is an important activity to undertake: as a researcher you must work to the highest ethical standards and act with integrity and professionalism. If you work with a company or provider who does not meet these standards, your research and/or reputation could be compromised.

There are a number of stages that you can work through to evaluate compliance of software companies and third-party providers:

1. Recognize and list all software companies and third-party suppliers that will be used in your research. This varies significantly, depending on your discipline, research topic, methodology and methods. It could include data collection and data analysis software companies (for online questionnaires, mobile interviews or statistical analysis, for example); audio, video and multimedia hardware and software manufacturers, creators and suppliers; and data controllers, processors and suppliers of primary and secondary data (census data, company records or customer data, for example).

2. Develop a list of questions that you can ask that will help you to undertake your evaluation. These will depend on whether you are evaluating manufacturers, creators or suppliers. Examples of questions concerning the use of primary and secondary data include:

   - Who owns the data?
   - How are data handled?
   - How are they procured, stored, managed, used and disposed of?

   - Who handles data within the business? Have all handlers signed confidentiality agreements?
   - What protections are in place to prevent the leak or misuse of sensitive data?
   - Are all relevant data governance and regulatory compliance commitments supported and enforced? Am I happy that they are met and conform to the standards required for my research?
   - Are data management policies credible, clear and transparent?

3. Undertake a third-party risk assessment to ensure that third parties or software companies do not bring risk to your research. This could be reputational risk (their actions bring your research into disrepute); operational risk (the way they operate causes problems with the way you conduct your research); security or privacy risks (they do not have the same data management and protection rules and assurances that are required for your research); or regularity risk (their actions bring legal liability to your research, to your university or to you).

Now consider your research. Build a checklist of the action you need to take to identify and evaluate compliance of software companies and third-party providers. Your checklist will be unique to your research: however, you might decide to share it with your peers to bounce ideas off each other and further develop your list. Once developed, use your checklist to ensure that you evaluate compliance as you move forward with your research.

Learning outcome: By the end of this activity, you will be able to define what is meant by compliance of software companies and third-party providers, and explain how you intend to identify and evaluate compliance when undertaking your research.

Activity • • • • • • • • • • → 48

Assessing the Reliability of Digital Tools and Software

The activity

Ask your students to produce a blog of no more than 600 words (for undergraduates) or 800 words (for postgraduates). The blog should provide information about how users can (and should) assess the reliability of digital tools and software. Encourage students to produce an informal, imaginative, creative and memorable blog from which their peers can learn.

Once students have produced their blog, it should be uploaded using a tool you have set up for this purpose (the blog tool in Moodle or Blackboard Learn, for example). Alternatively, your university may have its own blogging service that can be used for teaching and learning: these contain useful templates, guidance notes and advice on setting up the service for assessed and non-assessed work. If you decide to make this an assessed piece of work, explain the process to your students and give guidance on standards required. Students can use the dashboard to customize their blogs; add features such as images, links and multimedia; edit their work; and receive comments from their peers.

Give a deadline by which time all blogs should be posted. Ask students to read the blogs of their peers, and post constructive and informative comments, where relevant (check that the right visibility option is chosen so that students can read each other's blogs: default settings sometimes enable blogs to be shared only between student and educator). Read all blogs when they have been posted to ensure that information is correct and does not breach copyright rules. Monitor comments to make sure that they are supportive and constructive, and delete comments that do not meet these criteria, explaining why this has been done.

This activity can be run as a vlog production and sharing exercise, if you prefer. If you choose this option, run it as a small group exercise rather than on an individual basis: this allows for group support for students who do not have the necessary technology, or for those who are unfamiliar with the technology. Vlogs can be uploaded using a VLE-hosted tool that enables messages to be posted with media file attachments, such as Discussions in Canvas or Forum in Moodle, or using an external tool such as Vimeo or WeVideo. Ensure that settings enable sharing and comments.

Alternatively, this activity can be run as a simple written assignment (assessed or non-assessed). Ask students to produce a written piece of work that explains how users can (and should) assess the reliability of digital tools and software. Give guidance on length (appropriate to your cohort), include assessment criteria if this is to be an assessed piece of work, and provide a submission deadline.

Key issues

This activity provides the opportunity for students to undertake self-guided individual work, before sharing their work with their peers. This enables them to complete the work independently, share their knowledge, respond to each other, learn from each other and reinforce their learning. Students must first get to grips with how to assess the reliability of tools and software, before thinking about how they can best communicate this to their peers. Blogs have been chosen as a way to do this because they encourage students to think about how complex and detailed issues can be communicated effectively, creatively and imaginatively, in a way that can be understood by those who are new to these issues.

Topics that are covered in this activity tend to depend on students' subject and level of study, but can include:

- spotting design defects (tools and software work as they have been designed to, but the design is flawed);
- looking for bias in design (biases of the designer have an influence on outputs from software and tools: inherent bias, race bias, class bias or gender bias, for example);
- checking for errors in coding (tools and software do not work as they should do, but mistakes can be difficult to spot for those who are unfamiliar with coding);
- raising awareness of deceptive, fraudulent or intentionally misleading tools or software (for personal, political or religious gain, for example);

- recognizing biased data, or gaps in data: how this influences the way artificial intelligence is trained and the effect this has on subsequent outputs, for example;
- acknowledging problems associated with believing that digital tools and software are always flaw-free and that outputs are correct and cannot be challenged;
- considering the possibility of software testing, to look for faults and test for quality (can include a discussion on the different types of software testing and whether these mean that software is reliable);
- seeking expert advice on finding and using reliable tools and software;
- using additional tools and software to check on results.

Some of the topics raised in this activity are similar to, or the same as, those raised in Activity 51: Assessing the neutrality of online platforms, tools and data, and Activity 52: Assessing bias in search tools. Therefore, choose the most appropriate of the three activities for your students or combine them, if you have the time available.

Cautionary note

Check blog visibility when you set up your chosen tool. It is a good idea to ensure that blogs can be viewed only by students on your course and by yourself, at least until you have checked for potential problems such as breach of copyright, slander, libel or plagiarism. Educators have control over this activity: you have the opportunity to create or edit content; monitor comments; remove posts or blogs that are misleading, unsupportive or wrong; or prohibit users if they break the rules.

→ Related activities

Activity 51: Assessing the neutrality of online platforms, tools and data

Activity 52: Assessing bias in search tools

Activity 53: Overcoming problems with weak, restricted, non-existent or invisible data systems

→ Preparatory reading

Educators: If you are new to using blogs in teaching, Chawinga (2017) and Ifinedo (2018) provide interesting and useful reading.

Students: None required. Students will find their own resources for this activity.

Activity 48

→ **Useful resources**

Broussard, M. (2019) *Artificial Unintelligence: How Computers Misunderstand the World*. Cambridge, MA: MIT Press.

Chawinga, W.D. (2017) 'Taking social media to a university classroom: Teaching and learning using Twitter and blogs', *International Journal of Educational Technology in Higher Education*, 14 (3), open access, published 25 January 2017, doi: 10.1186/s41239-017-0041-6.

Criado Perez, C. (2020) *Invisible Women: Exposing Data Bias in a World Designed for Men*. London: Vintage.

Ifinedo, P. (2018) 'Determinants of students' continuance intention to use blogs to learn: An empirical investigation', *Behaviour & Information Technology*, 37 (4): 381–92, doi: 10.1080/0144929X.2018.1436594.

Kearns, M. and Roth, A. (2020) *The Ethical Algorithm: The Science of Socially Aware Algorithm Design*. New York, NY: Oxford University Press.

Turner Lee, N., Resnick, P. and Barton, G. (2019) 'Algorithmic bias detection and mitigation: Best practices and policies to reduce consumer harms', *Center for Technology Innovation*, published online 22 May 2019, www.brookings.edu/research/algorithmic-bias-detection-and-mitigation-best-practices-and-policies-to-reduce-consumer-harms/ [accessed 26 November 2021].

Turner Lee, N. (2018) 'Detecting racial bias in algorithms and machine learning', *Journal of Information, Communication and Ethics in Society*, 6 (3): 252–60, published 13 August 2018, doi: 10.1108/JICES-06-2018-0056.

Activity 48

Activity · · · · · · · · · · · → 49

Assessing the Ethical Implications of Data Mining

ACTIVITY 49: EDUCATOR NOTES

Purpose: This is a scenario-based activity that enables students to identify, discuss and assess the ethical implications of data mining.

Type: Scenarios for group discussion.

Alternative type(s): Scenarios for online asynchronous discussion; scenario-based individual exercise.

Level: Elementary, intermediate and advanced (the level will be reflected in scenarios and discussion).

Duration: Fifty minutes to one hour of contact time. If the online option is chosen, students will spend one or two hours over a week, working on scenarios and entering into online discussion. Educators will spend an hour or two monitoring posts and entering into discussion, where required. If the self-guided individual exercise option is chosen, students will spend one or two hours working on their own during independent study.

Equipment/materials: A suitable online discussion board, if the online option is chosen.

Learning outcome: By the end of this activity, students will be able to identify and assess various ethical implications of data mining.

The activity

Divide your students into groups and ask them to work through the scenarios provided in the Student Handout. This part of the activity usually takes 15-20 minutes. Walk among the groups, answering questions or helping with dilemmas, if they occur. Once this has concluded, bring the groups back together to lead a class discussion on the ethical implications that have arisen (see key issues).

This activity can be run as an online asynchronous discussion, if you prefer. Present the scenarios using a suitable tool, such as your VLE-hosted discussion board, and ask students to discuss each, over a period of a week. Monitor posts to ensure that information is correct, supportive, respectful and constructive.

You can also run this activity as a scenario-based individual exercise for students to work on during independent study. Adapt the Student Handout slightly and decide whether to make this an assessed piece of work: if you do, provide assessment criteria and a submission deadline.

Key issues

Issues that are raised in this activity depend on subject, level and research approach. Examples include:

Scenario 1

- Razi could think about issues surrounding privacy, security and the misuse or abuse of mined data, and look into the fairness of data mining practices, in particular from the point of view of the people whose data *are* being mined (Berendt and Preibusch, 2017; Hate et al., 2015; Kennedy et al., 2017).
- Razi should consider how human and machine-based reasoning have been used and combined to produce and structure data, and the subtle ways in which bias can be introduced and amplified when data are mined (Criado Perez, 2020).
- Razi should not take data at face value: raw data are not necessarily neutral (Activity 78).
- Razi must take steps to avoid predictive harm when building his model: will his model be flawed if he is using flawed data?

Scenario 2

- Giulia needs to consider how to tackle unequal access to, and ownership of, smartphones (Activity 55) and assess how this might bias her sample (Activity 64).
- Giulia will be able to obtain informed consent from those she intends to interview or observe, but how might she obtain informed consent from those whose data are mined, in particular, in cases where people are unaware of this practice?
- Issues of anonymity and identification will need to be considered: mined data can be in the form of aggregated statistics that help to prevent people being identified, but data from interviews or focus groups (and associated recordings) will need to be anonymized carefully (Activity 62).
- If Giulia intends to undertake some type of fieldwork, she will need to consider the challenges and potential negative effects (Activity 69). She will need to think about how she is going to record conversations and the ethical implications associated with participants choosing to disclose personal information in public spaces (when conducting mobile phone interviews, for example).

Scenario 3

- The researchers need to consider who owns education data (universities, educators or students, for example)? Who can access data? Do students have a right to see their data, decide who can use them and what is done with them?
- Team members need to consider how they will address issues of informed consent (Activity 57).
- How will team members protect students' privacy and prevent the possibility that de-identified data could be re-identified?
- The researchers need to ask whether their analyses can cause harm to students (stereotyping or profiling, for example). Or will their research benefit students (identify those who need additional support, for example)?
- How can team members ensure that they undertake ethical analyses and model-building? Can machines, algorithms and computational techniques be 'ethical'?
- How can team members ensure that data are accurate and reliable? If data are inaccurate the model's results will be unreliable (Activity 77).
- How can team members avoid bias in algorithm and technique choice?
- How do the researchers intend to share their data (Activity 83)?

The following questions can be used for the whole-class discussion:

- Can you be sure of data neutrality when mining data?
- How is bias built into data? How might it be amplified by machine learning and algorithms. How can we recognize built-in bias?
- How can data mining be performed within the bounds of privacy regulations and informed consent (when using previously collected data, for example)?
- What are the ethical implications of mining data when people are unaware (from location trackers or sensors, for example)?
- How can discrimination-aware and fairness-aware data mining be undertaken?
- How do individuals react to data mining? Might they try to fool, thwart or disrupt the process? What influences might these reactions have on research involving data mining?

→ Related activities

Activity 40: Understanding digital licences, laws and conventions

Activity 42: Obtaining informed consent in the digital world

Activity 46: Reclaiming datasets for social justice

Activity 49

Activity 51: Assessing the neutrality of online platforms, tools and data

Activity 67: Identifying unethical practice when collecting data

Activity 72: Assessing ethical issues in data analytics

→ **Preparatory reading**

Educators: Kennedy (2016) provides comprehensive coverage on social media data mining.

Students: None required. Some of the resources listed below can be recommended to students who wish to read more about the issues raised in this activity.

→ **Useful resources**

Berendt, B. and Preibusch, S. (2017) 'Toward accountable discrimination-aware data mining: The importance of keeping the human in the loop – and under the looking glass', *Big Data*, 5 (2): 135–52, first published 1 June 2017, doi: 10.1089/big.2016.0055.

Criado Perez, C. (2020) *Invisible Women: Exposing Data Bias in a World Designed for Men*. London: Vintage.

Custers, B., Calders, T., Schermer, B. and Zarsky, T. (eds) (2103) *Discrimination and Privacy in the Information Society: Data Mining and Profiling in Large Databases*. Heidelberg: Springer.

Fischer, C., Pardos, Z.A., Baker, R.S., Williams, J.J., Smyth, P., Yu, R., Slater, S., Baker, R. and Warschauer, M. (2020) 'Mining big data in education: Affordances and challenges', *Review of Research in Education*, 44 (1): 130–60, first published 21 April 2020, doi: 10.3102/0091732X20903304.

Kennedy, H. (2016) *Post, Mine, Repeat: Social Media Data Mining Becomes Ordinary*. London: Springer Nature.

Kennedy, H., Elgesem, D. and Miguel, C. (2017) 'On fairness: User perspectives on social media data mining', *Convergence*, 23 (3): 270 – 88, first published 28 June 2015, doi: 10.1177/1354856515592507.

O'Neil, C. (2017) *Weapons of Math Destruction: How Big Data Increases Inequality and Threatens Democracy*. London: Penguin.

Taylor, J. and Pagliari, C. (2018) 'Mining social media data: How are research sponsors and researchers addressing the ethical challenges?', *Research Ethics*, 14 (2): 1–39, first published 26 October 2017, doi: 10.1177/1747016117738559.

Završnik, A. (ed.) (2018) *Big Data, Crime and Social Control*. Abingdon: Routledge.

Activity 49

Activity • • • • • • • • • • • → 49

Assessing the Ethical Implications of Data Mining

STUDENT HANDOUT

This activity is about assessing the ethical implications of data mining. For the purposes of this activity, 'data mining' refers to the process of applying algorithms to extract hidden information in raw data to uncover patterns, relationships and trends, with the aim of building predictive or descriptive models for explanation and/or generalization.

Work through the following scenarios with your group members, discussing the ethical implications of each scenario. You have 15–20 minutes to complete this part of the activity. Once you have done this, we will hold a class discussion on the ethical issues you have raised.

Scenario 1

Razi has been mining crime data to discover patterns, relationships and trends within the data, with the aim of building an effective predictive model that could be used to inform policing practice. He began his research believing that raw data do not lie. However, he has found certain patterns within the data that do not seem quite right to him, especially concerning the high prevalence of anti-social behaviour among African Americans. He raises this issue with his supervisor. The outcome of the meeting is that Razi should investigate the ethical implications of data mining. What should Razi consider?

Scenario 2

Giulia is considering using ethno-mining techniques for her research. This combines ethnography (the study of individuals, groups or communities in their own environment over a period of time) with data mining techniques. She hopes that this approach will give her a more complete understanding of human behaviour. She intends to mine data from smartphones and apps, which she will explore using methods such as classification, clustering, anomaly detection, regression and summarization. Once she has done this, she will explore emerging patterns and trends using methods such as interviews, focus groups and participant observation (online or offline). What ethical issues does Giulia need to consider if she goes ahead with this research?

Scenario 3

A university research team intends to adopt educational data mining techniques to investigate patterns of online learning during the coronavirus pandemic, with the aim of predicting students' behaviour and future performance. They are in the process of putting together their application for ethical approval. What ethical issues do you think they need to consider?

Learning outcome: By the end of this activity, you will be able to identify and assess various ethical implications of data mining.

Activity • • • • • • • • • • • → 50

Evaluating Privacy Policies of Software Companies and Third-Party Providers

The activity

Run a workshop with your students. For the first part of the workshop ask students to list software companies and third-party providers that will be used in their studies and/or research. Write down their answers on a whiteboard, chalk board or flip chart. Once you have a suitable list, divide your students into pairs or small groups and allocate one or two items on the list to each pair/group (the number will depend on how many pairs/groups you have and how many items are in the list: ideally you need about 10–14 items for discussion so some items can be combined, if necessary, as illustrated in key issues, below). Ask students to work in their pairs/groups to consider the privacy issues that are pertinent to each company/provider identified.

After 15 minutes, bring the groups back together and ask each to give a brief summary of the main points from their discussion. Once this is complete, ask students to give examples of ways that privacy information can be accessed and evaluated. Write a bullet point list of the methods they mention. Conclude the session with a summary of the main points raised. If relevant to your cohort, ask them to work individually after the session to develop a checklist of action that they, personally, need to take to identify and evaluate privacy policies of software companies and third-party providers that they will use in their research.

This workshop can be held online, if you prefer, using a video/web conferencing tool such as Zoom Meetings, Blackboard Collaborate or Meetings in Microsoft Teams for Education. Set guidelines for constructive and supportive online discussion, use breakout rooms for the group discussions, and follow the same structure as that given for the in-class workshop, above.

This activity can also be run as a self-guided individual exercise. Ask students to work individually during independent study to:

1. List software companies and third-party providers that will be used in their studies and/or research.
2. Consider the privacy issues that are pertinent to each company/provider that has been identified.
3. Give examples of ways that privacy information can be accessed and evaluated.
4. Develop a checklist of action that they, personally, need to take to identify and evaluate privacy policies of software companies and third-party providers that they intend to use in their studies/research.

If you think that it will be useful for your students, ask them to upload, share and discuss their work with their peers. If you choose to make this an assessed piece of work, provide assessment criteria and a submission deadline.

Key issues

There are a wide variety of software companies and third-party providers that can be listed: these tend to depend on discipline, level of study, research topic, research methods and stage of research. Examples include companies or organizations that provide:

- access to the internet (internet service providers, internet browsers and search engines: specific companies or products might be mentioned);
- information retrieval tools to search documents, files, databases, digital libraries, digital repositories and digital archives;
- online collaboration tools such as file sharing and management (cloud-based file syncing and sharing services, peer-to-peer file sharing and web-based hyperlinked documents) and collaborative learning environments such as globally networked learning environments, wikis, online study groups and online reading groups;
- computer-mediated communication technology for online research, such as synchronous interviews that take place in real-time by video, webcam, text or instant messaging and asynchronous interviews over a period of time such as email, pre-recorded video, microblogs, blogs, wikis or discussion boards (specific platforms and tools might be mentioned);
- computer-assisted qualitative data analysis software, including NVivo, ATLAS.ti, MAXQDA, ANTHROPAC, hyperRESEARCH, QDA Miner, Qualrus and Quirkos (students often mention names of packages because they do not know the names of companies, especially if software is open source: this is not a problem as companies or developers can be researched later, if required);
- primary and secondary sources of data (census data, government databases, data from clinical trials, personal documents, raw statistical data, published results from research studies: students might mention specific creators, developers or researchers);
- organic or found sources of data, which have not been created for research purposes (social media, social networks, administrative data and business data: students might mention platforms and/or tools);
- tools for computer models and simulation (process mapping, discreet event simulation, linear static analyses, modal analysis and 3D model building, for example);
- data collection, conversion, storage, sharing, transferring and preservation tools or software;
- location tracking and location awareness data (real-time location systems embedded into mobile phones or navigation systems; patient tracking and healthcare monitors and devices; location-based services; smart home or smart office technology; and camera memory cards that tag the location of a picture, for example: students might mention tools, platforms, brands and companies).

Once students have identified relevant companies and providers, they can go on to think about privacy issues relevant to them. These can include keeping personal and/or research data safe and secure (Activity 85); protecting against hacking, theft or insertion of rogue data (Activity 86) and addressing issues of anonymity and confidentiality (Activities 9, 62 and 79). Examples of methods that can be used to access and evaluate privacy information include:

- identify parent company or third-party provider, owner, creator, developer or researcher;
- search company or third-party provider websites for privacy information;
- contact companies or providers direct to ask for privacy information;
- find examples of best practice or comprehensive privacy policies to compare and contrast or find privacy polices of a trusted organization to compare and contrast;
- consult the university privacy policy for guidance;
- carry out a privacy risk assessment;
- compare the company/provider policy against what researchers are required to do;
- seek advice from supervisors or personal tutors, if in doubt.

Activity 50

→ Related activities

Activity 9: Discussing privacy and confidentiality in the research context

Activity 31: Identifying and complying with local, regional and national law

Activity 47: Evaluating compliance of software companies and third-party providers

Activity 85: Keeping research data protected and secure

Activity 86: Protecting research data against hacking, theft, interception or insertion of rogue data

→ Preparatory reading

Educators: Garfinkel (2018) provides useful preparatory reading.

Students: None required.

→ Useful resources

The Global Privacy Assembly 'seeks to provide leadership at international level in data protection and privacy'. The website contains useful news, events and resources for educators and researchers interested in data protection and privacy: https://globalprivacyassembly.org [accessed 28 June 2021].

The Data Ethics Framework in the UK 'is a set of principles to guide the design of appropriate data use in the public sector': www.gov.uk/government/publications/data-ethics-framework [accessed 28 June 2021].

The Information Commissioner's Office (ICO) in the UK provides useful information, guidance and templates for producing a privacy notice: https://ico.org.uk/for-organisations/make-your-own-privacy-notice [accessed 30 June 2021].

Garfinkel, S.L. (2018) 'Privacy and security concerns when social scientists work with administrative and operational data', Annals of the American Academy of Political and Social Science, 675 (1): 83-101, first published 21 December 2017, doi: 10.1177/0002716217737267.

Greene, D. and Shilton, K. (2018) 'Platform privacies: Governance, collaboration, and the different meanings of "privacy" in iOS and Android development', New Media & Society, 20 (4): 1640-57, first published 27 April 2017, doi: 10.1177/1461444817702397.

O'Brien, J., Roller, S. and Lampley, S. (2017) 'LearningPad conundrum: The perils of using third-party software and student privacy', Journal of Cases in Educational Leadership, 20 (4): 17-26, first published 30 October 2017, doi: 10.1177/1555458917690191.

Ostherr, K., Borodina, S., Bracken, R.C., Lotterman, C., Storer, E. and Williams, B. (2017) 'Trust and privacy in the context of user-generated health data', Big Data & Society, first published 17 April 2017, doi: 10.1177/2053951717704673.

Sophus Lai, S. and Flensburg, S. (2020) 'A proxy for privacy uncovering the surveillance ecology of mobile apps', Big Data & Society, first published 16 July 2020, doi: 10.1177/2053951720942543.

Activity 50

Activity · · · · · · · · · · · → 51

Assessing the Neutrality of Online Platforms, Tools and Data

The activity

Ask your students to find one online platform, tool or source of data (or dataset) that they consider to be neutral, and one online platform, tool or source of data (or dataset) that they consider to be non-neutral. Once they have done this, they need to provide a summary of no more than 200 words for each of their choices that explains why they believe this platform, tool or data source to be neutral or non-neutral. Ask them to work on this task during independent study. Once they have made their choices and produced their summaries, these should be posted to the VLE-hosted discussion board or forum that you have set up for this purpose (Blackboard Discussion Board or Forum in Moodle, for example). Ensure that all students know where to find the discussions and know how to access them. Clear instructions and guidance are provided by your university if you are new to this type of activity. Ask students to read the posts made by their peers, and encourage discussion on the issues raised.

   This activity can be run as an in-class activity, if you prefer. Each student should be given a few minutes to present their choices and summaries, with 20 minutes for a class discussion to talk about the issues raised. If you have a large number of students and a short amount of contact time, ask students to complete this activity in pairs or in small groups.

Key issues

Students can choose any online platform, tool or data source they wish: the instructions in this activity are deliberately vague as this tends to lead to wider coverage. However, if you feel that your students need a little more guidance you can be more specific. For example, you could ask them to consider datasets that are relevant to their subject of study or to their research, or you could specify the type of online tool (search engines, for example: see Activity 52: Assessing bias in search tools).

An interesting outcome from this activity is that, on occasions, the same tool or data can appear in both the neutral and non-neutral category. This can lead to an interesting and productive discussion, in which students often have to think more deeply, ask further questions and engage in constructive dialogue with their peers and educator.

Examples of tools and data (along with a summary of some reasons) that have been discussed by students in this activity are listed below. As you will see, several are open to debate about placement and reasoning, and some reasons for placement are contradictory: these provide useful points for discussion.

- Suggestions for neutral:
  - Scopus:
    - open and transparent;
    - has an independent and international selection and advisory board of experts;
    - multidisciplinary.
  - Web of Science:
    - comprehensive and accessible;
    - covers multiple academic disciplines;
    - indexes peer-reviewed journals.
  - Zotero:
    - free and open source;
    - won awards;
    - highlights retracted articles and warns against citing them.
  - RefWorks:
    - commercial product aimed at universities and libraries;
    - comprehensive coverage;
    - ease of use.
  - Office for National Statistics online data in the UK (and equivalent in other countries):
    - statistics are independent of Government;
    - research methods are sound;

    - makes statistics available to the public.
  - UK Data Service (and international equivalents):
    - provides wide range of data;
    - ease of access: makes data discoverable;
    - emphasis on integrity.
- Suggestions for non-neutral:
  - Google search:
    - problems with the way machine learning creates conceptual connections;
    - issues surrounding confirmation bias;
    - influence of paid advertising;
    - dominance of wealthy people and nations;
    - influence of search engine optimization (SEO).
  - Google Scholar:
    - ranking algorithm is based on high citations: people cite papers that appear at the top and results are skewed;
    - includes predatory journals.
  - Facebook (see Mukerjee, 2016):
    - fake news;
    - personal and political agendas;
    - privacy issues;
    - tax avoidance.

As you can see from this list, some of the topics raised in this activity are similar to, or the same as, those raised in Activity 48: Assessing the reliability of digital tools and software, and Activity 52: Assessing bias in search tools. Therefore, choose the most appropriate of the three activities for your students or combine them, if you have the time available.

Cautionary note

Monitor posts and discussions: if the situation described above does occur (some tools or data are seen to be both neutral and non-neutral) it can lead to arguments. Ensure that these do not get out of hand. It is also important to ensure that this activity takes place on an internal, restricted space: students can highlight actual or perceived problems with large companies (Google and Facebook, for example) that are best discussed internally.

Activity 51

→ Related activities

Activity 48: Assessing the reliability of digital tools and software

Activity 52: Assessing bias in search tools

Activity 53: Overcoming problems with weak, restricted, non-existent or invisible data systems

Activity 72: Assessing ethical issues in data analytics

Activity 78: Assessing the neutrality of raw data

→ Preparatory reading

Educators: All the resources listed below provide useful preparatory reading.

Students: None required. Students will find their own resources for this activity.

→ Useful resources

Bogers, L., Niederer, S., Bardelli, F. and De Gaetano, C. (2020) 'Confronting bias in the online representation of pregnancy', *Convergence*, 26 (5–6): 1037–59, doi: 10.1177/1354856520938606.

Broussard, M. (2019) *Artificial Unintelligence: How Computers Misunderstand the World*. Cambridge, MA: MIT Press.

Criado Perez, C. (2020) *Invisible Women: Exposing Data Bias in a World Designed for Men*. London: Vintage.

Miorandi, D., Carreras, I., Gregori, E., Graham, I. and Stewart, J. (2013) 'Measuring net neutrality in mobile Internet: Towards a crowdsensing-based citizen observatory', *2013 IEEE International Conference on Communications Workshops (ICC)*, Budapest, Hungary, 2013, pp. 199–203, doi: 10.1109/ICCW.2013.6649228.

Mukerjee, S. (2016) 'Net neutrality, Facebook, and India's battle to #SaveTheInternet', *Communication and the Public*, 1 (3): 356–61, first published 22 August 2016, doi: 10.1177/2057047316665850.

O'Neil, C. (2017) *Weapons of Math Destruction: How Big Data Increases Inequality and Threatens Democracy*. London: Penguin.

Prates, M.O.R., Avelar, P.H. and Lamb, L.C. (2020) 'Assessing gender bias in machine translation: A case study with Google Translate', *Neural Computing and Applications*, 32: 6363–81, doi: 10.1007/s00521-019-04144-6.

Turner Lee, N. (2018) 'Detecting racial bias in algorithms and machine learning', *Journal of Information, Communication and Ethics in Society*, 6 (3): 252–60, published 13 August 2018, doi: 10.1108/JICES-06-2018-0056.

Activity 51

Activity · · · · · · · · · · · · · → 52

Assessing Bias in Search Tools

ACTIVITY 52: EDUCATOR NOTES

Purpose: This activity enables students to assess bias in search tools by asking them, in groups, to teach about these issues. One group is to plan a session to teach their peers, another to teach school pupils aged 14-16 and another to teach school pupils aged 8-10. When a particular group is teaching, their peers role-play the learners. This activity encourages students to think deeply about bias in search tools and work out how to communicate this to their specific learners.

Type: Peer-to-peer teaching in-class.

Alternative type(s): Peer-to-peer teaching online.

Level: Elementary, intermediate and advanced.

Duration: Students will spend a few hours during independent study researching, producing and practising their teaching session. One to two hours of contact time for students to teach their sessions will be required, depending on the number of students in your cohort. If the online option is chosen, students will spend a few hours during independent study researching, preparing, producing and uploading their teaching session. Educators will spend one or two hours setting up a suitable tool and monitoring uploaded teaching sessions and comments.

Equipment/materials: Students can use any presentation equipment they choose and this should be made available for their use. A suitable tool and the required student access will be required, if the online option is chosen.

Learning outcome: By the end of this activity, students will be able to explain how to assess bias in a variety of search tools.

The activity

A week before your next contact session, divide your students into three groups and give each group one of the Student Handouts (there are three Handouts: each one is slightly different). If you have a large number of students in your cohort, you can divide them into six groups and double-up with the Handouts. Students are to produce a 10-15-minute teaching session that explains how to assess bias in a variety of search tools. Each group has a different cohort to teach: peers (group 1), school pupils aged 14-16 (group 2) and school pupils aged 8-10 (group 3). Presentation equipment and materials should be made available for their use, if required.

When you next meet, introduce each group and ask each one to deliver their teaching session, in turn. Instruct other students to play the relevant learner role for each session (peers, school pupils aged 14-16 and school pupils aged 8-10) when you introduce each group. Allocate five minutes at the end of each session for students, in their role, to ask questions and receive answers. Conclude the session with a summary of the main points raised.

You can ask students to produce and upload a digital teaching session (video or text-based) if contact time is unavailable. Adapt the Student Handouts slightly to include information about where and how to upload sessions. Give a deadline by which time sessions should be uploaded, viewed and commented on. Monitor teaching sessions, posts and comments to ensure that information is correct, supportive and respectful.

Key issues

This activity enables students to learn about the topic through teaching others. Three different age groups are provided because it adds interest and encourages students to think about the different types and levels of searches undertaken, why and for what purpose. Aiming at different ages encourages students to explore a variety of ways to impart information (animations and comic strips for younger children and complex discussion on search engine bias, retrievability bias, race bias, gender bias and confirmation bias for university students, for example).

Some of the topics raised in this activity are similar to, or the same as, those raised in Activity 48: Assessing the reliability of digital tools and software, and Activity 51: Assessing the neutrality of online platforms, tools and data. Therefore, choose the most appropriate of the three activities for your students or combine them, if you have the time available.

→ Related activities

Activity 48: Assessing the reliability of digital tools and software

Activity 51: Assessing the neutrality of online platforms, tools and data

Activity 53: Overcoming problems with weak, restricted, non-existent or invisible data systems

→ Preparatory reading

Educators: Halavais (2018) and Noble (2018) provide interesting preparatory reading for educators.

Students: None required. Students will find their own resources for this activity.

→ Useful resources

Gregory, K.M., Cousijn, H., Groth, P., Scharnhorst, A. and Wyatt, S. (2020) 'Understanding data search as a socio-technical practice', *Journal of Information Science*, 46 (4): 459-75, first published 2 April 2019, doi: 10.1177/0165551519837182.

Halavais, A. (2018) *Search Engine Society*, 2nd edition. Cambridge: Polity Press.

Melucci, M. (2016) 'Impact of query sample selection bias on information retrieval system ranking', *2016 IEEE International Conference on Data Science and Advanced Analytics*, published online 26 December 2016, doi: 10.1109/DSAA.2016.43.

Noble, S.U. (2018) *Algorithms of Oppression: How Search Engines Reinforce Racism*. New York, NY: New York University Press.

Otterbacher, J. (2018) 'Addressing social bias in information retrieval'. In P. Bellot et al. (eds), *Experimental IR Meets Multilinguality, Multimodality, and Interaction*, CLEF 2018, Lecture Notes in Computer Science, 11018. Cham: Springer.

Sadeghi, M. and Vegas, J. (2017) 'How well does Google work with Persian documents?', *Journal of Information Science*, 43 (3): 316-27, first published March 23, 2016, doi: 10.1177/0165551516640437.

Samar, T., Traub, M., van Ossenbruggen, J., Hardman, L. and de Vries, A. (2018) 'Quantifying retrieval bias in Web archive search', *International Journal on Digital Libraries*, 19 (1): 57-75, published online 18 April 2017, doi: 10.1007/s00799-017-0215-9.

Zavadski, A. and Toepfl, F. (2019) 'Querying the Internet as a mnemonic practice: How search engines mediate four types of past events in Russia', *Media, Culture & Society*, 41 (1): 21-37, doi: 10.1177/0163443718764565.

Activity 52

Activity • • • • • • • • • • → 52

Assessing Bias in Search Tools

STUDENT HANDOUT 1

This activity is called 'Assessing bias in search tools'. Work with your group members to produce a 10- to 15-minute teaching session that explains how to assess bias in search tools. Your teaching session is aimed at your peers, so make sure that it is pitched at the right level. Think about what search tools your peers might use for their coursework and research. Consider both online and offline search tools if you think these are relevant to your peers, and think about search tools that are used for searching for different types of information and objects: documents, images, video, audio, maps and photos, for example.

The content, structure and style of your teaching session is a group choice. You can also choose to use any materials and equipment that you deem appropriate. Try to make your teaching session informative, interesting, creative and memorable, enabling you and your peers to achieve the learning outcome given below.

You will be required to present your teaching session to your peers when we next meet, so if you have any specific requirements for materials and equipment, please get in touch with me beforehand. Your peers will listen to your teaching session and will be able to ask questions at the end, so think about questions that might be asked, and research and prepare potential answers.

Learning outcome: By the end of this activity, you will be able to explain how to assess bias in a variety of search tools.

Activity • • • • • • • • • • → 52

Assessing Bias in Search Tools

STUDENT HANDOUT 2

This activity is called 'Assessing bias in search tools'. Work with your group members to produce a 10- to 15-minute teaching session that explains how to assess bias in search tools. Your teaching session is aimed at school pupils aged 14–16, so make sure that it is pitched at the right level. Think about what search tools this age group might use for their coursework and for their life outside school. Consider both online and offline search tools if you think these are relevant to your learners, and think about search tools that are used for searching for different types of information and objects: documents, news items, images, video, audio, games and photos, for example.

The content, structure and style of your teaching session is a group choice. You can also choose to use any materials and equipment that you deem appropriate. Try to make your teaching session informative, interesting, creative and memorable.

You will be required to present your teaching session to your peers when we next meet, so if you have any specific requirements for materials and equipment, please get in touch with me beforehand. Your peers will be asked to play the role of school pupils within this age group: they will listen to your session and then be encouraged to ask questions, in their role. Think about questions that might be asked, and research and prepare potential answers.

Learning outcome: By the end of this activity, you will be able to explain how to assess bias in a variety of search tools.

Activity • • • • • • • • • • → 52

Assessing Bias in Search Tools

STUDENT HANDOUT 3

This activity is called 'Assessing bias in search tools'. Work with your group members to produce a 10- to 15-minute teaching session that explains how to assess bias in search tools. Your teaching session is aimed at school pupils aged 8–10, so make sure that it is pitched at the right level. Think about what search tools this age group might use for their school work and for their life outside school. Consider both online and offline search tools if you think these are relevant to your learners, and think about search tools that are used for searching for different types of information or activities that are relevant to this age group.

The content, structure and style of your teaching session is a group choice. You can also choose to use any materials and equipment that you deem appropriate. Try to make your teaching session informative, interesting, creative and memorable.

You will be required to present your teaching session to your peers when we next meet, so if you have any specific requirements for materials and equipment, please get in touch with me beforehand. Your peers will be asked to play the role of school pupils within this age group: they will listen to your session and then be encouraged to ask questions, in their role. Think about questions that might be asked, and research and prepare potential answers.

Learning outcome: By the end of this activity, you will be able to explain how to assess bias in a variety of search tools.

Activity • • • • • • • • • • → 53

Overcoming Problems with Weak, Restricted, Non-Existent or Invisible Data Systems

The activity

Divide your students into groups of three to five people and give them a copy of the Student Handout. This asks them to craft a story that illustrates problems, difficulties or dilemmas associated with studying or researching communities or nations that have weak, restricted, non-existent or invisible data systems, before going on to provide possible solutions. Students can use any equipment, materials or props for their story, and can choose their own style, structure and content. They are encouraged to make sure that their story is entertaining, creative and enables their peers to meet the learning outcome given above.

When you next meet, ask each group, in turn, to tell their story. Request that students keep questions or comments until the end, until all stories have been told. Then lead a class discussion on the issues raised: students can ask general questions or questions related to a particular story, and discuss relevant problems, dilemmas and solutions. Conclude with a summary of the pertinent points.

This activity can be run online, if you prefer (adapt the Student Handout accordingly). Explain that students can use any technology or features that they wish, to entertain and bring their digital story to life (graphics, video, audio and photography, for example). Set up a suitable asynchronous tool for students to upload their stories. Give a deadline by which time stories should be uploaded and ask students to spend some time reading, and commenting on, each story, again giving a deadline for the completion of this task. Read each story and monitor the online discussion to ensure that information is correct, supportive and encouraging, and to ensure that students are able to learn from the stories presented.

Key issues

This activity tends to be enjoyable and memorable: students think about the best way to introduce problems, difficulties, dilemmas and solutions, while working out the most creative way to tell a story. Stories can be told in a number of different ways, including life histories, anecdotes, case studies, fiction, myth, reflective accounts, scenarios and personal examples from experience. Some students choose to use real examples from the research literature (invisibility in social media data or weak health data in poorer nations, for example), whereas others decide to use their imagination to create memorable stories (beings from another world expressing surprise at data inequality and invisible mythical creatures that no one cares about, for example). They also choose a wide variety of equipment, materials and props to bring their story to life. If the digital storytelling option is chosen, students have the opportunity to produce interactive and meaningful stories, using a wide variety of features such as narration, title screens, photography, music, text, graphics and sound effects.

   Not all students feel comfortable telling a story. This activity has been designed as a group activity because it enables students to choose who tells the story and who works on other aspects, such as the idea, research, development and required equipment, materials or props. Students are also able to pool strengths and bounce ideas off each other. Producing a story in a group can help students to understand others, help group cohesion, aid collaborative learning and enhance learning among group members. They are also able to help and support each other with technological requirements.

→ Related activities

Activity 6: Aligning with the UN's Sustainable Development Goals

Activity 45: Designing inclusive data systems

Activity 46: Reclaiming datasets for social justice

Activity 54: Understanding problems associated with unequal access to data

Activity 55: Assessing the ethical implications of ownership and use of digital technology

Activity 72: Assessing ethical issues in data analytics

→ Preparatory reading

Educators: If you are new to using storytelling in your teaching, Alterio and McDrury (2003) and Lambert and Hessler (2018) provide useful preparatory reading. A useful activity for educators who are interested in using storytelling with their students is Activity 46: Learning through storytelling, in Dawson (2019: 131-3).

Students: None required. Students will find their own resources for this activity.

→ Useful resources

Alterio, M. and McDrury, J. (2003) *Learning Through Storytelling in Higher Education: Using Reflection and Experience to Improve Learning*. London: Routledge.

Boccia Artieri, G., Brilli, S. and Zurovac, E. (2021) 'Below the radar: Private groups, locked platforms, and ephemeral content – introduction to the special issue', *Social Media + Society*, first published 19 January 2021, doi: 10.1177/2056305121988930.

Dawson, C. (2019) *100 Activities for Teaching Study Skills*. London: Sage.

Hoxha, K., Hung, Y.W., Irwin, B.R. and Grépin, K.A. (2020) 'Understanding the challenges associated with the use of data from routine health information systems in low- and middle-income countries: A systematic review', *Health Information Management Journal*, first published 30 June 2020, doi: 10.1177/1833358320928729.

Lambert, J. and Hessler, B. (2018) *Digital Storytelling: Capturing Lives, Creating Community*, 5th edition. New York, NY: Routledge.

Activity 53

Milan, S. and Treré, E. (2020) 'The rise of the data poor: The COVID-19 pandemic seen from the margins', *Social Media + Society*, first published 11 August 2020, doi: 10.1177/2056305120948233.

Neumayer, C., Rossi, L. and Struthers, D.M. (2021) 'Invisible data: A framework for understanding visibility processes in social media data', *Social Media + Society*, first published 21 January 2021, doi: 10.1177/2056305120984472.

Ohler, J. (2013) *Digital Storytelling in the Classroom: New Media Pathways to Literacy, Learning, and Creativity*, 2nd edition. Thousand Oaks, CA: Corwin.

Tromble, R. (2021) 'Where have all the data gone? A critical reflection on academic digital research in the post-API age', *Social Media + Society*, first published 19 January 2021, doi: 10.1177/2056305121988929.

Examples of digital stories can be found at www.storycenter.org/stories [accessed 29 September 2021].

Activity 53

Activity • • • • • • • • • • • → 53

Overcoming Problems with Weak, Restricted, Non-Existent or Invisible Data Systems

STUDENT HANDOUT

This activity is about overcoming problems with weak, restricted, non-existent or invisible data systems. For this activity I would like you, with your group members, to craft a story that illustrates problems, difficulties or dilemmas associated with studying or researching communities or nations that have weak, restricted, non-existent or invisible data systems. Your story should then go on to provide possible solutions to the issues you have identified. The content, style and structure of your story is a group choice and you can use any materials, equipment and props that you wish. The story can be based on real-life examples or it can be imaginary. You will be listening to a few stories when we meet, so try to make yours interesting, entertaining, creative and memorable.

When you craft your story, consider the following questions:

1. What is the key point, idea or lesson you want to transmit?
2. What do you want others to learn from your story?
3. How are you going to ensure that others learn from your story?

4. Will your story stimulate thought and reflection? Will it have emotional and intellectual impact on your peers?
5. Will your story enable your peers to achieve the learning outcome given below?

When we next meet, each group will have 10 minutes to tell their story. We will hear each story, one after the other. Then we will hold a class discussion: you will have the opportunity to ask general questions about the topic, ask specific questions about a particular story and clarify pertinent issues.

Learning outcome: By the end of this activity, you will be able to identify, and provide solutions to, problems that can occur when studying or researching communities or nations that have weak, restricted, non-existent or invisible data systems.

Activity · · · · · · · · · · · → 54

Understanding Problems Associated with Unequal Access to Data

The activity

Divide your students into small groups: the number of groups depends on the size of your cohort and the amount of contact time you have available. Ideally, each group will need up to 10 minutes for their presentation, with a further five minutes for discussion after each presentation. Give each group a copy of the Student Handout. This describes how this activity is old school, or retro, asking students to produce a paper collage that illustrates (or highlights) problems associated with unequal access to data. Their collage can relate specifically to research practice, or it can take a more general approach.

When you meet, ask each group to present their collage, in turn, explaining why items have been included, what they represent and how they help to illustrate problems associated with unequal access to data. Allocate up to 10 minutes for each presentation with a further five minutes for discussion and questions. Conclude the session with a discussion about the implications of unequal access to data for research practice.

This session works best when students are asked to produce a paper collage. However, if this is not possible, ask students to use a suitable collage maker tool to produce a digital collage that can be presented and discussed online (Canva or PicCollage, for example). Set up a suitable asynchronous tool to host collages and discussion, and ensure that all students have access details. Adapt the Student Handout and provide a deadline by which time all collages should be presented and discussed.

Key issues

This activity provides an entertaining and creative way for students to think about problems associated with unequal access to data. Paper collages are memorable, both in the production stage and when they are presented to peers. Students enjoy this activity, although they are sometimes surprised and consider it to be very old-fashioned (this is why this point is emphasized in the Student Handout).

Collages cover a number of issues and styles. In one session, for example, one group concentrated on global distribution and access to data, illustrating, with news headlines and images of poverty, how poorer nations and people are disadvantaged by difficulties accessing medical and health data. Another group considered how unequal access to data can lead to discrimination through the use of photos and a collage of words (or a word cloud). Another group considered the digital divide, placing images of cutting-edge technology on one side of a ravine with images of cave people, clubs and wheels on the other: it made students laugh, but the presentation raised some interesting and valid points. Note here that the line between a collage and infographic might seem a little blurred, but that is not important: the focus should, instead, be on the ideas presented.

→ Related activities

Activity 6: Aligning with the UN's Sustainable Development Goals

Activity 7: Promoting social good through research practice

Activity 45: Designing inclusive data systems

Activity 46: Reclaiming datasets for social justice

→ Preparatory reading

Educators: If you are new to using collages for teaching and research you might find Lahman et al. (2020) interesting.

Students: None required. Students will find their own resources for this activity.

→ Useful resources

Büchi, M., Just, N. and Latzer, M. (2016) 'Modeling the second-level digital divide: A five-country study of social differences in Internet use', *New Media & Society*, 18 (11): 2703-22, first published 9 September 2015, doi: 10.1177/1461444815604154.

Hoxha, K., Hung, Y.W., Irwin, B.R. and Grépin, K.A. (2020) 'Understanding the challenges associated with the use of data from routine health information systems in low- and middle-income countries: A systematic review', *Health Information Management Journal*, first published 30 June 2020, doi: 10.1177/1833358320928729.

Lahman, M.K.E., Taylor, C.M., Beddes, L.A., Blount, I.D., Bontempo, K.A., Coon, J.D., Fernandez, C. and Motter, B. (2020) 'Research falling out of colorful pages onto paper: Collage inquiry', *Qualitative Inquiry*, 26 (3-4): 262-70, first published 2 April 2019, doi: 10.1177/1077800418810721.

Ragnedda, M. and Muschert, G.W. (eds) (2019) *Theorizing Digital Divides*. Abingdon: Routledge.

Ragnedda, M. (2017) *The Third Digital Divide: A Weberian Approach to Digital Inequalities*. Abingdon: Routledge.

Scheerder, A.J., van Deursen, A.J. and van Dijk, J.A. (2019) 'Internet use in the home: Digital inequality from a domestication perspective', *New Media & Society*, 21 (10): 2099-118, first published 2 May 2019, doi: 10.1177/1461444819844299.

van Deursen, A.J. and van Dijk, J.A. (2019) 'The first-level digital divide shifts from inequalities in physical access to inequalities in material access', *New Media & Society*, 21 (2): 354-75, first published 7 September 2018, doi: 10.1177/1461444818797082.

The Organisation for Economic Co-operation and Development's (OECD) most recent analysis of the Digital Economy illustrates how digital transformation is affecting economies and societies. The *OECD Digital Economy Outlook 2020* can be found in the OECD library: www.oecd-ilibrary.org [accessed 29 September 2021].

A number of the UN's Sustainable Development Goals address problems associated with unequal access to data: https://sdgs.un.org/goals [accessed 29 September 2021]. See Activity 6 for more information on these goals.

Other useful references relating to technology ownership and use, and the digital divide, can be found in Activity 55: Assessing the ethical implications of ownership and use of digital technology.

Activity 54

Activity · · · · · · · · · · → 54

Understanding Problems Associated with Unequal Access to Data

STUDENT HANDOUT

This activity is called 'Understanding problems associated with unequal access to data'. For this activity, we're going old school, or perhaps you prefer the term 'retro'. You're going to channel your inner child to create an old-fashioned, paper collage (yes, a collage: a collection or combination of various things such as photos, fabric and news items) that illustrates, or highlights, problems associated with unequal access to data. For the purposes of this activity, we will use a broad definition of data: information, such as facts, statistics, figures, measurements, text, characters, symbols, images, objects or artefacts that are used for reasoning, analysis, discussion, reference, action and/or development. Your collage can relate specifically to research practice, or it can take a more general approach to aspects related to unequal access to data.

Work with your group members to create your collage. No digital collage makers allowed, just old-fashioned paper and glue: I can provide these for you, if you need them. When we next meet, you will be asked to present your collage to your peers, explaining why items have been included, what they represent and how they help to illustrate problems associated with unequal access to data. You will be given up to 10 minutes to present your collage, with a further few minutes for your peers to ask questions. Be creative and have fun!

Learning outcome: By the end of this activity, you will be able to identify and discuss problems associated with unequal access to data, and highlight the implications for research practice.

Activity • • • • • • • • • • • • → 55

Assessing the Ethical Implications of Ownership and Use of Digital Technology

The activity

Divide your students into small groups (or pairs or individuals, depending on the size of your student cohort: ideally 8–10 scenarios are good numbers for this activity). Give each group a copy of the Student Handout and ask that they work on the task during independent study ready for when you next meet. They are to develop two scenarios, each with three discussion points or questions, which will enable them and their peers to identify and assess the ethical implications of ownership and use of digital technology. They are asked to develop two scenarios even though they might only present one during the session: this provides an alternative choice if another group has presented a similar scenario, and it enables you to have more scenarios available if your students work through them more quickly than expected.

When you next meet, ask one group to present one of their scenarios. Spend five minutes discussing the scenario and discussion points/questions, then move on to the next group and so on, until all groups have presented one scenario. If a particular scenario is generating useful and interesting discussion, more time can be spent on the discussion: if it is not, less time can be spent. If your students are studying at intermediate or advanced level and are in the planning stages of their research, spend a few minutes at the end of the session discussing how the issues that have been raised might relate to their research (if this has not been brought up in the discussion).

You can run this activity online if you prefer (the Student Handout will need to be adapted slightly). This can be done synchronously (using a video/web conferencing tool) or asynchronously (using your VLE-hosted discussion board). If the asynchronous option is chosen, give a deadline by which time one scenario from each group should be uploaded and discussed. Monitor discussions to ensure that information is correct and that comments are supportive and constructive. Remove any incorrect posts and explain why this has been done. Provide assessment criteria with the Student Handout if you choose to make this an assessed piece of work.

This activity can also be run as a scenario-based individual exercise if you prefer. Use the scenarios given below, or develop your own, and ask students to work on them during independent study. Provide assessment criteria and a date for submission if you choose to make this an assessed piece of work.

Key issues

There are a number of different scenarios that can be presented in this activity (the topic has been left fairly vague to encourage a diverse range of scenarios, and these tend to vary, depending on discipline, level of study and research approach). Some examples of scenarios are given below and these can be used for a scenario-based individual exercise, if required.

Scenario 1

Smart glasses have been developed, manufactured and sold to a significant proportion of the UK population. People listen to music, take phone calls, make videos and record voices. They wear them travelling to work, at work and when they go out in the evening. The smart glasses are stylish and unobtrusive and customers think they are worth the rather hefty price tag.

1. The user can record and store information about anyone, anywhere at any time, without them knowing. What are the ethical implications of this?
2. Who owns the data that are collected (video and audio recordings, for example)?
3. Are these glasses legal?

Scenario 2

A daughter is worried about her father. She thinks he is developing dementia so convinces him to carry a tracker that sends an alert when her father leaves his home or a specific area.

1. How might this action affect her father's civil liberties?
2. Could this action lead to stigma?
3. Has her father consented to this action (Activity 57)?

Scenario 3

A researcher has decided to use a mobile app for his data collection. He requires participants to use the app to record their activities, while capturing real-time location data from smartphones. He expects participants to use their own devices.

1. What are the implications for location privacy?
2. How might these methods influence who is chosen for the research? What about people who don't have smartphones or don't know how to use them? Will this skew his results?
3. What burdens are placed on participants (financial or time, for example: Activity 66)?

Scenario 4

An organization has been mining data to uncover patterns, relationships and trends within their business. They have been reality mining, using mobile devices, GPS and sensors to provide a picture of what their customer do, where they go and who they communicate with. They will use this information to target customers with specific products and deals.

1. Is this type of reality mining fair? Can it lead to discrimination (Activity 49)?
2. Have people consented to this type of reality mining? Can people opt out (Activity 42)?
3. Can people be recognized from this data? If so, might this cause harm (Activities 62, 79 and 84)?

Scenario 5

A community group has decided to invite members of their community to tell their story of living in the community using digital technology. The stories will be uploaded onto the community website.

1. How can the community group take into account different experiences of storytelling and different experiences and knowledge of digital technology? Might some individuals be excluded?
2. What are the implications for informed consent when someone might tell their story that includes another member of the community who has not given their consent (Activity 42)?
3. How can the community respect privacy and protect privacy, in particular, if they intend to upload the stories onto a website, which can be accessed by anyone?

Activity 55

→ Related activities

Activity 6: Aligning with the UN's Sustainable Development Goals

Activity 45: Designing inclusive data systems

Activity 46: Reclaiming datasets for social justice

Activity 53: Overcoming problems with weak, restricted, non-existent or invisible data systems

Activity 54: Understanding problems associated with unequal access to data

→ Preparatory reading

Educators: Lutz (2019) provides a useful overview.

Students: None required. Students will find their own resources for this activity.

→ Useful resources

Camerini, A.-L., Schulz, P.J. and Jeannet, A.-M. (2018) 'The social inequalities of Internet access, its use, and the impact on children's academic performance: Evidence from a longitudinal study in Switzerland', *New Media & Society*, 20 (7): 2489–508, first published 22 August 2017, doi: 10.1177/1461444817725918.

Goedhart, N.S., Broerse, J.E., Kattouw, R. and Dedding, C. (2019) '"Just having a computer doesn't make sense": The digital divide from the perspective of mothers with a low socio-economic position', *New Media & Society*, 21 (11-12): 2347–65, first published 19 May 2019, doi: 10.1177/1461444819846059.

Helsper, E. (2021) *The Digital Disconnect: The Social Causes and Consequences of Digital Inequalities*. London: Sage.

Keusch, F., Leonard, M.M., Sajons, C. and Steiner, S. (2019) 'Using smartphone technology for research on refugees: Evidence from Germany', *Sociological Methods & Research*, first published 30 May 2019, doi: 10.1177/0049124119852377.

Kudina, O. and Verbeek, P.-P. (2019) 'Ethics from within: Google Glass, the Collingridge dilemma, and the mediated value of privacy', *Science, Technology, & Human Values*, 44 (2): 291–314, first published 21 August 2018, doi: 10.1177/0162243918793711.

Lutz, C. (2019) 'Digital inequalities in the age of artificial intelligence and big data', *Special Issue: Emerging Technologies: Perspectives from Behavioral Scientists*, 1 (2): 141–8, first published 26 April 2019, doi: org/10.1002/hbe2.140.

Mascheroni, G. and Ólafsson, K. (2016) 'The mobile internet: Access, use, opportunities and divides among European children', *New Media & Society*, 18 (8): 1657–79, first published 14 January 2015, doi: 10.1177/1461444814567986.

Tarrant, A. and Hughes, K. (2020) 'The ethics of technology choice: Photovoice methodology with men living in low-income contexts', *Sociological Research Online*, 25 (2): 289–306, first published 12 November 2019, doi: 10.1177/1360780419878714.

Other useful references relating to technology ownership and use, and the digital divide, can be found in Activity 54. Information relating to the ethics of data mining can be found in Activity 49 and information about the ethics of data analytics can be found in Activity 72.

Activity 55

Activity • • • • • • • • • • • → 55

Assessing the Ethical Implications of Ownership and Use of Digital Technology

STUDENT HANDOUT

This activity is about identifying and assessing the ethical implications of ownership and use of digital technology. These implications are wide and varied: they can concern individuals, communities, culture and society. They can involve privacy, rights, consent, discrimination, harm, human dignity, benefits, (dis)advantage, autonomy, security, social (in)justice, (in)equality and balance of power, for example.

Work with your group members during independent study to develop two scenarios that introduce one, two or a number of ethical implications of ownership and use of digital technology. The scenarios can relate to any type of digital technology, including social media, virtual and augmented reality, wearables, mobile apps, gaming, learning platforms, software and hardware, and they can relate to any type of use or ownership. Once you have developed your scenarios, provide three discussion points or questions, relating to your scenarios, that will enable your peers to assess the ethical implications that you have introduced.

Scenarios can be based on real examples, or they can be imagined. Try to make them interesting and creative: ensure that your discussion points or questions relate specifically to your scenario and check that your scenarios and discussion points will enable you and your peers to meet the learning outcome given below.

When we meet, each group will present a scenario. We will work through the discussion points before moving on to a scenario from another group. You have been asked to produce two scenarios even though you may only have time to present one: having two gives your group a choice if you find that a scenario similar to yours has already been presented. It also provides a few more scenarios to discuss if we find that we have time available.

Learning outcome: By the end of this activity, you will be able to identify and discuss various ethical implications of ownership and use of digital technology.

Activity · · · · · · · · · · · → 56

Citing Digital Tools and Software Correctly

The activity

This activity is a simple quiz that provides a number of statements about citing digital tools and software correctly, which students must work through, deciding whether the statements are correct or incorrect. The quiz can be educator-administered in-class, with each answer discussed, or it can be self-administered online, with students reading the correct answer once they have made their choice (or at the end of the quiz). If you choose the online option, use tools such as Quiz in Moodle, Tests, Surveys or Pools in Blackboard or open-source software such as Quiz, Survey, Test (https://qstonline.ca).

Key issues

Statements (along with answers) that can be used in the quiz are given below. Students are to answer correct or incorrect for each statement. A mix of levels and experiences have been included in this quiz: add to, or delete, statements so that they suit your cohort, level of study and country of study. Answers have been produced for general use: they can be modified to provide information specific to your university, if required.

Statement 1: All organizations, universities and university departments in my home country use the same referencing style for digital tools and software.

Answer 1: That is *incorrect*. There are several different referencing styles, all of which have distinct styles for referencing digital tools and software. These include the Modern Languages Association (MLA) style, the American

Psychological Association (APA) style, the Harvard style, the Vancouver style, the Chicago style and the Modern Humanities Research Association (MHRA) style. Organizations, universities and departments within the same university use different styles, so it is important that you find out which style you should use for your assignments, projects, theses and dissertations. Consult your university website, read your university referencing policy and speak to your tutor/supervisor if in doubt.

Statement 2: I do not need to check digital citations produced by referencing (or reference management) software when I produce my reference list and bibliography.

Answer 2: That is *incorrect*. Referencing (or reference management) software makes referencing easier, enabling you to save time and improve accuracy. However, mistakes can be made and digital references might not be cited in the style required at your university. Therefore, all references should be checked for accuracy and to ensure that the correct style is used. Your university will provide information about the software supported (EndNote, Mendeley, Zotero, and Paperpile, for example) and will provide guidance to ensure correct and accurate referencing and management.

Statement 3: I must check licensing terms and conditions on software I use in my research to find out whether I need to acknowledge or cite its use.

Answer 3: That is *correct*. Some software publishers include a clause in their licence or conditions of use that the software must be acknowledged or cited in reference sections or bibliographies of published research. All licences and terms and conditions must be checked when you use the software. In other cases, you might not need to cite software unless it has made a significant or critical contribution to your research (statistical analyses, for example), or it provided something new to your research (modelling and simulation, for example).

Statement 4: Digital object identifiers (DOI) can be used to identify journal articles, research reports and software.

Answer 4: That is *correct*. A DOI name can be assigned to physical, digital or abstract entities, including journal articles, research reports, software and digital tools. It is like a digital fingerprint and can be used to trace the particular entity through its lifespan. The DOI name is a unique number that enables identification of the entity in material form (physical or digital). All DOI names of work that you use in your studies or research must be included in your references using the correct referencing style.

Statement 5: I do not need to reference webpages because they are available online for all to see.

Answer 5: That is *incorrect*. All webpages you use for your research or studies must be referenced. The way in which you do this depends on the referencing style at your university or within your department but, in general, should include author (or organization), year, page title, name of site sponsor (if available), date of access and URL. Remember to record all this information as soon as you access the page so that it is available if you decide to use the work at a later date in your research or studies.

Statement 6: When I access a piece of work through a searchable database, I should include the database name in the reference.

Answer 6: That is *correct*. You might access the piece of work through a searchable database provided by your university, or through one provided online, for example. Always include the name of the database when you reference the piece of work, following the referencing style required at your university or in your department.

Statement 7: I don't need to cite work that is open access.

Answer 7: That is *incorrect*. All work you use in your studies or research must be cited, however it is published. Open access enables work to be made available, free of charge, to anyone who wishes to access it. However, the work must still be cited if it is used: suggested citation will be published with the work and you should ensure that you follow your university referencing policy when citing (some universities acknowledge that students may need to apply the refencing style of a particular journal and this will be made clear in the university refencing policy).

Statement 8: I don't need to cite the source of code when I modify it for my research.

Answer 8: This is *incorrect*. The source of any code you use must be cited in the same way that you cite sources when writing a paper. This must be done when you copy any code directly from another source and when you modify or paraphrase code that you have copied from an external source. When doing this, you should cite the URL and date of retrieval and use words such as 'adapted from' or 'based on': your university will provide specific guidelines about the words to use.

Statement 9: I must cite code I use from open-source software.

Answer 9: That is *correct*. When using code from open-source software, you must acknowledge the source. You must also take note of the Open Source licence and ensure that you comply with all terms. Licences can be obtained when you download the software or can be found on the website of the Open Source Initiative. When citing, you will need to include author, date of retrieval and URL, in line with your university's referencing policy.

Activity 56

Statement 10: When citing data and statistical tables, I only need to cite the author, date accessed and URL.

Answer 10: That is *incorrect*. You will need to cite the author or creator, date of publication, title or description, publisher and DOI or URL. You will also need to cite the edition or version, the data accessed online and a description of the format (this might differ slightly, depending on the referencing style used by your university and/or department).

Statement 11: If I produce a journal paper for a particular journal, I should automatically follow the citation style of my university (for both digital and non-digital works).

Answer 11: This is *incorrect*. You must always check first with the journal editor to find out their preferred style. You might be able to use the same style as you have used at your university, but this is not automatic: you must check first.

Statement 12: I can use statistical data for my research that we generated in a research group for another course, without the need for citation because I was involved in producing the data.

Answer 12: This is *incorrect*. You must check that you are able to use the data, first with the research team and with the tutor on that particular course (if possible: if not, check relevant university guidelines or policy, including that relating to intellectual property). If you are given permission to use the data, it must be cited correctly, using the correct referencing style of your department/university.

→ Related activities

Activity 23: Avoiding plagiarism

Activity 99: Communicating and reporting ethically

→ Preparatory reading

Educators: Read your university guidelines on citing digital tools and software, if you have not already done so, and become familiar with your university's referencing policy.

Students: The following can be recommended to students, if required:

Neville, C. (2016) *The Complete Guide to Referencing and Avoiding Plagiarism*, 3rd edition. Maidenhead: Open University Press.
Pears, R. and Shields, G. (2019) *Cite Them Right: The Essential Referencing Guide*, 11th edition. Basingstoke: Macmillan.
Williams, K. and Davis, M. (2017) *Referencing and Understanding Plagiarism*, 2nd edition. Basingstoke: Palgrave.

→ Useful resources

Information about how to cite and describe software can be obtained from the Software Sustainability Institute: www.software.ac.uk/how-cite-software [accessed 5 June 2021].

Cousijn, H. et al. (2018) 'A data citation roadmap for scientific publishers', *Scientific Data*, 5: 180259, published online 20 November 2018, doi: 10.1038/sdata.2018.259.
Fazilatfar, A.M., Elhambakhsh, S.E. and Allami, H. (2018) 'An investigation of the effects of citation instruction to avoid plagiarism in EFL academic writing assignments', *SAGE Open*, first published 11 April 2018, doi: 10.1177/2158244018769958.
Nilashi, M., Dalvi, M., Ibrahim, O., Zamani, M. and Ramayah, T. (2019) 'An interpretive structural modelling of the features influencing researchers' selection of reference management software', *Journal of Librarianship and Information Science*, 51 (1): 34–46, first published 18 September 2016, doi: 10.1177/0961000616668961.
Nitsos, I., Malliari, A. and Chamouroudi, R. (2021) 'Use of reference management software among postgraduate students in Greece', *Journal of Librarianship and Information Science*, first published 2 March 2021, doi: 10.1177/0961000621996413.
Soito, L. and Hwang, L.J. (2016) 'Citations for software: Providing identification, access and recognition for research software', *International Journal of Digital Curation*, 11 (2): 48–63, published online 4 July 2017, doi: 10.2218/ijdc.v11i2.390.

Activity 56

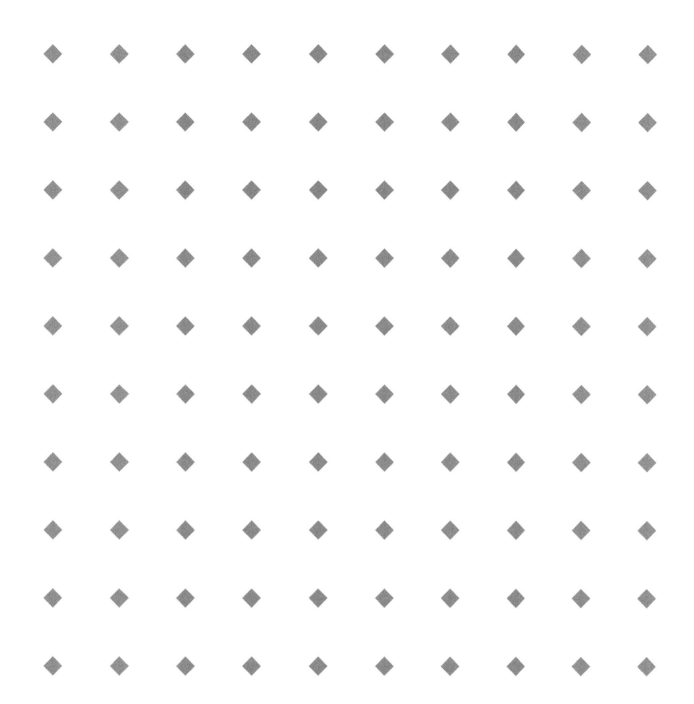

Section 5 Data Collection

Activity • • • • • • • • • • • → 57

Seeking Informed Consent

The activity

This activity can be run in several ways, depending on how much coverage you wish to give to this topic and the time that you have available.

1. Ask students to read your university's informed consent guidance, procedures, templates and forms. Once they have done this, they should think about useful questions they want answered about obtaining informed consent: these can be general questions about obtaining informed consent or questions related specifically to their research, the forms that are required and the information they need to provide. When you next meet, ask each student, in turn, to pose a question. Invite answers from other students before providing your own (if required).

2. Run this activity online: decide whether to run the session in real-time using a suitable video/web conferencing tool, or over a period of time using a discussion

board. Also, decide whether to make the activity compulsory (a set number of questions and answers must be given) or voluntary. Ask students to post their questions and provide answers to the questions posed by their peers, encouraging discussion, reflection and support. If necessary, begin the question-and-answer session with a few of your own. Monitor the posts or video discussion to make sure that information is correct, supportive, constructive and useful.

3. Run Activity 2: Discussing the ethics of consent and purpose. This is a theoretical (and part practical) discussion about the ethics of consent and purpose. It presents 12 questions on this topic for discussion: use all questions or choose those related specifically to informed consent. Once the discussion is complete, introduce your students to your university's informed consent information and invite questions about the informed consent process from your students.

4. Run Activity 42: Obtaining informed consent in the digital world. This asks students to develop two scenarios that introduce a difficulty, problem or dilemma relating to obtaining informed consent in the digital world. Once this activity is complete, introduce your students to your university's informed consent information and invite questions about the informed consent process.

5. Choose relevant questions from key issues in Activity 2 and Activity 42. Take 30–40 minutes to discuss these points, before introducing and discussing your university's informed consent information and inviting questions from students.

Key issues

A university's informed consent guidance, procedures, templates and forms differ, depending on the university. In general, this information will include:

- what informed consent is (fully informed consent, freely given consent and valid consent, for example);
- why informed consent is required;
- whether written or oral consent is required;
- guidance on participants' capacity to consent (relevant mental health legislation, for example);
- guidance for obtaining informed consent with children or vulnerable people (information about safeguarding, for example) and rules and regulations (including the relevant checks required, such as Disclosure and Barring Service (DBS) checks in the UK);
- information about collecting, storing and sharing sensitive personal data in line with the university's policy and relevant legislation;
- guidance on drafting consent forms and/or templates for consent forms (for different types of research and

- for different types of participants, including easy-read forms, for example);
- guidance for participant information sheets and/or templates;
- guidance and consent forms for photography and videoing in accordance with data protection legislation;
- what to do in circumstances where consent cannot be obtained;
- information about renewal of consent;
- protocol on reimbursement for research participants (Activity 65);
- information about what is required for ethical approval (Activity 41);
- guidance on external requirements for specific subjects such as health and medicine.

→ **Related activities**

Activity 2: Discussing the ethics of consent and purpose

Activity 11: Avoiding harm to others

Activity 14: Working with vulnerable people

Activity 15: Conducting research with children

Activity 41: Obtaining ethical approval

Activity 42: Obtaining informed consent in the digital world

Activity 65: Assessing the ethical implications of incentives and rewards

→ **Preparatory reading**

Educators: Become familiar with your university's informed consent guidance, procedures, templates and forms, if you have not already done so. These documents can be opened for reference purposes during the activity, if required.

Activity 57

Students: None required. Students should be encouraged to find their own way to your university's information, or if you prefer, provide relevant links.

....

→ Useful resources

Information about valid consent can be obtained from the Information Commissioner's Office (ICO) in the UK: https://ico.org.uk/for-organisations/guide-to-data-protection/guide-to-the-general-data-protection-regulation-gdpr/consent/what-is-valid-consent [accessed 7 July 2021].

Information about consent for data sharing can be obtained from the UK Data Service: www.ukdataservice.ac.uk/manage-data/legal-ethical/consent-data-sharing/overview.aspx [accessed 7 July 2021].

Biros, M. (2018) 'Capacity, vulnerability, and informed consent for research', *Journal of Law, Medicine & Ethics*, 46 (1): 72–8, first published 7 March 2018, doi: 10.1177/1073110518766021.

Campbell, L.M., Paolillo, E.W., Bryan, R., Marquie-Beck, J., Moore, D.J., Nebeker, C. and Moore, R.C. (2020) 'Informing informed consent for HIV research', *Journal of Empirical Research on Human Research Ethics*, 15 (4): 235–43, first published 19 June 2020, doi: 10.1177/1556264620933766.

Capron, A.M. (2018) 'Where did informed consent for research come from?', *Journal of Law, Medicine & Ethics*, 46 (1): 12–29, first published 27 March 2018, doi: 10.1177/1073110518766004.

Khabour, O.F., Alomari, M.A. and Al-sheyab, N.A. (2017) 'Parental perceptions about informed consent/assent in pediatric research in Jordan', *Journal of Empirical Research on Human Research Ethics*, 12 (4): 261–8, first published 12 July 2017, doi: 10.1177/1556264617718937.

Mayne, F. and Howitt, C. (2022) *The Narrative Approach to Informed Consent: Empowering Young Children's Rights and Meaningful Participation*. Abingdon: Routledge.

Tauri, J.M. (2018) 'Research ethics, informed consent and the disempowerment of First Nation peoples', *Research Ethics*, 14 (3): 1–14, first published 14 November 2017, doi: 10.1177/1747016117739935.

Thomas, M. and Pettitt, N. (2017) 'Informed consent in research on second language acquisition', *Second Language Research*, 33 (2): 271–88, first published 3 October 2016, doi: 10.1177/0267658316670206.

Activity 57

Activity · · · · · · · · · · · · → 58

Cultivating Sensitivity in Method

The activity

Give your students a copy of the Student Handout and ask that they work on the task during independent study. This asks them to imagine that they are a participant in a research study. It can be any type of study on any topic, using any methods: the choice is theirs. As the study progresses, they start to realise that the researcher(s) is acting insensitively and/or using insensitive methods. They must then produce a bullet point list of five actions and/or methods that they consider to be insensitive, within their role as research participant, before working through each item to provide a solution. Once the work is complete, they should upload it using the tool you have set up for this purpose. Encourage students to read the work of their peers and enter into constructive and supportive online discussion. Provide a date by which time this should be done.

This activity can be run as an in-class workshop, if you prefer or if it better suits your students (it is of particular use for a small number of students studying at advanced level, for example). Divide students into pairs and ask them to build their bullet point list. Then open the workshop up for discussion, working through each bullet point and asking your students to suggest solutions. Complete the workshop by asking students to think about how they intend to cultivate sensitivity in method in their own research.

Key issues

Examples of items that students might list vary considerably, depending on the role that students decide to play and the research topic, approach and methods they choose. Examples include the following (these have been edited and shortened, where required):

- not giving me time to get my head around the research and whether I should take part;
- providing information about the research that I don't understand;
- presuming that I will give consent and I'm happy to take part, even though I have concerns;
- passing over my worries and concerns, or trivializing them;
- not understanding that I'm really scared about the research process;
- lack of sympathy or empathy shown by the researcher;
- displaying cultural insensitivity;
- I don't think she took my race into account;
- he didn't respect me as a woman;
- not providing comfort or help when I get upset;
- talking down to me;
- using complicated terminology in questionnaires;
- not paying attention to my feelings;
- not listening to me in interviews;
- expecting me to answer far too many questions;
- using up too much of my time and not compensating me;
- expecting me to use my own devices, even if it costs me money;
- asking personal questions that are not relevant to the research topic;
- not offering to switch the recorder off when I'm saying something personal and private;
- looking bored when I'm speaking;
- fidgeting in interviews;
- not respecting my dignity in health research;
- they didn't have a clue about my mental health needs;
- spying on me in my online world;
- not giving enough detail about how my answers and personal information will be kept safe;
- doing what they want with the results of the research and not thinking about how it might impact me;
- sharing my information with other researchers or organizations when I haven't given my permission;
- using me to further their research careers.

Cautionary note

Monitor discussions carefully and intervene if required. Sometimes students raise quite personal issues in this activity and it is important to ensure that they treat each other with respect, take time to digest the comments and enter into supportive and constructive discussion.

→ Related activities

Activity 1: Respecting human dignity, privacy and rights

Activity 8: Conducting discrimination-aware and fairness-aware research

Activity 11: Avoiding harm to others

Activity 28: Evaluating biases with reference to equality, diversity and inclusion

Activity 60: Collecting personal information sensitively

Activity 61: Capturing data on sexual orientation and gender identity

....

→ Preparatory reading

Educators: All the resources listed below provide useful preparatory reading.

Students: None required. Students will find their own resources for this activity, if required.

....

→ Useful resources

Awad, G.H., Patall, E.A., Rackley, K.R. and Reilly, E.D. (2016) 'Recommendations for culturally sensitive research methods', *Journal of Educational and Psychological Consultation*, 26 (3): 283-303, published online 18 December 2015, doi: 10.1080/10474412.2015.1046600.

Activity 58

Bahn, S. and Weatherill, P. (2013) 'Qualitative social research: A risky business when it comes to collecting "sensitive" data', *Qualitative Research*, 13 (1): 19-35, first published 10 August 2012, doi: 10.1177/1468794112439016.

Burnette, C.E., Sanders, S., Butcher, H.K. and Rand, J.T. (2014) 'A toolkit for ethical and culturally sensitive research: An application with indigenous communities', *Ethics and Social Welfare*, 8 (4): 364-82, published online 25 February 2014, doi: 10.1080/17496535.2014.885987.

Cornejo, M., Rubilar, G. and Zapata-Sepúlveda, P. (2019) 'Researching sensitive topics in sensitive zones: Exploring silences, "the normal," and tolerance in Chile', *International Journal of Qualitative Methods*, first published 16 May 2019, doi: 10.1177/1609406919849355.

Kvande, M.E., Delmar, C., Lauritzen, J. and Damsgaard, J.B. (2021) 'Ethical dilemmas embedded in performing fieldwork with nurses in the ICU', *Nursing Ethics*, first published 8 April 2021, doi: 10.1177/0969733021996025.

Paton, J., Horsfall, D. and Carrington, A. (2018) 'Sensitive inquiry in mental health: A tripartite approach', *International Journal of Qualitative Methods*, first published 15 March 2018, doi: 10.1177/1609406918761422.

Sharma, J., McDonald, C.P., Bledsoe, K.G., Grad, R.I., Jenkins, K.D., Moran, D., O'Hara, C. and Pester, D. (2021) 'Intersectionality in research: Call for inclusive, decolonized, and culturally sensitive research designs in counselor education', *Counseling Outcome Research and Evaluation*, published online 3 June 2021, doi: 10.1080/21501378.2021.1922075.

Turhan, Z. and Bernard, C. (2021) 'Challenges and strategies of translation in a qualitative and sensitive research', *Qualitative Research*, first published 15 March 2021, doi: 10.1177/1468794121999003.

Activity 58

Activity • • • • • • • • • • • → 58

Cultivating Sensitivity in Method

STUDENT HANDOUT

This activity is called 'Cultivating sensitivity in method'. Imagine that you are a participant in a research study. It can be any type of study on any topic, using any methods: the choice is yours. Also, as a research participant, you can play any role you wish. As the study progresses, you start to realise that the researcher(s) is acting insensitively and/or using insensitive methods. But what, exactly, does this mean? What are they doing to make you think that they are acting insensitively or using insensitive methods?

Produce a bullet point list of five actions and/or methods that you consider to be insensitive, within your role as research participant. They can be points related to topic and method, or related to researcher actions and demeanour, for example. Try to be creative, but ensure that you are realistic. Situate your role-play in the real world: think about situations that could be encountered in actual research projects.

Once you have built your five-point list, work through each item to provide a solution. Suggest ways that the researcher(s) could or should have acted, or the methods that could or should have been used. Think about what the researcher(s) needs to do to cultivate sensitivity in method.

When your work is complete, upload it using the tool set up for this purpose by the given date. Read the work of your peers and enter into constructive and supportive online discussion. Remember to respect the views of others and keep comments on a professional level, avoiding personal comments and arguments.

Learning outcome: By the end of this activity, you will be able to list a number of insensitive methods and actions in research and provide solutions to the problems identified.

Activity • • • • • • • • • • • • • → 59

Critiquing Overt and Covert Methods

The activity

Print the dilemmas and associated solutions presented in the Student Handout onto separate pieces of card (about the size of a postcard). Produce several identical 'packs' of these cards to give the impression of this being a game. Adapt, delete or add to the dilemmas, depending on what you feel to be appropriate for your students and to better suit your country and type of institution.

When you meet, introduce the session by giving a definition of what is meant by overt and covert research. Then give a brief explanation of the game and its purpose (to encourage in-depth discussion, assessment and critique of overt and covert research methods). Explain that there are no right or wrong answers and that, in some cases, it is possible to reach consensus on more than one solution or provide an alternative solution. Finding the correct answer is not the goal of this activity (indeed, there are no correct answers): instead, it is the ability to discuss, listen, negotiate, compromise, respect others' views and build a deeper understanding of overt and covert methods that are important.

Divide your students into small groups and give each group a pack of the dilemma cards. Ask groups to work through the dilemmas and discuss and agree on a given solution(s). Some dilemmas are straightforward and students are able to reach consensus quickly, whereas others are more complex and require in-depth discussion. Students might decide that more than one solution is appropriate or they might decide that none of the given solutions are appropriate and, instead, develop their own solution(s). Allocate up to 40 minutes for this activity (depending on the number of dilemmas you choose), before bringing the groups together for an educator-led discussion on the issues raised (some questions for discussion are given below).

This activity can be run online if this option is preferable: choose a suitable tool to host the game (Zoom Meetings or Conferences in Canvas, for example). Use breakout rooms for the first part of the discussion. These can be set automatically or manually: ensure that breakout rooms are enabled and pre-assign students to breakout rooms prior to your session (or if you prefer, enable software to split students evenly into groups).

Provide a brief introduction to the session and set guidelines for constructive and supportive online discussion. Open the breakout rooms and broadcast dilemmas and solutions to your students, one at a time. Ask groups to work through each dilemma, before broadcasting the next. Visit breakout rooms to check on progress and to make sure that discussions are constructive and useful. When all dilemmas have been presented and discussed, end the breakout session and lead a discussion on the issues raised.

The dilemmas presented in the Student Handout can be adapted into a worksheet that students can work on during independent study, if preferred. Add to, delete or modify dilemmas, as appropriate.

Key issues

This activity can take place at the beginning of a research methods course: it provides an entertaining icebreaker on a topic that students can relate to, which is not too complex or off-putting. An important part of the activity is that students have the chance to discuss issues, negotiate, compromise and reach consensus, in addition to understanding more about overt and covert research methods. It is entertaining, informal and informative, and helps students to get to know their peers. The dilemmas are based on practical cases that help students to think more deeply about the issues presented. Topics that might be discussed include:

- when covert research might be justified;
- different levels of overt and covert research, and how they can be used together in a project;
- what is meant by deception, and immoral and unethical behaviour in research;
- differences between online and face-to-face overt and covert research, and whether online covert research is easier to justify;
- the value of overt and covert research;
- the importance of informed consent and the practicalities of obtaining informed consent, in particular in virtual spaces;
- weighing up the need for participation against the need for informed consent;

- respect, safety and dignity of research participants;
- the importance of privacy, confidentiality and anonymity;
- how taking part in research influences participants' behaviour;
- problems associated with changing approaches midway through a project (leading to sampling or selection bias, for example);
- the role of university policy and ethical review committees (or similar) and how these might constrain, restrict or guide choices;
- relationships with supervisors/personal tutors.

Questions that can be explored further during the educator-led discussion include:

1. Should all research be overt? Why (not)?
2. Are covert methods unethical? Why (not)?
3. Can covert methods be justified? If so, when and why? Roulet et al. (2017) provide an interesting discussion on this topic and Calvey (2017) provides an in-depth discussion with a variety of examples.
4. Is all overt research really overt? Can you think of examples where covert methods are used within an overt

project? McKenzie (2009) provides an interesting discussion on these issues.
5. What is the role of research ethics committees (or similar) in relation to overt or covert research?
6. What are institutional, professional body and national guidelines on overt and covert research?

Cautionary note

On occasions, groups may not be able to reach consensus and, on rare occasions, the discussion can develop into an argument (if you have two students with strong, opposing views, for example). Walk among the groups listening to discussions so that you can defuse any problems that may arise, before they escalate.

Activity 59

→ Related activities

Activity 17: Cultivating transparency and openness

Activity 34: Researching illegal, unlawful, illicit or dangerous behaviour

Activity 43: Critiquing the presentation of self in online worlds

Activity 44: Managing the researcher's online presence

→ Preparatory reading

Educators: The resources listed below provide useful preparatory reading. You might find it useful to have access to your university's policy on overt and covert research if you wish to cover this during the tutor-led discussion.

Students: None required.

→ Useful resources

Calvey, D. (2017) *Covert Research: The Art, Politics and Ethics of Undercover Fieldwork*. London: Sage.

Kluczewska, K. and Lottholz, P. (2021) 'Recognizing the never quite absent: De facto usage, ethical issues, and applications of covert research in difficult research contexts', *Qualitative Research*, first published 14 August 2021, doi: 10.1177/14687941211033084.

McKenzie, J.S. (2009) ''You don't know how lucky you are to be here!': Reflections on covert practices in an overt participant observation study', *Sociological Research Online*, 14 (2): 60-9, first published 11 December 2017, doi: 10.5153/sro.1925.

Roulet, T.J., Gill, M.J., Stenger, S. and Gill, D.J. (2017) 'Reconsidering the value of covert research: The role of ambiguous consent in participant observation', *Organizational Research Methods*, 20 (3): 487-517, first published 23 March 2017, doi: 10.1177/1094428117698745.

Virtová, T., Stöckelová, T. and Krásná, H. (2018) 'On the track of c/overt research: Lessons from taking ethnographic ethics to the extreme', *Qualitative Inquiry*, 24 (7): 453-63, doi: 10.1177/1077800417732090.

Activity 59

Activity • • • • • • • • • • • → 59

Critiquing Overt and Covert Methods

STUDENT HANDOUT

Dilemma 1

A student is thinking about undertaking research into the sale of counterfeit money on the dark web. She wants to pose as a seller, attract buyers and engage in dialogue to gather data for her research. What should she do?

- Choose another topic and approach: her suggestion is deceptive, unethical and immoral.
- Conduct the research as planned: this type of covert research is necessary and will provide valuable insight.
- Continue with the research but make sure that people (the buyers) know she is a researcher and that she gets their informed consent to take part.

- Discuss her research with her supervisor/personal tutor before she makes any further decisions.
- Contact her ethical review committee (or similar) to find out whether this research would receive ethical approval.

Dilemma 2

A doctoral student has received ethical approval for her research. She has negotiated access to two refuges for women who have suffered domestic violence. At the first refuge she found that women were unwilling to talk to her for fear of their abusers finding out. What should she do?

- Ask the manager at the second refuge whether she can pose as a member of staff to ask questions and get women to talk to her.
- Produce a more detailed privacy, confidentiality and anonymity document to give to women to try to convince them that it will be safe to participate.

- Ask the manager at the second refuge whether she can observe from a distance, without women knowing.
- Reassess her research approach and methods to find out if there is a better way to obtain the information.
- Try the same methods: the second refuge might yield better results and, if it doesn't, this will form the basis for a useful discussion in her research report.

Dilemma 3

A researcher has received ethical approval to undertake an ethnographic study into gang membership. Part of his application for approval was that he would obtain informed consent from everyone taking part in his research. However, he has been told that a rival gang will not give consent if they know that the researcher has already worked with 'their enemies'. What should the researcher do?

- Fully inform participants of the research and obtain informed consent, even if it means that a rival gang will not participate.
- Withhold some information from the rival gang: they do not need to know that he has already worked with

'their enemies' but he should still obtain informed consent.
- Decide to join the rival gang covertly, as a new member, rather than as a researcher.

- Change methods and approaches and put in a new application for ethical review.
- Find a different gang to work with.

- Evade questions, if asked. After all, other participants should not know who has taken part in the research due to confidentiality and anonymity issues.

Dilemma 4

A doctoral student believes that their use of covert methods is justified because of the importance and value of their research. However, their supervisor argues that covert research can never be justified due to the harm it causes, to participants and to research. What would you advise the doctoral student to do?

- Listen to their supervisor: this person knows best.
- Change supervisors to find someone more open to these methods.
- Think about the issues deeply and produce a detailed defence of their methods to put to their supervisor.

- Seek further advice from someone in the University Research Ethics Office (or similar).
- Tweak their methods to include some covert and some overt methods.

Dilemma 5

In a pilot study, a student notices that his research participants act differently when he is present. What should he do?

- Decide that he will make a case for undertaking covert research because it is important that natural behaviour is observed.
- Try another pilot study in which he does not disclose his researcher identity, and then compare the results of the two pilot studies.

- Continue with the study as planned: he knows seeking full informed consent is paramount to ethical research.
- Find out more about the observer effect and try to control for this effect.
- Scrap the project and try something different.

Learning outcome: By the end of this activity, you will be able to identify and discuss a number of ethical issues associated with the use of overt and covert research methods.

Activity 59

Activity • • • • • • • • • • • • → 60

Collecting Personal Information Sensitively

The activity

Give your students a copy of the Student Handout and ask that they undertake the task ready for when you next meet. They are asked to read and digest their university's guidelines and policy on collecting personal data, identify the type of personal data they need to collect for their research, justify the collection of this data and explain how they intend to do this sensitively. Students are also asked to note down any questions, comments or concerns they might have about collecting personal data sensitively.

When you next meet, discuss these points with your students (use the questions in the handout as a basis for your discussion, and refer to the points listed in key issues to ensure that pertinent issues are covered). Invite questions, comments and concerns from students: this will enable them to clarify thoughts, bounce ideas off one another and modify and develop their plans.

This discussion can be held in-class or online, using synchronous tools such as Zoom Meetings, Meetings in Microsoft Teams for Education or Blackboard Collaborate. It is also possible to run this activity as a self-guided individual exercise, without the discussion, if you prefer (adapt the Student Handout accordingly).

Key issues

This activity introduces students to a number of topics, depending on what is included in your university's guidelines and policy. These can include:

- limiting the collection of personal data to what is genuinely required for the research project (and knowing what to do with information that has been collected that is irrelevant or excessive);
- complying with relevant legislation, such as the General Data Protection Regulation (GDPR) and the Data Protection Act 2018 (DPA) in the UK (Activities 31 and 33);
- identifying the lawful basis that is relied on when collecting data (public task, legitimate interest, contract, legal obligation, vital interest and consent);
- complying with the common law duty of confidentiality for special categories of personal data (data that relate to physical and mental health, race or ethnicity, political opinions, religious beliefs, trade union membership, criminal convictions, sexual orientation, genetics and biometrics, for example);
- producing participant information sheets (guidance and templates);
- seeking informed consent (Activity 57);
- keeping personal data protected and secure (Activity 85);
- addressing issues of anonymity and confidentiality (Activity 62);
- capturing data on sexual orientation and gender identity (Activity 61);
- sharing data: ethical implications (Activity 89), your university's policy, forms and guidelines;
- guidelines on short-term storage and long-term preservation of data (Activity 87);
- obtaining ethical approval (Activity 41).

The final part of this activity asks students to consider how they can collect personal data sensitively. The discussion can include compliance with their university's policy and guidelines, as above, but can also include issues such as:

- asking questions sensitively in interviews and on questionnaires (being sensitive to diversity and enabling self-identification, for example: Activity 61);
- cultivating empathy and being aware of participants' feelings, experiences and needs (Activity 58);
- ensuring personal data and opinions are recorded accurately;
- enabling and respecting requests to update or delete personal data held;
- respecting confidentiality and ensuring that personal information is not disclosed to third parties;
- protecting against privacy breaches (see Kroes et al., 2021 for an interesting discussion on privacy and medical data);
- adopting new and creative methods (see Lupton and Watson, 2020 for a discussion on new and innovative methods).

Cautionary note

Before you run this activity, check that your university has comprehensive guidelines and policy on collecting personal data. If it does not, choose some of the useful resources listed below and refer your students to these as preparation for the discussion.

→ **Related activities**

Activity 42: Obtaining informed consent in the digital world

Activity 57: Seeking informed consent

Activity 58: Cultivating sensitivity in method

Activity 61: Capturing data on sexual orientation and gender identity

Activity 62: Addressing issues of anonymity and confidentiality

....

→ **Preparatory reading**

Educators: Read your university's guidelines and policy on collecting personal data if you have not already done so.

Students: None required. Students should be left to find their own way to your university's guidelines and policy, or if you prefer, provide relevant links.

....

Activity 60

→ **Useful resources**

A guide to the UK General Data Protection Regulation (UK GDPR) can be obtained from the Information Commissioner's Office (ICO) in the UK: https://ico.org.uk/for-organisations/guide-to-data-protection/guide-to-the-general-data-protection-regulation-gdpr [accessed 13 July 2021].

Information about issues raised in this activity can be found in 'Research Ethics Guidance', *Social Research Association*, 2021: www.the-sra.org.uk/common/Uploaded%20files/Resources/SRA%20Ethics%20guidance%202021.pdf [accessed 13 July 2021].

Fernandez, T., Godwin, A., Doyle, J., Verdin, D., Boone, H., Kirn, A., Benson, L. and Potvin, G. (2016) 'More comprehensive and inclusive approaches to demographic data collection', *School of Engineering Education Graduate Student Series*, Paper 60, http://docs.lib.purdue.edu/enegs/60.

Ioannou, A., Tussyadiah, I. and Miller, G. (2020) 'That's private! Understanding travelers' privacy concerns and online data disclosure', *Journal of Travel Research*, first published 11 September 2020, doi: 10.1177/0047287520951642.

Kroes, S.K., Janssen, M.P., Groenwold, R.H. and van Leeuwen, M. (2021) 'Evaluating privacy of individuals in medical data', *Health Informatics Journal*, first published 2 June 2021, doi: 10.1177/1460458220983398.

Lupton, D. and Watson, A. (2020) 'Towards more-than-human digital data studies: developing research-creation methods', *Qualitative Research*, first published 14 July 2020, doi: 10.1177/1468794120939235.

Activity 60

Activity • • • • • • • • • • • → 60

Collecting Personal Information Sensitively

STUDENT HANDOUT

This activity is called 'Collecting personal information sensitively' and has been designed to encourage you to think about how to collect personal information sensitively when you conduct your research. Before we next meet, find, read and digest our university's guidelines and policy on collecting personal information. As you do this, consider the following questions:

1. What personal data do I need to collect?
2. Why do I need to collect this data?
3. What legislation do I need to adhere to when collecting this data?
4. What university guidance, forms and templates are available?
5. How do I collect this data sensitively?

When we next meet, we will discuss your thoughts. If you have any questions, comments or concerns, note them down and we will address them during the class discussion.

Learning outcome: By the end of this activity, you will be able to summarize your university's policy on collecting personal data; identify the type of personal data you need to collect for your research; justify the need to collect this data; and explain how you will collect this data sensitively.

Activity • • • • • • • • • • • → 61

Capturing Data on Sexual Orientation and Gender Identity

ACTIVITY 61: EDUCATOR NOTES

Purpose: This activity encourages students to think about the ethical issues associated with capturing data on sexual orientation and gender identity, and reflect on how this data can be collected inclusively, sensitively, safely and without causing offence.

Type: Scenarios for group discussion (in-class).

Alternative type(s): Scenarios for discussion (online asynchronous).

Level: Intermediate and advanced (this activity is aimed at students who are planning their research project).

Duration: Fifty minutes to one hour for the in-class activity. Up to two hours for the online activity, spread over a few days.

Equipment/materials: VLE-hosted discussion board, if the online option is chosen.

Learning outcome: By the end of this activity, students will be able to identify, discuss and assess a number of ethical issues associated with capturing data on sexual orientation and gender identity; and demonstrate how this data can be collected inclusively, sensitively, safely and without causing offence.

The activity

This activity can be run with your usual cohort of students or you can invite together a number of students from different courses or research areas who have expressed an interest in this topic. Divide your students into small groups and give each group a copy of the Student Handout. Ask them to work through each scenario in their groups, discussing possible solutions. Allocate 30 minutes for groups to discuss the scenarios, before bringing students together to lead a class discussion on the issues raised.

Ensure that students understand that there are no right or wrong answers: the scenarios are to generate discussion and stimulate reflection. Walk between groups as they hold their discussions, answering questions and checking that students are being respectful, courteous and supportive, and keeping to the task in hand. On occasions, you may find that groups require a little longer to discuss scenarios: if you feel the discussions are fruitful and you have time available, a further 10 or 15 minutes can be allocated. Ensure that you have enough time available for a class discussion and to sum up the points raised (groups can arrive at quite different solutions: a class discussion illustrates this and enables students to think about solutions that differ from their own).

This activity can also be run as a VLE-hosted discussion board activity, and can be done on an individual or group basis. If you choose this option, give a deadline by which time students should provide their solutions for each scenario, and monitor posts to ensure that students are providing useful information in a supportive and constructive manner.

Key issues

The following issues arise from the scenarios and can be used as a basis for the class discussion (although there are no right or wrong answers, some suggestions are better than others, and some of these can be combined to arrive at a more complete solution: this should be made clear during the class discussion).

Scenario 1: Possible solutions include:

1. The researcher could undertake more research to back up their opinion and illustrate why it is important to capture data on sexual orientation and gender identity. Data should be collected only if they are vital to the research, there is a valid reason to collect the data and they are relevant to the research question. Once this has been done, the researcher can return to their supervisor and put forward a well-structured and reasoned argument.
2. The researcher should listen to their supervisor as that person is experienced and should know what they are talking about.
3. The researcher must be careful to avoid stereotypes. They should think about their own biases with reference to equality, diversity and inclusion (EDI) (Activity 28). This should be done alongside a careful assessment of their research question, and their research aims and objectives. Once this has been done, they should be in a better position to decide whether or not this data should be captured.
4. They should weigh up the pros and cons (or advantages or disadvantages) to collecting this type of data, and discuss further with their supervisor. Peers and the university LGBT+ network might provide useful sounding boards.

Scenario 2: Possible solutions include:

1. Respect the participant's wishes and recognize and record only their affirmed gender.
2. Ask two questions: one that enables the participant to self-identify and the other that asks about the sex they were assigned at birth, with an explanation of why it is important that this information is collected.
3. Decide not to ask this participant a question about gender identity as it might cause offence.
4. Presume that the chances of this participant being affected by the particular health issues that could arise are minimal, and that it is more important to respect their wishes. Therefore, only their affirmed gender should be recognized and recorded.
5. Consult the university's LGBT+ network and/or EDI office for guidance and act accordingly.

Scenario 3: Possible solutions include:

1. If the research is to be a global survey, the correct sampling procedures must be followed to avoid error and bias, to enable others to have trust in the outputs and conclusions, and for the researchers to make generalizations. Therefore, countries, organizations or employees cannot be omitted. However, the research team must take steps to avoid harm to participants or to employers (Activity 11). They should carry out a detailed risk assessment before starting the data collection phase of the project (Activity 27). They must also take time to work out a data protection, privacy, anonymity and confidentiality plan (Activities 81 and 85).
2. Don't collect data if these actions will cause harm to participants. Researchers should avoid conducting research in countries that have repressive regimes, or countries where people can be jailed for disclosing their sexual orientation. It should be made clear that these countries have been omitted when the research is reported/published.
3. Collect this data, but make sure that people taking part in the survey understand that they do not have to answer any questions that they feel might put them in danger. Also, ensure that answers given in the survey are fully anonymized and cannot be traced back to individuals (Activities 79 and 84).

Scenario 4: Possible solutions include:

1. Get hold of a well-respected publication and follow their guidelines (the Stonewall publication, for example: see below).
2. If the interviews are semi-structured, take time to get to know the participant. Talk about issues that are important to them. Listen to what they are saying, and the terms they are using. Once rapport has been established and the participant is better understood, the questions can be asked. This might be different for each interviewee. Flexibility is the key.
3. Develop a comprehensive interview schedule. Ask your supervisor to check through the questions on

Activity 61

gender identity and sexual orientation. Also, they can be checked by the university's LGBT+ group. Practise asking the questions with a few participants, and ask how they felt about answering them. Modify and improve the schedule as a result of the pilot test.

4. Produce a specific question that is asked to all participants, with answers such as 'female', 'male', 'non-binary', 'prefer not to disclose', 'prefer to self-identify' (with a space to elaborate on self-identity) or 'other' (with a space to elaborate). Or produce a free-response question, enabling respondents to identify themselves, although this can make analysis difficult in cases where gender is an important variable for the research question.

Cautionary note

It is important that you monitor discussions for this activity. On occasions, you might find students with strong points of view that are at odds with others in their group. Also, for a minority of students who come from countries where same-sex relationships are illegal, or where transgenders are not protected, it can be difficult to adjust to common practice, sensitivities or legalities of their host country.

→ Related activities

Activity 11: Avoiding harm to others

Activity 28: Evaluating biases with reference to equality, diversity and inclusion

Activity 30: Researching cross-culturally

Activity 58: Cultivating sensitivity in method

Activity 60: Collecting personal information sensitively

→ Preparatory reading

Educators: The title of this activity is based on a Stonewall publication, which provides useful preparatory reading for this activity:

Stonewall (2016) *Do Ask Do Tell: Capturing Data on Sexual Orientation and Gender Identity Globally*. Available at: www.stonewall.org.uk/sites/default/files/do_ask_do_tell_guide_2016.pdf [accessed 1 October 2021].

Students: None required.

→ Useful resources

Institute of Medicine (IOM) (2013) *Collecting Sexual Orientation and Gender Identity Data in Electronic Health Records: Workshop Summary*. Washington, DC: The National Academic Press.
Sauntson, H. (2020) *Researching Language, Gender and Sexuality: A Student Guide*. Abingdon: Routledge.
Vincent, B.W. (2018) 'Studying trans: Recommendations for ethical recruitment and collaboration with transgender participants in academic research', *Psychology & Sexuality*, 9 (2): 102-16, doi: 10.1080/19419899.2018.1434558.

In the UK, the Government Equality Office produced two blogs in association with its LGBT survey [accessed 1 October 2021]:

- asking about sex and gender identity: https://equalities.blog.gov.uk/2017/07/28/lgbtsurvey-asking-about-your-sex-and-gender-identity/

- asking about sexual orientation and intersex: https://equalities.blog.gov.uk/2017/09/29/lgbtsurvey-asking-about-sexual-orientation-and-intersex/

Activity 61

Activity • • • • • • • • • • • → 61

Capturing Data on Sexual Orientation and Gender Identity

STUDENT HANDOUT

This activity is called 'Capturing data on sexual orientation and gender identity'. Discuss each of the following scenarios with your group members. There are no right or wrong answers to these scenarios: they have been presented to encourage reflection and discussion on this topic. We will then come together to hold a class discussion on the issues raised. I will be walking between groups, so if you have any problems during your group discussion, or if you have any questions, please ask for advice.

Scenario 1

A researcher is planning a project that will consider public perceptions of western fashion. The researcher thinks that it is extremely important to capture data on sexual orientation and gender identity, believing that these will influence perceptions of fashion. However, the researcher's supervisor disagrees and thinks that these data should not be captured as they have no relevance to perceptions of western fashion. What would you advise this researcher to do?

Scenario 2

A transgender participant in a research study does not want to self-identify as transgender. Instead, the participant wants to have their affirmed gender recognized and recorded without it being connected to their transgender history. However, the researcher is aware that the findings of the research could have implications for the health of transgender people, related to the sex they were assigned at birth. What action would you advise this researcher to take?

Scenario 3

An international research team is carrying out a global survey of LGBT+ employees in start-up technology companies. They are aware that there are social, legal, political and cultural differences regarding LGBT+ equality in different countries, and they need to work out how this can be factored into their research design. In particular, they must ensure that research participants are not harmed or put in danger by disclosing their sexual orientation. What issues do they need to consider, and how can these be factored into their research design?

Scenario 4

A researcher has received ethical approval for their research project to go ahead, part of which is to collect data on sexual orientation and gender identity. The researcher intends to carry out in-depth, semi-structured interviews, and is in the process of constructing interview questions. How would you advise the researcher to collect information on sexual orientation and gender identity in a sensitive way, which will not cause upset or offence?

Learning outcome: By the end of this activity, you will be able to identify, discuss and assess a number of ethical issues associated with capturing data on sexual orientation and gender identity; and demonstrate how this data can be collected inclusively, sensitively, safely and without causing offence.

Activity · · · · · · · · · · → 62

Addressing Issues of Anonymity and Confidentiality

....

ACTIVITY 62: EDUCATOR NOTES

Purpose: This is a scenario-based activity that encourages students to address issues of anonymity and confidentiality when undertaking research. Four scenarios are presented, which must be discussed in groups, before opening up to a class discussion on the issues raised.

Type: Scenario-based discussion (in-class).

Alternative type(s): Scenario-based discussion (online, synchronous); scenario-based individual exercise.

Level: Intermediate and advanced (this activity is designed for students who are in the planning stages of their research).

Duration: Fifty minutes to one hour of contact time. If the scenario-based individual exercise option is chosen, students will spend up to an hour working on the scenarios during independent study.

Equipment/materials: A suitable video/web conferencing tool, if this option is chosen.

Learning outcome: By the end of this activity, students will be able to identify, and explain how to address, various issues associated with anonymity and confidentiality in research.

....

The activity

Divide your students into small groups (or pairs, if you have only a small number of students) and give each group a copy of the Student Handout. This presents four scenarios that they must work through with their group members (these can be adapted to make them more relevant to your students, if required). For each, they must identify potential issues related to anonymity and/or confidentiality that the researchers in the scenarios need to address before they begin to collect their data. Allocate up to 30 minutes for this part of the activity (the actual time depends on how quickly groups work through the task: walk among the groups, answering questions and helping them to overcome problems, while keeping an eye on when the task is complete). Once the discussions have run their course, bring the groups back together to lead a class discussion on the issues raised (possible topics and questions are given below).

   This activity can be run online, if you prefer. Use a suitable video/web conferencing tool such as Zoom Meetings or Blackboard Collaborate and breakout rooms for groups to work through the scenarios. These can be set automatically or manually: ensure that breakout rooms are enabled prior to your session. Provide a brief introduction to the session and set guidelines for constructive and supportive online discussion. Open the breakout rooms and broadcast the scenarios to your students. Ask groups to discuss each one, taking notes as they hold their discussion: they will need to discuss these issues with the whole class later. You can develop and use an online spreadsheet or document note-catcher to organize note-taking for each group, if required. This can be used to monitor their discussions and see how they are progressing. It can also help you to decide which breakout rooms to visit and ascertain when to conclude this part of the session. Bring the groups back together to lead a class discussion on the issues raised.

This activity can be run as a scenario-based individual exercise, if you prefer. Adapt the Student Handout and give a copy to each student. Give a submission deadline and provide assessment criteria if you choose to make this an assessed piece of work.

Key issues

A wide range of issues can be raised in this activity. Some of these are given below and, along with the additional two questions, can be used in your class discussion, if required.

Scenario 1: Potential issues that Paul needs to address include:

- Where will the participants be when they answer Paul's questions on their phone? Will they be in a crowded space? Could they be overheard? Paul must try to ensure that they are in a private place and that that they are not overheard. He should consider the time of day for contact (when people are more likely to be on their own, or when they are able to find a quiet space, for example). Given all these factors, Paul should consider whether he can guarantee confidentiality.
- Where will Paul be when he conducts the interviews? If he is writing down the answers, does that mean that he will use his speakerphone? If so, he must ensure that the interview is not overheard by others.
- Paul must ensure that he doesn't give away previous answers if he is asking the same questions to each

participant. Sometimes a participant might ask how another person has answered or Paul could provide this information inadvertently or by mistake.
- How has Paul chosen his 10 participants? Do they know each other? Do they know who else is taking part? If so, Paul cannot guarantee anonymity.
- Paul should consider relevant technology and make sure that this does not have an influence on anonymity or confidentiality (location trackers that could lead to the identification of research participants, for example).
- Paul must make sure that participants' phone numbers are kept safe and deleted as soon as possible. He must make sure that no one else has access to his phone, that it is kept secure (from viruses, spyware or malware) and that it is not lost or stolen, for example.

Scenario 2: Potential issues that Roshni needs to address include:

- Roshni must check all security features carefully and ensure that they are used effectively so that information provided in the groups remains confidential. This includes registration requirements in advance (and allowing only authenticated users to join); cloud recording security (and ensuring that she has disabled the sharing of recordings); using watermarks (image or audio to protect against unauthorized sharing); and locking the group to prevent anyone else joining when it is under way.
- Roshni needs to ensure that any platforms or tools she uses have the same strict anonymity and confidentiality codes that she applies to her research (Activity 50).

- Where will participants be located, when they take part in the group? Is it possible for Roshni to ensure that they are alone and that they, or other participants, cannot be overheard? If not, confidentiality cannot be guaranteed.
- How can Roshni address issues of anonymity when it is difficult or almost impossible to disguise individuals appearing on video? Are masking techniques necessary and what impact might these have on collection, analysis, sharing and reporting?
- Roshni needs to address issues of confidentiality and anonymity with participants. She should ensure that they understand that information provided in the focus groups, by others, must not be passed on to third parties.

Scenario 3: Potential issues that Peyton needs to address include:

- Peyton needs to consider how and where respondents complete the survey. Are they in public places? Can their answers be viewed by others, or are they discussed with others? Will the questionnaire be completed all at once or in short bursts? If so, is the respondent in different places, with different people, when filling in different parts of the questionnaire?
- Peyton needs to consider verification methods so that it is possible to tell who has completed a questionnaire and when.
- There might be situations where another person borrows the device: what are the implications for confidentiality and anonymity if anyone can access the questionnaire on a particular device? What mechanisms

should be put in place to prevent this from happening (sending out a unique link to the questionnaire in an email, for example)?
- How can Peyton ensure that respondents understand the importance of anonymity and confidentiality? If this information is provided as text that must be read, how can Peyton know whether respondents have read the information or have merely ticked the box without reading the information?
- If respondents are using their own devices, how can their information be kept safe and secure? How can questionnaire responses be protected against hacking, theft, interception or insertion of rogue data (Activity 86)?

Activity 62

Scenario 4: Potential issues that Niamh needs to address include:

- Niamh will need to consider rules, regulations and compliance of social media platforms, checking whether they adhere to strict anonymity and confidentiality policy (Activity 47). She will also have to decide whether it is possible to work within their policy (some platforms might insist that data are reported only in their original form and attributed to the original poster, for example).
- She will need to think about whether it is possible to assure anonymity and confidentiality when social media comments are traceable online.

- When undertaking social media analytics, people are often unaware that they are part of a research study. If individuals cannot be given information about anonymity and confidentiality at the start of the project, Niamh might need to address these issues further down the line, when she has collected and analysed data and when she knows what she wants to use in her research. Again, she needs to consider traceability.

Additional questions

If you have time, the following two questions can be explored:

1. What should researchers do if participants say that they want to be identified? Perhaps they have created something of which they are proud as part of the research project: see Mannay (2020) for an interesting discussion on creative research methods and anonymity. Or perhaps they are part of the elite and want to be identified (see Ellersgaard et al., 2021)?

2. Might anonymization further disadvantage marginalized groups? See Macleod and Mnyaka (2018) for an interesting discussion on these issues.

→ Related activities

Activity 9: Discussing privacy and confidentiality in the research context

Activity 79: Discussing the ethics, integrity and practice of anonymization in analysis, secondary analysis, re-analysis and third-party analysis

Activity 84: Anonymizing qualitative and quantitative data

Activity 85: Keeping research data protected and secure

→ Preparatory reading

Educators: All the resources listed below provide useful preparatory reading.

Students: None required. Some of the resources listed below can be recommended to students if they wish to follow up any of the issues raised in this activity.

→ Useful resources

Information about confidentiality and anonymity can be found in Section 2 of 'Research Ethics Guidance', *Social Research Association*, 2021: www.the-sra.org.uk/common/Uploaded%20files/Resources/SRA%20Ethics%20guidance%202021.pdf [accessed 13 July 2021].

Duclos, D. (2019) 'When ethnography does not rhyme with anonymity: Reflections on name disclosure, self-censorship, and storytelling', *Ethnography*, 20 (2): 175–83, first published 13 August 2017, doi: 10.1177/1466138117725337.

Ellersgaard, C.H., Ditlevsen, K. and Larsen, A.G. (2021) 'Say my name? Anonymity or not in elite interviewing', *International Journal of Social Research Methodology*, published online 6 June 2021, doi: 10.1080/13645579.2021.1932717.

Macleod, C.I. and Mnyaka, P. (2018) 'Introduction: The politics of anonymity and confidentiality'. In C. Macleod, J. Marx, P. Mnyaka and G. Treharne (eds), *The Palgrave Handbook of Ethics in Critical Research* (pp. 227–40). Cham: Palgrave Macmillan.

Mannay, D. (2020) 'Creative methods: Anonymity, visibility and ethical re-representation'. In R. Iphofen (ed.) *Handbook of Research Ethics and Scientific Integrity* (pp. 493–507). Cham: Springer.

Surmiak, A.D. (2018) 'Confidentiality in qualitative research involving vulnerable participants: Researchers' perspectives', *Forum Qualitative Sozialforschung / Forum: Qualitative Social Research*, 19 (3), published 26 September 2018, doi: 10.17169/fqs-19.3.3099.

Activity 62

Activity • • • • • • • • • • • → 62

Addressing Issues of Anonymity and Confidentiality

STUDENT HANDOUT

This activity is called 'Addressing issues of anonymity and confidentiality'. Work through the following scenarios with your group members. Take notes as you discuss each scenario: once this part of the activity is concluded, we will come back together to discuss the issues raised.

Scenario 1

Paul intends to undertake mobile phone interviews with his participants. He has identified 10 people to interview and will conduct the interviews over 10 days. He has developed a list of questions, some closed-ended, some open-ended. He will ask the same questions to all participants and write down their answers as they speak. What potential anonymity and confidentiality issues does Paul need to consider and how might he address them?

Scenario 2

Roshni intends to hold three online focus groups using Zoom Meetings. She has developed an interview schedule that has a number of topics listed, which she wants to discuss. She will use cloud recording so that she can replay the session as many times as she wishes when undertaking her analysis. What potential anonymity and confidentiality issues does Roshni need to consider and how might she address them?

Scenario 3

Peyton intends to administer an online questionnaire to a random sample of 500 respondents. The questionnaire will be adaptable and optimized so that it can be viewed on any device. Peyton will check how the questionnaire looks on a variety of devices, but the expectation is that most respondents will complete it on smartphones. What potential anonymity and confidentiality issues does Peyton need to consider and how might they address them?

Scenario 4

Niamh intends to undertake opinion mining of social media to track opinions expressed by people about the COVID-19 pandemic. She intends to look at social networking, microblogging, blogs and messaging sites. She has just completed a short course in social media analytics and feels confident in using the software and tools available for this type of research. What potential anonymity and confidentiality issues does Niamh need to consider and how might she address them?

Learning outcome: By the end of this activity, you will be able to identify, and explain how to address, various issues associated with anonymity and confidentiality in research.

Activity · · · · · · · · · · · → 63

Recognizing and Addressing Bias when Collecting Data

ACTIVITY 63: EDUCATOR NOTES

Purpose: This activity introduces students to different types of bias that can influence data collection. Students are asked to match the type of bias with the correct scenario, before going on to produce their own scenarios for other types of bias. Scenarios are then uploaded, along with useful references, to build a student-centred digital resource.

Type: Scenario-based, student-centred digital resource.

Alternative type(s): Scenarios for group discussion (in-class).

Level: Intermediate and advanced.

Duration: Students will spend up to two hours on this activity during independent study. If the in-class group activity is chosen, 50 minutes to one hour of contact time will be required.

Equipment/materials: A suitable tool for building the digital resource.

Learning outcome: By the end of this activity, students will be able to list a number of biases that can influence data collection and provide practical examples of the types of bias listed.

The activity

Give your students a copy of the Student Handout and ask that they work on the activity during independent study. They are asked to match three of the types of bias listed with the correct scenario before going on to develop their own scenarios for the remaining types of bias listed (you might need to produce other scenarios that are more relevant to your student cohort). They are then asked to find one more type of bias related to data collection and write a short scenario that illustrates this bias. Once they have done this, they are asked to upload their scenarios (with answers) to build a useful student-centred digital resource. They can also post links to useful references, if relevant. Post the correct answers to the three scenarios provided, so that students can check they have got it right before uploading their own for the remaining types of bias. Monitor posts and alter, amend or comment on any that are misleading or incorrect. Provide a deadline by which time students should upload and read scenarios.

This activity can be run as a group activity in-class, if you prefer. Divide your students into small groups and provide them with the three scenarios in the Student Handout, asking them to work out which of the biases listed is being described in each scenario. Allocate up to 15 minutes for groups to work on the exercise. Bring the groups back together and provide the correct answers. Then lead a class discussion: this can include a discussion on the other types of bias; a discussion on how these types of bias can be eliminated, reduced or avoided; and questions from students about bias that might be relevant to their own research.

Key issues

This activity is scenario-based because it encourages students to think about practical examples, or the practical application, of different types of bias. Initially, they were asked to match the type of bias with the relevant definition, and then produce their own definitions for the other types of bias listed. However, this was too easy and did not involve a great deal of thought as definitions were easy to find online. Therefore, an extra layer was introduced by asking them to produce a scenario relevant to each bias. The final part of the activity (find another type of bias not listed) was also added to encourage them to think more deeply about what is meant by bias in data collection and to make the student-centred resource even more useful. Additional types of bias that can be found and illustrated include information bias, participant bias, social desirability bias and channelling bias.

The answers to the three scenarios are:

Scenario 1: Selection bias is relevant here: Richard has chosen students who are in a bar. All students who do not go to the bar have been omitted from the study. This means that the students in Richard's study differ from the population of interest, which is all students. Some might not go to the bar because they do not drink alcohol, some might not like socializing, some might drink in other places and some might not go to the bar at the particular time Richard is present. They might have very different attitudes towards alcohol, but Richard will not know this because of selection bias.

Scenario 2: This is an example of volunteer bias. The people who have agreed to take part in this study might differ considerably from those who have not agreed: perhaps those who do not do very well in games are more reluctant to volunteer and those who do better want to show off their skills to the researcher (and to anyone else who takes an interest). There are a wide variety of reasons for people volunteering (or not volunteering) for research and this must be acknowledged in research that relies on volunteers.

Scenario 3: This is an example of interviewer bias. Mateo might be able to establish rapport better (or he might perceive that he establishes it better) because he is a football fan. This could mean that he is more interested in what they are saying (and this could be displayed through subtle signs as the interview progresses). It could also mean that he attaches more importance to what they are saying and, again, there could be subtle hints to this in body language, gestures and the way questions are asked, for example. All this could encourage football players to open up, whereas the opposite (subtle signs that display a lack of interest, for example) could lead to less productive interviews with rugby players.

Cautionary note

Monitor scenarios carefully when they are uploaded. Some types of bias are complex and students might struggle to produce a suitable scenario. If a scenario is incorrect or misleading, alter or comment on the post, pointing out issues and entering into discussion with students.

→ Related activities

Activity 28: Evaluating biases with reference to equality, diversity and inclusion

Activity 52: Assessing bias in search tools

Activity 64: Avoiding sampling bias

Activity 73: Recognizing and addressing bias when analysing qualitative data

Activity 74: Avoiding bias in quantitative analyses

Activity 97: Recognizing reporting bias

Activity 98: Understanding the influence of publication bias

→ Preparatory reading

Educators: The Catalogue of Bias is a useful place to start for educators new to teaching this topic (see useful resources).

Students: Some of the useful resources listed below can be placed on the digital resource, if relevant to your students.

Activity 63

→ Useful resources

A comprehensive list of bias in research studies, with definitions, can be obtained from the Catalogue of Bias: https:// catalogofbias.org [accessed 16 July 2021].

Bergen, N. and Labonté, R. (2020) '"Everything is perfect, and we have no problems": Detecting and limiting social desirability bias in qualitative research', *Qualitative Health Research*, 30 (5): 783–92, first published 13 December 2019, doi: 10.1177/1049732319889354.

Demir, M., Haynes, A., Orthel-Clark, H. and Özen, A. (2017) 'Volunteer bias in research on friendship among emerging adults', *Emerging Adulthood*, 5 (1): 53–68, first published 26 April 2016, doi: 10.1177/2167696816641542.

Kühne, S. (2020) 'Interpersonal perceptions and interviewer effects in face-to-face surveys', *Sociological Methods & Research*, first published 15 June 2020, doi: 10.1177/0049124120926215.

Mentges, A., Blowes, S.A., Hodapp, D., Hillebrand, H. and Chase, J.M. (2021) 'Effects of site-selection bias on estimates of biodiversity change', *Conservation Biology*, 35 (2): 688–98, first published 18 August 2020, doi: 10.1111/cobi.13610.

Schaurer, I. and Weiß, B. (2020) 'Investigating selection bias of online surveys on coronavirus-related behavioral outcomes', *Survey Research Methods*, 14 (2): 103–8, first published 2 June 2020, doi: 10.18148/srm/2020.v14i2.7751.

West, B.T. and Li, D. (2019) 'Sources of variance in the accuracy of interviewer observations', *Sociological Methods & Research*, 48 (3): 485–533, first published 25 September 2017, doi: 10.1177/0049124117729698.

Activity 63

Activity • • • • • • • • • • → 63

Recognizing and Addressing Bias when Collecting Data

STUDENT HANDOUT

In research, bias is the name given to an influence or prejudice that affects the research in some way. This can happen at all stages of the research process. This activity is called 'Recognizing and addressing bias when collecting data': it looks specifically at the different types of bias that can be introduced when gathering data. Six of these types are:

- observer bias
- recall bias
- selection bias

- question order bias
- volunteer bias
- interviewer bias

Consider the following three scenarios and match each one with the appropriate type of bias listed above. Read all three scenarios before you make your choices (scenarios might appear to relate to more than one bias, but matching them will become clearer if you read all three first).

Scenario 1

Richard is researching students' attitudes towards alcohol. He decides to go to the Students' Union bar where he hands out his questionnaire to every student he sees. He waits for students to return questionnaires to him. He does this over a period of four weeks so that he can access as many students as possible. He is surprised to find that attitudes towards alcohol are very favourable and that the sample of students he has chosen are drinking more than the national average.

Scenario 2

Marisha is undertaking research into how people interact with each other when playing massively multiplayer online games. She puts out a call for people to agree to take part in her research using Facebook. Twenty people get in touch and are happy to be part of the research project. When Marisha starts to observe game players who have agreed to take part, she finds that they are very good at their chosen game and are very keen to show off their skills. She begins to wonder whether the players are representative of all players of massively multiplayer online games.

Scenario 3

Mateo is a fanatic football supporter. He is part of a research team undertaking research into sports injuries in men. He, along with five other researchers, are to interview rugby and football players who identify as male. Mateo finds that, as his interviews progress, he obtains more detailed information from football players than he does from rugby players. He feels that he is able to build a better rapport with the football players because he understands their game.

Once you have matched the scenarios with the correct type of bias, go on to produce three more scenarios for the remaining types of bias listed. You can choose any type of scenario you wish, as long as each of the remaining three biases is illustrated by a different scenario. Then, go to the research literature to find one more type of bias related to data collection that has not been included in the list. Again, produce a short scenario that illustrates the type of bias you have found. Indicate the type of bias you are referring to at the end of each scenario.

Once you have produced your scenarios, upload them using the tool set up for this purpose by the given date. Read the scenarios produced by your peers and enter into online discussion, where appropriate. If you find any useful resources that would be of benefit to your peers, links to them can be added. This resource is for you and your peers, therefore, make it useful, interesting and informative.

Learning outcome: By the end of this activity, you will be able to list a number of biases that can influence data collection and provide practical examples of the types of bias listed.

Activity 63

Activity · · · · · · · · · · · · · → 64

Avoiding Sampling Bias

The activity

Decide whether you intend to run this session in-class, online synchronous (using video/web conferencing tools such as Zoom Meetings or Blackboard Collaborate) or online asynchronous (using a suitable VLE-hosted discussion board). If either of the online options is chosen, ensure that all students have the required access details.

Ask your students to work individually during independent study to answer two questions:

1. What is sampling bias?

2. How do you intend to address, reduce or eliminate sampling bias in your research?

Explain that their answers will be shared and discussed with their peers, so they should ensure that their work is thorough, correct and informative.

Once the work is complete, ask students to share it with their peers. This can be done in-class or online synchronous: ask each student, in turn, to present their ideas and invite questions or comments from their peers. Or it can be done online asynchronous: ask each student to upload their work by a given deadline, then read and discuss the work of their peers, again, by a specific deadline (for this option it might be prudent to give a word count limit of 500 so that students are not asked to read too much). Monitor posts to ensure that information is correct: if you notice any problems or mistakes, point them out, modify or amend them, explaining why this has been done. Monitor discussions to ensure that comments are respectful, constructive, supportive and correct.

Key issues

This activity is simple but extremely important: it encourages students to think about what is meant by sampling bias (including different types such as volunteer, self-selection and non-response bias), before going on to think about how this can be addressed, reduced or eliminated in their research. The content and type of discussion tends to depend on discipline and methodology. Some students believe that, if they follow correct procedures, it is possible to eliminate sampling bias. Others point out that, as both researchers and participants are human, some type of bias will always be present: all that can be done is to address bias (perhaps by acknowledging that it exists), while attempting to reduce it as much as possible. This is why students are asked to think about how sampling bias can be 'addressed, reduced or eliminated': it encourages them to explore sampling bias within their research more deeply and leads to interesting discussions about whether it is actually possible to eliminate sampling bias.

→ Related activities

Activity 28: Evaluating biases with reference to equality, diversity and inclusion

Activity 52: Assessing bias in search tools

Activity 63: Recognizing and addressing bias when collecting data

Activity 73: Recognizing and addressing bias when analysing qualitative data

Activity 74: Avoiding bias in quantitative analyses

Activity 97: Recognizing reporting bias

Activity 98: Understanding the influence of publication bias

→ Preparatory reading

Educators: The resources listed below provide perspectives from different disciplines and methodologies, and provide useful preparatory reading.

Students: None required. Students will find their own resources for this activity. Some of the relevant resources listed below can be recommended to students once the activity is complete.

→ Useful resources

Andringa, S. and Godfroid, A. (2020) 'Sampling bias and the problem of generalizability in applied linguistics,' *Annual Review of Applied Linguistics*, Cambridge University Press, 40: 134–42, doi: 10.1017/S0267190520000033.

Emmel, N. (2013) *Sampling and Choosing Cases in Qualitative Research: A Realist Approach.* London: Sage.

Lohr, S. (2019) *Sampling: Design and Analysis*, 2nd edition. Boca Raton, FL: CRC Press.

Napier-Munn, T.J., Whiten, W.J. and Faramarzi, F. (2020) 'Bias in manual sampling of rock particles,' *Minerals Engineering*, 153: 106260, published 1 July 2020, doi: 10.1016/j.mineng.2020.106260.

Thompson, S. (2012) *Sampling*, 3rd edition. Hoboken, NJ: John Wiley & Sons.

Valliant, R., Dever, J. and Kreuter, F. (2018) *Practical Tools for Designing and Weighting Survey Samples*, 2nd edition. Cham: Springer International.

Walters, W.H. (2021) 'Survey design, sampling, and significance testing: Key issues,' *Journal of Academic Librarianship*, 47 (3):102344, doi: 10.1016/j.acalib.2021.102344.

Webster, M.W. and Rutz, C. (2020) 'How STRANGE are your study animals?', *Nature*, 582: 337–40, published 15 June 2020, doi: 10.1038/d41586-020-01751-5.

The National Audit Office in the UK has produced a useful practical guide to sampling that can be downloaded from their website: www.nao.org.uk/report/sampling-guide [accessed 6 July 2021].

Activity 64

Activity · · · · · · · · · · · → 65

Assessing the Ethical Implications of Incentives and Rewards

The activity

Invite together students who are thinking about offering incentives or rewards to people who take part in their research (any number from six to 10 students is fine for this activity: if you have more, you will need longer than an hour to run the session). If possible, try to encourage students from different subjects, courses or research topics and methods: this adds depth and variety to this activity.

Begin the session by asking each student, in turn, to give a brief description of their research, a summary of the type of incentive or reward they intend to provide and a reason why they think this is necessary. As each student speaks, write down on a flip chart or white board the type of incentive or reward they intend to offer along with a precis of the reason they give.

Once students have provided their descriptions, work through the items you have written down. First, identify types of incentive to be offered. Discuss each type, asking students to consider the ethical implications, and whether these differ, depending on type. Second, consider the reasons given for offering incentives or rewards. Discuss whether the reasons are sound. Are there counter-arguments that can be put forward for each reason? The content and level of this discussion depends on subject and level of study: some examples of further questions that can be explored are given below.

Once this discussion has concluded, ask students to take a little time to reflect on their thoughts about incentives and rewards. Have they changed their mind (if so, why?)? Or do they feel that their choices are justified (why)? How can they justify and defend their choices? What action do they now need to take? If you still have time available, ask each student, in turn, to provide a brief summary of these thoughts and the action they intend to take. Conclude the session with a summary of the main points raised.

This workshop can be held online, if you prefer, using a video/web conferencing tool such as Zoom Meetings or Blackboard Collaborate. Set guidelines for constructive and supportive online discussion and follow the same structure as that given for the in-class workshop, above.

Key issues

There are a variety of issues that can be raised in this activity, including:

- Do incentives and rewards really encourage more people to take part in research? If they do, does this mean that research outcomes will be better and more people/society will benefit? Does this mean that incentives and rewards are justified?
- What is the connection between offering incentives and rewards and informed consent? Might people who need money provide their consent without understanding what is required (or the need for money outweighs the need to consider what is involved)? Or do people take extra time to consider risks when payments are high (Devine et al., 2013; Dickert, 2013)?
- How might incentives and rewards influence scientific methods and procedures (samples are skewed to groups from lower incomes, for example)?
- Should financial payment be made only if the risk of harm to the individual is negligible? Or should the amount of financial payment reflect the harm that could occur (in cases where patients could become unwell, for example)?
- If people expect a payment, might this stop people taking part in research that does not provide a payment (Zutlevics, 2016)?
- What is the effect of incentives and rewards on vulnerable members of society?
- Do incentives and rewards lead to unjust research burden on certain groups?
- How might incentives and rewards influence unethical behaviour of participants (exaggerating, lying or concealing the truth to become involved; fabricating results to continue in the study or receive rewards; serial research participants, for example; Devine et al., 2013)?

→ Related activities

Activity 2: Discussing the ethics of consent and purpose

Activity 42: Obtaining informed consent in the digital world

Activity 57: Seeking informed consent

Activity 66: Reducing participant burden

....

→ Preparatory reading

Educators: Dickert (2013) provides a brief editorial that sums up some of the main issues that can be raised in this activity.

Students: None required. However, you can recommend some of the resources listed below after the workshop has taken place, if required.

....

→ Useful resources

Bentley, J.P. and Thacker, P.G. (2004) 'The influence of risk and monetary payment on the research participation decision making process', *Journal of Medical Ethics*, 30: 293-8, first published June 1, 2004, doi: 10.1136/jme.2002.001594.

Brown, B., Marg, L., Zhang, Z., Kuzmanovi , D., Dubé, K. and Galea, J. (2019) 'Factors Associated with payments to research participants: A review of sociobehavioral studies at a large Southern California research university', *Journal of Empirical Research on Human Research Ethics*, 14 (4): 408-15, first published 21 August 2019 doi: 10.1177/1556264619869538.

Devine, E.G., Waters, M.E., Putnam, M., Surprise, C., O'Malley, K., Richambault, C., Fishman, R.L., Knapp, C.M., Patterson, E.H., Sarid-Segal, O., Streeter, C., Colanari, L. and Ciraulo, D.A. (2013) 'Concealment and fabrication by experienced research subjects', *Clinical Trials*, 10 (6): 935-48, first published 18 July 2013, doi: 10.1177/1740774513492917.

Dickert, N.W. (2013) 'Concealment and fabrication: The hidden price of payment for research participation?', *Clinical Trials*, 10 (6): 840-1, doi: 10.1177/1740774513506619.

Gelinas, L., White, S.A. and Bierer, B.E. (2020) 'Economic vulnerability and payment for research participation', *Clinical Trials*, 17 (3): 264-72, first published 17 February 2020, doi: 10.1177/1740774520905596.

Activity 65

Morgan, A.J., Rapee, R.M. and Bayer, J.K. (2017) 'Increasing response rates to follow-up questionnaires in health intervention research: Randomized controlled trial of a gift card prize incentive', *Clinical Trials*, 14 (4): 381–6, first published 8 April 2017 doi: 10.1177/1740774517703320.

Zutlevics, T. (2016) 'Could providing financial incentives to research participants be ultimately self-defeating?', *Research Ethics*, 12 (3): 137–48, first published 18 February 2016, doi: 10.1177/1747016115626756.

Activity 65

Activity • • • • • • • • • • → 66

Reducing Participant Burden

The activity

Find a suitable online brainstorming tool (Stormboard, MindMeister, SpiderScribe, Popplet or Miro are examples, but there are plenty more available). Practise with the tool if you have not used it before. Set up a suitable synchronous tool for your discussion (Zoom Meetings or Blackboard Collaborate, for example). Again, practise with the tool, if required.

Send a time, date and joining instructions to your students. Introduce the online session by giving a description of what is meant by participant burden (see below). Then run the brainstorm. Ask your students to give examples of different types of participant burden (provide one or two examples, if this helps to get the brainstorm started: see below). Write down their answers without judgement or critique. Continue with this until there are no more suggestions. This will take 10–15 minutes.

If students are unfamiliar with the brainstorming technique, ask them to give any answer they can think of in relation to the question, one at a time. Explain that their answers will not be judged, nor should they judge the answers of others (even if they do not agree with another's contribution). Each answer they give will be written down: the goal is to pool ideas and come up with a comprehensive list of types of participant burden.

Ask students to consider the list you have built from the brainstorm, in relation to their own research. Then go through each item, asking students to raise their hand if they think that the particular type of participant burden is relevant to their research. Identify the items that are most relevant to discuss further (those that had the most hands raised). Hold a discussion, asking questions and encouraging constructive and useful dialogue. Examples of questions that can be asked are given below.

This brainstorm and discussion can be held in-class, if you have the contact time available and if you think it will better suit your students.

Key issues

The term 'participant burden' (or 'respondent burden') can cover the:

- actual or perceived actions that need to be undertaken by people who take part in research relating to issues such as duration, intensity, frequency, invasiveness and finance;
- stresses and strains that these actual or perceived actions can place on people, psychologically, physically and emotionally (fear, anxiety or distress about methods, for example);
- effects this can have on people while taking part in research and after;
- effects this can have on the researcher, research methods and outputs (non-response and bias, for example).

Topics that have been mentioned in the brainstorm include the following (some have been shortened or modified for brevity and clarity):

- length of time for interviews;
- time required to complete questionnaires;
- length of experiments;
- complexity of questions;
- anxiety about perceived complexity;
- complexity of interventions;
- anxiety about health interventions;
- type of health interventions;
- fear of personal injury;
- distress when covering sensitive or upsetting topics;
- fear of emotional response;
- anxiety about technology;
- unfamiliarity with technology;
- privacy concerns;
- anxiety about confidentiality and/or anonymity;
- personal disclosure concerns;
- financial burden;
- concern about not answering 'in the right way';
- confusion or misunderstanding of purpose;
- confusion about methods.

Questions that can be asked in the discussion include:

- Why do you think this type of burden is relevant to your research?
- What effect do you think this type of burden might have on your participants?
- What effect do you think this type of burden might have on your research?
- Do you think this type of burden should be reduced? Why?
- How can you reduce this type of burden in your research?

→ **Related activities**

Activity 1: Respecting human dignity, privacy and rights

Activity 2: Discussing the ethics of consent and purpose

Activity 9: Discussing privacy and confidentiality in the research context

Activity 10: Working within the principle of beneficence

Activity 11: Avoiding harm to others

Activity 14: Working with vulnerable people

Activity 58: Cultivating sensitivity in method

Activity 62: Addressing issues of anonymity and confidentiality

Activity 85: Keeping research data protected and secure

Activity 66

➜ Preparatory reading

Educators: Useful preparatory reading covering monitoring and reducing burden in surveys has been produced by the Government Statistical Service in the UK: https://gss.civilservice.gov.uk/policy-store/monitoring-and-reducing-respondent-burden-2 [accessed 8 October 2021].

Students: None required in preparation for this activity. However, some of the resources listed below can be recommended, if required.

....

➜ Useful resources

Gieselmann, A., Efkemann, S.A. and Scholten, M. (2019) 'Commentary 2: Qualitative research with vulnerable persons – how to ensure that burdens and benefits are proportional and fairly distributed', *Journal of Empirical Research on Human Research Ethics*, 14 (5): 479–82, first published 28 November 2019, doi: 10.1177/1556264619847322b.

Golinelli, D., Ryan, G., Green, H.D., Kennedy, D.P., Tucker, J.S. and Wenzel, S.L. (2010) 'Sampling to reduce respondent burden in personal network studies and its effect on estimates of structural measures', *Field Methods*, 22 (3): 217–30, first published 20 May 2010, doi: 10.1177/1525822X10370796.

Kabacińska, K., Sharma, N., Kaye, J., Mattek, N., Kuzeljevic, B. and Robillard, J. (2020) 'Investigating the concept of participant burden in aging technology research', *BMC Geriatrics*, 20 (50), published 12 February 2020, doi: 10.1186/s12877-020-1441-3.

Lingler, J.H., Schmidt, K.L., Gentry, A.L., Hu, L. and Terhorst, L.A. (2014) 'A new measure of research participant burden: Brief report', *Journal of Empirical Research on Human Research Ethics*, 9 (4): 46–9, first published 11 August 2014, doi: 10.1177/1556264614545037.

Lingler, J., Coble, D.W., Bollinger, R., Edwards, D.F., Gabel, M., Grill, J.D., Knox, M. and Stark, S. (2020) 'Perceptions of research burden among participants in ADC cohorts', *Alzheimer's and Dementia*, 16 (Suppl 10): e044605, first published 7 December 2020, doi: 10.1002/alz.044605.

Naidoo, N., Nguyen, V.T., Ravaud, P., Young, B., Amiel, P., Schanté, D., Clarke, M. and Boutron, I. (2020) 'The research burden of randomized controlled trial participation: A systematic thematic synthesis of qualitative evidence', *BMC Medicine*, 18 (6), published 20 January 2020, doi: 10.1186/s12916-019-1476-5.

National Academies of Sciences, Engineering, and Medicine (2016) *Reducing Response Burden in the American Community Survey: Proceedings of a Workshop*. Washington, DC: The National Academies Press, doi: 10.17226/23639.

Activity 66

Activity · · · · · · · · · · · · → 67

Identifying Unethical Practice when Collecting Data

ACTIVITY 67: EDUCATOR NOTES

Purpose: This activity enables students to identify unethical practice when collecting data through the use of small group discussion and class brainwave. Students are able to discuss, share and remember examples of unethical practice in an entertaining and creative way, before going on to discuss how to overcome the types of unethical practice highlighted.

Type: Brainwave (in-class).

Alternative type(s): Online discussion.

Level: Intermediate and advanced.

Duration: Fifty minutes to one hour of contact time (in-class or online).

Equipment/materials: A suitable video/web conferencing tool, if the online option is chosen.

Learning outcome: By the end of this activity, students will be able to identify different types of unethical practice when collecting data and explain how to address the types of unethical practice identified.

The activity

Divide your students into small groups. The number and size of groups depend on the size of your class. Ideally, you need five or six groups with three or more students in each. Give each group a copy of the Student Handout. This asks them to discuss and develop a list of different types of unethical practice when collecting data.

When all groups have developed their list (usually after about 15 minutes) the brainwave can begin. This is a variation on the brainstorming method. It enables students to share their information in an entertaining way, while listening to others, thinking quickly and memorizing what has been said previously. Each answer is given quickly, without judgement or criticism from educators or peers.

To begin the brainwave, ask one member of the first group to stand up and offer one type of unethical practice. Write down their response on a flip chart or whiteboard (some will need to be summarized or shortened). Then ask a member of the second group to stand up and give a different example, then a member of the third group and so on. The groups do not have to make their contribution in any particular order: you can point randomly at the groups to keep your students motivated and alert.

Continue until a member from each group has provided an example. Carry on with the brainwave, starting again at the first group (with a different member speaking, if appropriate) until all ideas are exhausted and/or examples of unethical practice are beginning to be repeated (this usually takes about 10 minutes). Use your judgement about repetition: some examples of unethical practice are similar, but are described in a slightly different way (see below). Some can be allowed because they encourage students to think about the issues from different perspectives. Once this part of the activity has concluded, hold a whole-class discussion to cover the issues raised. Consider each type of unethical practice and ask students how they (or other researchers) could or should overcome or address the problems identified.

This activity can be run as an online group discussion followed by a whole-class discussion, if you prefer not to run the brainwave in-class. Use a suitable video/web conferencing tool (Blackboard Collaborate, Zoom Meetings or Conferences in Canvas, for example) and use breakout rooms for the group part of the discussion. Allocate 15 minutes for groups to discuss different types of unethical practice when collecting data, then bring the groups back together to present their main findings. Follow this with a whole-class discussion to talk about the issues raised and to identify ways to overcome or address the types of unethical practice that have been identified.

This activity can be followed by Activity 71: Identifying unethical practice when analysing data. This is a worksheet that provides specific examples for students to work through during independent study and, as such, will help to reinforce and consolidate learning on this topic.

Key issues

A wide variety of issues can be raised during the brainwave. These include the following (in students' own words, which illustrates how similar practices can be included because they are approached from a slightly different perspective):

- lying about the purpose of the research (Activity 2);
- not getting permission to do the research (Activity 57);
- presuming people have agreed when they haven't (Activities 42 and 57);
- collecting digital data without consent (Activity 42);
- using data without permission (Activity 35);
- harvesting and re-using social media data that isn't intended for research (Taylor and Pagliari, 2018; Stommel and Rijk, 2021; Activity 49);
- ignoring data rights (Activities 31 and 33);
- bullying people to take part;
- exploiting vulnerable people (Activity 14);
- exploiting people to get information;
- harming animals (Beauchamp and DeGrazia, 2020);
- making someone ill in a clinical trial (Activities 10 and 11);
- choosing people because they will give the best answers (Activity 64);
- choosing references to back up your viewpoint;
- choosing samples to back up your theory (Activity 64);
- being prejudiced when interviewing someone (Activity 63);

- discriminating against certain groups (Activity 8);
- breaking confidentiality (Activities 9 and 62);
- accidentally identifying someone to another person (Activities 9, 62 and 79);
- ignoring what someone has said (Activity 71);
- paying too much money for taking part in research (Activity 65);
- invading private digital spaces (Activity 9);
- collecting personal data that isn't required (Activities 60 and 61);
- not having the right identity questions and answers (Activity 61);
- cutting corners due to lack of time (Activities 18, 20 and 21);
- expecting too much from people (Activity 66);
- pinching other researchers' data (Activities 23 and 29);
- poor lab practice (Activities 19 and 21);
- cheating (Activity 24);
- using collection methods that weren't given ethical approval (Activity 41);
- manipulating data due to vested interest (Activity 25).

→ Related activities

Activity 8: Conducting discrimination-aware and fairness-aware research

Activity 11: Avoiding harm to others

Activity 42: Obtaining informed consent in the digital world

Activity 57: Seeking informed consent

Activity 71: Identifying unethical practice when analysing data

→ Preparatory reading

Educators: The references given below provide useful preparatory reading for this activity. Consult the relevant activity for further resources about a particular issue listed above.

Students: None required. Some of the resources listed below can be recommended after the activity, if required.

Activity 67

→ Useful resources

Ajunwa, I., Crawford, K. and Ford, J.S. (2016) 'Health and big data: An ethical framework for health information collection by corporate wellness programs', *Journal of Law, Medicine & Ethics*, 44 (3): 474-80, first published 1 September 2016, doi: 10.1177/1073110516667943.

Beauchamp, T. and DeGrazia, D. (2020) *Principles of Animal Research Ethics*. New York, NY: Oxford University Press.

Louis-Charles, H.M., Howard, R., Remy, L., Nibbs, F. and Turner, G. (2020) 'Ethical considerations for postdisaster fieldwork and data collection in the Caribbean', *American Behavioral Scientist*, 64 (8): 1129-44, first published 10 July 2020, doi: 10.1177/0002764220938113.

Stommel, W. and Rijk, L. de (2021) 'Ethical approval: None sought. How discourse analysts report ethical issues around publicly available online data', *Research Ethics*, first published 19 January 2021, doi: 10.1177/1747016120988767.

Taylor, J. and Pagliari, C. (2018) 'Mining social media data: How are research sponsors and researchers addressing the ethical challenges?', *Research Ethics*, 14 (2): 1-39, first published 26 October 2017, doi: 10.1177/1747016117738559.

Ethical guidelines to ensure 'that research on and about the Internet is conducted in an ethical and professional manner' can be obtained from The Association of Internet Researchers (AoIR): https://aoir.org/ethics/ [accessed 8 October 2021].
    Information about codes, declarations and ethical guidelines for research with humans can be obtained from Part 2 of this textbook:

Emanuel, E., Grady, C., Crouch, R., Lie Miller, F. and Wendler, D. (eds), *The Oxford Textbook of Clinical Research Ethics*. New York, NY: Oxford University Press.

Activity 67

Activity · · · · · · · · · · · → 67

Identifying Unethical Practice when Collecting Data

STUDENT HANDOUT

This activity is about unethical practice when collecting data. Work with your group members to discuss and develop a list of different types of unethical practice that could be used by researchers when they gather or collect data for their research. Think about examples from different disciplines and different types of research. This can include quantitative and qualitative research, primary or secondary research, digital methods, face-to-face methods and data harvesting and mining, for example. You have 15 minutes to discuss and develop your list.

Once you have done this, you will be asked to share your list with the rest of the class during a class 'brainwave'. This is a variation on the brainstorm technique and will require a member from each group to stand up, in turn, and give one example of unethical practice, taking care not to repeat what has come before. This method enables you to share ideas, while listening to others, thinking quickly and memorizing what has been said previously. Each answer is given promptly, without judgement or criticism, even if you do not agree with what has been said. The aim of the brainwave is to help you to discuss, share and remember useful information and advice about unethical practice when collecting data, in an entertaining and creative way.

When the brainwave has finished, we will consider the issues raised and discuss methods that can be used to tackle the problems you have identified.

Learning outcome: By the end of this activity, you will be able to identify different types of unethical practice when collecting data and explain how to address the types of unethical practice identified.

Activity · · · · · · · · · · · · → 68

Collecting Images and Using Visual Methods Ethically

ACTIVITY 68: EDUCATOR NOTES

Purpose: This activity encourages students to explore how to collect images and use visual methods ethically by asking them to take part in a student-led discussion (questions are posed by students and discussed by their peers so that topics that are of importance to students can be raised). It can be run together with Activity 100: Displaying and publishing images ethically, for greater coverage of the topic, if required.

Type: Student-led discussion (in-class or online).

Alternative type(s): Self-guided individual exercise.

Level: Intermediate and advanced.

Duration: Fifty minutes to one hour.

Equipment/materials: A suitable video/web conferencing tool if the online option is chosen.

Learning outcome: By the end of this activity, students will be able to identify, and provide solutions to, a number of ethical issues, challenges and dilemmas when collecting images and using visual methods in research.

The activity

This activity can be run with your whole student cohort or with students who intend to use visual methods for their research. Give your students a copy of the Student Handout. This asks them to think about how to collect images and use visual methods ethically. They are to produce three questions concerning this topic that they would like to discuss with their peers when you next meet (in-class or online). Questions should lead to an informative, interesting and thought-provoking discussion. This activity works best if there are 8-10 students in the discussion group. If you have more than this number in your student cohort, divide your students into groups (use a room big enough for separate groups if you choose the in-class option, and use breakout rooms if you choose the online option).

Your role is to act as facilitator. Set guidelines for constructive, respectful and courteous discussion. Ask a student to pose their first question, then encourage their peers to discuss the issues raised by the question, with the aim of providing a suitable solution/answer. Move on to the next student, when appropriate. Students might not have time to pose all three questions, but they are asked to produce three in case one of their questions has been posed by another student. Conclude the discussion with a summary of the main points raised.

This activity can be run as a self-guided individual exercise, if you prefer. Choose some of the questions listed below that are appropriate for your cohort and ask students to work through them on an independent basis.

Key issues

The questions posed by students tend to depend on the level of study, type of research and discipline. Examples include the following (questions have been edited, amalgamated and shortened, where appropriate):

- Can we use images found on Facebook for our research? How can we get permission to use images from Facebook?
- If images are freely available on the internet, can I use them for my research?
- How can privacy be protected when collecting and using images, especially photos?
- How should we deal with things like anonymity (when it is obvious who is in the picture)?
- Who owns the digital image? How do we find out who owns an image?
- Do we have to get permission to use visual material?
- Can I ask participants to produce their own images for my research? In this case, who owns the images they produce?
- Does anyone provide open-source images that we can use for our research?
- How can we get permission to use a photo, especially when other people might appear in it? Do people in a photo need to consent to my using it? If people give me a photo for my research, does that count as permission to use it in my dissertation?
- Are images protected by copyright? Are photos protected by copyright? How do we find out who is the copyright holder of visual material?

- Can I use maps in my research without asking anyone for permission?
- Do visual images represent reality?
- In what way do images differ from words?
- How might the 'truth' status of images differ from the 'truth' status of words?
- How credible and authentic are images?
- Is it okay to use Photoshop for images we want to use? Should researchers manipulate images? What are the implications for transparency?
- How should we analyse visual materials?
- What is the best (or correct way) to cite visual images that you might have referred to, but not published, in your work?
- How should we store photos that we are using for research?
- What is the best way to keep visual material safe and secure?
- How do we stop other researchers using images we have created?
- What is the best way to share visual materials with other researchers?
- What does 'using visual methods ethically' actually mean?

→ Related activities

Activity 46: Using visual methods, in Dawson (2016: 120-1)

Activity 62: Analysing visual data, in Dawson (2016: 166-8)

Activity 100: Displaying and publishing images ethically

→ Preparatory reading

Educators: All the resources listed below provide useful preparatory reading for this activity.

Students: None required. Relevant resources listed below can be recommended after the activity, if required.

→ Useful resources

The UK Research Integrity Office contains some useful information and links to resources about academic image integrity: https://ukrio.org/research-integrity-resources/research-integrity-resources/academic-image-integrity [accessed 6 July 2021].

Clark, A. (2013) 'Haunted by images? Ethical moments and anxieties in visual research', *Methodological Innovations Online*, 8 (2): 68-8, first published 1 August 2013, doi: 10.4256/mio.2013.014.

Dawson, C. (2016) *100 Activities for Teaching Research Methods*. London: Sage.

Dodd, S. (ed.) (2020) *Ethics and Integrity in Visual Research Methods*. Bingley: Emerald Publishing.

Mannay, D. (2016) *Visual, Narrative and Creative Research Methods: Application, Reflection and Ethics*. Abingdon: Routledge.

Nash, M. and Moore, R. (2019) 'Exploring research relationships and other ethical challenges of participatory visual research in remote environments', *Journal of Sociology*, 55 (3): 604-23, first published 3 October 2018, doi: 10.1177/1440783318802982.

Activity 68

Shepherd, L.J. (2017) 'Aesthetics, ethics, and visual research in the digital age: "Undone in the face of the otter"', *Millennium*, 45 (2): 214-22, first published 1 January 2017, doi: 10.1177/0305829816684255.

Warfield, K., Hoholuk, J., Vincent, B. and Camargo, A.D. (2019) 'Pics, dicks, tits, and tats: Negotiating ethics working with images of bodies in social media research', *New Media & Society*, 21 (9): 2068-86, first published 26 April 2019, doi: 10.1177/1461444819837715.

Warr, D., Guillemin, M., Cox, S. and Waycott, J. (eds) (2016) *Ethics and Visual Research Methods: Theory, Methodology, and Practice*. New York, NY: Palgrave Macmillan.

Activity 68

Activity • • • • • • • • • • • → 68

Collecting Images and Using Visual Methods Ethically

STUDENT HANDOUT

This activity is called 'Collecting images and using visual methods ethically'. It is a student-led activity in which you and your peers decide on, and lead, the discussion. Take a little time before we next meet to think about questions you would like answered about the ethical use of images in research and about the ethics of visual methods in research. Once you have done this, develop three questions related to this topic that you would like to explore with your peers.

When we next meet, each student, in turn, will have the chance to pose one of their questions, which will then be discussed by the group. It is important that we have an interesting, informative and thought-provoking discussion, so think about this when developing your questions. Try to choose something that will not have been chosen by your peers, while ensuring that your questions are relevant to the topic and will enable you and your peers to achieve the learning outcome given below.

You have been asked to produce three questions, but may have the chance to ask only one or two of them. It is important, however, that you produce three, so that you can choose which to ask and have alternatives available if one of your questions has already been posed by one of your peers.

Learning outcome: By the end of this activity, you will be able to identify, and provide solutions to, a number of ethical issues, challenges and dilemmas when collecting images and using visual methods in research.

Activity · · · · · · · · · · · · → 69

Assessing the Challenges and Potential Negative Effects of Fieldwork

The activity

Invite together a group of students who intend to undertake fieldwork for their research (some who are new to research may require a short definition of 'fieldwork'). Students can be from one course and one level or from a range of courses and levels. The group should not be too large: 7–14 participants is ideal. Explain the purpose and format of the structured peer support group:

- first, you will meet in a 50-minute to one-hour session (in-class or online) to assess potential challenges and possible negative effects of fieldwork;
- second, students will work on an action plan that will help them to address problems that have been identified (during independent study);

- third, students will undertake their fieldwork (the time-scale here depends on the type and level of research);
- fourth, the group will reconvene for another 50 minutes to one hour session (in-class or online) to discuss their fieldwork and any problems they may have encountered.

Students can also meet on an informal basis (face-to-face or online) at any time as the activity progresses and after the activity, if they feel that support and encouragement from group members will be of use.

Decide how you would like to run the sessions. They can be informal, enabling students to raise issues that are of concern in any order they wish, or you can develop a list of topics or questions to cover (see key issues, below). Encourage students to meet with their peers if they need support as their fieldwork progresses and be flexible about calling another meeting part-way through their research, if students feel this would be of help (this may not be possible for some types of fieldwork, and for others it will only be possible online).

A similar structured support group is used in Activity 34: Researching illegal, unlawful, illicit or dangerous behaviour. Some research projects may cover both this activity and Activity 34, and similar issues can be raised in each. Therefore, take a little time to look at students' proposed research and choose the activity that is the most appropriate to run with your students.

Key issues

This activity enables students to discuss worries and concerns about undertaking fieldwork, while gaining support and encouragement from each other. They can pool experiences, knowledge and understanding, which will help them to develop and implement a constructive and effective plan of action. Group members are available for support and encouragement throughout the activity (and often throughout their research). This provides the opportunity for peers to offer support if unforeseen problems occur during their fieldwork and after the research has been completed.

Challenges that are identified depend on the subject, level of study and type of research, and can cover:

- risk, personal security and researcher safety (Activities 26 and 27);
- the unpredictable and dynamic nature of risk (Sampson, 2019);
- avoiding harm to participants and maintaining their welfare (Activities 11 and 10);
- vulnerable groups and people (Activity 14);
- access and seeking informed consent (Activities 42 and 57);
- organizational, institutional and political access and barriers to access (Mukeredzi, 2012; Fuchs et al., 2019);

- gender, ethnicity, age and emotions (Benz, 2014; Zubair et al., 2012);
- researching cross-culturally (Activity 30);
- toilet facilities and ablutions (Frøystad, 2020);
- privacy and confidentiality (Activity 9);
- using technology when in the field (van Baalen, 2018)
  - o keeping data protected and secure (Activity 85);
  - o storing and transferring sensitive data safely;
  - o keeping hardware safe and secure;
  - o protecting against hacking, theft, interception or insertion of rogue data (Activity 86).

The following can be included in plans of action:

- carrying out a risk assessment (Activity 27) and a digital risk assessment;
- producing a Data Management Plan (Activity 81);
- keeping a personal journal or research diary (Browne, 2013);
- taking time to talk to, and connect with, others undertaking fieldwork;

- conducting detailed background reading to find out more about relevant issues;
- identifying and working on specific coping strategies;
- working out how to stay connected with supervisors, tutors and/or peers, even when in the field.

➜ Related activities

Activity 26: Ensuring researcher safety

Activity 27: Carrying out a risk assessment

Activity 34: Researching illegal, unlawful, illicit or dangerous behaviour

Activity 70: Critiquing representation of the researcher in qualitative research

....

➜ Preparatory reading

Educators: All the resources listed below provide useful preparatory reading for educators.

Students: None required for the first stage of the activity. Some of the references listed below can be recommended if they are relevant to the challenges and concerns that have been raised.

....

Activity 69

→ Useful resources

Benz, T. (2014) 'Flanking gestures: Gender and emotion in fieldwork', *Sociological Research Online*, 19 (2): 1–8, first published 2 June 2014, doi: 10.5153/sro.3326.

Browne, B.C. (2013) 'Recording the personal: The benefits in maintaining research diaries for documenting the emotional and practical challenges of fieldwork in unfamiliar settings', *International Journal of Qualitative Methods*, February 2013: 420–35, first published 1 February 2013, doi: 10.1177/160940691301200121.

Frøystad, K. (2020) 'Failing the third toilet test: Reflections on fieldwork, gender and Indian loos', *Ethnography*, 21 (2): 261–79, first published 15 October 2018, doi: 10.1177/1466138118804262.

Fuchs, D., Fuk-Ying Tse, P. and Feng, X. (2019) 'Labour research under coercive authoritarianism: Comparative reflections on fieldwork challenges in China', *Economic and Industrial Democracy*, 40 (1): 132–55, doi: 10.1177/0143831X18780337.

Lunn, J. (ed.) (2014) *Fieldwork in the Global South: Ethical Challenges and Dilemmas*. Abingdon: Routledge.

Mukeredzi, T.G. (2012) 'Qualitative data gathering challenges in a politically unstable rural environment: A Zimbabwean experience', *International Journal of Qualitative Methods*, February 2012: 1–11, first published 1 February 2012, doi: 10.1177/160940691201100101.

Sampson, H. (2019) '"Fluid fields" and the dynamics of risk in social research', *Qualitative Research*, 19 (2): 131–47. doi: 10.1177/1468794117746085.

van Baalen, S. (2018) '"Google wants to know your location": The ethical challenges of fieldwork in the digital age', *Research Ethics*, 14 (4): 1–17, first published 1 January 2018, doi: 10.1177/1747016117750312.

Zubair, M., Martin, W. and Victor, C. (2012) 'Embodying gender, age, ethnicity and power in "the field": Reflections on dress and the presentation of the self in research with older Pakistani Muslims', *Sociological Research Online*, 17 (3): 73–90, first published 21 September 2012, doi: 10.5153/sro.2667.

Activity 69

Activity · · · · · · · · · · · · → 70

Critiquing Representation of the Researcher in Qualitative Research

---

ACTIVITY 70: EDUCATOR NOTES

Purpose: This activity has been designed for postgraduate students who are in the process of planning their research. It is an informal discussion (in-class or online) for invited students who have an interest in critiquing the representation of the researcher in qualitative research.

Type: Informal discussion for invited students (in-class or online).

Alternative type(s): Written assignment (individual self-guided activity during independent study).

Level: Advanced.

Duration: Students will spend one or two hours during independent study reading a journal paper and preparing their questions/topics. You will need 50 minutes to one hour of contact time for the in-class or online discussion. If the written assignment option is chosen, students will spend a few hours working on the assignment and educators will spend an hour or two reading/marking assignments.

Equipment/materials: A suitable video/web conferencing tool, if the online discussion option is chosen.

Learning outcome: By the end of this activity, students will be able to provide a critique of the representation of the researcher in qualitative research and explain the relevance to their research.

The activity

Explain to your students that you are running a voluntary session that will enable them to explore the representation of the researcher in qualitative research. Once you have your volunteers, ask them to read Langley and Klag (2019) prior to the session. As they read, they should jot down some questions or topics that they wish to explore when you meet. These can be general issues related to the paper, or issues related specifically to their research that they would like to discuss with their peers. When you meet (either in-class or online synchronous), ask students to discuss the paper. What do they think about the paper and the points raised? Then ask each student, in turn, to ask a question or introduce their topic for discussion. Spend a few minutes on the discussion, before moving on to the next question/topic. Continue until time runs out or all questions/topics have been discussed. Conclude with a summary of the main points raised.

This activity can be run as a written assignment if you prefer. Ask your students to produce a critique of Langley and Klag (2019), before going on to illustrate the relevance to their research. Provide a submission date and assessment criteria, if you choose to make this an assessed piece of work.

Key issues

This activity has been designed as a voluntary discussion because it might not be relevant to all your students. However, if you feel that all students could benefit from attendance, make it compulsory instead. Langley and Klag (2019) raise a number of important issues about the representation of the researcher and their paper provides useful, interesting and real examples that enable students to see the relevance to their research. The questions or topics students present for discussion depend on their research topic and methodology, but can include how they present themselves to participants, how their identity influences participants, how they write their research and whether their choices are acceptable for research ethics committees and examiners.

→ Related activities

Activity 43: Critiquing the presentation of self in online worlds

Activity 44: Managing the researcher's online presence

Activity 59: Critiquing overt and covert methods

→ Preparatory reading

Educators: Langley and Klag (2019) should be read prior to the discussion. Gregory (2018) provides useful preparatory reading for educators who are working with students who intend to conduct online qualitative research.

Students: Langley and Klag (2019) should be read in preparation for the discussion.

→ Useful resources

Cheek, J. and Øby, E. (2019) '"Getting attention" creating and presenting the visible, online, researcher self', *Qualitative Inquiry*, 25 (6): 571–82, first published 31 October 2018, doi: 10.1177/1077800418806593.

Gregory, K. (2018) 'Online communication settings and the qualitative research process: Acclimating students and novice researchers', *Qualitative Health Research*, 28 (10): 1610–20, first published 11 June 2018, doi: 10.1177/1049732318776625.

Lahman, M.K.E., De Oliveira, B., Cox, D., Sebastian, M.L., Cadogan, K., Rundle Kahn, A., Lafferty, M., Morgan, M., Thapa, K., Thomas, R. and Zakotnik-Gutierrez, J. (2021) 'Own your walls: Portraiture and researcher reflexive collage self-portraits', *Qualitative Inquiry*, 27 (1): 136–47, first published 6 February 2020, doi: 10.1177/1077800419897699.

Langley, A. and Klag, M. (2019) 'Being where? Navigating the involvement paradox in qualitative research accounts', *Organizational Research Methods*, 22 (2): 515–38, first published 20 November 2017, doi: 10.1177/1094428117741967.

Leaney, S. and Webb, R. (2021) 'Representation as politics: Asserting a feminist ethic in ethnographic research', *Ethnography and Education*, 16 (1): 44–59, published online 2 February 2020, doi: 10.1080/17457823.2020.1722952.

Manning, J. (2018) 'Becoming a decolonial feminist ethnographer: Addressing the complexities of positionality and representation', *Management Learning*, 49 (3): 311–26, first published 2 January 2018, doi: 10.1177/1350507617745275.

Mao, L., Mian Akram, A., Chovanec, D. and Underwood, M.L. (2016) 'Embracing the spiral: researcher reflexivity in diverse critical methodologies', *International Journal of Qualitative Methods*, first published 8 December 2016, doi: 10.1177/1609406916681005.

Ntanyoma, R.D. (2021) 'Fieldnotes, field research, and positionality of a "contested-native researcher"', *International Journal of Qualitative Methods*, first published 21 June 2021, doi: 10.1177/16094069211025454.

Shai, P.N. (2020) 'A local researcher's experiences of the insider–outsider position: An exercise of self-reflexivity during ethnographic GBV and HIV prevention research in South Africa', *International Journal of Qualitative Methods*, first published 28 July 2020, doi: 10.1177/1609406920938563.

Activity 70

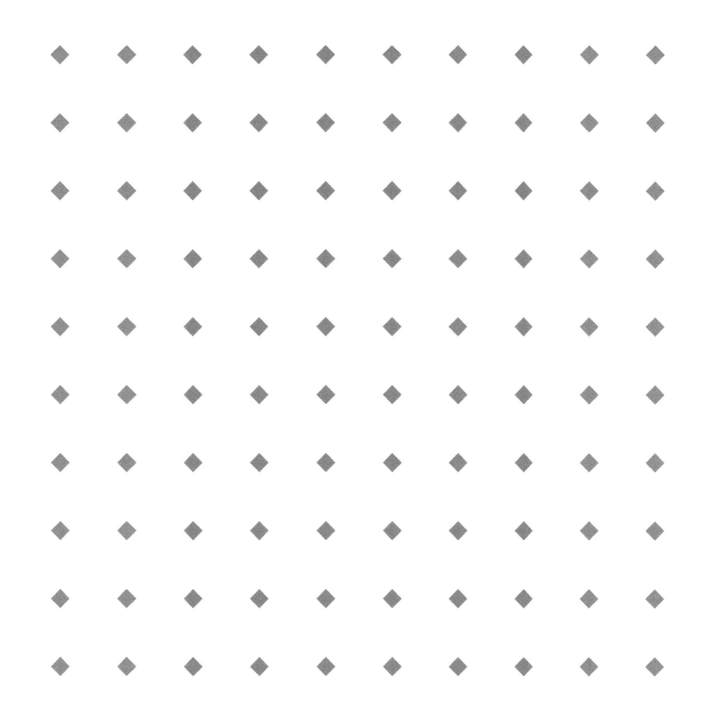

Section 6 Data Analysis

Activity • • • • • • • • • • • → 71

Identifying Unethical Practice when Analysing Data

The activity

Give your students a copy of the Student Handout and ask that they work through the questions in their own time during independent study. The worksheet can be completed as a self-contained exercise. Alternatively, you can bring students together to discuss their answers, or ask them to post these on your VLE-hosted discussion board for review and comments from peers. Five examples are given in the worksheet, but these can be modified to suit the subject and level of study of your students, if required.

This activity can also be run as a synchronous online discussion using a video/web conferencing tool such as Zoom Meetings or Blackboard Collaborate, and a suitable online polling tool such as Kwiqpoll, Mentimeter or Answer Garden. Set guidelines for constructive and supportive online discussion. Introduce the session and then ask students to read the examples given in the Handout (these can be produced in a pre-prepared document or through using features such as Whiteboard or Annotate). Once they have read the examples, ask each question one at a time. Use your chosen polling tool to receive answers to the first two questions (it is interesting for students to see how others vote), before discussing them in more depth. Take time to receive answers for the remaining three questions (students can write these answers using the chat facility or you can ask them to answer by video). Conclude the session with a summary of the main points raised.

Key issues

Asking students to think about which of the types of unethical practice is the most severe (and using polling tools, if the online option is chosen) is a useful exercise because it can illustrate that your students have different ideas about what constitutes unethical behaviour when analysing data. The activity can also illustrate that they have different ideas about how this sort of behaviour should be tackled. However, most students tend to think that genuine mistakes (examples 2 and 5) are less severe than deliberate unethical practice, and that mistakes can be avoided through developing knowledge and understanding of techniques and methods.

This activity provides an introduction to the topic. If you wish to study this topic further, combine this activity with one of the activities below, for deeper coverage. Alternatively, pick one or two of the references in the resource section to give to students to discuss when you next meet.

➜ Related activities

Activity 67: Identifying unethical practice when collecting data

Activity 72: Assessing ethical issues in data analytics

Activity 73: Recognizing and addressing bias when analysing qualitative data

Activity 74: Avoiding bias in quantitative analyses

Activity 75: Avoiding wrong conclusions

Activity 76: Recognizing false, fabricated or misleading analyses

➜ Preparatory reading

Educators: The resources listed below provide useful preparatory reading.

Students: None required. Students can find their own resources if they need them when completing the worksheet.

➜ Useful resources

Gibbert, M., Nair, L.B., Weiss, M., and Hoegl, M. (2021) 'Using outliers for theory building', *Organizational Research Methods*, 24 (1): 172-81, first published 10 January 2020, doi: 10.1177/1094428119898877.

Jones, M., Walker, M. and Attia, J. (2017) 'Understanding statistical principles in correlation, causation and moderation in human disease', *Medical Journal of Australia*, 207 (3): 104-6, published online 7 August 2017, doi: 10.5694/mja16.00697.

Levitin, D. (2018) *A Field Guide to Lies and Statistics: A Neuroscientist on How to Make Sense of a Complex World*. London: Penguin.

Rohrer, J.M. (2018) 'Thinking clearly about correlations and causation: Graphical causal models for observational data', *Advances in Methods and Practices in Psychological Science*, 1 (1): 27-42, doi: 10.1177/2515245917745629.

Smith, G. (2020) 'Data mining fool's gold', *Journal of Information Technology*, 35 (3): 182-94, first published 11 May 2020, doi: 10.1177/0268396220915600.

Wasserman, R. (2013) 'Ethical issues and guidelines for conducting data analysis in psychological research', *Ethics & Behavior*, 23 (1): 3-15, doi: 10.1080/10508422.2012.728472.

Activity 71

Identifying Unethical Practice when Analysing Data

STUDENT HANDOUT

This activity is called 'Identifying unethical practice when analysing data'. Please read the following examples of unethical practice, before answering the questions below.

Example 1

Not including data outliers, obscuring data or taking only data points that validate a researcher's view or reinforce their theory.

Example 2

Making genuine mistakes when analysing data and then hiding, obscuring or denying the mistakes when they are detected.

Example 3

Using quotations from transcripts that back up the developing theory, and discarding quotations and whole transcripts that don't back-up the theory.

Example 4

Data-dredging to find specific relationships between data points that are then presented as statistically significant.

Example 5

Thinking that correlation suggests causation or not understanding what statistical evidence is required to warrant or support causal conclusions.

Question 1

Which of these examples, in your opinion, is the most serious type of unethical practice? Explain your answer.

Question 2

Which of these examples, in your opinion, is the least serious type of unethical practice? Explain your answer.

Question 3

How might you spot each type of unethical practice in a research project?

Example 1:

Example 2:

Example 3:

Example 4:

Example 5:

Question 4

How can researchers avoid each of these types of unethical practice?

Example 1:

Example 2:

Example 3:

Example 4:

Example 5:

Question 5

What do you need to do in your research to avoid unethical practice when analysing data?

Learning outcome: By the end of this activity, you will be able to identify different types of unethical practice in data analysis; differentiate between their severity; recognize unethical practice when it occurs; and describe how to avoid unethical practice in analysis, including your own.

Activity 71

Activity • • • • • • • • • • • • → 72

Assessing Ethical Issues in Data Analytics

The activity

Divide your students into groups (the number of groups depends on the size of your cohort and the amount of contact time you have available). About three to five students in each group is a good number for this activity (if you have a large number of students in your cohort and only 50 minutes to one hour of contact time, you may need to allocate more students to each group). Give half the groups Student Handout 1 and the other half Student Handout 2. These provide a definition of data analytics, before going on to outline the task. Students are asked to build a vision of the future in which data analytics are rampant and all-encompassing. In Handout 1 students are told that ethical issues associated with data analytics are not important and have been ignored. In Handout 2 students are told that ethical issues associated with data analytics are extremely important and great emphasis has been placed on ensuring that data analytics is conducted to the highest ethical standards. Both Handouts instruct students to build their visions and prepare a presentation for their peers.

When you next meet, ask each group, in turn, to present their vision. Before they start, tell them that half the groups have been asked to present a different picture from the others (there is no need to tell them exactly how, as they soon work this out for themselves and it provides an interesting point for discussion). Allocate 10 minutes for each presentation and five minutes for questions and discussion. Conclude the session with a summary of the main points raised.

This activity can be run online, if preferred. Students will need to create and upload a video of their presentation, which can then be viewed and discussed using a suitable synchronous tool. The Student Handouts will need to be adapted slightly.

Key issues

This activity introduces students to ethical issues in data analytics in a creative, enjoyable and memorable way. Groups are asked to present ethical issues from negative and positive sides because it provides variety and interest, while enabling students to consider the issues from different viewpoints. To undertake this activity successfully, they must identify ethical issues associated with data analytics, before going on to produce their vision. Examples of issues that can be included are:

- negative impact on disadvantaged groups (Activity 45);
- harm to individuals (Activity 11);
- social (in)justice (Activity 46);
- informed consent (Activity 42);
- neutrality (Activity 78);
- transparency and openness (Activity 17).

More information about ethical issues associated with data analytics can be obtained from Chapter 10, Dawson (2020: 66-72).

→ Related activities

Activity 42: Obtaining informed consent in the digital world

Activity 45: Designing inclusive data systems

Activity 46: Reclaiming datasets for social justice

Activity 49: Assessing the ethical implications of data mining

Activity 51: Assessing the neutrality of online platforms, tools and data

Activity 78: Assessing the neutrality of raw data

....

→ Preparatory reading

Educators: O'Neil (2017) provides interesting preparatory reading.

Students: O'Neil (2017), Criado Perez (2020) and Kearns and Roth (2020) can be recommended after the activity, if required.

....

→ Useful resources

Braunack-Mayer, A.J., Street, J.M., Tooher, R., Feng, X. and Scharling-Gamba, K. (2020) 'Student and staff perspectives on the use of Big Data in the tertiary education sector: A scoping review and reflection on the ethical issues', *Review of Educational Research*, 90 (6): 788-823, first published 23 September 2020, doi: 10.3102/0034654320960213.
Criado Perez, C. (2020) *Invisible Women: Exposing Data Bias in a World Designed for Men*. London: Vintage.
Dawson, C. (2020) *A–Z of Digital Research Methods*. Abingdon: Routledge.
Kearns, M. and Roth, A. (2020) *The Ethical Algorithm: The Science of Socially Aware Algorithm Design*. New York, NY: Oxford University Press.
Metcalf, J. and Crawford, K. (2016) 'Where are human subjects in Big Data research? The emerging ethics divide', *Big Data & Society*, first published 1 June 2016, doi: 10.1177/2053951716650211.
O'Neil, C. (2017) *Weapons of Math Destruction: How Big Data Increases Inequality and Threatens Democracy*. London: Penguin.
Pink, S. and Lanzeni, D. (2018) 'Future anthropology ethics and datafication: Temporality and responsibility in research', *Social Media + Society*, first published 2 May 2018, doi: 10.1177/2056305118768298.

Activity 72

Richterich, A. (2018) *The Big Data Agenda: Data Ethics and Critical Data Studies*. London: University of Westminster Press.

Siege, E. (2016) *Predictive Analytics: The Power to Predict Who Will Click, Buy, Lie, or Die.* Hoboken, NJ: Kogan Page.

Someh, I., Davern, M., Breidbach, C.F. and Shanks, G. (2019) 'Ethical issues in big data analytics: A stakeholder perspective', *Communications of the Association for Information Systems*, 44, doi: 10.17705/1CAIS.04434.

Activity 72

Activity • • • • • • • • • • • • → 72

Assessing Ethical Issues in Data Analytics

STUDENT HANDOUT 1

This activity is called 'Assessing ethical issues in data analytics' and will be undertaken in groups. First of all, read the following quotation:

> Data analytics refers to the process of examining datasets, or raw data, to make inferences and draw conclusions. The term also encompasses the tools, techniques and software that are used to scrape, capture, extract, categorise, analyse, visualise and report data, and the models, predictions and forecasts that can be made. This differentiates data analytics from data analysis, which refers to the processes and methods of analysing data, rather than the tools, techniques and outcomes. As such, data analysis can be seen to be a subset, or one component, of data analytics. (Dawson, 2020: 66)

For this activity, I would like you to imagine a future in which data analytics is used worldwide to inform and influence business, government, communities, groups and individuals. The use of, and reliance on, analytics is rampant and all-encompassing. People believe that data analytics provides a true and correct representation of reality. Within this future, ethical issues in data analytics are unimportant and have been ignored. Analysts, commissioning organizations and users have no ethical standards to adhere to. What ethical issues would be ignored? What would be the consequences? What would this future look like?

Work with your group members to build a description or picture of this future. You can consider any or all types of analytics (learning, game, business and big data analytics, for example) and any or all methods (descriptive, diagnostic, location, network, real-time and predictive analytics, for example). You can imagine any type of future: this can be in the near future or far into the future.

Once you have built a description or picture, think about how to present it to your peers. You will be given 10 minutes when we next meet to make your group presentation. Your peers will be given five minutes to ask questions and make comments about your vision, before we move on to the next.

Have fun with this activity: it is an entertaining, creative and memorable way to introduce important ethical issues in data analytics. The focus and content of your vision is a group choice: all you need to do is make sure that your vision is interesting and enables your peers to meet the learning outcome given below.

Learning outcome: By the end of this activity, you will be able to list ethical issues associated with data analytics, and assess potential outcomes or consequences of adherence and non-adherence to ethical standards when undertaking data analytics.

Reference

Dawson, C. (2020) *A–Z of Digital Research Methods*. Abingdon: Routledge.

Activity • • • • • • • • • • • • → 72

Assessing Ethical Issues in Data Analytics

STUDENT HANDOUT 2

This activity is called 'Assessing ethical issues in data analytics' and will be undertaken in groups. First of all, read the following quotation:

> Data analytics refers to the process of examining datasets, or raw data, to make inferences and draw conclusions. The term also encompasses the tools, techniques and software that are used to scrape, capture, extract, categorise, analyse, visualise and report data, and the models, predictions and forecasts that can be made. This differentiates data analytics from data analysis, which refers to the processes and methods of analysing data, rather than the tools, techniques and outcomes. As such, data analysis can be seen to be a subset, or one component, of data analytics. (Dawson, 2020: 66)

For this activity, I would like you to imagine a future in which data analytics is used worldwide to inform business, government, communities, groups and individuals for the benefit of society. Within this future, ethical issues in data analytics are extremely important and great emphasis has been placed on ensuring that data analytics is conducted to the highest ethical standards. Analysts, commissioning organizations and users have strict ethical standards to which they must adhere. What might these ethical standards be? How would adherence to these standards affect outcomes? What would this future look like?

Work with your group members to build a description or picture of this future. You can consider any or all types of analytics (learning, game, business and big data analytics, for example) and any or all methods (descriptive, diagnostic, location, network, real-time and predictive analytics, for example). You can imagine any type of future: this can be in the near future or far into the future.

Once you have built a description or picture, think about how to present it to your peers. You will be given 10 minutes when we next meet to make your group presentation. Your peers will be given five minutes to ask questions and make comments about your vision, before we move on to the next.

Have fun with this activity: it is an entertaining, creative and memorable way to introduce important ethical issues in data analytics. The focus and content of your vision is a group choice: all you need to do is make sure that your vision is interesting and enables your peers to meet the learning outcome given below.

Learning outcome: By the end of this activity, you will be able to list ethical issues associated with data analytics, and assess potential outcomes or consequences of adherence and non-adherence to ethical standards when undertaking data analytics.

Reference

Dawson, C. (2020) *A–Z of Digital Research Methods*. Abingdon: Routledge.

Activity • • • • • • • • • • → 73

Recognizing and Addressing Bias when Analysing Qualitative Data

ACTIVITY 73: EDUCATOR NOTES

Purpose: This activity encourages students to recognize and address bias when analysing qualitative data through role-play and educator-led discussion.

Type: Role-play and discussion (in-class).

Alternative type(s): Text-based role-play (self-guided individual exercise with digital document sharing).

Level: Intermediate and advanced.

Duration: Fifty minutes to one hour of contact time. If the text-based role-play option is chosen, students will spend an hour or two during independent study working on the task, uploading their work and discussing ideas with their peers. Educators will spend up to an hour monitoring posts.

Equipment/materials: A suitable tool for students to upload their work, if the text-based role-play option is chosen.

Learning outcome: By the end of this activity, students will be able to recognize and address bias when analysing qualitative data.

The activity

Divide your students into pairs and give them a copy of the Student Handout. This asks them to undertake a role-play in which one student is to play a qualitative research sceptic who thinks that qualitative data analysis is unscientific and open to bias. The other student is to play an experienced qualitative researcher who has undertaken comprehensive qualitative data analysis, who believes that qualitative data analysis is rigorous and trustworthy. Students are asked to choose a role and then take 10 minutes working individually to think about what they would like to say in their role, referring, in particular, to bias when analysing qualitative data. They are told not to worry if some of the ideas are new to them as they will be discussed and clarified later in the activity.

After 10 minutes, ask students to undertake their role-plays. These take place simultaneously: walk between pairs to ensure that students remain polite, courteous and respectful of each other's views and arguments (they are asked to do this in the Student Handout). After 10 minutes, lead a class discussion on the issues raised. Questions that can be considered are given in 'Key issues' below.

This activity can be run as a text-based role-play, if you prefer. Ask students to play the role of an experienced qualitative researcher who has to persuade a sceptical colleague that they know how to recognize and address bias in qualitative data analysis. They should do this in no more than 500 words. Once they have produced their work, it should be uploaded using a suitable tool by a given date so that it can be shared and discussed with peers. If you choose to make this an assessed piece of work, include assessment criteria.

Key issues

This activity enables students to learn about bias in qualitative data analyses in a memorable way. The role-play does not put pressure on students as they are told that no one will watch them and all the issues will be discussed and clarified later. This is reassuring for students who might be new to issues of bias in qualitative data analysis.

Questions that can be discussed include:

1. What is bias? Students will already have thought about this for the role-play, so this will help to clarify issues and consolidate learning. It can include a discussion on how the notion of 'bias' might be very different from that in quantitative research and subjectivity should not be construed as bias (see Roulston and Shelton, 2015 for a useful discussion on this topic and others).
2. What types of bias might be present in qualitative data analysis? This gives an opportunity to introduce and discuss types of bias that might have been touched on in the role-play, but perhaps did not have a specific name.
3. What methods can we use to recognize bias? This can include reflection or self-evaluation (perhaps with references to equality, diversity and inclusion: Activity 28);

reading around the topic; developing understanding and becoming familiar with problems that can occur.
4. What specific methods can we use to address bias? This can include verifying with more or different data sources; asking participants to check analyses and conclusions; viewing and interpreting data from several and different perspectives; asking other researchers/coders to undertake analysis/coding; considering alternative explanations; and undertaking peer review, for example.
5. How can we ensure rigour, transparency and trustworthiness in qualitative data analyses? Again, these issues will probably have been touched on in the role-play and can include cultivating openness and transparency (Activity 17) and fostering research integrity through practice (Activity 20), for example.

Cautionary note

Some students might be nervous or unsure about the role-play: if so, spend a little time reassuring them. Also, walk among the pairs to check that the role-play is not getting heated or argumentative. Answer any queries or address problems that students might encounter as you walk among them.

→ Related activities

Activity 28: Evaluating biases with reference to equality, diversity and inclusion

Activity 52: Assessing bias in search tools

Activity 63: Recognizing and addressing bias when collecting data

Activity 64: Avoiding sampling bias

Activity 74: Avoiding bias in quantitative analyses

Activity 97: Recognizing reporting bias

Activity 98: Understanding the influence of publication bias

....

→ Preparatory reading

Educators: Roulston and Shelton (2015) provide an interesting preparatory read.

Students: None required. The Catalogue of Bias (see useful resources) can be recommended once the activity has taken place, if appropriate.

....

→ Useful resources

A comprehensive list of bias in research studies, with definitions, can be obtained from the Catalogue of Bias: https://catalogofbias.org [accessed 16 July 2021].

Activity 73

Abraham, T.H., Finley, E.P., Drummond, K.L., Haro, E.K., Hamilton, A.B., Townsend, J.C., Littman, A.J. and Hudson, T. (2021) 'A method for developing trustworthiness and preserving richness of qualitative data during team-based analysis of large data sets', *American Journal of Evaluation*, 42 (1): 139–56, first published 20 August 2020, doi: 10.1177/1098214019893784.

Eakin, J.M. and Gladstone, B. (2020) '"Value-adding" analysis: Doing more with qualitative data', *International Journal of Qualitative Methods*, first published 27 August 2020, doi: 10.1177/1609406920949333.

Mackieson, P., Shlonsky, A. and Connolly, M. (2019) 'Increasing rigor and reducing bias in qualitative research: A document analysis of parliamentary debates using applied thematic analysis', *Qualitative Social Work*, 18 (6): 965–80, first published 10 July 2018, doi: 10.1177/1473325018786996.

McSweeney, B. (2021) 'Fooling ourselves and others: Confirmation bias and the trustworthiness of qualitative research – Part 1 (the threats)', *Journal of Organizational Change Management*, published online 1 July 2021, doi: 10.1108/JOCM-04-2021-0117.

O'Kane, P., Smith, A. and Lerman, M.P. (2021) 'Building transparency and trustworthiness in inductive research through computer-aided qualitative data analysis software', *Organizational Research Methods*, 24 (1): 104–39, first published 21 August 2019, doi: 10.1177/1094428119865016.

Roulston, K. and Shelton, S.A. (2015) 'Reconceptualizing bias in teaching qualitative research methods', *Qualitative Inquiry*, 21 (4): 332–42, first published 17 February 2015, doi: 10.1177/1077800414563803.

Activity 73

Activity • • • • • • • • • • • → 73

Recognizing and Addressing Bias when Analysing Qualitative Data

STUDENT HANDOUT

This activity is called 'Recognizing and addressing bias when analysing qualitative data'. The first part of this activity is a role-play that you will undertake in pairs. Student 1 is to play a qualitative research sceptic. You think that qualitative data analysis is unscientific and open to bias. Student 2 is to play an experienced qualitative researcher who has undertaken comprehensive qualitative data analysis. You believe that qualitative data analysis is rigorous and trustworthy, with bias addressed.

Discuss roles with your partner and agree on which you would both like to play. Take 10 minutes working individually to think about what you might like to say in your role. Think also about what your opposite role-player might try to argue and think about how you will counter those arguments. As this activity is about bias in data analysis, think about what this means. What is bias and how might different types of bias influence analyses? How might biases in qualitative analyses differ from biases found in quantitative analyses? Don't worry if some of these ideas are new to you: they will be discussed and clarified in our discussion after the role-play.

After 10 minutes, we will begin the role-play: each pair will conduct their role-play simultaneously, so no one will be listening to you apart from your partner. When you undertake the role-play, remain courteous and polite: give each other a chance to put forward their views and listen to what the other person is saying before presenting your own arguments. Keep your views and arguments at an academic level. Avoid personal attacks. Most of all, have fun. This part of the activity should serve to introduce some of the topics that we will discuss later. The role-play will last for 10 minutes.

Once you have completed your role-play, we will go on to discuss the issues raised, looking, in particular, at how you can recognize and address bias when analysing qualitative data.

Learning outcome: By the end of this activity, you will be able to recognize and address bias when analysing qualitative data.

Activity • • • • • • • • • • • → 74

Avoiding Bias in Quantitative Analyses

The activity

Invite together a group of students who intend to undertake quantitative data analysis in their research. Explain that this will be an informal and practical discussion that will introduce them to different types of bias that could influence their data analysis, before going on to consider practical ways in which bias can be avoided when they analyse their data.

When you meet (either in-class or online synchronous), provide a brief definition of bias, then ask students to suggest any types of bias they can think of that could, potentially, have an influence on data analysis. Some suggestions are given in key issues below. Take a little time to discuss each type of bias mentioned. You might find that students mention a variety of types of bias that are also connected with research design and data collection (such as sampling bias or selection bias). Use your judgement as to how far you wish to discuss these, as they do have an impact on data analysis but might be discussed elsewhere in your course (Activities 63 and 64, for example).

After 25-30 minutes ask students to think of ways that the types of bias mentioned could be avoided (or if not avoided, reduced). Some suggestions are given in 'Key issues' below and these can be used if students find it difficult to think of suitable suggestions. Conclude the session with a summary of the main points raised.

Key issues

Types of bias that can be mentioned in this activity tend to depend on understanding, discipline and research approach. They include the following (students might not know the name, but instead will describe what they mean: put a name to their description, where appropriate):

- confounding bias;
- confounding by indication (or indication bias);
- collider bias;
- data-dredging bias (p-hacking or data fishing, for example);
- confirmation bias;
- information bias;
- misclassification bias;

- cognitive bias;
- behavioural bias;
- emotional bias;
- inherent bias;
- implicit or unconscious bias;
- sampling bias;
- selection bias.

Suggested action for avoiding (or reducing) bias include:

- undertake a thorough examination and exploration of raw data;
- become familiar with your data;
- look for mistakes (this can include in data entry, but also in sampling and selection methods: Activity 64);
- choose the right statistical procedures or tests;
- check all data analysis software and tools for bias in design (and assess personal choice of tools for bias);
- handle missing data (undertake a missing value analysis to describe patterns of missing data; estimate means, standard deviations, covariances and correlations; and impute missing values, for example);
- identify and handle outliers (consider performing the analysis with and without the outlier, reporting both upfront and providing an interpretation of how results are influenced by the outlier, for example);

- do not add or omit data without clear justification;
- keep a meticulous record of all analyses, interpretations and justifications;
- consider alternative explanations or interpretations, or look at ways to disprove your model;
- recognize false assumptions and identify flaws in analyses and/or arguments;
- use alternative and varied data sources to validate your results;
- recognize, acknowledge and address bias in all stages of the research process, not just during analysis;
- consider your own bias (inherent bias, implicit or unconscious bias, for example) that could influence your analyses and evaluate biases with reference to equality, diversity and inclusion: Activity 28);
- read around the subject, take statistics courses and seek advice from supervisors, tutors and peers.

→ **Related activities**

Activity 28: Evaluating biases with reference to equality, diversity and inclusion

Activity 52: Assessing bias in search tools

Activity 63: Recognizing and addressing bias when collecting data

Activity 64: Avoiding sampling bias

Activity 73: Recognizing and addressing bias when analysing qualitative data

Activity 97: Recognizing reporting bias

Activity 98: Understanding the influence of publication bias

→ **Preparatory reading**

Educators: The Catalogue of Bias (see useful resources) provides useful preparatory reading.

Students: None required. You can recommend the Catalogue of Bias once the activity has taken place, if appropriate.

→ **Useful resources**

A comprehensive list of bias in research studies, with definitions, can be obtained from the Catalogue of Bias: https://catalogofbias.org [accessed 16 July 2021].

Barnett, L.A., Lewis, M., Mallen, C.D. and Peat, G. (2017) 'Applying quantitative bias analysis to estimate the plausible effects of selection bias in a cluster randomised controlled trial: Secondary analysis of the Primary care Osteoarthritis Screening Trial (POST)', *Trials*, 18 (585), published 4 December 2017, doi: 10.1186/s13063-017-2329-1.

Activity 74

Griffith, G.J., Morris, T.T., Tudball, M.J. et al. (2020) 'Collider bias undermines our understanding of COVID-19 disease risk and severity', *Nature Communications*, 11 (5749), first published 12 November 2020, doi: 10.1038/s41467-020-19478-2.

Head, M.L., Holman, L., Lanfear, R., Kahn, A.T. and Jennions, M.D. (2015) 'The extent and consequences of p-hacking in science', *PLoS Biology*, 13(3), e1002106, published March 13 2015, doi: 10.1371/journal.pbio.1002106.

Lash, T.L., Ahern, T.P., Collin, L.J., Fox, M.P. and MacLehose, R.F. (2021) 'Bias analysis gone bad', *American Journal of Epidemiology*, kwab072, published 29 March 2021, doi: 10.1093/aje/kwab072.

Lash, T.L., Fox, M.P., Cooney, D., Lu, Y. and Forshee, R.A. (2016) 'Quantitative bias analysis in regulatory settings', *American Journal of Public Health*, 106 (7): 1227-30, published online 10 June 2016, doi: 10.2105/AJPH.2016.303199.

Salway, T., Plöderl, M., Liu, J. and Gustafson, P. (2019) 'Effects of multiple forms of information bias on estimated prevalence of suicide attempts according to sexual orientation: An application of a Bayesian misclassification correction method to data from a systematic review', *American Journal of Epidemiology*, 188 (1): 239-49, published 5 September 2018, doi: 10.1093/aje/kwy200.

van Smeden, M., Penning de Vries, B.B.L., Nab, L. and Groenwold, R.H.H. (2021) 'Approaches to addressing missing values, measurement error, and confounding in epidemiologic studies', *Journal of Clinical Epidemiology*, 131: 89-100, doi: 10.1016/j.jclinepi.2020.11.006.

Activity 74

Activity • • • • • • • • • • • → 75

Avoiding Wrong Conclusions

ACTIVITY 75: EDUCATOR NOTES

Purpose: This activity encourages students to think about how researchers can avoid wrong conclusions through the development of scenarios, which are presented and discussed with peers. This activity can be combined with Activity 91: Building trust in inferences and conclusions, for students studying at advanced level, if required.

Type: Scenarios developed by students for discussion (in-class or online synchronous or asynchronous).

Alternative type(s): None.

Level: Elementary, intermediate and advanced (the level of study tends to be reflected in the content of scenario and discussion).

Duration: Students will spend one or two hours during independent study developing their scenarios. Fifty minutes to one hour of contact time will be required to present and discuss scenarios (synchronous online or in-class), and an hour or two over a period of time if the asynchronous online option is chosen.

Equipment/materials: A video/web-conferencing tool if the online synchronous option is chosen, and a suitable discussion board/forum if the asynchronous online option is chosen.

Learning outcome: By the end of this activity, students will be able to provide examples of ways in which wrong conclusions can be reached in research, summarize reasons for reaching wrong conclusions and explain how wrong conclusions can be avoided.

The activity

Divide your students into small groups (or pairs, depending on the size of your cohort: ideally, 8–10 scenarios are a good number for this activity). Give each group a copy of the Student Handout and ask that they work on the task during independent study ready for when you next meet. They are to develop two scenarios that illustrate how a researcher (or research team) can come to the wrong conclusion in their research. They can consider any type of research approach, topic and methodology.

When you next meet, ask the first group to present one of their scenarios. Spend five minutes discussing the scenario, then move on to the next group and so on, until all groups have presented a scenario. Groups can choose which scenario to present, if they find that another group has already touched on one of their topics (you probably will not have time for groups to present two scenarios). Questions that can be discussed after each scenario include:

1. What is the wrong conclusion identified in the scenario?
2. Has the researcher made a mistake or was the wrong conclusion deliberate (if so, to what end)?
3. What should the researcher have done differently, to ensure that the wrong conclusion was not reached?
4. What lessons can we learn from this scenario?

You can run this activity online, if you prefer (the Student Handout will need to be adapted slightly). This can be done synchronously (using a video/web conferencing tool) or asynchronously (using your VLE-hosted discussion board, for example). If the asynchronous option is chosen, give a deadline by which time scenarios should be uploaded and discussed. Monitor discussions to ensure that information is correct, supportive and constructive. Remove any incorrect posts and explain why this has been done. If you choose to make this an assessed piece of work, provide assessment criteria with the Student Handout.

Key issues

Scenarios produced by students cover a number of issues including:

- providing false conclusions to make the research more publishable (Activity 98);
- fabricating results to further their research careers (Activity 76);
- failing to evaluate and address personal bias (Activity 28);
- lacking knowledge and experience;
- having inadequate training in research methods/statistical analysis;
- confusing correlation with causation;
- lacking robustness and credibility in qualitative analyses;
- ignoring evidence/only using data that supports argument/hypothesis;
- misunderstanding/misconstruing what someone has said;
- failing to check analyses and conclusions with research participants;
- failing to provide a justification, or evidence, for conclusions;
- omitting a description/step-by-step account of how conclusions have been reached.

➜ Related activities

Activity 17: Cultivating transparency and openness

Activity 18: Appraising disciplinary standards of acceptable academic conduct

Activity 22: Avoiding research misconduct

Activity 71: Identifying unethical practice when analysing data

Activity 91: Building trust in inferences and conclusions

➜ Preparatory reading

Educators: All the resources listed below provide useful preparatory sources.

Students: None required. Students will find their own resources for this activity. Some of the resources listed below can be recommended once the activity has concluded, if appropriate.

➜ Useful resources

Cian, H. (2021) 'Sashaying across party lines: Evidence of and arguments for the use of validity evidence in qualitative education research', *Review of Research in Education*, 45 (1): 253-90, first published 18 April 2021, doi: 10.3102/0091732X20985079.

Dunn, E.W., Chen, L., Proulx, J.D.E., Ehrlinger, J. and Savalei, V. (2020) 'Can researchers' personal characteristics shape their statistical inferences?', *Personality and Social Psychology Bulletin*, 47 (6): 969-84, first published 31 August 2020, doi: 10.1177/0146167220950522.

Ritchie, S. (2021) *Science Fictions: Exposing Fraud, Bias, Negligence and Hype in Science*. London: Vintage.

Rouder, J.N., Haaf, J.M. and Snyder, H.K. (2019) 'Minimizing mistakes in psychological science', *Advances in Methods and Practices in Psychological Science*, 2 (1): 3-11, first published 30 January 2019, doi: 10.1177/2515245918801915.

Sibulkin, A.E. and Butler, J.S. (2019) 'Learning to give reverse causality explanations for correlations: Still hard after all these tries', *Teaching of Psychology*, 46 (3): 223-9, first published 30 May 2019, doi: 10.1177/0098628319853936.

Suter, W.N. and Suter, P.M. (2015) 'How research conclusions go wrong: A primer for home health clinicians', *Home Health Care Management & Practice*, 27 (4), 171-7, first published 14 May 2015, doi: 10.1177/1084822315586557.

Bad Science (www.badscience.net) is a website containing articles, videos and blogs about bad science, produced by Dr Ben Goldacre. The articles were written for the Bad Science column in the *Guardian* newspaper in the UK and highlight the misuse of science and statistics in the news, by politicians and others.

Activity 75

Activity · · · · · · · · · · · · → 75

Avoiding Wrong Conclusions

STUDENT HANDOUT

This activity is about avoiding wrong conclusions in research. Work with your group members during independent study to develop two scenarios about a researcher (or research team) who comes to the wrong conclusions when analysing data. This can be a deliberate action or a mistake. If you choose to develop scenarios in which the researcher has come to the wrong conclusion deliberately, think about why this is the case. Why have they been motivated to act in the way that they have? Their motivation can be written into your scenario, if you wish.

When we meet, the first group will present one of their scenarios for class discussion. Questions that we will discuss include:

1. What is the wrong conclusion identified in the scenario?
2. Has the researcher made a mistake or was the wrong conclusion deliberate (if so, to what end)?
3. What could or should the researcher have done differently, to ensure that they did not jump to the wrong conclusion?
4. What lessons can we learn from this scenario?

After five minutes, we will move on to the next group. You have been asked to produce two scenarios even though you may only have time to present one: having two gives your group a choice if you find that a scenario similar to yours has already been presented. It also provides a few more scenarios to discuss if we find that we have time available.

Scenarios should be no longer than 200 words: be concise, but include all relevant information. Try to ensure that they will lead to interesting and fruitful discussion that will enable you and your peers to meet the learning outcome given below.

Learning outcome: By the end of this activity, you will be able to provide examples of ways in which wrong conclusions can be reached in research, summarize reasons for reaching wrong conclusions and explain how wrong conclusions can be avoided.

Activity • • • • • • • • • • • ➔ 76

Recognizing False, Fabricated or Misleading Analyses

The activity

Divide your students into groups. The number and size of group depends on the amount of contact time you have available (if you have an hour, three to four groups will be required: if you have two hours you can have up to eight groups). Give each group a copy of Student Handout 1 and ask that they prepare their teaching session, during independent study. When you meet, ask each group, in turn, to run their teaching session, leaving a little time for questions after each one. Summarize the main findings once all the groups have presented their session.

Teaching sessions can be produced as a video, if you prefer. For this option, give students a copy of Student Handout 2 and ask them to produce and upload their video using a suitable tool (an internal VLE-hosted tool or an external tool such as a Facebook group or Vimeo, for example). Advice about producing the video is given in the Handout. Give a deadline by which time this task should be completed. Ask students to view the videos produced by their peers and encourage them to spend a little time discussing the issues raised.

Key issues

This activity provides the opportunity for students to use their imagination and creativity to produce a teaching session that is interesting and informative. Some students choose to produce their session using software such as Google Slides, Visme or Keynote. They insert videos, images or animations to add interest and bring the presentation to life.

Others choose not to use software at all, instead basing their session on actual case studies that illustrate where and how researchers have falsified or fabricated results. Some choose a more interactive approach, providing a number of scenarios or examples, and asking peers to discuss which might be false, fabricated or misleading analyses.

→ Related activities

Activity 17: Cultivating transparency and openness

Activity 18: Appraising disciplinary standards of acceptable academic conduct

Activity 22: Avoiding research misconduct

Activity 71: Identifying unethical practice when analysing data

Activity 75: Avoiding wrong conclusions

Activity 91: Building trust in inferences and conclusions

→ Preparatory reading

Educators: All the resources listed below provide useful preparation.

Students: None required. Groups will find their own resources when they prepare their session.

→ Useful resources

Andersen, L.E. and Wray, K.B. (2019) 'Detecting errors that result in retractions', *Social Studies of Science*, 49 (6): 942–54, first published 12 September 2019, doi: 10.1177/0306312719872008.

Bouter, L.M., Tijdink, J., Axelsen, N., Martinson, B.C. and ter Riet, G. (2016) 'Ranking major and minor research misbehaviors: Results from a survey among participants of four world conferences on research integrity', *Research Integrity and Peer Review*, 1 (17), published 21 November 2016, doi: 10.1186/s41073-016-0024-5.

Dal-Ré, R., Bouter, L.M., Cuijpers, P., Gluud, C. and Holm, S. (2020) 'Should research misconduct be criminalized?', *Research Ethics*, 16 (1-2): 1–12, first published 16 January 2020, doi: 10.1177/1747016119898400.

Goldacre, B. (2015) *I Think You'll Find It's a Bit More Complicated Than That*. London: Fourth Estate.

Ritchie, S. (2021) *Science Fictions: Exposing Fraud, Bias, Negligence and Hype in Science*. London: Vintage.

Bad Science (www.badscience.net) is a website containing articles, videos and blogs about bad science, produced by Dr Ben Goldacre. The articles were written for the Bad Science column in the *Guardian* newspaper in the UK and highlight the misuse of science and statistics in the news, by politicians and others.

'More or Less' is a radio programme that is broadcast on BBC Radio 4 in the UK, produced together with the Open University. The programme discusses the use, abuse and misuse of statistics in the news and everyday life. Downloads and podcasts are available from the BBC website (www.bbc.co.uk/programmes).

Activity 76

Activity · · · · · · · · · · · · → 76

Recognizing False, Fabricated or Misleading Analyses

STUDENT HANDOUT 1

This activity is called 'Recognizing false, fabricated or misleading analyses'. Work with your group members to produce a teaching session of up to 10 minutes that teaches your peers how to recognize false, fabricated or misleading analyses in the work of other researchers. The style, content and structure of your teaching session is a group choice. Choose any software, tools or visual aids that you wish.

   The goal of this activity is to teach your peers something new about the topic and help them to remember what they have learnt. Therefore, ensure that your session is interesting, creative, informative and memorable. Consider the learning outcome given below and ensure that your session will enable your peers to achieve this outcome. You will be given up to 10 minutes to make your presentation. Your peers will then be able to ask questions, if they wish.

Learning outcome: By the end of this activity, you will be able to recognize false, fabricated and/or misleading analyses in research projects and reports.

Recognizing False, Fabricated or Misleading Analyses

STUDENT HANDOUT 2

This activity is called 'Recognizing false, fabricated or misleading analyses'. Work with your group members to produce a video that teaches your peers how to recognize false, fabricated or misleading analyses in the work of other researchers. Your video can be any length, up to 10 minutes. The approach, style and content of your video is a group choice: use your creativity and imagination to produce a video that is entertaining, informative and memorable. If you need to borrow video equipment, please contact me, otherwise smartphones or webcams are fine for this activity. Ensure that you pay attention to audio, lighting and camera stabilization, and use basic editing software, if required.

Once you have produced your video, share it with your peers by uploading it using the given tool. Make sure that this is done by the deadline. View the videos that are uploaded by your peers and, if you want to make any comments, do so on the discussion board. Ensure that you have viewed the videos and participated in the discussion by the given deadline.

The goal of this activity is to teach your peers something new about the topic and help them to remember what they have learnt. Therefore, ensure that your video is interesting, creative, informative and memorable. Consider the learning outcome given below and ensure that your video will enable your peers to achieve this outcome.

Learning outcome: By the end of this activity, you will be able to recognize false, fabricated and/or misleading analyses in research projects and reports.

Activity ⟶ 77

Critiquing the Origin and Provenance of Data

The activity

Divide your students into groups: the size of group depends on the number of students in your cohort (ideally, four to six posters are good numbers for this activity). Give each group a copy of the Student Handout. This provides definitions of 'data, 'origin' and 'provenance' before going on to ask students to produce a digital poster presentation that illustrates steps and procedures and/or provides advice to their peers, about how to critique the origin and provenance of data. Advice about producing a digital poster presentation is given for those who are new to this type of software or app. Once students have produced their poster, they should upload it using a suitable tool (Padlet or Canvas, for example), and take a little time viewing and discussing the posters produced by their peers. Both Padlet and Canvas enable discussion and questions. View posters when they are uploaded to check that information is correct and monitor discussion to check that it is constructive, supportive and respectful.

This activity can be run as an in-class poster session, if you prefer. Ask students, in their groups, to produce a poster that illustrates steps and procedures and/or provides advice to their peers, about how to critique the origin and provenance of data. Groups should produce their poster during independent study. Give a date, time and venue when posters are to be presented so that each group can work to the deadline (if you choose a time that is outside your usual teaching hours, ensure that all students are able to attend the session). Give details of the venue so that groups know what equipment and space is available for their poster presentation. Give students a copy of the Student Handout in Activity 26 if they are unfamiliar with the poster presentation technique. If you require more information about running a poster presentation session, see Activity 26.

Key issues

This activity is a creative and memorable way to strengthen knowledge and increase awareness of the topic. Students are asked to work in groups for this activity so that they can pool knowledge and bounce ideas off each other, while supporting group members in the use of relevant technology. Digital posters tend to be varied and creative: some concentrate on specific steps required to check origin and provenance, others use scenarios or case studies to illustrate how to critique origin and provenance. Some take a more holistic approach, considering why and for what purpose data are created and illustrating how data change as politics and culture change, whereas others consider the life of data or the data journey (see Bates et al., 2016 for an interesting discussion on this journey).

→ Related activities

Activity 51: Assessing the neutrality of online platforms, tools and data

Activity 52: Assessing bias in search tools

Activity 53: Overcoming problems with weak, restricted, non-existent or invisible data systems

Activity 72: Assessing ethical issues in data analytics

Activity 78: Assessing the neutrality of raw data

→ Preparatory reading

Educators: Poirier (2021) provides an interesting preparatory read for this activity. The Technology Enhanced Learning (TEL) team at the University of Sussex in the UK produces a regular blog on using technology to support teaching and learning, and some of these cover digital poster presentations. This provides useful preparatory reading for educators who are new to teaching with this technology: https://blogs.sussex.ac.uk/tel/2021/04/27/poster-presentations-online [accessed 22 October 2021].

Students: None required. Students will find their own resources for this activity.

→ Useful resources

Bates, J., Lin, Y.-W. and Goodale, P. (2016) 'Data journeys: Capturing the socio-material constitution of data objects and flows', *Big Data & Society*, first published 13 July 2016, doi: 10.1177/2053951716654502.

Doyle, S. and Senske, N. (2018) 'Digital provenance and material metadata: Attribution and co-authorship in the age of artificial intelligence', *International Journal of Architectural Computing*, 16 (4): 271-80, first published 28 November 2018, doi: 10.1177/1478077118800887.

Ford, H. and Graham, M. (2016) 'Provenance, power and place: Linked data and opaque digital geographies', *Environment and Planning D: Society and Space*, 34 (6): 957-70, first published 27 September 2016, doi: 10.1177/0263775816668857.

Halford, S., Weal, M., Tinati, R., Carr, L. and Pope, C. (2018) 'Understanding the production and circulation of social media data: Towards methodological principles and praxis', *New Media & Society*, 20 (9): 3341-58, first published 31 December 2017, doi: 10.1177/1461444817748953.

Imran, M., Hlavacs, H., Haq, I.U., Jan, B., Khan, F.A. and Ahmad, A. (2017) 'Provenance based data integrity checking and verification in cloud environments', *PLoS ONE*, 12 (5): e0177576, published 17 May 2017, doi: 10.1371/journal.pone.0177576.

Poirier, L. (2021) 'Reading datasets: Strategies for interpreting the politics of data signification', *Big Data & Society*, first published 1 July 2021, doi: 10.1177/20539517211029322.

Activity 77

Activity · · · · · · · · · · · · · → 77

Critiquing the Origin and Provenance of Data

STUDENT HANDOUT

This activity is called 'Critiquing the origin and provenance of data'. For the purposes of this activity, we will use a broad definition of data: information, such as facts, statistics, figures, measurements, text, characters, symbols, images, objects or artefacts that are used for reasoning, calculation, analysis, discussion or reference. 'Origin' refers to the moment or time when data are created, and 'provenance' refers to the record attached to data: when they were created and what has happened to them from creation to the time when you access them (amendment, modification, addition and deletion record, for example).

Within these definitions, work with your group members to produce a digital poster that illustrates steps and procedures and/or provides advice to your peers, about how to critique the origin and provenance of data. The content, style, structure and type of digital poster is a group choice. You can also choose which app or software to use to create your poster (PowerPoint, MS Sway, Adobe Spark, Piktochart or Glogster are examples, but there are many more available). All you need to do is ensure that your digital poster enables you and your peers to meet the one simple learning outcome given below. The following tips might help:

- use templates if available;
- read all tutorials to get the most out of software;
- work out what you want to include and the best way to present this information;
- produce a short and attention-grabbing title;
- work out the main message you want to convey: ensure that all information is relevant to this message and delete anything that is not;
- use multi-media to make your poster interesting (images, sound, interactive features, etc.);

- keep text short and to the point;
- link to external sources, if relevant (and if software allows);
- ensure that you do not breach copyright or plagiarize materials: ensure that any third-party materials are cited correctly;
- ensure your poster style and content is suitable for the intended audience;
- edit, proofread, check that multi-media works and ensure compatibility before the deadline is due.

Once you have created your poster, upload it using the tool provided by the given deadline. Take a little time to view and discuss the posters created by your peers. Remember to keep all comments constructive, supportive and respectful. Have fun with this activity: it is a creative, entertaining and memorable way to learn about the topic.

Learning outcome: By the end of this activity, you will be able to critique the origin and provenance of data.

Activity • • • • • • • • • • • • → 78

Assessing the Neutrality of Raw Data

The activity

This activity is a group debate in which one group of students argue that raw data are neutral and the other that raw data are not neutral. Divide your students into two groups: allocate one group to argue for neutrality, the other against. Give both groups a copy of the Student Handout. This explains the activity and provides advice about how to prepare for, and take part in, a debate. Ideally, you should not have more than six students in each group. Therefore, if you have more than 12 students in your cohort you may need to run the debate twice.

The debate is to be held when you next meet either in-class or online (using a suitable video conferencing tool such as Zoom Meetings, Blackboard Collaborate or Google Meet). Introduce the debate, explain procedures, set ground rules and act as chairperson and timekeeper, ensuring that the debate remains on track, is constructive and takes place within the allotted time. Ensure that students listen to, and respect, the views of their peers and that arguments remain academic, rather than personal. For online debates, you may need to use messaging or raise hand functions, and invite students to speak. Encourage your students to present their arguments in a confident and persuasive way, and ask them to pay attention to speed, tone, volume and clarity. The debate should last for 40 minutes (in four 10-minute slots with each group speaking twice), with a debrief of 10-20 minutes on the issues that have been raised.

Key issues

This activity requires students to prepare a structured argument in which two sides speak for and against the neutrality of raw data. They need to think about what is meant by raw data; how they are collected or generated; who collects or generates them and why; how and why they are presented or made public; and how they are used by others. Students have to work out how to argue as part of a team and ensure that they do not contradict the arguments of their team members. They also need to pay close attention to the content: their introduction, their argument (and the evidence that is used to back up their argument), their rebuttal of the arguments used by the other team, and their conclusion. This activity enables them to understand the complexities of raw data in an enjoyable and memorable way, while also enhancing their researching, collaboration, debating and presentation skills.

Cautionary note

Debates tend to be lively, interesting and memorable. However, it is essential that you monitor the debate carefully, to ensure that everyone respects each other's opinion and listens to what their opponents have to say. If you feel that issues have arisen that may upset students, or cause offence, flag them for discussion after the debate.

→ Related activities

Activity 48: Assessing the reliability of digital tools and software

Activity 51: Assessing the neutrality of online platforms, tools and data

Activity 52: Assessing bias in search tools

Activity 53: Overcoming problems with weak, restricted, non-existent or invisible data systems

Activity 72: Assessing ethical issues in data analytics

→ Preparatory reading

Educators: if you are new to running debates, a brief but useful blog by Ian Glover from Sheffield Hallam University in the UK provides some useful information: https://blogs.shu.ac.uk/shutel/2014/09/02/debate-an-approach-to-teaching-and-learning [accessed 5 August 2021]. Karlsen et al. (2017) also provide interesting preparatory reading.

Students: None required. Students will find their own resources for this activity.

→ Useful resources

Denis, J. and Goëta, S. (2017) 'Rawification and the careful generation of open government data', *Social Studies of Science*, 47 (5): 604–29, first published 21 June 2017, doi: 10.1177/0306312717712473.

Fisher, M. and Keil, F.C. (2018) 'The binary bias: A systematic distortion in the integration of information', *Psychological Science*, 29 (11): 1846–58, first Published 4 October 2018, doi: 10.1177/0956797618792256.

Gitelman, L. (2013) *Raw Data Is an Oxymoron*. New York, NY: MIT Press.

Jürgens, P., Stark, B. and Magin, M. (2020) 'Two half-truths make a whole? On bias in self-reports and tracking data', *Social Science Computer Review*, 38 (5): 600–15, first published 28 February 2019, doi: 10.1177/0894439319831643.

Karlsen, R., Steen-Johnsen, K., Wollebæk, D. and Enjolras, B. (2017) 'Echo chamber and trench warfare dynamics in online debates', *European Journal of Communication*, 32 (3): 257–73, first published 3 April 2017, doi: 10.1177/0267323117695734.

Marbach, M. (2018) 'On imputing UNHCR data', *Research & Politics*, 5 (4), first published 12 October 2018, doi: 10.1177/2053168018803239.

Poirier, L. (2021) 'Reading datasets: Strategies for interpreting the politics of data signification', *Big Data & Society*, first published 1 July 2021, doi: 10.1177/20539517211029322.

Räsänen, M. and Nyce, J.M. (2013) 'The raw is cooked: Data in intelligence practice', *Science, Technology, & Human Values*, 38 (5): 655–77, first published 15 April 2013, doi: 10.1177/0162243913480049.

Ugwudike, P. (2020) 'Digital prediction technologies in the justice system: The implications of a "race-neutral" agenda', *Theoretical Criminology*, 24 (3): 482–501, first published 22 January 2020, doi: 10.1177/1362480619896006.

Activity 78

Activity • • • • • • • • • • • → 78

Assessing the Neutrality of Raw Data

STUDENT HANDOUT

This activity is called 'Assessing the neutrality of raw data'. For this activity, we are going to hold a debate. This is a structured argument in which two sides speak for and against a particular contention. In this case, one group is to argue that raw data are neutral and the other that raw data are not neutral. You might disagree with the position you have been given, or you might feel that this activity presents a false dichotomy. However, you are still required to take part in the debate as it is a useful and memorable way to introduce, assess and critique the neutrality of raw data. You will have the chance to identify your actual position during discussion after the debate.

Questions you may need to consider when you prepare for your debate include:

- What is 'raw data'?
- How are they collected or generated?
- Who collects or generates them and why?

- How and why are they made available?
- How and why are they used by others?

Prepare, in your group, your arguments ready for debate when we next meet. Your group will be given two 10-minute slots in which to debate (alternating with your opponents). You will also need to prepare a rebuttal of the arguments presented by your opponents.

The advice below will help you to prepare for the debate:

- Prepare for the debate:
  - define your topic;
  - find relevant sources and research the topic (and your side of the argument);
  - prepare enough material to fill two 10-minute slots;
  - produce notes to aid your memory;
  - pay close attention to your introduction, main argument (and evidence to back up your argument) and conclusion;
  - divide your material and time between team mates so that you know who is speaking at what time and what they are going to say;
  - avoid arguments that are factually, morally or logically flawed;
  - avoid rhetorical questions (this could enable your opponents to attack your arguments);
  - practise presenting your material within the allotted time.
- Prepare for your defence and rebuttal:
  - think about how your opponents will refute your arguments and prepare a defence;

  - understand the key arguments that will be put forward by your opponents and prepare a suitable rebuttal;
  - offer evidence for your defence and rebuttal.
- During the debate:
  - argue as part of a team and take care not to contradict the arguments of your team members;
  - for in-class debates, make good eye contact with team mates and with your opponents;
  - present your arguments in a confident and persuasive manner;
  - keep all arguments on an academic level and avoid personal comments: counter the arguments, not the person;
  - ensure that other students can understand what you are saying and vary your tone for interest;
  - avoid shouting or raising your voice;
  - listen to your opponents and respect what they say;
  - do not interrupt each other;
  - have fun: this is an enjoyable and memorable way to meet the learning outcome given below.

Learning outcome: By the end of this activity, you will be able to assess and critique the neutrality of raw data.

Activity • • • • • • • • • • → 79

Discussing the Ethics, Integrity and Practice of Anonymization in Analysis, Secondary Analysis, Re-Analysis and Third-Party Analysis

ACTIVITY 79: EDUCATOR NOTES

Purpose: This activity is a student-led discussion that enables students to discuss the ethics, integrity and practice of anonymization in data analysis, secondary analysis, re-analysis or third-party analysis. This activity can be combined with Activity 62: Addressing issues of anonymity and confidentiality, or with Activity 84: Anonymizing qualitative and quantitative data, for greater coverage of this topic, if required.

Type: Student-led discussion (in-class or online synchronous).

Alternative type(s): Student worksheet.

Level: Intermediate and advanced.

Duration: Students will spend up to an hour thinking about, and developing, their discussion points or questions. Fifty minutes to one hour of contact time will be required (in-class or online synchronous). If the worksheet option is chosen, educators will spend up to an hour developing the worksheet and students will spend an hour or two working on the task during independent study.

Equipment/materials: A suitable video/web conferencing tool, if the online option is chosen.

Learning outcome: By the end of this activity, students will be able to assess and critique the ethics, integrity and practice of anonymization in analysis, secondary analysis, re-analysis and third-party analysis.

The activity

Give your students a copy of the Student Handout and ask that they work on the task ready for when you next meet (in-class or online). They are provided with useful definitions before being asked to think of three discussion points or questions that they would like to discuss about the ethics, integrity and/or practice of anonymity in analysis, secondary analysis, re-analysis or third-party analysis.

When you meet (in-class or online, using a suitable synchronous tool such as Blackboard Collaborate, Google Meet or Zoom Meetings), ask each student in turn to present one of their discussion points or questions. Spend a little time discussing the issues before moving on to the next. Students are asked to produce three points or questions, but they might not get the chance to ask all three (this depends on the size of your cohort). However, if they have three discussion points or questions available, they can choose which to ask, depending on what has been discussed previously. Continue to invite a new question/discussion point until you have five minutes of the session left. Conclude with a summary of the main points raised.

This activity can be run as a student worksheet, if you prefer. Develop a worksheet using some of the questions given below and ask students to work on the activity during independent study. Provide assessment criteria and a submission deadline if you choose to make this an assessed piece of work.

Key issues

This activity enables students to discuss issues that they deem important about the topic. Some choose to ask very specific questions about practicalities, whereas others consider wider ethics and integrity issues about anonymization. Examples of questions and discussion points that can be raised by students tend to depend on discipline and level of study. They include the following (some have been edited and shortened for clarity and brevity):

- Is anonymization about more than just changing names?
- What is the difference between 'anonymous' and 'confidential'?
- Is it immoral to promise anonymity?
- Social media data is available online for all to see. Do we need to ensure anonymity when people posting their comments haven't?
- When I'm analysing data from my questionnaires, I need to know about gender and identity. But how can I do this according to the definition of anonymization?
- If you are working with First Nations or indigenous knowledge, what right do we have to anonymize their voices?
- How can we know or ensure that third-party analysts work to the same standards and ethical codes as we do?
- What are the dangers of identification?
- Who does anonymization protect?
- If we're analysing secondary data, how do we know that people cannot be identified?
- When you're working with recordings, it must be very difficult to keep them anonymous, especially if you're working with an easily identifiable group of people (politicians or celebrities, for example).
- What do you do if another researcher asks to see your transcripts when you've told participants that they will be kept confidential and that no one will be able to identify them from the transcripts?
- What anonymization techniques can I use for my quantitative data?
- What is K-anonymization and can we use it?
- Can we trust big tech companies to anonymize data?
- In large-scale health research, what if researchers find that someone has got a really bad disease and they need to tell them, but they can't because all the data are anonymous?
- Is it possible for data analysis software to identify people, even if we've been really careful?
- How much valuable data are lost through anonymization and does it matter?
- What is the difference between anonymization and pseudonymization?

→ **Related activities**

Activity 9: Discussing privacy and confidentiality in the research context

Activity 62: Addressing issues of anonymity and confidentiality

Activity 84: Anonymizing qualitative and quantitative data

Activity 85: Keeping research data protected and secure

→ **Preparatory reading**

Educators: The UK Data Service (details below) provides useful preparatory reading.

Students: None required. Students will find their own resources for the first part of this activity. Useful resources below can be recommended on conclusion of the activity, if required.

Activity 79

→ Useful resources

The UK Data Service provides comprehensive information about anonymization, including qualitative and quantitative data, and a step-by-step approach to anonymize a data file: www.ukdataservice.ac.uk/manage-data/legal-ethical/anonymisation.aspx [accessed 6 August 2021].

The Information Commissioner's Office (ICO) in the UK has produced a code of practice for anonymization and managing data protection risk. Section 9 covers the Data Protection Act research exemption and provides useful information relating to this activity: https://ico.org.uk/media/1061/anonymisation-code.pdf [accessed 6 August 2021].

Corti, L., Van den Eynden, C., Bishop, L. and Woollard, M. (2020) *Managing and Sharing Research Data: A Guide to Good Practice*, 2nd edition. London: Sage.

Kroes, S.K., Janssen, M.P., Groenwold, R.H. and van Leeuwen, M. (2021) 'Evaluating privacy of individuals in medical data', *Health Informatics Journal*, first published 2 June 2021, doi: 10.1177/1460458220983398.

Rhoads, R.A. (2020) '"Whales tales" on the run: Anonymizing ethnographic data in an age of openness', *Cultural Studies ↔ Critical Methodologies*, 20 (5): 402-13, first published 10 July 2020, doi: 10.1177/1532708620936994.

Saunders, B., Kitzinger, J. and Kitzinger, C. (2015) 'Anonymising interview data: Challenges and compromise in practice', *Qualitative Research*, 15 (5): 616-32, first published 23 September 2014, doi: 10.1177/1468794114550439.

Vainio, A. (2013) 'Beyond research ethics: Anonymity as "ontology", "analysis" and "independence"', *Qualitative Research*, 13(6): 685-98, first published 18 September 2012, doi: 10.1177/1468794112459669.

Vokinger, K.N., Stekhoven, D.J. and Krauthammer, M. (2020) 'Lost in anonymization – a data anonymization reference classification merging legal and technical considerations', *Journal of Law, Medicine & Ethics*, 48 (1): 228-31, first published 28 April 2020, doi: 10.1177/1073110520917025.

Activity 79

Activity • • • • • • • • • • • • → 79

Discussing the Ethics, Integrity and Practice of Anonymization in Analysis, Secondary Analysis, Re-Analysis and Third-Party Analysis

STUDENT HANDOUT

This activity is called 'Discussing the ethics, integrity and practice of anonymization in analysis, secondary analysis, re-analysis and third-party analysis'. 'Anonymization' refers to the process or procedure used to remove personal, identifiable information from data sets and transcripts. When analysing data, it refers to the process of undertaking the analysis without knowing the identity of those who have provided data (personal, identifying information is not included in the analysis). Secondary analysis is the process of analysing data that have been collected by others; re-analysis is the process of re-analysing your own data, perhaps to check the original analysis or to look for new insight; and third-party analysis involves the process of passing on data to someone else to analyse (another research team or industry collaborator, for example). If suitable and correct anonymization procedures have been used, participants cannot be identified in any of these types of analysis, either directly or indirectly, and their privacy is protected.

I would like you to prepare for our next class by producing three separate discussion points, or questions, that you would like to talk about with your peers. These can relate to:

- ethical issues associated with anonymization in analysis (for example, is it possible and desirable? Can people be harmed by identification or the anonymization process?);

- research integrity (how to approach anonymization to the highest academic and professional standards);
- practical issues (how to go about anonymizing qualitative and quantitative data).

Your discussion points or questions can be very specific, relating to your own research and any dilemmas or concerns you might have about anonymization, or more general points related to ethics and integrity of anonymization and data analysis. Try to think of questions or points that will generate useful discussion, which will enable you to bounce ideas off each other, learn something new and meet the learning outcome given below.

When we meet you will be asked, in turn, to give one question or discussion point. We will spend a few minutes in discussion, before moving on to the next student and so on. You may not have time to deliver all your points or questions. However, you will have a choice if you find that one of your questions or points has already been discussed.

Learning outcome: By the end of this activity, you will be able to assess and critique the ethics, integrity and practice of anonymization in analysis, secondary analysis, re-analysis and third-party analysis.

Activity • • • • • • • • • • • • → 80

Avoiding Unethical or Inappropriate Action Resulting from Analyses

> ### ACTIVITY 80: EDUCATOR NOTES
>
> **Purpose:** This activity is aimed at students who are concerned that their research analyses could, potentially, lead to unethical or inappropriate action by others, which could result in some kind of harm to those taking part in the research, or to those affected by the research. It is an informal discussion for invited students that enables them to discuss their concerns, and obtain advice and support from their peers.
>
> **Type:** Discussion (informal, for invited students, in-class or online).
>
> **Alternative type(s):** None.
>
> **Level:** Intermediate and advanced.
>
> **Duration:** Fifty minutes to one hour of contact time (in-class or online synchronous).
>
> **Equipment/materials:** A suitable video/web conferencing tool, if the online option is chosen.
>
> **Learning outcome:** By the end of this activity, students will be able to identify potential unethical and inappropriate action that could result from their analyses, and list possible ways to mitigate the types of action identified.

The activity

Invite together a number of students who feel that their analyses could, potentially, lead to unethical or inappropriate action, which could cause harm to those involved in the research or those affected by the research. Explain that you are going to hold an informal discussion in which students can express their concerns, gain support from each other and discuss potential ways to mitigate the problems identified. Up to 10 students is a good number for this activity: if you have more who wish to attend, run the session twice or expand the session to one and a half to two hours, so that all students get a chance to talk about their concerns.

This activity can be run either in-class or online, using a synchronous video/web conferencing tool such as Zoom Meetings, Blackboard Collaborate or Conferences in Canvas. When you meet, ask a student to start the discussion off by expressing their concerns, then invite comments and advice from their peers, while also offering your own. Continue until all students have had a chance to speak. Conclude the session with a summary of the main points raised, and find out whether students would like to have a follow-up discussion at a later date.

Key issues

This activity provides the opportunity to pass on useful advice and support for students who are concerned about what might happen as a result of their analyses. Examples of situations that students might face include:

- analyses that could, potentially, lead to policy change or legislation that causes suffering or harm, even if it is well-intentioned;
- analyses that lead to sanctions or disciplinary action (employers who feel their employees have been 'disloyal' or 'lazy', for example);
- analyses that lead to inappropriate intervention (in health and medicine or social work, for example);
- stakeholders who misinterpret or misappropriate analyses, whether intentionally or unintentionally (Activity 4);

- gatekeepers who misunderstand, or who want to take control of or influence, the analysis to the detriment of participants;
- regimes, authorities or governments that can use analyses to further their own aims or agendas;
- media misreporting, interfering with or affecting analyses to sell newspapers or improve ratings;
- co-researchers, or community participants, who are well-intentioned but lack training in, or understanding of, data analysis.

It is useful to ask if students want to reconvene for further discussion at a later date because some of these issues might not be easily resolved or could, potentially, get worse after analysis and during the writing up, sharing and publication processes.

Cautionary note

Students often perceive this activity to be irrelevant, which means that you might not have any volunteers for the discussion. This might be because these issues will not be encountered in their research, students have not realised that they could encounter such problems or problems only manifest as research gets under way. Although this is a voluntary activity, it might be prudent to spend a little extra time speaking to, and inviting, students who could, potentially, encounter such problems in their research.

→ Related activities

Activity 4: Meeting the ethical needs of stakeholders

Activity 11: Avoiding harm to others

Activity 90: Critiquing the misuse and abuse of research data

Activity 94: Ensuring against exploitation of results and outputs

→ Preparatory reading

Educators: The resources listed below cover some of the different issues that can be raised in this activity and can be useful preparatory reading.

Students: None required.

→ Useful resources

Criado Perez, C. (2020) *Invisible Women: Exposing Data Bias in a World Designed for Men.* London: Vintage.

Hoffman, S. and Podgurski, A. (2013) 'The use and misuse of biomedical data: Is bigger really better?', *American Journal of Law & Medicine*, 39 (4): 497-538, published online by Cambridge University Press 6 January 2021, doi: 10.1177/009885881303900401.

Larsen, B.R. (2021) 'The (un)celebrated asylum centre: How Danish media hijacked an ethnographic fieldwork and altered local realities', *Ethnography*, first published 19 August 2021, doi: 10.1177/14661381211038516.

Natow, R.S. (2020) 'Research use and politics in the federal higher education rulemaking process', *Educational Policy*, first published 14 May 2020, doi: 10.1177/0895904820917363.

Ogden, J. (2019) 'Do no harm: Balancing the costs and benefits of patient outcomes in health psychology research and practice', *Journal of Health Psychology*, 24 (1): 25-37, first published 31 May 2016, doi: 10.1177/1359105316648760.

O'Neil, C. (2017) *Weapons of Math Destruction: How Big Data Increases Inequality and Threatens Democracy.* London: Penguin.

Wiley, J.L., Marusich, J.A., Huffman, J.W., Balster, R.L. and Thomas, B.F. (2011) 'Hijacking of basic research: The case of synthetic cannabinoids', *Methods Report (RTI Press)*, 2011, 17971, doi: 10.3768/rtipress.2011.op.0007.1111.

Activity 80

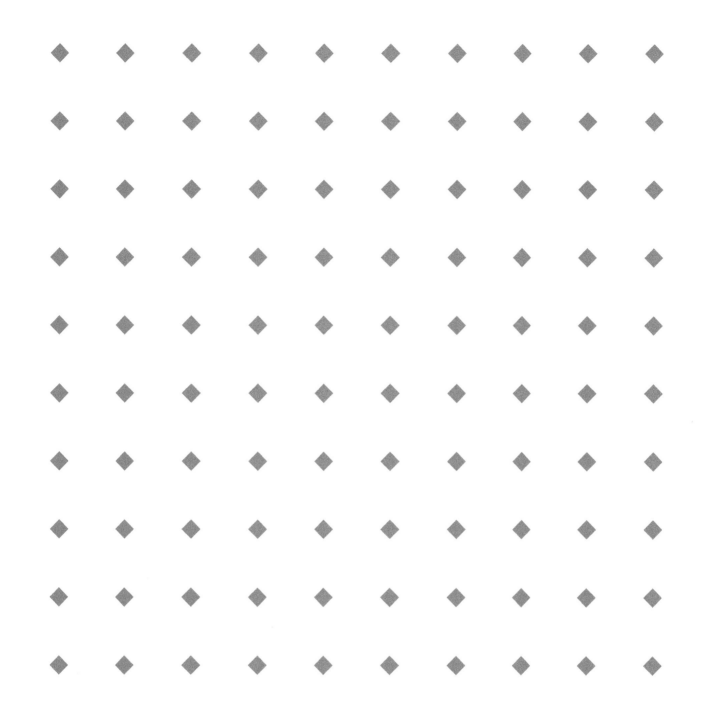

Section 7

Data
Management

Activity • • • • • • • • • • • • • → 81

Producing a Data Management Plan

The activity

Ask your students to read your university guidelines and view templates (if available) about producing a DMP (or equivalent, such as a Data Management and Sharing Plan). If they are funded students, they will also need to view any relevant guidelines and templates provided by their funding body. As they do this, set up a suitable asynchronous tool such as a VLE-hosted discussion board. Provide joining instructions and ask that, once students have read university/funding body guidelines, they pose questions they might have about producing a DMP. Students can ask questions and answer those posed by their peers. You can also answer questions, or pass them on to the relevant DMP member of staff at your university, if specific expertise is required. Monitor answers given by students to ensure that they are correct: if not, modify and explain why this has been done. Keep the discussion open until all students have produced their DMP.

This activity can be run in-class, if you prefer. Ask students to read all relevant university/funding body guidance and view templates, before developing some questions they want answering. Ask students to pose questions one at a time, when you meet. Lead a class discussion on the issues raised. Invite a DMP member of staff from the relevant university office, if you feel that specific expertise is required.

Key issues

This is a practical activity that enables students to find out how to produce their DMP in the required format. Any queries and concerns can be addressed before they go on to produce their plan. It is preferable to make the question-and-answer part of this activity voluntary as not all students will need to take part: some are able to produce their plan without needing any help or advice.

→ Related activities

Activity 82: Aligning with the FAIR principles

Activity 83: Producing a data access (or availability) statement

Activity 85: Keeping research data protected and secure

Activity 86: Protecting research data against hacking, theft, interception or insertion of rogue data

Activity 87: Assessing short-term storage and long-term data preservation strategies

Activity 89: Assessing the ethical implications of data sharing

→ Preparatory reading

Educators: Read your university's DMP guidelines and view templates, if you have not already done so. It might also be useful to read DMP guidelines from funding bodies that fund your students (these can be found on the Digital Curation Centre website for those studying in the UK: details below).

Students: Are required to read their university's and relevant funding body's guidelines and view templates. You can also recommend the DMPonline tool, if relevant to your students (details in the 'Useful resources').

→ Useful resources

The Digital Curation Centre (DCC) in the UK has useful information and guidance about producing a DMP, including a summary of funders' expectations, a useful checklist, FAQs, templates and examples: www.dcc.ac.uk/resources/data-management-plans [accessed 10 August 2021].

   The DCC also has an online service that enables students to create, review and share DMPs that meet institutional and funder requirements. Some universities in the UK ask students to use this service instead of providing their own templates: https://dmponline.dcc.ac.uk [accessed 10 August 2021].

   Information about producing a DMP in Australia can be obtained from the Australian National Data Service: www.ands.org.au/working-with-data/data-management/data-management-plans [accessed 10 August 2021].

Carey, P. (2018) *Data Protection: A Practical Guide to UK and EU Law*, 5th edition. Oxford: Oxford University Press.

Corti, L., Van den Eynden, V., Bishop, L. and Woollard, M. (2019) *Managing and Sharing Research Data: A Guide to Good Practice*. London: Sage.

Cox, A. and Verbaan, E. (2018) *Exploring Research Data Management*. London: Facet Publishing.

Elsayed, A.M. and Saleh, E.I. (2018) 'Research data management and sharing among researchers in Arab universities: An exploratory study', *IFLA Journal*, 44 (4): 281–99, first published 19 July 2018, doi: 10.1177/0340035218785196.

Maienschein, J., Parker, J.N., Laubichler, M. and Hackett, E.J. (2019) 'Data management and data sharing in science and technology studies', *Science, Technology, & Human Values*, 44 (1): 143–60, first published 18 September 2018, doi: 10.1177/0162243918798906.

Pryor, G. (ed.) (2012) *Managing Research Data*. London: Facet Publishing.

Van Loon, J.E., Akers, K.G., Hudson, C. and Sarkozy, A. (2017) 'Quality evaluation of data management plans at a research university', *IFLA Journal*, 43 (1): 98–104, first published 1 March 2017, doi: 10.1177/0340035216682041.

Activity 81

Activity · · · · · · · · · · · · · → 82

Aligning with the FAIR Principles

The activity

Explain that this activity requires students to collaborate on discussing, creating and editing a wiki. If students are new to wikis, provide written guidelines or hold a discussion about the technique prior to the activity. Set guidelines about respect for the contribution of others and offering supportive and encouraging peer feedback.

Ask your students to work together to produce a wiki that, first, describes what is meant by the FAIR principles and, second, illustrates how they can align their research to these principles. Set up a suitable wiki for this purpose (the wiki activity in Moodle or wikis in Blackboard Learn, for example) ensuring that you choose the collaborate option. Guidance notes and video tutorials are provided on these platforms for educators who are new to using wikis in their courses, including information about grading, if you choose to make this an assessed piece of work.

Encourage students to discuss, create, edit and refine their wiki until everybody is happy with the result. Monitor the wiki as it progresses: the wiki tools enable you to see who has created or edited comments and at what time. They also enable you to modify or delete pages or comments. Once the wiki has been produced it can be used for later cohorts, if appropriate (they too can discuss, edit and refine the wiki: it builds a useful resource covering a wide variety of research projects).

This activity is aimed at students studying at advanced level and, therefore, has been designed on the assumption that there are only a small number of students in your cohort. If you have a larger number of students, divide them into smaller groups and ask each group to produce their own wiki.

Key issues

Wikis provide a useful way for students to collaborate and engage with each other, without having to meet face-to-face. This activity enables them to work together to find out about the FAIR principles, and describe them in a way that every-one can understand. It also enables them to personalize the wiki by considering how the FAIR principles align with each of their research projects. This makes the wiki more interesting and relevant, keeping students motivated and engaged.

Cautionary note

As we have seen above, the collaborative nature of this project, and the part of the activity that asks students to illustrate how to align the FAIR principles with their research, tend to result in an in-depth, useful and relevant wiki. However, note that there is an entry on Wikipedia covering FAIR data: make sure that students do not plagiarize this work. If you feel this could be a problem, provide written guidelines or hold a short discussion covering these issues before the activity gets under way.

→ Related activities

Activity 81: Producing a Data Management Plan

Activity 83: Producing a data access (or availability) statement

Activity 88: Discussing the ethics of data ownership in the research context

Activity 89: Assessing the ethical implications of data sharing

Activity 90: Critiquing the misuse and abuse of research data

....

→ Preparatory reading

Educators: If you are new to using wikis, Huang (2019) and Salaber (2014) provide useful preparatory reading.

Students: None required. Students will find their own resources for this activity.

....

→ Useful resources

Boeckhout, M., Zielhuis, G.A. and Bredenoord, A.L. (2018) 'The FAIR guiding principles for data stewardship: Fair enough?', *European Journal of Human Genetics*, 26: 931–6, published 17 May 2018, doi: 10.1038/s41431-018-0160-0.

Huang, K. (2019) 'Design and investigation of cooperative, scaffolded wiki learning activities in an online graduate-level course', *International Journal of Educational Technology in Higher Education*, 16 (11), published 25 April 2019, doi: 10.1186/s41239-019-0141-6.

Leonelli, S., Lovell, R., Wheeler, B.W., Fleming, L. and Williams, H. (2021) 'From FAIR data to fair data use: Methodological data fairness in health-related social media research', *Big Data & Society*, first published 3 May 2021, doi: 10.1177/20539517211010310.

Peeters, L.M. (2018) 'Fair data for next-generation management of multiple sclerosis', *Multiple Sclerosis Journal*, 24 (9): 1151–6, first published 19 December 2017, doi: 10.1177/1352458517748475.

Salaber, J. (2014) 'Facilitating student engagement and collaboration in a large postgraduate course using wiki-based activities', *International Journal of Management Education*, 12 (2): 115–26, available online 22 April 2014, doi: 10.1016/j.ijme.2014.03.006.

Wilkinson, M., Dumontier, M., Aalbersberg, I. et al. (2016) 'The FAIR Guiding Principles for scientific data management and stewardship', *Scientific Data*, 3:160018, published 15 March 2016, doi: 10.1038/sdata.2016.18.

Information about the FAIR principles, along with practical guidance about how to go FAIR, can be found at www.go-fair.org/fair-principles [accessed 25 October 2021].

Guidance for researchers on how to make data FAIR can be obtained from Open Access Infrastructure for Research in Europe (OpenAIRE): www.openaire.eu/how-to-make-your-data-fair [accessed 25 October 2021].

Activity 82

Activity • • • • • • • • • • • • → 83

Producing a Data Access (or Availability) Statement

The activity

This activity can be approached in a number of ways:

1. Provide students with the link https://journals.plos.org/plosone/s/data-availability. Ask them to read and digest the content, then go ahead and produce their own data access (or availability) statement, during independent study. PLOS journals cover a wide variety of subject areas and this information about making data available is clear and comprehensive. Other publishers provide similar information and some of these are listed in useful resources: choose a different link if it is better suited to your students.

2. Ask students to find their own resources and work independently to:

   • provide a definition of a data access (or availability) statement;

   • explain why these statements are important;

   • produce their own data access (or availability) statement that is suitable for publications resulting from their research.

3. Ask students to find your university guidance or policy on producing a data access (or availability) statement. They should read and digest the information and produce their own statement, based on the information provided by your university.

4. Undertake 1, 2 or 3 and, once complete, bring students together to share and discuss their statements. This can be done in-class or online (using either a synchronous video tool or an asynchronous discussion board).

Key issues

Data access (or availability) statements are short descriptions of where data that are directly related to a specific publication can be found and the conditions under which they can be accessed. Although they are clear and concise statements, there is considerable thought and action involved in their production. For example, students might need to consider:

- openly available digital data (trustworthy repositories, funder-mandated repositories, archives and persistent identifiers);
- non-digital data (locations of, and access to, data if they are not possible to digitize, and information asset registers);
- source codes (model codes or codes for statistical analyses relevant to the reported results, for example);
- metadata (a description of data);
- access restrictions (and legal, political and ethical justification for restrictions), including:
  - sensitive data;
  - commercial restrictions (patents pending, contractual restrictions, embargos or non-disclosure agreements, for example);
  - participants not giving consent for sharing data;
- conditions of access:
  - open licences (Activity 40);
  - data sharing agreements (bilateral agreements, for example);
  - embargo release period;
- high volume data (practical and cost limitations);
- qualitative data (epistemological and ethical challenges: Feldman and Shaw, 2019; Mannheimer et al., 2019);
- secondary analysis of data (sources and access arrangements);
- third-party data (sources and search parameters);
- citing data (and citing multiple datasets);
- licensing conditions of publishers;
- no new data (stated clearly that no new data were collected for the research);
- timing of statement preparation (prior to final submission);
- location of statement (checking journal policy).

➔ **Related activities**

Activity 81: Producing a Data Management Plan

Activity 82: Aligning with the FAIR principles

Activity 89: Assessing the ethical implications of data sharing

Activity 96: Discussing Open Research, Open Science and Open Access

Activity 99: Communicating and reporting ethically

....

➔ **Preparatory reading**

Educators: All the resources listed below provide useful preparatory reading. Become familiar with your university's policy and guidance on data access and availability, if you have not already done so.

Students: Should read the PLOS information about data availability, find their own resources or find their university's guidance, depending on the way you decide to run this activity.

....

➔ **Useful resources**

Clear information about data access and availability can be obtained from the PLOS ONE website: https://journals.plos.org/plosone/s/data-availability [accessed 25 October 2021].

Most publishers include information on their websites about structure and content of statements, along with examples and/or templates. Examples of these include:

Wellcome Open Research: https://wellcomeopenresearch.org/for-authors/data-guidelines [accessed 25 October 2021].

Wiley: https://authorservices.wiley.com/author-resources/Journal-Authors/open-access/data-sharing-citation/data-sharing-policy.html [accessed 25 October 2021].

Elsevier: www.elsevier.com/authors/tools-and-resources/research-data/data-statement [accessed 25 October 2021].

Activity 83

Springer Nature: www.springernature.com/gp/authors/research-data-policy/data-availability-statements/12330880 [accessed 25 October 2021].

Taylor and Francis: https://authorservices.taylorandfrancis.com/data-sharing-policies/data-availability-statements/# [accessed 25 October 2021].

The Digital Curation Centre in the UK provides comprehensive advice about citing datasets and linking to publications: www.dcc.ac.uk/guidance/how-guides/cite-datasets [accessed 25 October 2021].

More information about a joint statement from leading journals committed to greater data access and research transparency can be accessed at www.dartstatement.org/2014-journal-editors-statement-jets [accessed 25 October 2021].

Denny, S.G., Silaigwana, B., Wassenaar, D., Bull, S. and Parker, M. (2015) 'Developing ethical practices for public health research data sharing in South Africa: The views and experiences from a diverse sample of research stakeholders', *Journal of Empirical Research on Human Research Ethics*, 10 (3): 290–301, first published 21 August 2015, doi: 10.1177/1556264615592386.

Feldman, S. and Shaw, L. (2019) 'The epistemological and ethical challenges of archiving and sharing qualitative data', *American Behavioral Scientist*, 63 (6): 699–721, first published 6 September 2018, doi: 10.1177/0002764218796084.

Houtkoop, B.L., Chambers, C., Macleod, M., Bishop, D.V.M., Nichols, T.E. and Wagenmakers, E.-J. (2018) 'Data sharing in psychology: A survey on barriers and preconditions', *Advances in Methods and Practices in Psychological Science*, 70–8, first published 15 February 2018, doi: 10.1177/2515245917751886.

Mannheimer, S., Pienta, A., Kirilova, D., Elman, C. and Wutich A. (2019) 'Qualitative data sharing: data repositories and academic libraries as key partners in addressing challenges', *American Behavioral Scientist*, 63 (5): 643–64, first published 28 June 2018, doi: 10.1177/0002764218784991.

Sterett, S.M. (2019) 'Data access as regulation', *American Behavioral Scientist*, 63 (5): 622–42, first published 12 October 2018, doi: 10.1177/0002764218797383.

Activity 83

Activity • • • • • • • • • • • • → 84

Anonymizing Qualitative and Quantitative Data

The activity

Ask your students to read and digest the information about anonymization provided by the UK Data Service (see the link given in useful resources below). If you are located elsewhere, choose information provided by your national data service (or equivalent). Once they have read the information, they should produce an action plan that demonstrates how they intend to anonymize their research data. Explain that when you next meet (in-class or online using synchronous tools such as Zoom Meetings, Blackboard Collaborate or Google Meet) they will be asked to share and discuss their action plan with their peers. There may be some students in your cohort who do not intend to anonymize data: if this is the case, ask these students to produce a justification for non-anonymization, instead of an action plan, which will be shared and discussed.

When you meet, ask each student in turn to present their plan/justification. Spend a little time discussing each one, before moving on to the next. Invite questions from students and conclude the session with a summary of the main points raised.

Key issues

The key issues for this activity are those covered in the information provided by the UK Data Service. In summary, these are:

- primary anonymization techniques for quantitative data:
  - o removing direct identifiers;
  - o aggregating or reducing the precision;
  - o generalizing the meaning;
  - o restricting the upper or lower ranges;
  - o anonymizing relational data;
  - o anonymizing geo-referenced data;
- anonymizing qualitative data:
  - o best practices for anonymizing text;
  - o anonymizing audio-visual data;
- step-by-step guide:
  - o finding and highlighting direct identifiers;
  - o assessing indirect identifiers;
  - o assessing the wider picture;
  - o removing (or pseudonymizing) direct identifiers;
  - o aggregating or blurring (in)direct identifiers;
  - o redacting indirect identifiers;
  - o re-assessing any remaining disclosure risk.

→ Related activities

Activity 9: Discussing privacy and confidentiality in the research context

Activity 62: Addressing issues of anonymity and confidentiality

Activity 79: Discussing the ethics, integrity and practice of anonymization in analysis, secondary analysis, re-analysis and third-party analysis

Activity 85: Keeping research data protected and secure

→ Preparatory reading

Educators: The information provided by the UK Data Service (see link in useful resources), or a national equivalent, provides useful preparatory reading.

Students: Should read the information provided by the UK Data Service (or national equivalent).

→ Useful resources

The UK Data Service provides detailed information about anonymization: www.ukdataservice.ac.uk/manage-data/legal-ethical/anonymisation [accessed 10 August 2021].

Corti, L., Van den Eynden, C., Bishop, L. and Woollard, M. (2020) *Managing and Sharing Research Data: A Guide to Good Practice*, 2nd edition. London: Sage.

Duclos, D. (2019) 'When ethnography does not rhyme with anonymity: Reflections on name disclosure, self-censorship, and storytelling', *Ethnography*, 20 (2): 175-83, first published 13 August 2017, doi: 10.1177/1466138117725337.

Macleod, C.I. and Mnyaka, P. (2018) Introduction: The Politics of anonymity and confidentiality. In: Macleod, C., Marx, J., Mnyaka, P. and Treharne, G. (eds) *The Palgrave Handbook of Ethics in Critical Research* (pp. 227-40). Cham: Palgrave Macmillan.

Rhoads, R.A. (2020) '"Whales Tales" on the run: Anonymizing ethnographic data in an age of openness', *Cultural Studies ↔ Critical Methodologies*, 20 (5): 402-13, first published 10 July 2020, doi: 10.1177/1532708620936994.

Saunders, B., Kitzinger, J. and Kitzinger, C. (2015) 'Anonymising interview data: challenges and compromise in practice', *Qualitative Research*, 15 (5): 616-32, first published 23 September 2014, doi: 10.1177/1468794114550439.

Vainio, A. (2013) 'Beyond research ethics: Anonymity as "ontology", "analysis" and "independence"', *Qualitative Research*, 13 (6): 685-98, first published 18 September 2012, doi: 10.1177/1468794112459669.

Activity 84

Activity • • • • • • • • • • • → 85

Keeping Research Data Protected and Secure

The activity

Ask your students to work independently to produce a bullet point list of what they perceive to be the 10 best tools, methods, people and/or resources that can be used or consulted to help them to keep their research data safe and secure. Items listed should be succinct (one-word items, or short terms, for example, as you are going to rank them by popularity: if students need guidance on this, use two or three of the items listed below as examples). Ask them to upload their lists using the digital tool you have set up for this purpose. Use ranking tools (or a word cloud tool) to rank the lists in order of popularity: you might need to summarize lists, depending on how they have been produced. If you want to make this a more complete student-centred resource you can also upload the game descriptions and comments produced in Activity 86, which cover identifying and finding solutions to threats to research data from hacking, theft, interception or insertion of rogue data.

Ensure that this student-centred resource is available throughout the data collection, analysis and storage stages of students' research. Ask students to add to the resource if they feel they have any useful information for their peers and encourage students to enter into online discussion about the items listed, where appropriate.

This activity can be run as a wordsearch (see the Student Handout), which can be given to your students as a paper or digital copy. Ask them to complete the wordsearch: this introduces a number of methods that can be used to keep research data protected and secure. The wordsearch can be used as a simple standalone activity, or can be followed with an online asynchronous discussion or in-class discussion, to talk about the methods found in the wordsearch.

If you choose the wordsearch option, the answers to the wordsearch provided in the Student Handout are:

antivirus	firewall
backup	keys
checksum	lock
code	password
disposal	permission
encryption	verification

Key issues

Bullet point items listed in this activity include the following (some of these can be added to the resource if they are not mentioned by students):

- antivirus software;
- firewalls;
- classification;
- encryption;
- access restrictions;
- permissions;
- passwords;
- checksums;
- verification checks;

- integrity checks;
- back-ups;
- locked filing cabinets;
- secure buildings;
- controlled access to buildings;
- approved storage;
- trustworthy repositories;
- up-to-date software;
- secure servers;

Activity 85

- power surge protection;
- Data Managements Plans (Activity 81);
- data access statements (Activity 83);
- safe disposal;
- GDPR;
- university policy;
- research ethics committees;

- Data Protection Officer approval;
- university data protection handbook;
- personal tutors/supervisors;
- computer science students/researchers;
- IT technicians/computer services;
- university research/governance office.

→ Related activities

Activity 83: Producing a data access (or availability) statement

Activity 84: Anonymizing qualitative and quantitative data

Activity 86: Protecting research data against hacking, theft, interception or insertion of rogue data

Activity 87: Assessing short-term storage and long-term data preservation strategies

Activity 89: Assessing the ethical implications of data sharing

→ Preparatory reading

Educators: Read your university's guidelines on protecting data and keeping them secure, if you have not already done so. The EDUCAUSE website has a detailed section on cybersecurity (see useful resources).

Students: None required.

→ Useful resources

Detailed information, resources and toolkits covering data security concerns for researchers can be obtained from the EDUCAUSE website: www.educause.edu/focus-areas-and-initiatives/policy-and-security/cybersecurity-program/resources/information-security-guide/toolkits/top-information-security-concerns-for-researchers [accessed 23 March 2021].

The UK Data Service provides detailed information about keeping research data protected and secure: www.ukdataservice.ac.uk/manage-data/store.aspx [accessed 26 March 2021].

A comprehensive guide to data protection and research data has been produced by Andrew Charlesworth for Jisc: www.jisc.ac.uk/full-guide/data-protection-and-research-data [accessed 26 March 2021].

Researchers in Australia can obtain comprehensive information from *Management of Data and Information in Research: A Guide Supporting the Australian Code for the Responsible Conduct of Research* (2019), produced by the National Health and Medical Research Council, Australian Research Council and Universities Australia. It is available from: www.nhmrc.gov.au/about-us/publications/australian-code-responsible-conduct-research-2018#download [accessed 22 March 2022].

Guides covering topics raised in this activity can be obtained from OpenAIRE, the European project supporting Open Science: www.openaire.eu/guides [accessed 26 March 2021].

Activity 85

Activity • • • • • • • • • • • • • → 85

Keeping Research Data Protected and Secure

STUDENT HANDOUT

This activity is called 'Keeping research data protected and secure'. Find 12 words in the puzzle that relate to keeping research data protected and secure.

```
G T Q R D V C H E C K S U M
O A N T I V I R U S R Y V A
S L P A S S W O R D O G E V
Q R E W P I N U S W P U R A
H Q R A O L K A F Q W W I A
W W M E S V H C K A Z P F F
F L I Z A Y K V U B I K I K
E V S Q L N X R M A P C C S
F Y S K Z P U A D C S O A M
P F I R E W A L L K L D T L
P U O K K C K P M U M E I P
K V N N E N C R Y P T I O N
M W B F Y Q X Q P U I U N Q
V F V E S X G D H S Y P A G
```

Learning outcome: By the end of this activity, you will be able to identify and discuss a number of ways to keep your research data protected and secure.

Activity • • • • • • • • • • • • → 86

Protecting Research Data Against Hacking, Theft, Interception or Insertion of Rogue Data

The activity

Divide your students into groups (up to six groups is a good number for this activity to provide variety: it does not matter how many students are in each group). Give each group a copy of the Student Handout. This asks them to work with their group members to produce a description of a game that addresses the issue of protecting research data against hacking, theft, interception or insertion of rogue data. The game can be any type: computer, board or card game, for example. Students should use their creativity and imagination to invent a game that will help their peers to meet the learning outcome given above. Students do not need to produce the game itself, just a detailed description of the game.

Set up a suitable tool for uploading, viewing and commenting on game descriptions. Use a polling tool to enable students to vote on the game they feel to be the most interesting, entertaining and effective at helping them to meet the learning outcome given above (if you feel this is appropriate).

This activity can be run as an in-class activity, if you prefer. Ask students to describe their game in a group presentation of up to six minutes in length. Spend a little time at the end of the presentations to discuss the issues raised and finish with a vote on the most creative, entertaining and effective game.

Key issues

Students tend to enjoy this activity, using their creativity and imagination to invent a game that is interesting, entertaining and enables their peers to meet the learning outcome given above. Most students now choose to invent a computer game. For some, the researcher is the good guy who has to work through a series of levels, hazards or bad guys who are intent on disrupting data collection, sharing or archiving through hacking, stealing, intercepting or inserting rogue data. Students use university guidelines, rules or procedures as a talisman, badge or weapon to thwart the bad guys, avoid hazards or move up a level. They also incorporate actions such as installing firewalls and antivirus software, classification, encryption, restricting access and permissions, using passwords, running checksums and saving back-ups (Activity 85). Board games that use dice throws to represent different threats to data, or card games that contain scenarios and different solutions, have also been described.

→ Related activities

Activity 83: Producing a data access (or availability) statement

Activity 84: Anonymizing qualitative and quantitative data

Activity 85: Keeping research data protected and secure

Activity 87: Assessing short-term storage and long-term data preservation strategies

Activity 89: Assessing the ethical implications of data sharing

....

→ Preparatory reading

Educators: Read your university's guidelines on protecting data and keeping them secure. The EDUCAUSE website has a detailed section on cybersecurity (see useful resources).

Students: None required.

....

→ Useful resources

Detailed information, resources and toolkits covering data security concerns for researchers can be obtained from the EDUCAUSE website: www.educause.edu/focus-areas-and-initiatives/policy-and-security/cybersecurity-program/resources/information-security-guide/toolkits/top-information-security-concerns-for-researchers [accessed 23 March 2021].

The UK Data Service provides useful information about protecting research data [accessed 25 March 2021]:

Security: www.ukdataservice.ac.uk/manage-data/store/security.aspx

Encryption: www.ukdataservice.ac.uk/manage-data/store/encryption.aspx

Back-up: www.ukdataservice.ac.uk/manage-data/store/backup.aspx

Checksums: www.ukdataservice.ac.uk/manage-data/store/checksums.aspx

Tempini, N. and Leonelli, S. (2018) 'Concealment and discovery: The role of information security in biomedical data re-use', *Social Studies of Science*, 48 (5): 663–90, first published 15 October 2018, doi: 10.1177/0306312718804875.

Activity 86

Activity · · · · · · · · · · · · → 86

Protecting Research Data Against Hacking, Theft, Interception or Insertion of Rogue Data

STUDENT HANDOUT

This activity is called 'Protecting research data against hacking, theft, interception or insertion of rogue data'. Work with your group members to produce a detailed description of a game that addresses some or all of these issues. The game can be any type: computer, word, board or card game, for example. Use your creativity and imagination to invent a game that will help your peers to meet the learning outcome given below. Note that you do not need to produce the game itself, just a detailed description of the game.

Once you have produced your description, upload it using the tool provided for this purpose. Your peers will read each description, provide comments and vote on the game that they feel is the most creative, entertaining and effective at helping them to meet the learning outcome given below. Therefore, work hard with your group members to invent and describe a game that is inventive, interesting, creative, entertaining and memorable.

Learning outcome: By the end of this activity, you will be able to identify threats to research data from hacking, theft, interception or insertion of rogue data, and provide solutions to the threats identified.

Activity • • • • • • • • • • • → 87

Assessing Short-Term Storage and Long-Term Data Preservation Strategies

The activity

Provide your students with a link to the document *Five steps to decide what data to keep: a checklist for appraising research data*, v.1 produced by the Digital Curation Centre (DCC, 2014), listed in the useful resources. This document has been produced in the UK: if you work in another country, find a similar national document, if available. Alternatively, if your university has produced comprehensive policy and guidance, ask students to consult that information instead. Once students have read and digested the information, they should produce their own strategy for the short-term storage and long-term preservation of their research data. If students are funded, they may also need to refer to their funding body guidelines or policy when producing their strategies. Explain that they will be asked to share and discuss their strategies with their peers.

When you next meet (either in-class or online, using a synchronous tool such as Zoom Meetings, Google Meet or Blackboard Collaborate), ask students, one at a time, to present their strategies for discussion. Spend a little time discussing each one, before moving on to the next. Refer students to your university policy and guidance, and to funding body policy and guidance, where applicable, during the session. Conclude with a summary of the main points raised.

Key issues

This is a practical activity that can be undertaken during the research planning and design stage, when students are thinking about producing their Data Management Plan (see Activity 81). Strategies produced in this activity can be incorporated into their DMP. In some cases, however, you might feel that this session is better left until students have collected and analysed their data, as they will be able to address some of the steps in the document more specifically. Strategies for short-term storage and long-term data preservation should be viewed as dynamic and evolving, and this should be made clear during the discussion. As strategies can change during the research process, it might be useful to have a follow-up session later, once students have undertaken their data collection.

➜ **Related activities**

Activity 81: Producing a Data Management Plan

Activity 82: Aligning with the FAIR principles

Activity 83: Producing a data access (or availability) statement

Activity 89: Assessing the ethical implications of data sharing

➜ **Preparatory reading**

Educators: Read the DCC (2014) step-by-step guidance document listed in useful resources as preparation. The DCC website also contains other useful information about data storage and preservation: www.dcc.ac.uk/guidance [accessed 11 August 2021]. Become familiar with your university's policy and guidance on storing and preserving data.

Students: Should read the DCC (2014) step-by-step guidance document.

➜ **Useful resources**

Burgi, P.-Y., Blumer, E. and Makhlouf-Shabou, B. (2017) 'Research data management in Switzerland: National efforts to guarantee the sustainability of research outputs', *IFLA Journal*, 43 (1): 5–21, first published 1 March 2017, doi: 10.1177/0340035216678238.

Corti, L., Van den Eynden, V., Bishop, L. and Woollard, M. (2019) *Managing and Sharing Research Data: A Guide to Good Practice*. London: Sage.

Cox, A. and Verbaan, E. (2018) *Exploring Research Data Management*. London: Facet Publishing.

DCC (2014) *Five steps to decide what data to keep: a checklist for appraising research data*, v.1. Edinburgh: Digital Curation Centre. Available online: www.dcc.ac.uk/guidance/how-guides/five-steps-decide-what-data-keep [accessed 11 August 2021].

Dearborn, C. and Meister, S. (2017) 'Failure as process: Interrogating disaster, loss, and recovery in digital preservation', *Alexandria: The Journal of National and International Library and Information Issues*, 27 (2): 83–93, first published 16 August 2017, doi: 10.1177/0955749017722076.

Herzinger, K., Daniels, C. and Fox, H. (2020) 'Preservation not paralysis: Reflections on launching a born-digital preservation program', *Collections*, first published 11 December 2020, doi: 10.1177/1550190620978221.

Joo, S. and Peters, C. (2020) 'User needs assessment for research data services in a research university', *Journal of Librarianship and Information Science*, 52 (3): 633–46, first published 1 July 2019, doi: 10.1177/0961000619856073.

Schaefer, S.K., McGovern, N.Y., Zierau, E.M., Goethals, A.L. and Wu, C.C. (2021) 'Deciding how to decide: Using the digital preservation storage criteria', *IFLA Journal*, first published 11 May 2021, doi: 10.1177/03400352211011490.

Tripathi, M., Chand, M., Sonkar, S.K. and Jeevan, V.K.J. (2017) 'A brief assessment of researchers' perceptions towards research data in India', *IFLA Journal*, 43 (1): 22–39, first published 1 March 2017, doi: 10.1177/0340035216686984.

Activity 87

Activity • • • • • • • • • • • • → 88

Discussing the Ethics of Data Ownership in the Research Context

The activity

This session can be run in-class or online, using a suitable video/web conferencing tool such as Zoom Meetings or Blackboard Collaborate. Divide students into small groups or pairs, or if you only have a small number of students, they can work on an individual basis (ideally, you need about eight different groups, pairs or individuals). Set guidelines for courteous and respectful discussion. Ask students to work together (or individually) to develop two open questions that they would like to discuss concerning the ethics of data ownership in the research context. These questions can relate to specific ownership issues related to their research, or to more general issues about who owns research data. They can cover any type of research and any research topic. Some questions are given in 'Key issues' below: provide some of these as examples, if your students need more guidance. Students usually spend around five minutes on this task. Use breakout rooms for this part of the activity if you are running it online.

Bring students back together and ask the first group, pair or student to present a question. Spend a little time discussing the question before moving on to the next. Continue until all questions have been asked or time has run out (some questions may be duplicated, so these can be skipped). Conclude the session with a summary of the main points raised.

Key issues

A wide variety of questions can be produced for this activity. A selection of those that have generated interesting discussion for different levels of study is given below (questions have been edited and amalgamated, where appropriate):

- What is meant by 'data ownership in the research context'?
- Are data property that can be owned?
- Surely, as the researcher, I own all my data and reports, after all, I've done all the hard work?
- Do we need to talk about these issues for an undergraduate dissertation (they don't seem relevant to me)?
- Personal data must be owned by the person, therefore, if they give it to us voluntarily, have they passed on ownership to us?
- Can you own truth or facts and, if so, who owns what truth and what facts?
- Should participants retain ownership over research outputs? If so, what is the best way to ensure that they can retain ownership?
- Can you think of specific examples where researchers and research subjects might come into conflict about who owns research data?
- How have researchers and universities appropriated ownership among First Nations or indigenous people?
- Will participants want to take ownership? Do they understand what this means?
- How do we tackle ownership issues for people who don't understand the complexities?
- If we talk about data ownership to research subjects, won't they run a mile?
- What is the relevance of ownership when researching big data or when data mining?
- Who owns data from social media research?
- Who owns data collected from the internet?
- Who owns data in crowd-sourced science or citizen science?
- Do patients own their medical samples used for research?
- If we use images of, or produced by, participants, who owns them?
- Are data intellectual property (IP)?
- What is the relevance of data ownership to my IP?
- If researchers and participants contribute ideas to research, whose IP is it? How do you decide?
- Does our university own all our personal data and all our research data?
- It is important to share data, but how can we do this when taking into account ownership of data?
- We need to publish, but what if participants say they own the data and don't want us to publish?

Cautionary note

This activity can sometimes generate heated discussion, in particular in cases where students are approaching it from different methodological standpoints. Monitor the discussion carefully to ensure that students remain respectful and courteous. Move on if you feel that problems cannot be overcome, the discussion is getting too heated or it is straying too far off topic. Remind students of the guidelines that were set at the beginning, concerning courtesy and respect.

→ Related activities

Activity 1: Respecting human dignity, privacy and rights

Activity 2: Discussing the ethics of consent and purpose

Activity 5: Assessing research accountability

Activity 89: Assessing the ethical implications of data sharing

Activity 90: Critiquing the misuse and abuse of research data

Activity 94: Ensuring against exploitation of results and outputs

....

→ Preparatory reading

Educators: All the resources listed below provide useful preparatory reading.

Students: None required, although some of the resources listed below can be recommended, once the discussion has taken place.

Activity 88

→ **Useful resources**

Corti, L., Van den Eynden, V., Bishop, L. and Woollard, M. (2020) *Managing and Sharing Research Data: A Guide to Good Practice*, 2nd edition. London: Sage.

de Koning, M., Meyer, B., Moors, A. and Pels, P. (2019) 'Guidelines for anthropological research: Data management, ethics, and integrity', *Ethnography*, 20 (2): 170-74, first published 24 April 2019, doi: 10.1177/1466138119843312.

Kostkova, P., Brewer, H., de Lusignan, S., Fottrell, E., Goldacre, B., Hart, G., Koczan, P., Knight, P., Marsolier, C., McKendry, R.A., Ross, E., Sasse, A., Sullivan, R., Chaytor, S., Stevenson, O., Velho, R. and Tooke, J. (2016) 'Who owns the data? Open data for healthcare', *Frontiers in Public Health*, 4 (7), published online 17 February 2016, doi: 10.3389/fpubh.2016.00007.

Marley, T.L. (2019) 'Indigenous data sovereignty: University institutional review board policies and guidelines and research with American Indian and Alaska Native Communities', *American Behavioral Scientist*, 63 (6): 722-42, first published 12 September 2018, doi: 10.1177/0002764218799130.

Moodie, S. (2010) 'Power, rights, respect and data ownership in academic research with indigenous peoples', *Environmental Research*, 110 (8): 818-20, doi: 10.1016/j.envres.2010.08.005.

Russell, L. and Barley, R. (2020) 'Ethnography, ethics and ownership of data', *Ethnography*, 21 (1): 5-25, first published 17 July 2019, doi: 10.1177/1466138119859386.

Williamson, B. (2017) 'Who owns educational theory? Big data, algorithms and the expert power of education data science', *E-Learning and Digital Media*, 14 (3): 105-22, first published 18 September 2017, doi: 10.1177/2042753017731238.

Activity 88

Activity • • • • • • • • • • • • → 89

Assessing the Ethical Implications of Data Sharing

The activity

Divide students into groups and ask them to work through the scenarios provided in the Student Handout. This part of the activity usually takes 20–25 minutes. Walk among the groups, answering questions or helping with dilemmas, if they occur. Once this part of the activity has concluded (students have covered each scenario), bring the groups back together to lead a class discussion on the ethical implications that have arisen (see key issues, below). As you do this, ask whether and how the implications raised relate to students' proposed research and, if so, how they can be addressed.

This activity can be run as an online asynchronous discussion, if you prefer. Present the scenarios online and ask students to discuss each, over a period of a week. Once they have done this, ask them to consider how the ethical implications raised in the scenarios might relate to their own research, and post thoughts about how they might address the issues raised. Encourage students to offer advice and ask questions. Monitor posts to ensure that information is correct and supportive.

You can also run this activity as a scenario-based individual exercise for students to work on during independent study. Adapt the Student Handout slightly and decide whether to make this an assessed piece of work: if you do, provide assessment criteria and a submission deadline.

Key issues

The scenarios given in the Student Handout present different types of research from different disciplines to provide a variety of ethical implications for students to think about and discuss. Examples of issues that can be raised (and can be used as prompts if discussions stall) include the following:

Scenario 1

- If Jaya shares her data and analyses, it increases transparency, enables others to replicate the research, helps to reduce research burden and makes better use of research funded with public funds. It will enable others to take the research further and find out things that could be of benefit to the health of women.
- Data can be misused and abused: is there a possibility that Jaya's datasets could be exploited? Is there a possibility that women could be harmed from people misusing data she has collected and shared? Jaya should read up on ways that this can happen and address

them. Techniques can include careful anonymization (to protect identity and disguise research location, for example) and consideration of the spectrum of access (open, partial or controlled, for example).
- Jaya should adhere to all relevant legislation (Activities 31, 32 and 33).
- Jaya needs to think about informed consent: are participants agreeing to their information being used by researchers in the future? How will she obtain this consent?
- Jaya should consult university policy and guidelines on sharing data.

Scenario 2

- Sharing and collaborating helps build science, capacity, fairness and respect.
- Researchers need to consider how unequal access to data impacts on different countries (Activity 54). They also need to think about and address problems that can occur with weak, restricted, non-existent or invisible data systems (Activity 53).
- Researchers must ensure all direct identifiers are removed (unless explicit consent from participants for public sharing has been obtained). They must pay attention to privacy and confidentiality, ensuring that participants cannot be identified when datasets are merged.

- When data are used at a distance from where they were collected, researchers need to consider whether future researchers will take into account the context in which data were collected, and take into account the expectations of those providing and collecting the data.
- The team will need to hold a frank discussion on benevolence and competition.
- The team will need to discuss the ethical implications of sharing data with repressive, aggressive or rogue nations.
- Problems could be addressed by ensuring that the team have a robust and comprehensive data sharing policy, following institutional, national and international guidelines.

Scenario 3

- Sharing data in animal research reduces the need for further research on animals, reduces the costs of further research, saves time and resources and increases collaboration. It enables researchers to extend their research, and the impact of their research in a sustainable way (Morrissey et al., 2017).
- Sharing provides a use for surplus materials.
- The team will need to consider issues such as public and private funding, competition and intellectual property.

- They will need to work with their university to produce a Materials Transfer Agreement (MTA).
- Problems could be addressed by ensuring that the team have a robust and comprehensive data sharing policy, following institutional, national and international guidelines. They should also consult the NC3Rs website for information (see useful resources).

Scenario 4

- Richard needs to think about informed consent (Activity 57). As he has now finished his research, did he ask participants at the start of the project whether they would be happy for him to share transcripts? What did he tell them he would do with the transcripts? Did he talk about anonymity and confidentiality (Activity 62)?
- Is there information contained within the transcripts that could be used to identify participants? If people could be identified, would it cause them harm or upset? What anonymization techniques would he use?
- Where does he intend to share transcripts? If he is talking about sharing with the actual interviewee, it can be useful as the interviewee can discuss, and add to, information and/or collaborate on interpretations.

- Richard could think about whether it is possible to go back to participants to seek consent for sharing transcripts. He could show how they have been anonymized and ask whether participants are happy for them to be shared. He will need to talk about the limits to, and challenges of, anonymity (Saunders et al., 2015). Or perhaps he could choose relevant exerpts from a number of different transcripts, to illustrate how he has built his theory. In either case, he needs to think about the emotional response of participants seeing their words in writing, in particular, when it covers sensitive topics.
- Richard should consult university policy and guidelines on sharing data.

Activity 89

Cautionary note

Scenario 3 covers animal research: students may feel very strongly about this and, on occasions, some students are unwilling to discuss this scenario. They state that animals should never be used in research and, therefore, the scenario is irrelevant. Other students in the group, however, may try to point out that sometimes animal research is necessary. Monitor the discussion and step in if it gets too heated. Alternatively, delete this scenario and provide another in its place.

➜ Related activities

Activity 51: Assessing the neutrality of online platforms, tools and data

Activity 81: Producing a Data Management Plan

Activity 83: Producing a data access (or availability) statement

Activity 90: Critiquing the misuse and abuse of research data

➜ Preparatory reading

Educators: Become familiar with your university's data sharing policy and guidelines. All the resources listed below provide useful preparatory reading.

Students: None required.

➜ Useful resources

Feldman, S. and Shaw, L. (2019) 'The epistemological and ethical challenges of archiving and sharing qualitative data', *American Behavioral Scientist*, 63 (6): 699-721, first published 6 September 2018, doi: 10.1177/0002764218796084.

Forbat, L. and Henderson, J. (2005) 'Theoretical and practical reflections on sharing transcripts with participants', *Qualitative Health Research*, 15 (8): 1114-28, first published 1 October 2005, doi: 10.1177/1049732305279065.

Hate, K., Meherally, S., Shah More, N., Jayaraman, A., Bull, S., Parker, M., and Osrin, D. (2015) 'Sweat, skepticism, and uncharted territory: A qualitative study of opinions on data sharing among public health researchers and research participants in Mumbai, India', *Journal of Empirical Research on Human Research Ethics*, 10 (3): 239-50, first published 21 August 2015, doi: 10.1177/1556264615592383.

Hoeyer, K., Tupasela, A. and Rasmussen, M.B. (2017) 'Ethics policies and ethics work in cross-national genetic research and data sharing: Flows, nonflows, and overflows', *Science, Technology, & Human Values*, 42 (3): 381-404, first published 20 October 2016, doi: 10.1177/0162243916674321.

Levenstein, M.C. and Lyle, J.A. (2018) 'Data: Sharing is caring', *Advances in Methods and Practices in Psychological Science*, 95-103, first published 28 February 2018, doi: 10.1177/2515245918758319.

Morrissey, B., Blyth, K., Carter, P., Chelala, C., Jones, L., Holen, I. and Speirs, V. (2017) 'The Sharing Experimental Animal Resources, Coordinating Holdings (SEARCH) framework: Encouraging reduction, replacement, and refinement in animal research', *PLoS Biology*, 15 (1): e2000719, published online 12 January 2017, doi: 10.1371/journal.pbio.2000719.

Saunders, B., Kitzinger, J. and Kitzinger, C. (2015) 'Anonymising interview data: Challenges and compromise in practice', *Qualitative Research*, 15 (5): 616-32, first published 23 September 2014, doi: 10.1177/1468794114550439.

Zhu, Y. (2020) 'Open-access policy and data-sharing practice in UK academia', *Journal of Information Science*, 46 (1): 41-52, first published 21 January 2019, doi: 10.1177/0165551518823174.

Information about the 3Rs in animal research can be obtained from the website of the National Centre for the Replacement, Refinement and Reduction of Animals in Research: https://nc3rs.org.uk/the-3rs [accessed 26 October 2021].

A new Data Sharing Code of Practice has been produced in the UK by the Information Commissioner's Office (ICO). It covers issues such as data sharing agreements, data protection principles, security and the rights of individuals. It came into force in October 2021 and is available on the ICO website: https://ico.org.uk/for-organisations/data-sharing-information-hub [accessed 21 March 2022].

Activity 89

Activity • • • • • • • • • • • → 89

Assessing the Ethical
Implications of Data Sharing

STUDENT HANDOUT

This activity is called 'Assessing the ethical implications of data sharing'. Work through the following scenarios with your group members, discussing the ethical implications of each scenario. You have 20-25 minutes to complete this part of the activity. Once you have done this, we will hold a discussion on the ethical issues you have raised, and discuss how these issues might relate to your own research.

Scenario 1

Jaya's research is about the alcohol consumption of people who identify as female. Her supervisor has told her that she should share her data and her statistical analyses. This is not something that Jaya has thought about and she is slightly uneasy about the ethical implications of sharing sensitive data and her analyses. What do you think are the ethical implications of sharing her data? How might she address the ethical issues you have identified?

Scenario 2

A research team based in a country in West Africa has collected thousands of human blood samples along with curated clinical data on gender, ethnicity, age and number of parasites in the blood. They intend to share the data across the globe. What do you think are the ethical implications of sharing blood samples and curated clinical data? How can the research team address the ethical issues you have identified?

Scenario 3

Two postgraduate students are part of a biomedical research team that are using animals in their research. They have followed the correct protocols: undertaking an animal ethics course and adhering to all policies and codes of practice governing humane animal use in research, in particular, the 3Rs of replacement, reduction and refinement. They intend to share their animal tissue samples on a collaborative basis. What do you think are the ethical implications of sharing animal tissue samples? How can the research team address the ethical issues you have identified?

Scenario 4

Richard has just completed his dissertation for his undergraduate degree. His research was a grounded theory study of how adults experienced bullying when they were at school. He has a number of transcripts from interviews that were coded and categorized to enable him to build his theory. He feels that it is important to share the transcripts and his analysis because they illustrate how he built his theory. What do you think are the ethical implications of sharing his transcripts? How can Richard address the ethical issues you have identified?

Learning outcome: By the end of this activity, you will be able to assess the ethical implications of data sharing and consider these implications in relation to your own research.

Activity · · · · · · · · · · · · → 90

Critiquing the Misuse and Abuse of Research Data

The activity

Discuss the following questions with your students, either in-class or online (using a suitable video/web conferencing tool such as Zoom Meetings, Google Meet or Blackboard Collaborate). This can be run as a whole-class discussion, but if you have a large number of students in your cohort, divide students into smaller groups and ask each group to work through the questions (use breakout rooms if the online option is chosen). Conclude the session with a summary of the main points raised.

1. Who might misuse or abuse research data?
2. Why might individuals or organizations misuse or abuse research data?
3. What methods do these people or organizations use to misuse or abuse research data?

4. Is there anything that researchers can do to prevent or address the misuse or abuse of their research data? If so, what?
5. What can you do to prevent or address people misusing or abusing your research data? (This question is for students who are planning or conducting their research.)

These questions can be developed into a student worksheet, if you prefer. Ask students to work on the questions during independent study and provide assessment criteria and a submission date if you choose to make this an assessed piece of work.

Key issues

Examples of issues that can be discussed for each question include:

1. Individuals and organizations that can misuse or abuse research data (whether intentionally or unintentionally) include other researchers, students, universities, politicians, journalists, governments, regimes, non-governmental organizations (NGOs), members of the public, community groups, pressure groups and employers.

2. Reasons are varied:

   - enhance careers/career prospects;
   - competition;
   - rivalry/jealousy;
   - make money/sell newspapers;
   - get rid of unwanted members of staff;
   - genuine mistakes (even if well-intentioned);
   - misunderstanding/lack of training;
   - persuade others to back (or fund) a particular cause;
   - hold on to power and/or wealth;
   - political beliefs/ideology/dogma.

3. A variety of methods can be used:

   - deliberate manipulation or fabrication of another researcher's findings/results;
   - creating misleading/sensationalist headlines;
   - cherry-picking to confirm a political view or standpoint;
   - ignoring evidence;
   - censorship;
   - coercion, harassment, intimidation or bribery;
   - passing on/retweeting/posting incorrect information about research data;
   - trying to undermine or discredit the researcher (or academics/experts);
   - failure to quote source, or quote source incorrectly/misattribute the source.

4. Researchers can prevent or address misuse or abuse by:

   - publishing in respected journals (Activity 95);
   - ensuring that they act with integrity (Activities 19, 20 and 21);
   - monitoring their outputs and reactions to them (paper and online);
   - responding to problems in a professional, academic manner;
   - avoiding conflict of interest;
   - ensuring that their research is open and transparent so that data are freely available and others can replicate or reproduce the research (Activities 17, 92, 93 and 96).

5. Students can prevent or address misuse and abuse by:

   - ensuring that they know what they are doing and produce the best piece of research they can;
   - understanding research methods and knowing how to justify methods and results;
   - making conclusions clear and to the point, so that they cannot be misunderstood or misinterpreted (Activity 91);
   - paying attention to validity and reliability, and being able to argue that this has been done;
   - ensuring that they are open and transparent, and work with integrity (Activities 17, 18, 19 and 20);
   - monitoring reactions to their research if they choose (or if they are required) to make it public;
   - responding to problems politely and professionally;
   - seeking advice from tutors and supervisors if problems occur.

→ **Related activities**

Activity 17: Cultivating transparency and openness

Activity 91: Building trust in inferences and conclusions

Activity 92: Repeating, reproducing and replicating research

Activity 94: Ensuring against exploitation of results and outputs

Activity 96: Discussing Open Research, Open Science and Open Access

→ **Preparatory reading**

Educators: The resources listed below provide information about a variety of issues that can be raised in this activity and, therefore, all provide useful preparatory reading.

Students: None required, although you can recommend some of the relevant resources below, if your students want to follow up any of the issues raised.

Activity 90

→ **Useful resources**

Doan, S. (2021) 'Misrepresenting COVID-19: Lying with charts during the second golden age of data design', *Journal of Business and Technical Communication*, 35 (1): 73-9.

Fedina, L. (2015) 'Use and misuse of research in books on sex trafficking: Implications for interdisciplinary researchers, practitioners, and advocates', *Trauma, Violence, & Abuse*, 16 (2): 188-98.

Gibbs, B.G., Shafer, K. and Dufur, M.J. (2015) 'Why infer? The use and misuse of population data in sport research', *International Review for the Sociology of Sport*, 50 (1): 115-21.

Grahe, J. (2022) *A Journey into Open Science and Research Transparency in Psychology*. Abingdon: Routledge.

Haupt, M.R., Li, J. and Mackey, T.K. (2021) 'Identifying and characterizing scientific authority-related misinformation discourse about hydroxychloroquine on Twitter using unsupervised machine learning', *Big Data & Society*, first published 6 May 2021, doi: 10.1177/20539517211013843.

Heise, C. and Pearce, J.M. (2020) 'From Open Access to Open Science: the path from scientific reality to open scientific communication', *SAGE Open*, first published 10 May 2020, doi: 10.1177/2158244020915900.

Hoffman, S. and Podgurski, A. (2013) 'The use and misuse of biomedical data: Is bigger really better?', *American Journal of Law & Medicine*, 39 (4): 497-538, published online by Cambridge University Press, 6 January 2021, doi: 10.1177/009885881303900401.

Yang, K.-C., Pierri, F., Hui, P.-M., Axelrod, D., Torres-Lugo, C., Bryden, J. and Menczer, F. (2021) 'The COVID-19 infodemic: Twitter versus Facebook', *Big Data & Society*, first published 5 May 2021, doi: 10.1177/20539517211013861.

A joint Biotechnology and Biological Sciences Research Council (BBSRC), Medical Research Council (MRC) and Wellcome Trust policy statement on managing risks of research misuse can be found at: www.ukri.org/publications/managing-risks-of-research-misuse-joint-policy-statement/ [accessed 25 November 2021].

Activity 90

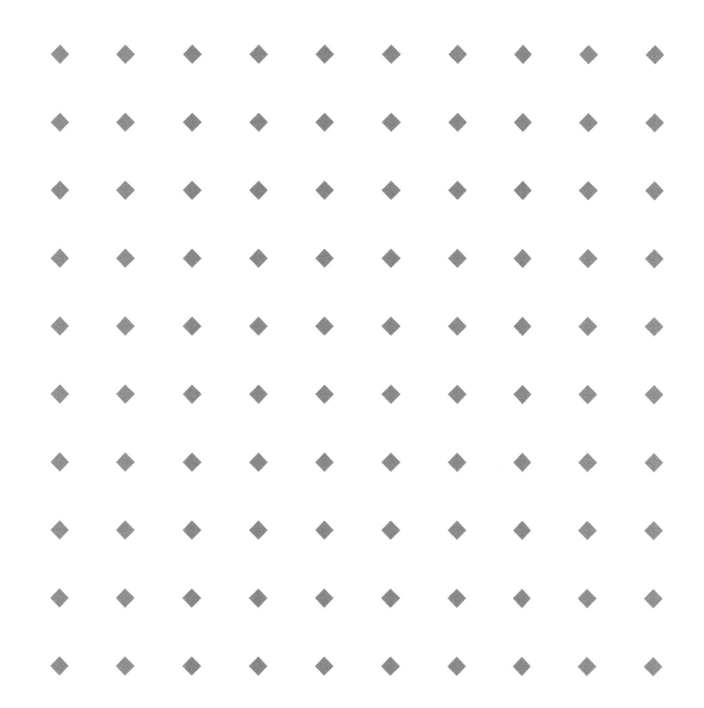

Section 8

Results and Outputs

Activity • • • • • • • • • • • • → 91

Building Trust in Inferences and Conclusions

The activity

Ask your students to find two peer-reviewed journal papers that are relevant to their research. As they read the papers, they should address the following questions:

- Do they trust the inferences and conclusions presented? Why (not)?
- What methods and techniques have (or haven't) been used to help build this trust?

- How can they factor successful methods and techniques for building trust in inferences and conclusions into their own research design? What action do they need to take?

Students should construct a plan of action that will enable them to build trust in their own inferences and conclusions, and factor these methods and techniques into their research design. If you feel it to be appropriate, and you have time available, bring your students together (in-class or online) to discuss their findings. This enables them to pool ideas, learn from each other and modify and improve their plans of action.

Key issues

This is a simple activity that is of great importance and should be undertaken early in the planning stages of research projects. This enables students to think about these issues as they read journal papers and monographs for their background reading. It also helps them to further develop and refine their own methods and techniques for building trust in their inferences and conclusions as their research progresses. Plans cover a number of issues including working with integrity (Activities 19, 20 and 21), cultivating openness and transparency (Activity 17), working within disciplinary standards (Activity 18) and taking care to avoid or address all forms of bias (Activities 52, 62, 64, 73, 74, 97 and 98).

→ Related activities

Activity 17: Cultivating transparency and openness

Activity 73: Recognizing and addressing bias when analysing qualitative data

Activity 74: Avoiding bias in quantitative analyses

Activity 75: Avoiding wrong conclusions

Activity 76: Recognizing false, fabricated or misleading analyses

Activity 90: Critiquing the misuse and abuse of research data

Activity 92: Repeating, reproducing and replicating research

Activity 93: Debating the replication crisis

→ Preparatory reading

Educators: All the resources listed below provide useful preparatory reading.

Students: None required. Students will find their own resources for this activity.

→ Useful resources

Dunn, E.W., Chen, L., Proulx, J.D.E., Ehrlinger, J. and Savalei, V. (2020) 'Can researchers' personal characteristics shape their statistical inferences?', *Personality and Social Psychology Bulletin*, first published 31 August 2020, doi: 10.1177/0146167220950522.

Forstmeier, W., Wagenmakers, E.-J. and Parker, T.H. (2017) 'Detecting and avoiding likely false-positive findings - a practical guide', *Biological Reviews*, 92: 1941-68, open access, first published 23 November 2016, doi: 10.1111/brv.12315.

Grigsby, T.J. and McLawhorn, J. (2019) 'Missing data techniques and the statistical conclusion validity of survey-based alcohol and drug use research studies: A review and comment on reproducibility', *Journal of Drug Issues*, 49 (1): 44-56, first published 29 August 2018, doi: 10.1177/0022042618795878.

Guillemin, M., Gillam, L., Barnard, E., Stewart, P., Walker, H. and Rosenthal, D. (2016) '"Doing trust": How researchers conceptualize and enact trust in their research practice', *Journal of Empirical Research on Human Research Ethics*, 11 (4): 370-81, doi: 10.1177/1556264616668975.

Kerasidou, A. (2017) '"Trust me, I'm a researcher!": The role of trust in biomedical research', *Medicine, Health Care, and Philosophy*, 20 (1): 43-50, doi: 10.1007/s11019-016-9721-6.

Rubin, A. and Parrish, D. (2007) 'Problematic phrases in the conclusions of published outcome studies: Implications for evidence-based practice', *Research on Social Work Practice*, 17 (3): 334-47, first published 1 May 2007, doi: 10.1177/1049731506293726.

Stavseth, M.R., Clausen, T. and R islien, J. (2019) 'How handling missing data may impact conclusions: A comparison of six different imputation methods for categorical questionnaire data', *SAGE Open Medicine*, doi: 10.1177/2050312118822912.

Activity 91

Activity • • • • • • • • • • → 92

Repeating, Reproducing and Replicating Research

ACTIVITY 92: EDUCATOR NOTES

Purpose: This activity encourages students to find out what is meant by, and consider the importance of, repeating, reproducing and replicating research; consider methods and techniques used to undertake these tasks; and think about this in relation to their own research.

Type: Self-guided individual exercise.

Alternative type(s): None.

Level: Intermediate and advanced.

Duration: Students will need to spend several hours during independent study working on this activity.

Equipment/materials: None required.

Learning outcome: By the end of this activity, students will be able to define what is meant by repeating, reproducing and replicating research, and differentiate between the terms; summarize techniques that can be used to repeat, reproduce and replicate research; and identify how to make it possible for others to repeat, reproduce and replicate their research.

The activity

Give your students a copy of the Student Handout and ask that they work on the activity during independent study. They are asked to provide a definition of 'repeating', 'reproducing' and 'replicating' research and illustrate how these terms differ from each other. They are then asked to find a journal paper, related to their research topic. They should illustrate how it would be possible to repeat, reproduce and replicate the research (or illustrate why this cannot be done: in this case, they will need to demonstrate why and suggest ways that the author could have made it easier to undertake these tasks).

Give a date by which time this task should be completed. You can make this an assessed piece of work, or if you have time available, you can meet (in-class or online) to discuss their findings. The Student Handout can be adapted if you choose either of these options.

Key issues

There are a number of key issues that can be raised in this activity: a summary of these is given below.

- The following definitions tend to be given. However, other definitions might also be given, which may be due to students' discipline, misinterpretation or the sources they use (Clemens, 2017; Gilbert et al., 2016; Patil et al., 2016; Plesser, 2018):

  o Repeat: the same researcher is able to repeat the research and achieve the same results, following the same methods and procedures and within the same conditions.

- o Reproduce: a different researcher is able to duplicate the results of a study through using the same data and same methods as the original study.
- o Replicate: a different researcher is able to achieve the same (or similar) results using the same methods with new samples (from the original population) and new data. Some students break this down into three types that provide slightly different defintions (Aguinis and Solarino, 2019):
    - exact replication: same methods, samples and procedures are used to get the same results;
    - empirical replication: same procedures with a different population;
    - conceptual replication: different procedures with the same population.
- Information that researchers need to share for others to repeat, reproduce and replicate research include the following (if these are missing, students find it harder to suggest how the research could be repeated, reproduced and replicated):
    - o a discussion on methodology (and perhaps epistemology and theoretical perspective, in some disciplines);
    - o a precise description of the methods and techniques used for data collection and data analysis:
        - sample sizes and criteria;

- all data (raw or processed);
- metadata;
- coding;
- software used;
- statistical tests;
- methods of qualitative analysis;
    - o an honest report of assumptions, preferences and bias;
    - o transparency concerning error, problems and challenges.
- Students need to ensure that they adopt a systematic approach and provide a complete record of methods, techniques and procedures used as their research progresses. They should use power calculations, multiple comparison tests and descriptive statistics to ensure statistics are sound. They should develop techniques for building trust in inferences and conclusions (Activity 91). Pre-registration of approaches, hypotheses and data analysis plans are suggested to prevent students choosing the most significant results, but some feel that this would not work for all research methodologies.
- When reporting results, students need to provide a detailed report on methods, techniques and procedures and highlight each step they have taken so that they are easy for others to follow.

→ **Related activities**

Activity 17: Cultivating transparency and openness

Activity 75: Avoiding wrong conclusions

Activity 76: Recognizing false, fabricated or misleading analyses

Activity 90: Critiquing the misuse and abuse of research data

Activity 91: Building trust in inferences and conclusions

Activity 93: Debating the replication crisis

Activity 95: Knowing where and how to publish

→ **Preparatory reading**

Educators: All the resources listed below provide useful preparatory reading.

Students: None required. Students will find their own resources for this activity.

→ **Useful resources**

Aguinis, H. and Solarino, A. (2019) 'Transparency and replicability in qualitative research: The case of interviews with elite informants', *Strategic Management Journal*, 40 (8): 1291-315, first published 6 March 2019, doi: 10.1002/smj.3015.

Clemens, M. (2017) 'The meaning of failed replications: A review and proposal', *Journal of Economic Surveys*, 31 (1): 326-42, first published 26 December 2015, doi: 10.1111/joes.12139.

Gilbert, D.T., King, G., Pettigrew, S. and Wilson, T.D. (2016) 'Comment on "Estimating the reproducibility of psychological science"', *Science*, 351 (6277): 1037, published 4 March 2016, doi: 10.1126/science.aad7243.

Goodman, S.N., Fanelli, D. and Ioannidis, J.P.A. (2016) 'What does research reproducibility mean?', *Science Translational Medicine*, 8 (341): 341ps12, published 1 Jun 2016, doi: 10.1126/scitranslmed.aaf5027.

Activity 92

Patil, P., Peng, R.D. and Leek, J.T. (2016) 'What should researchers expect when they replicate studies? A statistical view of replicability in psychological science', *Perspectives on Psychological Science*, 11 (4): 539-44. doi: 10.1177/1745691616646366.

Plesser, H.E. (2018) 'Reproducibility vs. replicability: A brief history of a confused terminology', *Frontiers in Neuroinformatics*, 11 (76), published online 18 January 2018, doi: 10.3389/fninf.2017.00076.

Thaler, K. (2021) 'Reflexivity and temporality in researching violent settings: Problems with the replicability and transparency regime', *Geopolitics*, 26 (1), 18-44, published online 23 July 2019, doi: 10.1080/14650045.2019.1643721.

The UK Reproducibility Network (UKRN) is a national peer-led consortium that seeks to improve the trustworthiness and quality of research through training, best practice and investigation: www.ukrn.org [accessed 27 October 2021].

Activity 92

Activity · · · · · · · · · · · → 92

Repeating, Reproducing and Replicating Research

STUDENT HANDOUT

This activity is about repeating, reproducing and replicating research. It is a self-guided individual exercise for you to undertake during independent study. Please complete the work on your own and hand it back to me by the specified date.

1. Think about what is meant by the three terms: 'repeating', 'reproducing' and 'replicating' in relation to research practice. Provide a definition for each that illustrates how they differ from each other.

2. Choose a journal paper that reports the results of a particular research project and is related to your proposed research (if you haven't yet decided on your research, choose a paper that is of personal interest). Read through the paper and suggest how researchers could go about repeating, reproducing and replicating the research (methods and techniques for each of these processes might be slightly different, so ensure that this is illustrated in your answer). If you cannot show how to repeat, reproduce and replicate the research, explain why not. What information is missing? What should the author have included that would make it easier for the research to be repeated, reproduced and replicated?

3. Think about your own research. How can you ensure that others will be able to repeat, reproduce and replicate your research? What do you need to include when writing up your research? How should you factor this into your research design? What do you need to consider in the planning stages of your research?

Learning outcome: By the end of this activity, you will be able to define what is meant by repeating, reproducing and replicating research and differentiate between the terms; summarize techniques that can be used to repeat, reproduce and replicate research; and identify how to make it possible for others to repeat, reproduce and replicate your own research.

Activity · · · · · · · · · · · → 93

Debating the Replication Crisis

ACTIVITY 93: EDUCATOR NOTES

Purpose: This activity is an entertaining and memorable way to introduce students to issues surrounding the replication crisis. It is a group debate in which one side argues for the existence of a replication crisis, and the other argues against its existence. It encourages students to think about what is meant by the replication crisis, why replicating research is important and how it can be done. This activity can be run together with Activity 92: Repeating, reproducing and replicating research, for a more complete understanding of this topic.

Type: Debate (group, in-class or online).

Alternative type(s): None.

Level: Intermediate and advanced.

Duration: Students will need to spend a few hours during independent study working with their group members to research, form and rehearse their argument. Fifty minutes to one hour of contact time will be required for the debate (in-class or online).

Equipment/materials: A suitable video/web conferencing tool, if this option is chosen.

Learning outcome: By the end of this activity, students will be able to define what is meant by the replication crisis and summarize arguments for and against the existence of a replication crisis in research.

The activity

This activity is a group debate in which students speak for and against the existence of a replication crisis in research. Divide your students into two groups. One group is to argue for the existence of a replication crisis and the other is to argue against its existence. They then have the chance to refute each other's argument. Ask your students to discuss the issues and prepare points for their debate with their group members during independent study. If your students are new to debating, give them a copy of the Student Handout, which they can use for guidance when preparing for the debate.

The debate is to be held when you next meet (in-class or online). Introduce the activity, explain debating procedures, set ground rules and act as chairperson and timekeeper, ensuring that the debate is constructive, remains on track and takes place within the allotted time. Ensure that students listen to, and respect, the views of their peers and that arguments remain academic, rather than personal. Encourage your students to be confident and persuasive, while paying attention to clarity, tone, speed and volume. The debate should last for 40 minutes (in four 10-minute slots with each group speaking twice), with a 10- to 20-minute debrief on the issues that have been raised.

It is possible to run this activity together with Activity 92: Repeating, reproducing and replicating research, for more complete coverage of these topics. Ask your students to hold the debate first, before completing the self-guided individual exercise to add to, and consolidate, their learning.

Key issues

This activity requires students to prepare a structured argument in which two sides speak for and against a particular contention. They have to work out how to argue as part of a team, ensuring that they do not contradict the arguments of their team members. They also need to pay close attention to the content: their introduction, their argument (and the evidence that is used to back up their argument), their rebuttal of the arguments used by the other team, and their conclusion.

In this activity, students might be asked to argue for something with which they do not agree: this enables them to come to terms with, and understand, alternative scientific and popular viewpoints (and misconceptions). It also encourages them to move beyond what Chopik et al. (2018: 159) describe as 'quite radical, superficial, and even emotional' opinions about the replication crisis.

Key issues that arise in this debate concern scientific evidence for or against the existence of a replication crisis; reviews and journal papers that discuss whether or not the problem is as bad as has been reported; and misleading reports on social media and in the newspapers, over-emphasizing or sensationalizing the issue. Students might also decide that this activity has presented a false dichotomy, that the two sides are not clear cut and that, although they had to present one particular argument, they will look at the issue from a variety of viewpoints as their studies progress. This is a useful issue to unpack during the discussion once the debate has concluded.

Cautionary note

Debates tend to be lively, interesting and memorable. However, it is essential that you monitor the debate carefully, to ensure that everyone respects each other's opinion and listens to what their opponents have to say. If you feel that issues have arisen that may upset students, or cause offence, take a note of them ready for discussion after the debate.

→ Related activities

Activity 17: Cultivating transparency and openness

Activity 75: Avoiding wrong conclusions

Activity 76: Recognizing false, fabricated or misleading analyses

Activity 91: Building trust in inferences and conclusions

Activity 92: Repeating, reproducing and replicating research

→ Preparatory reading

Educators: This paper might be of interest:

Chopik, W. J., Bremner, R.H., Defever, A.M. and Keller, V.N. (2018) 'How (and whether) to teach undergraduates about the replication crisis in psychological science', *Teaching of Psychology*, 45 (2), 158-63, first published 11 March 2018, doi: 10.1177/0098628318762900.

Students: None required. Students will find their own resources for this activity.

→ Useful resources

Anvari, F. and Lakens, D. (2018) 'The replicability crisis and public trust in psychological science', *Comprehensive Results in Social Psychology*, 3 (3): 266-86, published online 19 November 2019, doi: 10.1080/23743603.2019.1684822.

Block, J. and Kuckertz, A. (2018) 'Seven principles of effective replication studies: Strengthening the evidence base of management research', *Management Review Quarterly*, 68: 355-9, published 27 September 2018, doi: 10.1007/s11301-018-0149-3.

Flis, I. (2019) 'Psychologists psychologizing scientific psychology: An epistemological reading of the replication crisis', *Theory & Psychology*, 29 (2): 158-81, first published 7 April 2019, doi: 10.1177/0959354319835322.

Mansell, W. and Huddy, V. (2018) 'The assessment and modeling of perceptual control: A transformation in research methodology to address the replication crisis', *Review of General Psychology*, 22 (3): 305-20, first published 1 September 2018, doi: 10.1037/gpr0000147.

Activity 93

Mede, N.G., Schäfer, M.S., Ziegler, R., and Weißkopf, M. (2021) 'The "replication crisis" in the public eye: Germans' aware-ness and perceptions of the (ir)reproducibility of scientific research', *Public Understanding of Science*, 30 (1): 91-102, first published 14 September 2020, doi: 10.1177/0963662520954370.

Milfont, T.L. and Klein, R.A. (2018) 'Replication and reproducibility in cross-cultural psychology', *Journal of Cross-Cultural Psychology*, 49 (5): 735-50, first published 21 May 2018, doi: 10.1177/0022022117744892.

Stroebe, W. and Strack, F. (2014) 'The alleged crisis and the illusion of exact replication', *Perspectives on Psychological Science*, 9 (1): 59-71, first published 14 January 2014, doi: 10.1177/1745691613514450.

Suter, W.N. and Suter, P.M. (2019) 'Understanding replication: Trust but verify', *Home Health Care Management & Practice*, 31 (4): 207-12, first published 25 May 2019, doi: 10.1177/1084822319850501.

Activity 93

Activity · · · · · · · · · · · · → 93

Debating the Replication Crisis

STUDENT HANDOUT

This activity is called 'Debating the replication crisis'. A 'debate' is a structured argument in which two sides speak for and against a particular contention. In this case, one group is to argue for the existence of a replication crisis in research and the other is to argue against its existence. Prepare, in your group, your arguments ready for a debate for when we next meet (even if you, personally, disagree with the side of the argument you must debate). Your group will be given two 10-minute slots in which to debate (alternating with your opponents). You will also need to produce a rebuttal of arguments put forward by your opponents.

The following tips will help you to prepare for your debate:

- Prepare for the debate:
  - define your topic;
  - find relevant sources and research the topic (and your side of the argument);
  - prepare enough material to fill two 10-minute slots;
  - produce notes to aid your memory;
  - pay close attention to your introduction, main argument (and evidence to back up your argument) and conclusion;
  - divide your material and time between team members so that you know who is speaking at what time and what they are going to say;
  - avoid arguments that are factually, morally or logically flawed;
  - avoid rhetorical questions as these will help your opponents to attack your arguments;
  - practise presenting your material within the allotted time.
- Prepare for your defence and rebuttal:
  - think about how your opponents will refute your arguments and prepare a defence;
  - understand the key arguments that will be put forward by your opponents and prepare a suitable rebuttal;
  - offer evidence for your defence and rebuttal.
- During the debate:
  - argue as part of a team and take care not to contradict the arguments of your team members;
  - make good eye contact with team members and with your opponents;
  - present your arguments in a confident and persuasive manner;
  - keep all arguments on an academic level and avoid personal comments: counter the arguments, not the person;
  - ensure that other students can understand what you are saying and vary your tone for interest;
  - avoid shouting or raising your voice;
  - be courteous, listen to your opponents and respect what they say;
  - enjoy yourself.

Learning outcome: By the end of this activity, you will be able to define what is meant by the replication crisis and summarize arguments for and against the existence of a replication crisis in research.

Activity • • • • • • • • • • → 94

Ensuring Against Exploitation of Results and Outputs

The activity

Contact your students to find out whether any of them have concerns that their research results or outputs could be exploited in a negative or harmful way by others. Decide whether to provide detailed information about what you mean by exploitation of results or outputs (see key issues, below) or leave it up to your students to decide for themselves. If any students feel that this could be a problem as their research progresses, invite them to join a peer support group. Explain that the purpose of the group is to enable students to meet others who may be experiencing similar problems, to discuss the type of problems that could be encountered, and identify possible solutions. It will also enable students to form pairs or small groups to meet up together, to offer guidance and support as they continue with their research.

Choose a suitable time and date, and a venue that is conducive to frank and open discussion (or if you prefer, this can be run online using video/web conferencing tools such as Zoom Meetings, Google Meet or Blackboard Collaborate). Set guidelines for supportive and constructive discussion, and make sure that students understand that what is discussed in this support group should be kept confidential and not disclosed to third parties. Invite a student to give a brief description of their research, before outlining their concerns about exploitation of results or outputs. Spend a little time discussing the issues before moving on to the next student. Once all students have had a chance to speak, lead a discussion on possible ways to address the problems identified.

When the activity is complete, ask students to form pairs or small groups and suggest that they arrange to meet, or contact their peers, whenever they feel they are encountering problems that they need to discuss.

Key issues

There are various types of exploitation of results or outputs that might concern students, as illustrated in the following cases:

- A student is sponsored by his employer to undertake some research into employee work practices, with the aim of improving these practices. However, the student begins to suspect that the employer will use the research results as a way to get rid of what the employer perceives to be unproductive workers, or workers that have the 'wrong attitude', in her opinion.
- A student is a member of a research team working in collaboration with an industry partner. Although the team and partner have a strict collaboration agreement that outlines all roles and responsibilities, ownership of intellectual property and describes what will happen to research results and outputs, the student is worried that the industry partner will use the outputs unethically.

- A student is working as part of a research team developing a new type of fertilizer that can be used effectively on parched or arid land. However, there is potential for their product to be used in the development or production of harmful agents, which could pose a threat to national security. The student is beginning to feel uneasy about working on the team.
- A student is working on a new drug treatment together with a pharmaceutical company. The student is aware of similar drugs that have been sold illegally, which are highly addictive. He wants to make sure that, when his drug is developed, it cannot be used and abused by others.

Methods that can be used to deal with exploitation of results or outputs include:

- increase knowledge, understanding and awareness;
- find out who is commissioning/funding research and look into their background, motivation and justification for the research;
- read all contracts, guidelines and collaboration agreements carefully: if you feel these are being breached, speak to your supervisor;
- university policy and guidelines can be used to counteract unethical pressure from others (funding bodies or employers, for example);

- undertaking a potential misuse risk assessment (following funding body/university guidelines, if available);
- adhering, and/or referring others, to relevant codes of ethics;
- cultivating openness and transparency (Activity 17);
- working with integrity and professionalism (Activities 19, 20 and 21).

Cautionary note

You might find that none of your students is interested in this activity: they may think that their results will not be exploited, or that they can deal with problems should they arise. In these cases, let students know that the activity remains open: if they find problems occurring as their research progresses, a support group can be held. On other occasions, you may find that students encounter difficult and upsetting problems with which their peers are unable to help: if so, ensure that you are available to offer help or provide guidance about where additional support can be obtained.

➜ Related activities

Activity 82: Avoiding conflict of interest, in Dawson (2016: 221-2)

Activity 83: Understanding biased financial relationships, in Dawson (2016: 223-4)

Activity 84: Recognizing and managing the funding effect, in Dawson (2016: 225-6)

Activity 90: Critiquing the misuse and abuse of research data

Activity 91: Building trust in inferences and conclusions

....

➜ Preparatory reading

Educators: The statement, guidance notes and explanatory notes referenced below provide useful preparatory reading.

Students: None required.

....

Activity 94

→ Useful resources

A joint Biotechnology and Biological Sciences Research Council (BBSRC), Medical Research Council (MRC) and Wellcome Trust policy statement on managing risks of research misuse can be found at: www.ukri.org/publications/managing-risks-of-research-misuse-joint-policy-statement/ [accessed 25 November 2021].

An EU guidance note on potential misuse of research can be found at http://ec.europa.eu/research/participants/data/ref/h2020/other/hi/guide_research-misuse_en.pdf [accessed 25 November 2021].

An EU explanatory note on potential misuse of research can be found at https://ec.europa.eu/research/participants/portal/doc/call/h2020/fct-16-2015/1645168-explanatory_note_on_potential_misuse_of_research_en.pdf   [accessed   25   November 2021].

Dawson, C. (2016) *100 Activities for Teaching Research Methods*. London: Sage.

Wiley, J.L., Marusich, J.A., Huffman, J.W., Balster, R.L. and Thomas, B.F. (2011) 'Hijacking of basic research: The case of synthetic cannabinoids', *Methods Report (RTI Press)*, 2011, 17971, doi: 10.3768/rtipress.2011.op.0007.1111.

Activity 94

Activity • • • • • • • • • • • • → 95

Knowing Where and How to Publish

The activity

Divide your students into pairs or small groups (four pairs or small groups is a good number for this activity). Give them a copy of the Student Handout. This asks them to work in their pairs/groups to find two suitable senior researchers from your university to interview about where and how to publish research. They are to develop a list of questions, paying attention to issues of ethics and integrity when publishing, ready for the interview. In their pairs/groups, one person will ask the questions in the first interview while someone else videos it, with roles swapped for the second interview (these should be no longer than three minutes). Students tend to use smartphones or webcams: if they do not have this technology, make sure that video equipment is available for their use.

Once all interviews are complete, they are to be uploaded so that they can be shared with peers. Ask students to view each video and open an asynchronous discussion for them to ask questions, clarify information and provide further advice for their peers. Set a deadline by which time this task should be completed. If you choose to make this an assessed piece of work, provide assessment criteria.

You can choose to run this activity in-class, if you prefer. Ask students to produce and upload videos as above, then play them in class. Allocate 15-20 minutes to hold a discussion on the issues raised.

Key issues

This activity is dual purpose: it enables students to find out about where and how to publish their research, ethically and with integrity, while also giving them the chance to practise their interview technique. Students are able to learn a considerable amount from senior researchers who have published work using a variety of methods and media. Senior researchers are able to share their experience, and provide useful tips and advice for students.

Topics depend on who has been interviewed and what they decide to say, but can include the following issues:

- discussing and reaching agreement on any communication and publication methods with your supervisor, especially when using social media;
- publishing in peer-reviewed journals, what is meant by peer-review and why it is important;
- finding and knowing about journals that are relevant to your research topic and discipline;
- avoiding predatory journals and conferences (Dobusch and Heimstädt, 2019; Yeo et al., 2021);
- Open Access publishing: what it means, the process and why it is important (Activity 96), and the costs and benefits (May, 2020);
- different types of online publishing and the advantages, opportunities and challenges (Corti and Fielding, 2016);
- turning research into publishable content and how to be successful in getting published, for example, publishing with an experienced researcher/supervisor and choosing the right journal (Yeo et al., 2021);
- the importance of creativity and using your imagination;
- the importance of ensuring research is robust, validated and sound methodologically, before you publish or put it into the public domain;
- the importance of checking publishing protocols when collaborating;
- sharing data when publishing research (Activities 82 and 83);
- dealing with the pressures to publish and avoiding misconduct such as honorary authorship (Paruzel-Czachura et al., 2020);
- communicating and reporting ethically (Activity 99);
- understanding rules, regulations and legal issues concerning plagiarism, copyright, libel, slander and breaches of confidentiality, in particular when using social media and publishing online (activities in Section 3);
- recognizing and avoiding reporting bias (Activity 97);
- publishing images: where, how and ensuring it is done ethically (Activity 100);
- knowing how publication practices are changing (Antell et al., 2016);
- registering for a unique researcher identifier;
- preparing for, and dealing with, rejections (Yeo et al., 2021).

→ **Related activities**

Activity 96: Discussing Open Research, Open Science and Open Access

Activity 97: Recognizing reporting bias

Activity 98: Understanding the influence of publication bias

Activity 99: Communicating and reporting ethically

Activity 100: Displaying and publishing images ethically

→ **Preparatory reading**

Educators: All the resources listed below provide useful preparatory reading.

Students: None required. Students will learn from senior researchers.

→ **Useful resources**

Antell, K., Foote, J.S. and Foote, J.B. (2016) 'Scholarly publishing's evolving landscape: Impact metrics, electronic-only journals, and Open Access in journalism and communication research', *Journalism & Mass Communication Educator*, 71 (3): 309-28, first published 15 September 2016, doi: 10.1177/1077695816668864.

Corti, L. and Fielding, N. (2016) 'Opportunities from the digital revolution: Implications for researching, publishing, and consuming qualitative research', *SAGE Open*, first published 1 November 2016, doi: 10.1177/2158244016678912.

Dobusch, L. and Heimstädt, M. (2019) 'Predatory publishing in management research: A call for open peer review', *Management Learning*, 50 (5): 607-19, first published 22 October 2019, doi: 10.1177/1350507619878820.

Activity 95

Gastel, B. and Day, R. (2016) *How to Write and Publish a Scientific Paper*, 8th edition. Cambridge: Cambridge University Press.

May, C. (2020) 'Academic publishing and open access: Costs, benefits and options for publishing research', *Politics*, 40 (1): 120–35, first published 25 June 2019, doi: 10.1177/0263395719858571.

Paruzel-Czachura, M., Baran, L. and Spendel, Z. (2020) 'Publish or be ethical? Publishing pressure and scientific misconduct in research', *Research Ethics*, first published 18 December 2020, doi: 10.1177/1747016120980562.

Yeo, M.A., Renandya, W.A. and Tangkiengsirisin, S. (2021) 'Re-envisioning academic publication: From "publish or perish" to "publish and flourish"', *RELC Journal*, first published 3 February 2021, doi: 10.1177/0033688220979092.

The Open Science project is dedicated to writing and releasing free and open source scientific software: http://open-science.org [accessed 1 November 2021].

Creative Commons licences provide a simple, standardized way to grant copyright permissions to creative work: https://creativecommons.org [accessed 1 November 2021].

The Journal of Brief Ideas is an online platform that publishes 200-word 'idea' articles from a variety of disciplines that enable researchers to share their ideas efficiently with the wider research community: http://beta.briefideas.org [accessed 1 November 2021].

Activity 95

Activity • • • • • • • • • • • • → 95

Knowing Where and How to Publish

STUDENT HANDOUT

This activity is called 'Knowing where and how to publish'. Work together in your pair or small group to find two senior researchers at this university who have published widely and are willing to undertake a short interview (of up to three minutes) about how and where to publish research. You will need to let them know that you would like to video the interview and that this video will be shared with peers for teaching and learning purposes. Senior researchers can be from your department or from another department in the university: your peers will also be undertaking this activity, so try to choose someone who has not been approached. Think about approaching senior researchers from different disciplines, research methodologies or topics to add variety and interest to this activity.

Once you have found two senior researchers who have agreed to be interviewed, develop a list of questions that you can ask during the interview. When you do this, think about how issues of ethics and integrity when publishing can be included. In your pairs/groups, one person will ask the questions in the first interview while someone else videos it, then you will swap roles for the second interview. You can choose to use the same questions for each interview, or you can develop different questions for each. Use the learning outcome given below to guide you and to ensure that questions remain on topic. Find out how to probe for more detail so that you can obtain useful information and advice that will be shared with your peers.

When videoing the interview smartphones or webcams are fine for this activity: if you don't have this equipment, I can provide it for you. Ensure that you pay attention to audio, lighting and camera stabilization, and use basic editing software, if required. Once both interviews are ready, upload them using the tool provided. View the interviews posted by your peers and enter into the online discussion. Ensure that this is done by the given deadline.

Learning outcome: By the end of this activity, you will be able to identify a variety of methods and media that can be used to publish research, and explain how to publish your research effectively, ethically and with integrity.

Activity • • • • • • • • • • • • → 96

Discussing Open Research, Open Science and Open Access

The activity

Inform your students that you are going to run a student-led discussion on Open Research, Open Science and Open Access. Ask them to spend a little time during independent study researching these topics and developing three questions that they would like to discuss with their peers about these topics. Questions can be general, or relate specifically to students' thoughts about sharing and publishing their research. Explain that when you next meet (either in-class or online) students will lead the discussion and have the opportunity to ask their questions, one at a time, until all questions have been asked and discussed, or time has run out. Ask them to think of questions that will be of interest and relevance to all members of the group, and enable them to discuss important issues about the Open movement.

This activity works best if there are 8–12 students in the session, so you may need to divide your students into groups if you have more than this number in your cohort. Your role is to act as facilitator: introduce the session and request that a student volunteer their first question. Invite others to discuss possible answers, before moving on to another question from another student. Monitor the discussion: if it strays off topic, ask them to return to the topic or move on to the next question. Continue in this way until all questions have been asked or time has run out. Conclude the discussion with a summary of the issues raised.

This activity can be extended for students studying at advanced level by asking them to produce a plan of action, illustrating how they intend to address the Open movement when sharing and publishing their research.

Key issues

This activity is student-led so that each cohort can raise issues that they deem important. Some students concentrate on the practicalities of Open Access publishing and issues surrounding the protection of their work and ideas (this tends to be students studying at advanced level). Licensing (Activity 40), copyright (Activities 35 and 39) and intellectual property (Activity 38) are all raised. Some also discuss Open Data, Open Analysis and Open Materials and the practical issues associated with this type of data sharing, knowledge transfer and publication. Students may also choose to discuss the wider issues, such as why this movement is needed; the benefits of openness and transparency; the benefits to students, researchers, stakeholders and society (promoting diversity and justice, and leading to social change, for example); and how this movement relates to their studies and research.

→ Related activities

Activity 35: Seeking permission with regard to data ownership

Activity 38: Protecting intellectual property

Activity 39: Avoiding copyright infringement

Activity 40: Understanding digital licences, laws and conventions

Activity 83: Producing a data access (or availability) statement

Activity 89: Assessing the ethical implications of data sharing

→ Preparatory reading

Educators: The resources listed below all provide useful preparatory reading.

Students: None required as students will find their own resources for this activity. If appropriate, they can be directed to some of the resources listed below, once the discussion has concluded.

→ Useful resources

Eve, M.P. (2014) *Open Access and the Humanities: Contexts, Controversies and the Future.* Cambridge: Cambridge University Press.

Grahe, J.E., Cuccolo, K., Leighton, D.C. and Cramblet Alvarez, L.D. (2020) 'Open Science promotes diverse, just, and sustainable research and educational outcomes', *Psychology Learning & Teaching*, 19 (1): 5-20, first published 18 August 2019, doi: 10.1177/1475725719869164.

Heise, C. and Pearce, J.M. (2020) 'From Open Access to Open Science: The path from scientific reality to open scientific communication', *SAGE Open*, first published 10 May 2020, doi: 10.1177/2158244020915900.

Herb, U. and Schöpfel, J. (2018) *Open Divide: Critical Studies on Open Access.* Sacramento, CA: Litwin Books.

Pinfield, S., Wakeling, S., Bawden, D. and Robinson, L. (2021) *Open Access in Theory and Practice: The Theory-Practice Relationship and Openness.* Abingdon: Routledge.

Rockhold, F., Bromley, C., Wagner, E.K. and Buyse, M. (2019) 'Open science: The open clinical trials data journey', *Clinical Trials*, 16 (5): 539-46, first published 26 July 2019, doi: 10.1177/1740774519865512.

van Dijk, W., Schatschneider, C. and Hart, S A. (2021) 'Open science in education sciences', *Journal of Learning Disabilities*, 54 (2): 139-52, first published 31 July 2020, doi: 10.1177/0022219420945267.

Information about sharing knowledge, licences and public domain tools can be obtained from Creative Commons: https://creativecommons.org [accessed 12 April 2021].

Information about open source licences that enable software to be used, modified and shared can be obtained from the Open Source Initiative: https://opensource.org/licenses [accessed 12 April 2021].

The Open Science Project provides information about free and open source scientific software: http://openscience.org [accessed 12 April 2021].

Information about Open Hardware licences can be obtained from the Open Hardware Repository: https://ohwr.org/welcome [accessed 12 April 2021].

Wellcome Open Research provides open access to Wellcome-funded research and source data: https://wellcomeopen-research.org [accessed 12 April 2021].

Activity 96

Activity · · · · · · · · · · · · → 97

Recognizing Reporting Bias

....

ACTIVITY 97: EDUCATOR NOTES

Purpose: This activity enables students to understand what is meant by reporting bias and recognize when and how it occurs through the creation and editing of a wiki.

Type: Wiki creation and editing.

Alternative type(s): None.

Level: Elementary, intermediate and advanced.

Duration: Students spend several hours during independent study researching, discussing, creating and editing the wiki. Educators spend a few hours setting up and monitoring the wiki activity.

Equipment/materials: A suitable wiki tool.

Learning outcome: By the end of this activity, students will be able to provide a definition of reporting bias, give examples, explain why it occurs and summarize how it can be avoided.

....

The activity

Ask your students to work together to produce a wiki about reporting bias (if you have fewer than 12 students in your cohort, this can be run as a whole-class exercise: if you have more than this number, divide your students into groups and ask that they work on separate wikis in their groups). Set up a suitable wiki for this purpose (the wiki activity in Moodle or wikis in Blackboard Learn, for example) ensuring that you choose the collaborate option. Guidance notes and video tutorials are provided on these platforms for educators who are new to using wikis in their courses. This includes information about grading, if you choose to make this an assessed piece of work.

   This activity requires students to collaborate on discussing, creating and editing a wiki. If students are new to wikis, provide written guidelines or hold a discussion about the technique prior to the activity. Set guidelines about respect for the contribution of others and offering supportive and encouraging peer feedback. Encourage students to discuss, create, edit and refine their wiki until everybody is happy with the result. Monitor the wiki as it progresses: the wiki tools enable you to see who has created or edited comments and at what time. They also enable you to modify or delete pages or comments. Once the wiki has been produced it can be used for later cohorts, if appropriate (they too can discuss, edit and refine the wiki).

Key issues

This activity enables students to decide on pertinent issues and work collaboratively on what should be included in the wiki. Most are familiar with wikis and understand that they need to provide all the required information in an accessible and informative way. The wikis they produce tend to include a definition of reporting bias, information about the different types of reporting bias, a discussion on why reporting bias might occur and information about how to spot and address reporting bias (with examples). They also tend to provide useful resources and links.

One type of reporting bias is publication bias: this is covered in Activity 98: Understanding the influence of publication bias. The two activities can be run together, if greater coverage of the topic is required and if you have the time available.

Cautionary note

The collaborative nature of this project tends to result in an in-depth, useful and relevant wiki. However, there is an entry on Wikipedia covering reporting bias: it is advisable to become familiar with this entry so that you can check that students do not plagiarize the work. If you feel this could be a problem, provide written guidelines or hold a short discussion covering these issues before the activity gets under way. Activity 23 covers plagiarism.

→ Related activities

Activity 63: Recognizing and addressing bias when collecting data

Activity 73: Recognizing and addressing bias when analysing qualitative data

Activity 74: Avoiding bias in quantitative analyses

Activity 91: Building trust in inferences and conclusions

Activity 95: Knowing where and how to publish

Activity 98: Understanding the influence of publication bias

Activity 99: Communicating and reporting ethically

→ Preparatory reading

Educators: Huang (2019) and Salaber (2014) provide useful preparatory reading for educators who are new to using wikis in their teaching.

Students: Recommendations are not required as students will find their own resources for this activity.

→ Useful resources

Bradley, S.H., DeVito, N.J., Lloyd, K.E., Richards, G.C., Rombey, T., Wayant, C. and Gill, P.J. (2020) 'Reducing bias and improving transparency in medical research: a critical overview of the problems, progress and suggested next steps', *Journal of the Royal Society of Medicine*, 113 (11): 433-43, first published 10 November 2020, doi: 10.1177/0141076820956799.

Dawson, P. and Dawson, S.L. (2018) 'Sharing successes and hiding failures: "reporting bias" in learning and teaching research', *Studies in Higher Education*, 43 (8): 1405-16, published online 24 November 2016, doi: 10.1080/03075079.2016.1258052.

Huang, K. (2019) 'Design and investigation of cooperative, scaffolded wiki learning activities in an online graduate-level course', *International Journal of Educational Technology in Higher Education*, 16 (11), published 25 April 2019, doi: 10.1186/s41239-019-0141-6.

McLeroy, K.R., Garney, W., Mayo-Wilson, E. and Grant, S. (2016) 'Scientific reporting: Raising the standards', *Health Education & Behavior*, 43 (5): 501-8, first published 13 September 2016, doi: 10.1177/1090198116668522.

Page, M.J., Sterne, J.A.C., Higgins, J.P.T. and Egger, M. (2020) 'Investigating and dealing with publication bias and other reporting biases in meta-analyses of health research: A review', 12 (2): 248-59, first published 9 November 2020, doi: 10.1002/jrsm.1468.

Richards, G.C. and Onakpoya, I.J. (2019) 'Reporting biases'. In: *Catalogue of Bias*, 2019: https://catalogofbias.org/biases/reporting-biases/ [accessed 22 March 2022].

Salaber, J. (2014) 'Facilitating student engagement and collaboration in a large postgraduate course using wiki-based activities', *International Journal of Management Education*, 12 (2): 115-26, available online 22 April 2014, doi: 10.1016/j.ijme.2014.03.006.

Shah, K., Egan, G., Huan, L., Kirkham, J., Reid, E. and Tejani, A.M. (2020) 'Outcome reporting bias in Cochrane systematic reviews: a cross-sectional analysis,' *BMJ Open 2020*: 10: e032497, first published 16 March 2020, doi: 10.1136/bmjopen-2019-032497.

Activity 97

Activity · · · · · · · · · · · · · · → 98

Understanding the Influence of Publication Bias

The activity

Divide your students into groups (or pairs, if you have only a small number of students in your cohort) and give each group a copy of the Student Handout. This asks them to imagine a future in which publication bias is rampant and out of control. They are to present their visions of the future to their peers (in-class or online). The number of groups depends on the size of your cohort and the amount of contact time you have available: each group will need up to 10 minutes to present their vision, with 15-20 minutes for a class discussion once all visions have been presented.

When you next convene, ask each group to present their vision of the future. Ask students to keep questions and comments until the end, when all groups have made their presentation. Once they have done this, ask for comments and questions, and lead a class discussion on the issues raised. Suggestions for questions are given below. This activity can be carried out in-class or online, using a suitable video/web conferencing tool such as Zoom Meetings or Blackboard Collaborate (the Student Handout will need to be adapted accordingly).

Publication bias is one type of reporting bias. Other types of reporting bias can be raised in Activity 97: Recognizing reporting bias, which can be combined with this activity for greater coverage of the topic, if required.

Key issues

This activity enables students to develop imaginative, creative and thought-provoking visions of the future that provide an entertaining and memorable way to learn about publication bias and possible consequences. Some students present a bleak picture where researchers (and research) cannot be trusted and politicians use science to further their aims. Others present a more positive vision, imagining a backlash to rampant publication bias, believing that researchers would never stoop so low. Some imagine a future far ahead, whereas others look forward just a few years.

The visions that are presented usually generate questions and comments: give students time to work through these in the class discussion. Examples of general questions that can be asked, if required, include:

1. What are the consequences of publication bias?
2. Why should we be concerned about publication bias?
3. What do you think are the main reasons for publication bias?
4. How do we know that publication bias is taking place?
5. How can we recognize publication bias?
6. How can we avoid publication bias? Methods include:

- pre-registration of research studies;
- peer-review of study protocols;
- open accessibility of data;
- comprehensive ethics and integrity training;
- knowing how to build trust in inferences and conclusions (see Activity 91).

→ Related activities

Activity 91: Building trust in inferences and conclusions

Activity 95: Knowing where and how to publish

Activity 97: Recognizing reporting bias

Activity 99: Communicating and reporting ethically

→ Preparatory reading

Educators: All the resources listed below provide useful preparatory reading.

Students: None required. Students will find their own resources for this activity.

→ Useful resources

Cook, B.G. and Therrien, W.J. (2017) 'Null effects and publication bias in special education research', *Behavioral Disorders*, 42 (4): 149–58, first published 31 May 2017, doi: 10.1177/0198742917709473.

Franco, A., Malhotra, N. and Simonovits, G. (2014) 'Publication bias in the social sciences: Unlocking the file drawer', *Science*, 345 (6203): 1502-5, first published 19 September, 2014, doi: 10.1126/science.1255484.

Gage, N.A., Cook, B.G. and Reichow, B. (2017) 'Publication bias in special education meta-analyses', *Exceptional Children*, 83 (4): 428–45, first published 9 August 2017, doi: 10.1177/0014402917691016.

Harrison, J.S., Banks, G.C., Pollack, J.M., O'Boyle, E.H. and Short, J. (2017) 'Publication bias in strategic management research', *Journal of Management*, 43 (2): 400-25, first published 28 May 2014, doi: 10.1177/0149206314535438.

Lin, L. (2020) 'Hybrid test for publication bias in meta-analysis', *Statistical Methods in Medical Research*, 29 (10): 2881–99, first published 15 April 2020, doi: 10.1177/0962280220910172.

Scheel, A.M., Schijen, M.R.M.J. and Lakens, D. (2021) 'An excess of positive results: Comparing the standard psychology literature with registered reports', *Advances in Methods and Practices in Psychological Science*, first published 16 April 2021, doi: 10.1177/25152459211007467.

Tumin, D., Akpan, U.S., Kohler, J.A., and Uffman, J.C. (2020) 'Publication bias among conference abstracts reporting on pediatric quality improvement projects', *American Journal of Medical Quality*, 35 (3): 274-80, first published 13 September 2019, doi: 10.1177/1062860619873716.

Williams, I., Ayorinde, A.A., Mannion, R., Skrybant, M., Song, F., Lilford, R.J. and Chen, Y.-F. (2020) 'Stakeholder views on publication bias in health services research', *Journal of Health Services Research & Policy*, 25 (3): 162-71, first published 3 February 2020, doi: 10.1177/1355819620902185.

Activity 98

Activity · · · · · · · · · · · · → 98

Understanding the Influence of Publication Bias

STUDENT HANDOUT

This activity is about publication bias. This is a tendency for researchers to disseminate and submit research with statistically significant positive outcomes and ignore or suppress research with negative or null results. It also refers to journal editors and publishers who are more likely to publish research with positive outcomes. The result is that published studies are not representative of completed studies and the published research base is skewed. This can lead to further research being conducted, and policy and decisions being made, on incomplete data. Reasons for publication bias might include a belief that others are interested only in positive outcomes; the need to publish widely to enhance academic careers; concern that mistakes have been made if results differ from, or contradict, other research; and conflict of interest.

   Imagine a future world in which publication bias is rampant and out of control. What would this world look like? What would the consequences be for researchers, stakeholders, the wider community and humanity? Work with your group members to develop your vision. Use your imagination and be creative. When we next meet, you will have up to 10 minutes to present your vision. You can use any props, presentation equipment and materials that you wish: ensure that they are used to full effect to make your presentation entertaining and memorable. Once all groups have presented their vision, we will hold a class discussion on the issues raised.

Learning outcome: By the end of this activity, you will be able to summarize what is meant by publication bias; discuss reasons for, and consequences of, publication bias; describe how to recognize publication bias; and explain how publication bias can be avoided.

Activity • • • • • • • • • • • • → 99

Communicating and Reporting Ethically

The activity

This activity is a workshop that can be run in-class or online (using a suitable video/web conferencing tool such as Zoom Meetings, Blackboard Collaborate or Google Meet). Provide a short introduction to the workshop, explaining that it is about communicating and reporting ethically. Then divide your students into five groups (or pairs, if you have only a small number of students in your cohort). Allocate one of the following words to each group and ask that they take 10 minutes to discuss their word in relation to communicating and reporting ethically (use breakout rooms if you choose to run this activity online):

- inclusivity;
- equity;
- diversity;

- fairness;
- sensitivity.

After 10 minutes, bring the groups back together. Ask each group, in turn, to report back on the main points from their discussion. Encourage students to ask questions so that the issues can be explored further. After 15-20 minutes of discussion, ask students to think about their own communication and reporting strategy, in relation to the discussion you have just held. Ask them to take 10 minutes, working on their own, to think about their strategy: how do they intend to communicate and report their research ethically, with reference to inclusivity, equity, diversity, fairness and sensitivity?

After 10 minutes, bring your students back together to lead a class discussion on their intended communication and reporting strategies. Conclude the session with a summary of the main points raised.

This activity can be run as a self-guided individual exercise, if you prefer. Ask students to develop their communication and reporting strategies with reference to inclusivity, equity, diversity, fairness and sensitivity. When they do this, they will need to think about how they intend to communicate, with whom, when and why. If students feel they need to discuss any of these issues with you, provide a date and time when this can be done.

Key issues

The activity encourages students to think about whom they need to communicate with and how this can be done sensitively and fairly so that all parties are included and no one is, or feels, marginalized. This includes different people at different stages of the project: research participants as the research progresses and stakeholders (those who have an interest in, or are implicated by, the topic, methods, results and/or outcomes of their research) at the end of the project, for example. They also think about the methods that they will use to communicate so that people from a range of backgrounds and abilities are included. This can include various forms of online communication, co-production, visual methods, storytelling, narratives, scientific reports and conference papers, for example, and how these are written and produced to meet the needs of the audience.

Topics that are raised in this activity connect well with those raised in Activity 95: Knowing where and how to publish. The two activities can be combined for greater coverage, if required (by showing the videos produced by students in Activity 95 after this workshop has concluded, for example).

→ Related activities

Activity 95: Knowing where and how to publish

Activity 97: Recognizing reporting bias

Activity 98: Understanding the influence of publication bias

Activity 100: Displaying and publishing images ethically

→ Preparatory reading

Educators: The resources listed below discuss ethical considerations for a number of different communication and reporting methods. They all provide useful preparatory reading.

Students: None required prior to the activity. Some of the relevant resources listed below can be recommended to students once the workshop has concluded, if required.

→ Useful resources

Davey, N.G. and Benjaminsen, G. (2021) 'Telling tales: Digital storytelling as a tool for qualitative data interpretation and communication', *International Journal of Qualitative Methods*, first published 23 June 2021, doi: 10.1177/16094069211022529.

Dahlstrom, M.F. and Ho, S.S. (2012) 'Ethical considerations of using narrative to communicate science', *Science Communication*, 34 (5): 592-617, first published 13 September 2012, doi: 10.1177/1075547012454597.

Hintz, E.A. and Dean, M. (2020) 'Best practices for returning research findings to participants: Methodological and ethical considerations for communication researchers', *Communication Methods and Measures*, 14 (1): 38-54, published online 21 August 2019, doi: 10.1080/19312458.2019.1650165.

Jonsen, K., Fendt, J. and Point, S. (2018) 'Convincing qualitative research: What constitutes persuasive writing?', *Organizational Research Methods*, 21 (1): 30-67, first published 14 May 2017, doi: 10.1177/1094428117706533.

MacGregor, S. and Cooper, A. (2020) 'Blending research, journalism, and community expertise: A case study of coproduction in research communication', *Science Communication*, 42 (3): 340-68, first published 28 May 2020, doi: 10.1177/1075547020927032.

MacKenzie, C.A., Christensen, J. and Turner, S. (2015) 'Advocating beyond the academy: Dilemmas of communicating relevant research results', *Qualitative Research*, 15 (1): 105-21, first published 4 November 2013, doi: 10.1177/1468794113509261.

Medvecky, F. and Leach, J. (2019) *An Ethics of Science Communication*. London: Palgrave Macmillan.

Priest, S., Goodwin, J. and Dahlstrom, M.F. (eds) (2018) *Ethics and Practice in Science Communication*. Chicago, IL: University of Chicago Press.

Activity 99

Activity • • • • • • • • • • • → 100

Displaying and Publishing Images Ethically

ACTIVITY 100: EDUCATOR NOTES

Purpose: This activity encourages students to think about how images can be displayed and published ethically by asking them to develop brief scenarios that illustrate unethical practice. These are discussed by peers, who then go on to suggest ways to avoid or address the types of unethical practice identified.

Type: Student-developed scenarios and class discussion (in-class or online, synchronous).

Alternative type(s): None.

Level: Elementary, intermediate and advanced.

Duration: Fifty minutes to one hour of contact time.

Equipment/materials: A suitable video/web conferencing tool, if the online option is chosen.

Learning outcome: By the end of this activity, students will be able to list different types of unethical practice when displaying and publishing images, and explain how to avoid or address the types of unethical practice listed.

The activity

This session can be run in-class or online (using a suitable synchronous tool such as Zoom Meetings, Google Meet or Blackboard Collaborate). Provide a brief introduction to the session before dividing students into groups (ideally, you need five or six scenarios for discussion, so the number of students in each group will depend on the size of your cohort). If you are running this session online, use breakout rooms (or similar) for this part of the activity.

Ask each group to develop a short scenario that illustrates unethical practice in the display or publication of images. Scenarios can involve researchers, journalists or other individuals/groups involved in using images in their work. Ask students to be creative and imaginative: they should develop a scenario that illustrates any type of unethical practice relating to the display and/or publishing of images (they can include more than one type of unethical practice in their scenario, if they wish). The aim is to develop a plausible and memorable scenario that can be discussed with peers to identify types of unethical practice and provide solutions. Allocate 10 minutes for this part of the activity.

Bring the groups back together. Ask one group to present their scenario, then lead a class discussion in which the unethical practice is identified and discussed, before moving on to finding solutions: what should/could the person or organization in the scenario do differently to ensure that images are displayed and/or published ethically? Conclude the session with a summary of the main points raised.

This activity works well when combined with Activity 68: Collecting images and using visual methods ethically. Hold the student-led question-and-answer session first (Activity 68) before asking students to develop their scenarios described above.

Key issues

There are various unethical practices identified in this activity, including:

- not seeking informed consent for the use of images (Activity 57);
- failing to anonymize images (Activities 62, 79 and 84);
- using images in a way that can harm participants (Activity 11);
- publishing images for commercial gain (to sell newspapers or increase website/blog traffic, for example);
- publishing images for personal gain (to increase career prospects or publication record, for example);
- publishing images to influence behaviour (see Geise et al., 2021 for a discussion on how media coverage can influence willingness to participate in protests);
- breaching data protection rules (Activity 33);
- not paying attention to privacy and confidentiality (Activity 9);
- bias in the choice of images to publish and display (Activities 63, 73 and 74);
- cherry-picking images to back up a particular viewpoint or ideology;
- manipulating, altering or changing images and the implications for transparency (Activity 17);
- choosing publishing or display methods to influence who sees the image and how they see it (public and private settings, page visibility, password protection and licences, for example);
- not understanding, or not taking account of, image ownership (Activity 35);
- using digital images to reinforce existing power structures;
- breaching copyright rules (Activity 39);
- infringing intellectual property rights (Activity 38).

Cautionary note

This activity has been expanded to cover journalists and other individuals or organizations that work with images, as well as researchers. This is to give broader coverage of the topic as, on occasions, scenarios developed by students all covered the same types of unethical practice (informed consent and privacy, for example). It is useful to have some additional discussion points that can be developed from the list above if you find that there is not enough variety presented in the scenarios.

→ Related activities

Activity 46: Using visual methods, in Dawson (2016: 120-1)

Activity 62: Analysing visual data, in Dawson (2016: 166-8)

Activity 68: Collecting images and using visual methods ethically

→ Preparatory reading

Educators: Chapter 7 in Mannay (2016) and Part 2 of Warr et al. (2016) provide useful preparatory reading.

Students: None required for this activity, although some of the relevant resources listed below can be recommended when the activity has concluded, if required.

→ Useful resources

Chen, Y., Sherren, K., Smit, M. and Lee, K.Y. (2021) 'Using social media images as data in social science research', *New Media & Society*, first published 18 August 2021, doi: 10.1177/14614448211038761.

Dawson, C. (2016) *100 Activities for Teaching Research Methods*. London: Sage.

Dodd, S. (ed.) (2020) *Ethics and Integrity in Visual Research Methods*. Bingley: Emerald Publishing.

Geise, S., Panke, D. and Heck, A. (2021) 'Still images–moving people? How media images of protest issues and movements influence participatory intentions', *International Journal of Press/Politics*, 26 (1): 92-118, first published 3 November 2020, doi: 10.1177/1940161220968534.

Mäenpää, J. (2021) 'Distributing ethics: Filtering images of death at three news photo desks', *Journalism*, first published 15 February 2021, doi: 10.1177/1464884921996308.

Mann, D. (2018) '"I Am Spartacus": individualising visual media and warfare', *Media, Culture & Society*, 41 (1): 38-53, first published 16 March 2018, doi: 10.1177/0163443718764805.

Mannay, D. (2016) *Visual, Narrative and Creative Research Methods: Application, Reflection and Ethics*. Abingdon: Routledge.

Activity 100

Thomas, K.C. (2021) 'An alternative dynamics of research dissemination? The case of the *g word* tour', *Qualitative Research*, first published 27 December 2020, doi: 10.1177/1468794120981234.

Warr, D., Guillemin, M., Cox, S. and Waycott, J. (eds) (2016) *Ethics and Visual Research Methods: Theory, Methodology, and Practice*. New York, NY: Palgrave Macmillan.

The National Archives Image Library (https://images.nationalarchives.gov.uk/assetbank-nationalarchives/action/viewHome) in the UK contains over 70,000 images available to download, covering hundreds of years of history [accessed 26 November 2021].

Activity 100

Index